Lecture Notes in Computer Scie

Commenced Publication in 1973
Founding and Former Series Editors:
Gerhard Goos, Juris Hartmanis, and Jan van Leeuwer

John Field   Vasco T. Vasconcelos (Eds.)

Coordination Models and Languages

11th International Conference, COORDINATION 2009
Lisboa, Portugal, June 9-12, 2009
Proceedings

 Springer

Volume Editors

John Field
IBM T. J. Watson Research Center
H1-B24, P.O. Box 704
Yorktown Heights, NY 10598, USA
E-mail: jfield@us.ibm.com

Vasco T. Vasconcelos
University of Lisbon, Faculty of Sciences
Department of Informatics
Campo Grande, 1749-016 Lisboa, Portugal
E-mail: vv@di.fc.ul.pt

Library of Congress Control Number: Applied for

CR Subject Classification (1998): D.2, C.2.4, F.1.2, C.3

LNCS Sublibrary: SL 2 – Programming and Software Engineering

ISSN 0302-9743

ISBN 978-3-642-02052-0 Springer Berlin Heidelberg New York

springer.com

© Springer-Verlag Berlin Heidelberg 2009

Typesetting: Camera-ready by author, data conversion by Scientific Publishing Services, Chennai, India
Printed on acid-free paper   SPIN: 12688784   06/3180   5 4 3 2 1 0

Foreword

This year's edition of the international federated conferences on Distributed Computing Techniques (DisCoTec) took place in Lisbon during June 9–11, 2009. It was hosted by the Faculty of Sciences of the University of Lisbon, and formally the organized by the Instituto de Telecomunicações.

The DisCoTec conferences jointly cover the complete spectrum of distributed computing topics, ranging from theoretical foundations to formal specification techniques to practical considerations. This year's event consisted of the 11th International Conference on Coordination Models and Languages (COORDI-NATION), the 9th IFIP International Conference on Distributed Applications and Interoperable Systems (DAIS), and the IFIP International Conference on Formal Techniques for Distributed Systems (FMOODS/FORTE). COORDINA-TION focused on languages, models, and architectures for concurrent and distributed software. DAIS covered methods, techniques, and system infrastructures for designing, building operating, evaluating, and managing modern distributed applications in any application environment. FMOODS (the 11th Formal Methods for Open Object-Based Distributed Systems) joined forces with FORTE (the 29th Formal Techniques for Networked and Distributed Systems), creating a forum for fundamental research on theory and applications of distributed systems.

Each of the three days of the federated event began with a plenary speaker nominated by one of the conferences. In addition, there was a joint technical session consisting of one paper from each of the conferences. The common program also included a tutorial series on Global Computing, a joint initiative of the EU projects Mobius (Mobility, Ubiquity and Security) and Sensoria (Software Engineering for Service-Oriented Overlay Computers).

There were five satellite events: the Second Workshop on Context-Aware Adaptation Mechanisms for Pervasive and Ubiquitous Services (CAMPUS 2009), focusing on approaches in the domain of context-aware adaptation mechanisms supporting the dynamic evolution of the execution context; the Third Workshop on Middleware-Application Interaction (MAI 2009), focusing on middleware support for multiple cross-cutting features such as security, fault tolerance, and distributed resource management; the 10th International Conference on Feature Interactions in Telecommunications and Software Systems (ICFI); and meetings of the EU COST action on Formal Verification of Object-Oriented Software and the Sensoria project.

I hope this rich program offered every participant interesting and stimulating events. It was only possible thanks to the dedicated work of the members of the Organizing Committee—Ana Matos, Carla Ferreira, Francisco Martins, João Seco and Maxime Gamboni—and to the sponsorship of the Center of Informatics and Information Technology (CITI), the Portuguese research foundation

Fundação para a Ciência e a Tecnologia (FCT), the Instituto de Telecomunicações (IT), and the Large-Scale Informatics Systems Laboratory (LaSIGE).

June 2009   António Ravara

Preface

The 11th International Conference on Coordination Models and Languages, part of the IFIP federated event on Distributed Computing Techniques, took place in Lisbon, Portugal June 9–11, 2009. Since 1996, COORDINATION has been a leading forum for researchers and graduate students to present solutions to problems in distributed and concurrent programming, and to exchange new ideas and challenges.

COORDINATION 2009 focused on the design and implementation of models that allow compositional construction of large-scale concurrent and distributed systems, including both practical and foundational models, run-time systems, and related verification and analysis techniques. The Program Committee received 33 submission, covering a variety of topics, including foundations of distributed and concurrent interaction; specification, verification, and types; high-level optimization techniques; quality of service management; distributed software deployment and configuration; system support for programming models; and applications of novel distributed and concurrent techniques.

Each submission was reviewed by at least three Program Committee members. The review process included a rebuttal period during which authors were given the opportunity to react to the reviews. The Program Committee selected 14 papers for publication after a careful and thorough review process, based on the papers' significance, originality, and technical soundness.

Manuel Serrano of INRIA Sophia-Antipolis delivered an invited talk; his contribution "Hop, a Fast Server for the Diffuse Web," is included in these proceedings.

The success of COORDINATION 2009 was due to the dedication of many people. First, we would like to thank the authors for submitting high quality papers. We would also like to thank the members of the Program Committee and the external reviewers for their careful reviews and for thorough and balanced deliberations during the selection process. We are also indebted to the providers of the EasyChair conference management system, which was used to run the review process and to facilitate the preparation of these proceedings. Finally, we thank the Distributed Computing Techniques Organizing Committee.

June 2009

John Field
Vasco T. Vasconcelos

Organization

Conference Committee

Chairs

John Field	IBM Research, USA
Vasco T. Vasconcelos	University of Lisbon, Portugal

Program Committee

Gérard Boudol	INRIA, France
Dave Clarke	Katholieke Universiteit Leuven, Belgium
William R. Cook	University of Texas, USA
David Gay	Intel Research, USA
Rachid Guerraoui	EPFL, Switzerland
Thomas Hildebrandt	IT University, Denmark
Kohei Honda	Queen Mary, University of London, UK
Radha Jagadeesan	DePaul University, USA
Shriram Krishnamurthi	Brown University, USA
Doug Lea	State University of New York, USA
Frank Leymann	University of Stuttgart, Germany
Amy L. Murphy	ITC-IRST, Italy and University of Lugano, Switzerland
Uwe Nestmann	Technical University of Berlin, Germany
Rocco De Nicola	University of Florence, Italy
Gruia-Catalin Roman	Washington University in Saint Louis, USA
Jan Vitek	Purdue University, USA
Franco Zambonelli	University of Modena and Reggio Emilia, Italy

Publicity Chair

Herbert Wiklicky	Imperial College London, UK

Additional Reviewers

Tobias Anstett	Pepijn Crouzen	David Kitchin
Lamia Benmouffok	Hanna Eberle	Philipp Küfner
Mario Bravetti	Jens Chr. Godskesen	Alessandro Lapadula
Thomas Brihaye	Arjun Guha	Alex Loh
Mikkel Bundgaard	Espen Højsgaard	Louis Mandel
Luis Caires	Claude Jard	Daniel Martin
Antonio Cisternino	Einar Broch Johnsen	Eleftherios Matsikoudis
Greg Cooper	Chris King	Leonardo Gaetano Mezzina

Anja Monakova
Johan Östlund
Wojciech Penczekw
Kirstin Peters
Dumitru Potop-Butucaru
Damien Pous
José Proença

Gregor Richards
Judith Rohloff
Sidney Rosario
Sven Schneider
Ilya Sergey
Steve Strauch
Jean-Ferdinand
Susini

Daniel Tang
Ian Wehrman
Matthias Wieland
Tobias Wrigstad
Gianluigi Zavattaro
Luke Ziarek

Coordination Steering Committee

Farhad Arbab	CWI, The Netherlands
Rocco De Nicola (Chair)	University of Florence, Italy
Chris Hankin	Imperial College London, UK
Jean-Marie Jacquet	University of Namur, Belgium
Doug Lea	State University of New York, USA
Amy L. Murphy	ITC-IRST, Italy and University of Lugano, Switzerland
Gruia-Catalin Roman	Washington University in Saint Louis, USA
Carolyn Talcott	SRI International, USA
Jan Vitek	Purdue University, USA
Herbert Wiklicky	Imperial College London, UK
Gianluigi Zavattaro	University of Bologna, Italy

Distributed Computing Techniques Federated Event Organizing Committee

António Ravara (General Chair)	Technical University of Lisbon, Portugal
Carla Ferreira	New University of Lisbon, Portugal
Maxime Gamboni	Technical University of Lisbon, Portugal
Ana Almeida Matos	Technical University of Lisbon, Portugal
João Costa Seco	New University of Lisbon, Portugal
Martin Steffen (Publicity Chair)	University of Oslo, Norway
Francisco Martins (Workshops Chair)	University of Lisbon, Portugal

Table of Contents

Verification and Modeling

Hop, a Fast Server for the Diffuse Web

Manuel Serrano

Inria Sophia Antipolis, INRIA Sophia Antipolis 2004 route des Lucioles - BP 93
F-06902 Sophia Antipolis, Cedex, France

Abstract. The *diffuse* Web is an alternative way of using the Web 2.0 infrastructure for building personal diffuse applications. Systems that let users tune the temperature of their house with a cell-phone, check that the shutters are closed with a PDA, or select the music to be played on a Hi-Fi system with a PC are examples of the targeted applications.

Diffuse Web applications have similarities with Web 2.0 applications: *i)* they rely on fast bi-directional interactions between servers and clients, and *ii)* they make extensive use of non-cachable dynamic contents. On the other hand, diffuse applications have also an important difference with respect to traditional Web applications: they generally do not need to deal with a huge number of simultaneous users. That is, diffuse Web applications are built on top of standard technologies but they use it differently. Therefore they demand different optimizations and tunings.

Hop (`http://hop.inria.fr`) is a platform designed for building and running diffuse Web applications. Its software development kit contains two compilers, one interpreter, and a *bootstrapped* Web server. That is, the Hop Web server is implemented in Hop. This paper shows that this implementation strategy allows Hop to dramatically outperform the popular mainstream Web servers for delivering dynamic contents. Contrary to most servers, Hop delivers static and dynamic contents at a comparable pace. The paper details the implementation of the Hop Web server.

1 Introduction

The Web is the new ubiquitous platform where applications of tomorrow will be deployed. Though already wide, the Web will eventually become even wider when it connects all the appliances that surround us. The Web has already produced amazing new applications such as Google Map but a radically new way of thinking will be required.

Our answer to the challenge of programming ubiquitous Web applications relies on a small number of principles [31]. A Web application is not a federation of dynamic pages but a single, coherent program with multiple projections on servers or (perhaps roaming) clients. A typical application syndicates multiple data sources and, at the same time, is driven by multiple event streams.

Managing home appliances and organizing multimedia streams are typical targets for these new Web applications. Building these applications requires appropriate programming languages whose semantics, compilation process and

J. Field and V.T. Vasconcelos (Eds.): COORDINATION 2009, LNCS 5521, pp. 1–26, 2009.

runtime environment must fit the technologies offered by the Web. This paper focuses on this latter aspect.

Hop is a platform for programming ubiquitous, or *diffuse*, Web applications [31,33,34]. Its development kit contains two compilers, one interpreter, and one Web server. The first compiler is in charge of generating the native code executed by the server-side of the application. The second compiler produces JavaScript code executed by the client-side. The interpreter, which resides on the server, is used for fast prototyping. It has poor speed performance but since it may call compiled code and vice versa without any overhead, its speed is generally not a performance bottleneck.

The Hop Web server has been specially designed and tuned for serving efficiently the HTTP requests needed by diffuse applications. This paper focuses on studying its performance. It will be shown that using a *bootstrapped* software architecture where the server is implemented and executed in the same runtime environment as that used to execute user programs, may lead to a major speed improvement in comparison to mainstream Web servers that rely on CGI or FastCGI protocols. More precisely, it will be shown that for serving dynamic contents, Hop outperforms traditional generalist Web servers by a factor that increases with the number of dynamic responses. The paper presents the software architecture and the implementation techniques deployed in Hop.

1.1   The Context

The diffuse applications targeted by Hop use the Web differently than traditional Web 1.0 and 2.0 applications. They mostly use HTTP as a general purpose communication channel and they merely consider HTML and JavaScript as intermediate languages such as the ones used by compilers. The most important characteristics of diffuse Web applications are as follows.

- Most devices involved in the execution of a diffuse application may both act as server and as client. For instance, in a multimedia application, a PDA can be used to control the music being played as it can serve music files itself. That is, diffuse Web applications do not strictly implement a client-server architecture. They share some similarities with a peer-to-peer application.
- The applications frequently involve server-to-server, server-to-client, and client-to-server communications. For instance, a multimedia application playing music uses these communications for updating the state of all the GUIs controlling the music being played back.
- Programs are associated with URLs. Programs start when a Web browser requests such an URL. This generally loads a GUI on that browser. Apart from that initial transfer, most other communications will involve *dynamic contents* which can either be dynamic HTML documents or serialized data structures.
- The number of simultaneous concurrent requests is small because in general, only one user raises the temperature of the heating system or raises the volume of the Hi-Fi system. Hence dealing efficiently with a large number of connections is not a topmost priority for the servers considered here.

These characteristics have consequences on the implementation strategy a diffuse Web server should use. For instance, the first one, requires servers to have a small enough memory footprint to be embeddable inside small devices such as mobile phones. The second one requires servers to handle persistent connections efficiently. The third one demands short response times for dynamic documents. The fourth one impacts the concurrency model that should be deployed. Therefore, although diffuse Web applications probably have workloads that resemble those of Web 2.0 applications [25], they demand dedicated implementation strategies. In practice, general purpose Web servers that are mostly optimized for dealing with a large number of simultaneous connections are not suitable for most diffuse applications.

The vast majority of studies concerning the performance of Web servers concentrate on one crucial problem as old as the Web itself: sustaining the maximal throughput under heavy loads. This problem has been mostly addressed from a network/system programming perspective. For instance, a paper by Nahum et al. [26] surveys the impact on the performance of using various system services combinations. Another paper by Brech et al. explores and compares the different ways to accept new connections on a socket [6]. The seminal events-versus-threads dispute is more active than ever [1,40] and no clear consensus emerges. Hop is agnostic with respect to the concurrency model. Its software architecture supports various models that can be selected on demand.

The long debated question regarding kernel-space servers versus user-space servers seems to be now over. Initially it has been observed that kernel-space servers outperformed user-space servers [13], independently of the hosting operating systems. Adding zero-copy functions in the system API, such as the `sendfile`, has changed the conclusion [29]. In addition, another study [35] has shown that the gap between kernel-space and user-space that prevailed in older implementations unsurprisingly becomes less significant when the percentage of requests concerning dynamically generated content increases. Since Hop is designed mainly for serving dynamic contents, this study is of premium importance.

1.2   Organization of the Paper

Section **2** presents the general Hop's software architecture. Then Section **3** shows how the architecture is actually implemented. Section **4** presents the overall performance evaluation of the Hop Web server and compares it to other Web servers. It shows that Hop is significantly faster than all mainstream Web servers for serving dynamic documents. Section **5** presents related work.

2   The Implementation of the HOP Web Server

This section presents the general implementation of the Hop Web server. It first briefly sketches the Hop programming language and its execution model. Then, it shows the general architecture of the server.

2.1   The HOP Programming Language and Its Implementation

Since the Hop programming language has already been presented in a previous paper [31], only its main features are exposed here. Hop shares many characteristics with JavaScript. It belongs to the functional languages family. It relies on a garbage collector for automatically reclaiming unused allocated memory. It checks types dynamically at runtime. It is fully polymorphic (i.e., the *universal* identity function can be implemented). Hop has also several differences with JavaScript, the most striking one being its parenthetical syntax closer to HTML than to C-like languages. Hop is a full-fledged programming language so it offers an extensive set of libraries. It advocates a CLOS-like object oriented programming [5]. Finally, it fosters a model where a Web application is conceived as a whole. For that, it relies on a single formalism that embraces simultaneously server-side and client-side of the applications. Both sides communicate by means of function calls and signal notifications. Each Hop program is automatically associated with an unique URL that is used to start the program on the server. The general execution pattern of a Hop program is as follows:

- When an URL is intercepted by a server for the first time, the server *automatically* loads the associated program and the libraries it depends on.
- Programs first authenticate the user they are to be executed on behalf of and they check the permissions of that user.
- In order to *load* or *install* the program on the client side, the server elaborates an abstract syntax tree (AST) and compiles it on the fly to generate a HTML document that is sent to the client.
- The server side of the execution can be either executed by natively compiled code or by the server-side interpreter. If performance matters compiled code has to be preferred. However, for most applications, interpreted code turns out to be fast enough.

Here is an example of a simple Hop program.

```
(define-service (hello)
   (<HTML> (<DIV> :onclick ~(alert "world!") "Hello")))
```

Provided a Hop server running on the local host, browsing the URL http://-localhost:8080/hop/hello loads the program and executes the hello service. Contrary to HTML, Hop's markups (i.e., <HTML> and <DIV>) are node *constructors*. That is, the service hello *elaborates* an AST that is compiled on-the-fly into HTML when the result is transmitted to the client. It must be emphasized here, that a two phased evaluation process is strongly different from embedded scripting language such as PHP. The AST representing the GUI exists on the client as well as on the server. This brings flexibility because it gives the server opportunities to deploy optimized strategies for building and manipulating the ASTs. For instance, in order to avoid allocating an new AST each time a hello request is intercepted by the server, the AST can be elaborated at load-time and stored in a global variable that is reused for each reply.

```
(define hello-ast
  (<HTML> (<DIV> :onclick ~(alert "world!") "Hello"))))

(define-service (hello) hello-ast)
```

2.2   The Overall HOP Web Server Architecture

As most servers, when Hop intercepts a request it builds a reifying data structure which contains general informations such as the requested URL, the IP address of the client, and the date of the connection. In addition, Hop also proceeds to an early request authentication. That is, using the optional HTTP `authorization` field, it automatically searches in its database of declared users one whose login matches. If this query fails, a default *anonymous* user is associated with the request. This allows Hop to handle all requests on behalf of one particular user. Permissions to access the file system and to execute programs are granted individually, user by user.

Once users are authenticated and the request fully reified Hop builds a response object. This transformation is accomplished by a Hop program that can be changed as needed by users [32]. This gives flexibility to Hop that can therefore be used in various contexts such as smart proxies, application servers, load balancers, etc. It also strongly constraints its implementation because it forbids some classical optimizations. For instance it prevents Hop from re-using already allocated objects for representing requests because since these objects are used by user-defined programs they have dynamic extent.

Hop uses a traditional pipeline for processing HTTP requests, whose graphical representation is given in Figure 1. The advantages of using such an architecture for implementing Web servers have been deeply studied and are now well understood [42,44,9]. This Section presents the Hop pipeline without addressing yet the problem of scheduling its execution flow. In particular, it is not assumed here any sequential or parallel execution of the various stages. The scheduling strategies will be described in Sections 2.3 and 2.4.

In the Hop's pipeline, the first stage ("Accept"), establishes connections with clients. The second stage ("Request"), parses HTTP requests and builds the data structure reifying the authenticated requests. The stage "Response" elaborates responses to the requests. As suggested by the work on SEDA [42], provision

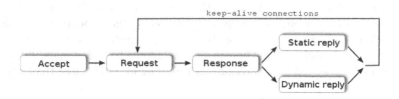

Fig. 1. The 4-stage HOP's pipeline

is taken to let the Hop scheduler handle static replies and dynamic replies differently. This is reflected by the pipeline fork after the "Response" stages. Persistent connections are handled by looping backward in the pipeline after the "Reply" stages. In order to avoid cluttering the next pipeline figures, keep-alive connections will be no longer presented.

The last two stages of the pipeline spawn user Hop programs executions. Services, such as `hello` defined in Section 2.1, are executed during the "Response" stage. For instance, when the server handles the request `http://-localhost:8080/hop/hello` the "Response" stage establishes the connection between the absolute path of the request URL, namely `/hop/hello`, and the defined service `hello`. It then invokes the latter. In this particular case, this service returns an AST representing a HTML tree. The "Response" stage wraps the values returned by services into `response` objects that are used by the final "Reply" stages. The "Static reply" stage handles static files or constant strings. It simply sends the characters composing the response to the clients. The "Dynamic reply" stage handles all other cases. When a dynamic response is an AST, this stage traverses the structure for compiling it on the fly into a regular HTML or XHTML document. That traversal can be controlled by user programs. The AST is represented by an object hierarchy that can be extended by user programs and the methods that implement the traversal can·be overridden.

Server side executions can either involve compiled codes or interpreted codes. Server-side interpreted code has not been optimized for performance but for flexibility. Hence the performance ratio between the two execution modes is strongly in favor of the former.

Flexibility is the main motivation for separating the elaboration of an AST and its compilation into a final document. As already mentioned in Section 2.1 this gives users the opportunity to *cache* ASTs. It also allows programs to re-use the same tree in different contexts. For instance, a same tree can be once compiled to HTML 4.01 and once to XHTML 1.0, depending on the capacities of the requesters that are identified in the HTTP request header.

2.3   HOP Concurrency

Hop aims at alleviating as much as possible the complexity of programming diffuse applications on the Web. This motivation has deeply impacted the overall design of the language. For instance, the language relies on a garbage collector, higher order functions, full polymorphism, and transparent serialization for function calls that traverse the network, because all these features make programs easier to write and to maintain. Obviously, the concurrency model is also another fundamental aspect of the language which has been impacted by the general Hop's philosophy. The concurrency model has been mainly designed with expressiveness and simplicity of programming in mind, more than runtime speed.

In Hop, responses to HTTP requests are all produced by user defined programs. This characteristic allows users to change the whole behavior of the server. This also deeply impacts its implementation because the concurrency model has to accommodate the spawning of user programs from various pipeline stages. Since running these programs may be unpredictably long, provisions have to be taken to execute them without blocking the entire server. That is, the server must still be able to answer other requests while executing user programs. This requires the server to be able to process multiple requests in parallel.

Although some previous studies might lead us to think that avoiding processes and threads by using an event-driven model can increase the speed [28,42], this form or concurrency forces programs to adopt a discipline that consists in splitting execution into a list of small call-backs that are scheduled by an event loop. Each of these call-backs must be as fast and short as possible in order to avoid monopolizing the CPU for too long. We have considered that organizing user programs into a well balanced list of call-backs was an unacceptable burden for the programmers. Hence, in spite of any performance considerations, we have decided to give up with pure event-driven models for Hop.

Currently Hop relies on a preemptive multi-threaded execution for user programs. However, the server and more precisely, the pipeline scheduler, is *independent* of the concurrency model of user programs, as long as they are executed in parallel with the stages of the pipeline. Hence, alternative concurrency models such as *cooperative threads* or *software memory transactions* could be used in Hop. This independence also allows many Web architectures to be used for scheduling the Hop pipeline. For instance, Hop may use multi-processes, multi-threads, pipeline [44,9], AMPED [28] or SYMPED [29], or a mix of all of them. In order to avoid early decisions, we have extracted the Hop scheduler from the core implementation of the server. That is, when the server is spawned, the administrator can select his scheduler amongst a set of predefined schedulers or provide his own. Hop pipeline schedulers are actually regular Hop user programs because the API that connects the scheduler to the server is part of the standard Hop library. The rest of this section emphasizes the simplicity of developing and prototyping new schedulers. In particular, it will be shown that adding a new scheduler is generally as simple as defining a new class and a couple of new methods. Using the server interpreter this can even been tested without any recompilation.

2.4   Hop Pipeline Scheduler

The Hop pipeline scheduler is implemented using a class hierarchy whose root is an abstract class named `scheduler`. Three methods `accept`, `spawn`, and `stage` implement the pipeline machinery. The Hop Web server provides several concrete subclasses of `scheduler` that can be selected using command line switches or by user programs. Extra user implementations can also be provided to Hop on startup. This feature might be used to easily test new scheduling strategies.

```
(abstract-class scheduler)

(define-generic (accept s::scheduler socket))
(define-generic (spawn s::scheduler proc . o))
(define-generic (stage s::scheduler th proc . o))
```

In this section, the general pipeline implementation is presented, followed by several concrete schedulers. For the sake of simplicity many details of the actual implementation are eluded. Exception handling is amongst them.

The pipeline implementation. When the Hop Web server is started, it first creates a socket that listens to new connections. The function make-server--socket of the Hop standard API takes one mandatory argument, a port number, and one optional argument, a backlog size:

```
(define-parameter port 8080)
(define-parameter somaxconn 128)

(define socket-server (make-server-socket (port) :backlog (somaxconn)))
```

Once the command line is parsed and the *Runtime Command* file loaded, the pipeline scheduler is created by instantiating the class corresponding to the selected scheduler.

```
(define-parameter scheduling-strategy 'pool)
(define-parameter max-threads 20)

(define pipeline-scheduler
   (case (scheduling-strategy)
      ((nothread) (instantiate::nothread-scheduler))
      ((one-to-one) (instantiate::one-to-one-scheduler))
      ((pool) (instantiate::pool-scheduler (size (max-threads))))
      ...))
```

The main server loop is entered with:

```
(accept pipeline-scheduler socket-server)
```

The function accept is a *generic function* function [5]. That is, a function whose default implementation might be overridden by *methods*. When a generic function is called, the actual implementation, i.e., the method to be executed, is chosen according to the dynamic types of the arguments of the call. The default implementation of accept is as follows:

```
1:  (define-generic (accept S::scheduler serv)
2:     (let loop ()
3:        (let ((sock (socket-accept serv)))
4:           (spawn S stage-request sock 0)
5:           (loop))))
```

On line *3*, a new connection is established. The request starts to be processed on line *4*. The function `spawn` being also a generic function, its actual implementation depends on the dynamic type of the scheduler.

The `spawn` function requires at least two parameters: a scheduler (S) and a function (`stage-request`) which can be considered as a *continuation*. The function `spawn` starts an *engine* which calls the function with the scheduler S, the engine itself, and all the other optional parameters `spawn` has received. As it will be presented in the next sections, the concurrency model used for executing the pipeline entirely depends on the actual implementation of the scheduler which may override the definition of `spawn`. This gives the freedom to each scheduler to use an implementation of its own for *creating* and *spawning* new engines. That is, one scheduler may implement its engine with sequential functional calls, another one may implement it with threads, and a third one could implement it with processes.

The function `stage-request` implements the second stage of the pipeline. It parses the HTTP header and body in order to create the object denoting the HTTP request.

```
1:  (define (stage-request S th sock tmt)
2:    (let ((req (http-parse-request sock tmt)))
3:      (stage S th stage-response req)))
```

The request is parsed on line *2*. The function `http-parse-request` reads the characters available on the socket `sock` with a timeout `tmt`. A value of 0 means no timeout at all. Parsing the request may raise an error that will be caught by an exception handler associated with the running thread. This handler is in charge of aborting the pipeline. Once the *request* object is created and bound to the variable `req` (see on line *2*), the third stage of the pipeline is entered. The function `stage` is the last generic function defined by the `scheduler` class. Although its semantics is equivalent to that of `spawn` there is a point in supporting two different functions. As it will be illustrated in the next sections, distinguishing `spawn` and `stage` is needed for enlarging the scope of possible scheduler implementations.

The function `stage-response` creates a *response* object from a *request* object. It is implemented as:

```
1:  (define (stage-response S th req)
2:    (let* ((rep (request->response req))
3:           (p (if (http-response-static? rep)
4:                  stage-static-answer
5:                  stage-dynamic-answer)))
6:      (stage S th p req rep)))
```

The two functions `stage-static-answer` and `stage-dynamic-answer` being similar only one is presented here:

```
(define (stage-static-answer S th req rep)
  (stage-answer S th req rep))
```

Using two functions instead of one gives the scheduler the opportunity to deploy different strategies for dealing with static and dynamic requests [42].

```
(define (stage-answer S th id req rep)
  (let* ((sock (http-request-socket req))
         (conn (http-response rep sock)))
    (if (keep-alive? conn)
        (if (= (scheduler-load S) 100)
            ;; use a minimal timeout (1mus)
            (stage S th stage-request sock 1))
            ;; use the default timeout (3ms)
            (stage S th stage-request sock 3000))
        (socket-close sock))))
```

After this sketch of the pipeline implementation the next sections present several actual scheduler implementations.

The row pipeline scheduler. Several Hop schedulers execute the stages of the pipeline sequentially, that is, they associate a new thread or a new process with each newly established connection that is used all along the pipeline. In order to alleviate the implementation of new schedulers that belong to this category, Hop provides a dedicated abstract class, namely **row-scheduler**, that overrides the **stage** generic function.

```
(abstract-class row-scheduler::scheduler)

(define-method (stage S::row-scheduler t p . o) (apply p S t o))
```

When no threads are used, jumping from one stage to another is implemented as a traditional function call. Hence, the implementation of the **stage** method of a **row-scheduler**, just consists in calling the function it has received as second argument.

The nothread pipeline scheduler. The simplest form of scheduler implements no parallelism at all. Within an infinite loop, the **nothread** scheduler waits for a new connection to be established, it then executes in sequence all the stages of the pipeline and it loops back, waiting for new connections (see Figure 2).

Implementing the **nothread** scheduler is straightforward because it only requires to override the generic function **spawn** with a method that merely calls the procedure it receives with the optional arguments and a dummy thread that is created by the scheduler. This thread is never used but it is required for the sake of compatibility with the other schedulers.

```
(class nothread-scheduler::row-scheduler)

(define *dummy* #f)
(define-method (spawn S::nothread-scheduler p . o)
  (unless (thread? *dummy*) (set! *dummy* (instantiate::hopthread)))
  (apply stage S *dummy* p o))
```

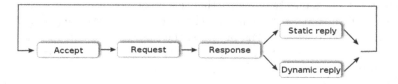

Fig. 2. The nothread pipeline scheduler

The **nothread** scheduler is fast but unrealistic since it cannot handle more than one request at a time. Using such a scheduler would prevent Hop from being used for serving long lasting requests such as music broadcasting.

The one-to-one scheduler. The **one-to-one** scheduler creates one new thread per connection (see Figure 3). Within an infinite loop it waits for connections. As soon as such a connection is established, it creates a new thread for processing the request. The main loop starts this new thread and waits for a new socket again.

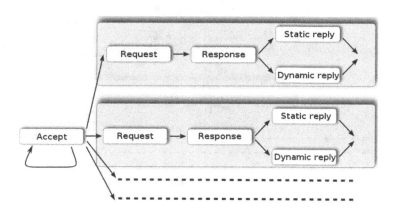

Fig. 3. The one-to-one pipeline scheduler

Implementing the **one-to-one** scheduler is as simple as implementing the **nothread** scheduler. It only requires to override the **spawn** generic function.

```
(class one-to-one-scheduler::row-scheduler)

(define-method (spawn S::one-to-one-scheduler p . o)
   (letrec ((th (instantiate::hopthread
                  (body (lambda () (apply p S th o)))))))
      (thread-start! th)))
```

The **one-to-one** scheduler supports parallel execution for requests so it overcomes the major drawback of the **nothread** scheduler. It is easy to implement persistent HTTP connections using this scheduler because after a response is sent to the client, the same thread can check if new requests are pending on the socket. However, in spite of this progress, the `one-to-one` scheduler is still inefficient because the system operations involved in creating and freeing threads are expensive.

The thread-pool scheduler. To eliminates the costs associated with the thread creation of the `one-to-one` scheduler, the `thread-pool` scheduler has been implemented. It is almost identical to the `one-to-one` scheduler with two noticeable differences: *i)* it uses a pool of early created threads, and *ii)* the *accept loop* is implemented inside each thread loop. That is, all the threads implement the same loop that executes all the stages of the pipeline (see Figure 4). Persistent connections are handled inside the same thread as the initial request. In scenarios where HTTP requests are sent to the server in sequence, this scheduler is able to avoid all context switches because a single thread executes the entire pipeline, from the "Accept" stage to the "Reply" stage. Context switches only occur when several requests are accepted in parallel.

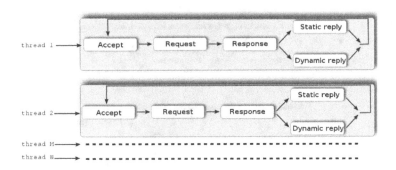

Fig. 4. The thread-pool pipeline scheduler

The bookkeeping needed to manage the pool of threads makes the implementation of the `thread-pool` scheduler obviously more complex than the previous ones. As this is a classical problem of concurrent programming it is probably not useful to present it here. Therefore all the details that are not strictly specific to Hop are therefore omitted.

The `pool-scheduler` class inherits from the `row-scheduler` class which it extends with two fields for holding the threads of the pool.

```
(class pool-scheduler::row-scheduler
   (threads::list read-only)
   (size::int read-only))
```

Each thread in the pool executes an infinite loop. When its action is completed a thread goes to `sleep` state. It will be awaken by the scheduler when a new connection will be assigned to this sleeping thread. Two functions implement this interface: `get-thread-pool` and `resume-thread-pool`.

```
(define-method (spawn S::pool-scheduler p . o)
  ;; get a free thread from the pool (may wait)
  (let ((th (get-thread-pool S)))
    (with-access::hopthread th (proc)
      ;; assign the new task to the thread
      (set! proc (lambda (S t) (stage S t p o)))
      ;; awake the sleeping thread
      (resume-thread-pool! th)
      th)))
```

Contrary to other schedulers, the call to `socket-accept` that waits for new connections is not invoked from the server main loop but inside each thread started by the scheduler. This is implemented by overriding the generic function `accept` for the `pool-scheduler` class and by creating an new function for implementing the "Accept" stage.

```
(define-method (accept S::pool-scheduler serv)
  (for (i 0 (pool-scheduler-size S))
    (spawn S stage-accept)))

(define (stage-accept S th)
  (let loop ()
    (let ((sock (socket-accept serv)))
      (stage S th stage-request sock 0)
      (loop))))
```

Other schedulers. Other schedulers have been implemented inside Hop. In particular we have tried a scheduler inspired by the `cohort` scheduling [16] (see Figure 5), a scheduler using an `accept-many` strategy [6], and a scheduler using a queue of waiting tasks. Early observations yield us to think that none performs faster than the `thread-pool` scheduler for our targeted application field.

The cohort scheduling experienced in Hop consists in grouping threads by tasks rather than by requests. It is hard to implement and even harder to optimize so up to now we have not been able to achieve good performance with it.

The *queue* strategy consists in associating stages of the pipeline to tasks. When a task must be executed, one thread is extracted from the pool. When the task completes, the thread goes back to the pool. A straightforward optimization of this scheduler removes superfluous queue operations and allows this scheduler to handle request in a row. When a thread should go back to the queue, if first checks if is queue of available threads is empty or not. If not empty, the same thread is used to execute the next stage of the pipeline.

The *accept-many* strategy consists in modifying the `accept` stage of the `thread-pool` scheduler in order to accept many connections at a time for purging as quickly as possible the socket backlog. All the connections that are established at a time are then processed by a pool of threads as the `thread-pool` scheduler

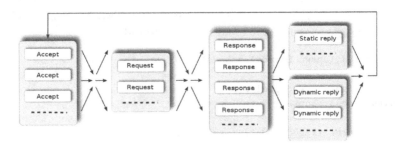

Fig. 5. The cohort pipeline scheduler

does. Although the authors of the `accept-many` technique report significant speed acceleration when deploying this strategy in mainstream Web servers, it fails at accelerating Hop. The reason for this different behavior is probably to be searched in the application field targeted by Hop where massively parallel requests burst are rare.

3   Optimizations

The online paper *Server Design* [10] highlights three major reasons for a Web server to behave inefficiently: *i)* data copies, *ii)* memory allocations, and *iii)* context switches. According to this paper, an ideal server would be a server that avoids them all. Of course, this is not practically feasible but still, working as hard as possible on these issues improves the chances of success in the quest of a fast server. Section 2.4 has shown that some Hop schedulers are able to *accept, parse*, and *reply* to requests without any context switch. Section 2.4 has presented an example of such a scheduler. This section shows how Hop addresses the two other points.

3.1   Limiting the Memory Allocation

High level programming languages such as Hop help programmers by supporting constructions that abstract low level mechanisms involved at runtime. Providing high level powerful forms alleviates programmers from tedious tasks but it also generally comes with a price: it makes writing efficient programs more difficult. A major reason for this inefficiency is excessive memory allocations.

Excessive memory allocation dramatically limits the performance for two main reasons: *i)* programs spend a significant percentage of their execution to allocate and free memory chunks and, *ii)* it introduces additional context switches for parallel executions that run in shared-memory environments. When the heap is a shared resource, allocating and freeing memory require some sort of synchronization. In general this is implemented with locks that eventually conduct to context switches. Hence, polishing a thread scheduling strategy can be pointless if, at the same time, memory allocation is not tamed.

Version 1.8.7 of Hop allocates 47.5MB for serving 10,000 times a file of 512 bytes. The same test run on the version 1.10.0-pre3 allocates only 4.3MB, that is 457 bytes per request. This section presents the two transformations that have lead us to shrink memory by more than 10 times.

BglMem. Contrary to a popular belief, garbage collectors generally used in high level languages impose no or minor runtime overhead [45]. The inefficiency of high level languages is more to be searched in the *implicit* memory allocations that are potentially hidden everywhere in the programs. For instance, calling a function might allocate lists if it accepts a variable number of arguments, declaring a function might yield to creating a closure if it makes use of free variables, opening a file or a socket might allocate inadequate buffers, etc.

In order to help programmers tame memory allocations, the Hop development kit provides an exact memory profiler. A dynamic tool keeps trace of the exact call graph at each allocation points. An offline tool produces histograms that, for each function of the programs, show: *i)* the number of data structures that have been allocated *by this function* and the overall size in bytes these allocations represent, and *ii)* the number of data structures and the size in bytes for all the functions the function dynamically calls. Using BglMem, we have, for instance, easily discovered that during a Hop test consisting in replying to 10,000 requests, the Hop function `http-parse-method-request` has allocated 60,006 pairs for a total of 468KB and 30,003 strings for a total of 654KB. In addition, the histograms produced by BglMem show that one of the children of this function has allocated 10,000 data structures representing the HTTP requests for a total size of 976KB.

The next sessions shows how BglMem has been used to reduce the Hop allocation and memory footprint.

One transformation. Because of the size constraint of the paper, it is not possible to present the exhaustive list of optimizations that have been applied to Hop to reduce its memory allocation. Hence only one exemplar transformations is presented here. It gets rid of implicit memory allocations that, once spotted are straightforward to eliminate.

Optimizing IO buffers: The function `socket-accept` waits for new connections on a socket. Once established the connection is associated with an input port for reading incoming characters and an output port for writing outgoing characters. BglMem reported that with Hop 1.8.7, `socket-accept` was responsible for allocating about 10MB of strings of characters! These 10MB came from the default configuration of `socket-accept` that creates a buffer of 1024 bytes for the input port associated with a connection. Removing these buffers has saved *10000 * 1024* bytes of memory.

Hop uses sockets in a way that allows it to use its own memory management algorithm which is more efficient than any general purpose memory manager. Hop needs exactly as many buffers as there are simultaneous threads parsing HTTP requests. Hence, the obvious idea is to associate one buffer per thread not by socket. This can be implemented more or less efficiently depending on

the nature of the scheduler. Some schedulers such as the `nothread-scheduler`
or `pool-scheduler` (see Section 2.4 and Section 2.4) accept an optimal solution
that totally eliminates the need to allocate buffers when the server is ready to
accept requests. It consists in allocating one buffer per thread when the scheduler
is initialized. These buffers are then simply reset each time the thread they are
associated with is about to parse characters. The modification in the source code
is minor. It only requires one additional line of code:

```
(define-method (accept S::nothread-scheduler serv)
  ;; create a buffer before the thread loop
  (let ((buf (make-string 1024)))
    (let loop ()
      ;; reuse buffer for each connection
      (let ((sock (socket-accept serv :inbuf buf)))
        (spawn S stage-request sock 0)
        (loop)))))
```

Wrap up. Memory allocation has been measured on a test that consists in
serving 10,000 a 512 bytes long file, without persistent connection. Each HTTP
request of this memory test contained 93 bytes. Parsing each request produces a
data structure made of strings (for denoting the path of the request, the client
hostname, etc.), lists (for holding the optional lines of the HTTP header), symbols (for the HTTP version, the transfer encoding, the mime type, etc.) and an
instance of the class `http-request` for packaging the parsed values plus some
extra values such as a time stamp, an authenticated user, etc. In the test this
structure uses the whole 457 bytes allocated per request. That is, applying the
optimizations described in this section has successfully removed *all* the memory
allocations not strictly needed for representing the HTTP requests. In particular, all the hidden allocations that can take place in high level languages such as
Hop have been eliminated. The current version of Hop is then close to optimal
regarding memory allocation.

3.2   Persistent Connections

Persistent connections have been one of the main reasons of the creation of
HTTP/1.1. Two early papers report that significant accelerations can be expected from implementing persistent connections [21,27]. A client has two means
for discovering that it has received the full body of a response: *i)* the connection
is closed by the server or, *ii)* the length of the response to be read is explicitly
provided by the server. Persistent connections, of course, can only use the second
method.

   Providing the length of a static response, i.e, a file or a string of characters, is
straightforward (although some Web servers, such as Lighttpd, implement caches
to eliminate repetitive calls to the expensive `fstat` system operation). Providing
the size of a dynamic response is more challenging. One solution consists in
writing the response in an auxiliary buffer first, then getting the length of that
buffer and then writing the length and the buffer to the socket holding the

connection. This technique is generally inefficient because it is likely to entail data copies. The characters have to be written to the buffer first which might need to be expanded if the response is large. Then, this buffer has to be flushed out to the socket, which is also likely to use a buffer of its own.

Hop uses a solution that avoids auxiliary buffers. It relies on *chunked* HTTP responses that break the response body in a number of chunks, each prefixed with its size. Using chunked responses in Hop is possible because of a dedicated facility provided by its runtime system. The Hop I/O system allows programs to associate *flush hooks* with input and output ports. Output flush hooks are functions accepting two arguments: the port that is to be flushed and the number of characters that are to be flushed out. The values produced by calling these hooks are directly written out to the physical file associated with the port before the characters to be flushed out.

Using output flush hook, chunked responses can be implemented as:

```
(define (chunked-flush-hook port size)
  (format "\r\n~x\r\n" size))
```

Using output port flush hooks is efficient because it imposes no overhead to the I/O system. The written characters are stored in a buffer associated with the output port, *as usual*. When the buffer is flushed out, the chunk size is written by the hook. Writing the chunk size is the only extra operation that has been added to answering responses. It is thus extremely lightweight and it allows persistent connections to be implemented efficiently (i.e., without extra copy nor extra memory allocation) for dynamic documents as well. Chunked HTTP responses have probably been designed for enabling this kinds of optimization but we have found no trace of equivalent techniques in the literature.

3.3   Operating System Interface

Implementing fast I/Os with sockets requires some operating system tunings and optimizations. This section presents two of them.

Non-copying output. Several studies have measured the benefit to be expected from using *non-copying* output functions such as the Linux `sendfile` facility [26,29]. This system service is supported by Hop. In addition to be fast because it avoids data copies and user-space/kernel-space traversals, it also simplifies the implementation of servers because it makes memory caches useless for serving static files. As in a previous study [29], we have noticed no acceleration when using memory cache for serving files instead of using a pure `sendfile`-based implementation. Using `sendfile` or a similar function actually *delegates* the caching to the operating system which is likely to perform more efficiently than a user-land application.

Network programming. The default setting of sockets uses the Nagle algorithm [24] that is aimed at avoiding TCP packets congestion. We know from previous studies that this algorithm combined with the acknowledgment strategy used by TCP may cause an extra 200ms or 500ms delay for delivering the last packet of a connection [12]. This is called the *OF+SFS* effect that has been identified to be due to the *buffer tearing* problem [22]. Persistent HTTP connections are particularly keen to exhibit this problem and thus it is recommended to disable the Nagle algorithm for implementing more efficiently Web servers that support persistent HTTP connections [27]. Therefore, Hop supports configuration flags that can enable or disable the Nagle algorithm.

The TCP_CORK hybrid solution (or a *super-Nagle* algorithm) is supported by some operating systems. However, as reported by Mogul & Mingall [22] this socket option does not solve the OF+SFS problem in presence of HTTP persistent connections. We confirm this result because in spite of several attempts we have failed to eliminate the 200ms delay it sometimes imposes (in between 8 and 20% of the responses according to Mogul & Mingall, much more according to our tests) between two persistent connections. Hence, we gave up on using it.

Other configurations impact the overall performance of socket based applications. For instance, previous studies have suggested that an adequate calibration on the backlog of a listen socket (controlled by the system limit somaxconn) may improve significantly the performance [4]. For the workloads used to test Hop we have found that mid-range values (such as 128) yield better results.

4   Performance Study

Although most HTTP requests involved in diffuse applications address dynamic contents, they also use static file transfers for cascading style sheets, images, and client-side libraries. Hence a fast server for the diffuse Web should be able to deliver efficiently dynamic *and* static documents. In this section we compare Hop to other Web servers for serving the two kinds of requests.

4.1   Performance Evaluation Caveat

This paper focuses on the performance evaluation of the Hop Web server, which is not to be confused with a performance evaluation of the Hop server-side programming language. Hop relies on the Bigloo compiler for generating server-side native code. It has already been shown that this compiler delivers native code whose performance is only 1.5 to 2 times slower than corresponding C code [30]. That is, the Hop server-side compiled code significantly outperforms the popular scripting languages such as PHP, Ruby, Python, as well as bytecode interpreted languages such as Java. In order to avoid overemphasizing the performance of the Hop programming language against PHP, Ruby, Java, or even C, we have only used simplistic generated documents that require minimalist computations. Our typical generated documents only require a few "prints" to be produced. Restricting to simple documents minimizes the performance penalty imposed by slow scripting languages implementations and allows us to focus on the evaluation of the mechanisms used by the server for running user programs on the server-side of the application.

4.2   Experimental Environment

Our experimental environment consists of three computers connected to a LAN: *i)* a server made of a bi-processor Intel PIV Xeon, 3Ghz with 1GB of RAM running Linux-2.6.27, *ii)* a first client running Linux-2.6.27 executed by an Intel Core 2 Duo ULV 1.06Ghz with 1.5GB of RAM, and *iii)* a second client running Linux-2.6.27 executed by an Intel Code 2 Duo 2.0Ghz with 2GB of RAM. The network traffic is ensured by a Cisco Gigabit ethernet router Catalyst 3750G. Using the Unix tool `iperf` we have experimentally verified that this setting indeed permits ethernet frames to be transferred at the pace of one gigabit per second.

In this paper, the workloads used for our tests are generated by `httperf` [23] version 0.9.0, a tool dedicated to measuring the performance of Web servers.

Before concentrating on the actual performance of the servers, we have measured the requests rate our setting can sustain. Following the protocol suggested by Titchkosky *et al* [38], we have observed that our clients can sustain a combined workload of more than 6,000 requests per second, which is enough to saturate the tested servers.

4.3   Hop vs. Other Web Servers

There are so many Web servers in vicinity that it is impossible to test them all[1]. Hence, we have tried to select a representative subset of existing servers. We have used two mainstream servers implemented in C, one mainstream server implemented in Java, and two servers implemented in functional languages:

- **Apache-2.2.10**, a popular Web server implemented in C. For producing dynamic documents with Apache, we have measured the performance of **mod_perl-2.0.4** and **mod_php5**, which both rely on the FastCGI protocol.
- **Lighttpd-1.4.20**, another popular Web server implemented in C. It is frequently used as a replacement of Apache on embedded devices such as routers and NASes.
- **Tomcat-5.5.27**, the popular Web server implemented in Java that relies on JSP for producing dynamic documents.
- **Yaws-1.77**, a small server implemented in Erlang [3].
- **PLT Web server-4.1.2**, a web server implemented in PLT-Scheme [14,15,43].

For this experiment all servers are used with their default configuration except for logging that has been disabled when possible. The Hop default configuration is as follows: *i)* use the `thread-pool` pipeline scheduler with 20 threads, *ii)* `somaxconn` = 128, *iii)* initial heap size = 4MB, *iv)* keep-alive timeout = 5 seconds, *v)* the socket send buffer size is 12KB (as recommended by [27]).

---

[1] At the time this paper has been written, the wikipedia articles comparing Web servers described 68 general purpose servers and 79 lightweight Web servers! See `http://en.wikipedia.org/wiki/Comparison_of_web_servers`.

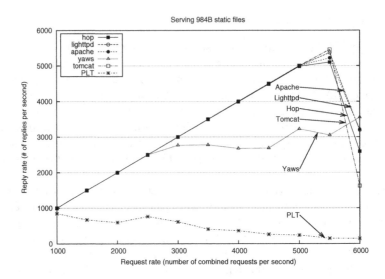

Fig. 6. Server performance. These tests measure the throughput a web server can sustain when delivering 984 bytes long static files. Each session consists in 5 consecutive requests that are sent using a single persistent connection.

As much as possible we have tried to write comparable versions of the dynamic test. That is for each of the tested languages, namely PHP, Perl, JSP, Erlang, Scheme, and Hop, we have tried to write a *fair* version of the test, that is a version as equivalent as possible to the version of the other languages.

Figures 6 and 7 presents the performance evaluation which calls for several observations:

Observation 1: In the considered application context where only a small number of users simultaneously connect to the server, Hop is one of the fastest server for delivering static content. In particular, it is as fast as C servers such as Apache and Lighttpd. The test presented in the paper involves serving a file of about 1KB. We have conducted a second test that involves a file of 64KB. This second test confirms the results presented in Figure 6. The speed hierarchy of Web servers for serving a 64KB file is roughly the same as the one found when serving the 1KB file.

Observation 2: Hop is the fastest server for delivering dynamic content.

Observation 3: Hop and Yaws are the only two servers that deliver static content and dynamic content at approximately the same speed.

Observation 4: Yaws runs remarkably steady. In particular, its performance seems hardly impacted when the server load increases. Further investigation would be needed but this early result seems to demonstrate that the advantage claimed by the Erlang programming language [2] for dealing with massively

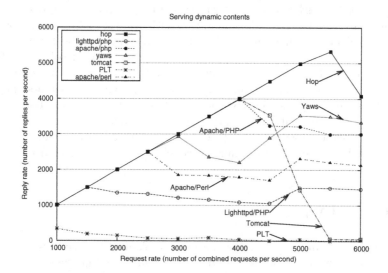

Fig. 7. Server performance. These tests measure the throughput a web server can sustain when delivering dynamic contents. Each session consists in 5 consecutive requests that are sent using a single persistent connection.

concurrent applications is also observable for Web servers. Those concerned by overloaded servers should probably consider using message passing as fostered by Erlang.

Observation 5: PHP and Perl present comparable performance. They are both significantly slower than Hop.

Tomcat performance drops dramatically around 4000 requests per second because its memory footprint becomes too large (more than 700MB), which forces the operating system to start swapping the main memory. It should be noticed here that none of the servers is stopped and restarted when the load increases. Hence if a Web server leaks memory its performance will continuously slow down. The PLT Scheme server suffers from the same problem as Tomcat. Its memory footprint rapidly approaches 1GB of memory. Hence, very soon it is not able to do anything useful because it is swapped out. Tomcat and PLT show how important it is to restrain memory allocation. An excessive memory allocation dramatically reduces the performance of a server.

From these observations, we can draw some conclusions. The experiment emphasizes persistent connections even for dynamic content delivery because each client emits consecutively 5 requests using the same connection. This corresponds to a real use-case for the targeted applications but it strongly penalizes all the systems that are not able to implement them efficiently. This might explain the poor performance of Apache and Lighttpd servers.

The file 984 bytes long file used for testing static delivery is exactly the file that gets generated by the dynamic content test. Hence, the static delivery and the dynamic delivery end up with the same characters written to the socket. The only difference between the two tests is the way these characters are obtained: from a static file in the first case, from an in-memory computation in the second. Hop and Yaws are the two fastest servers for delivering dynamic contents. They are both bootstrapped. This might be considered as an indication that bootstrapped Web servers should outperform other servers for delivering dynamic content. Tomcat is bootstrapped too but since its performance is deeply impacted by its excessively large memory footprint, no conclusion can be drawn from studying its performance.

5   Related Work

Many high level languages have been used to implement Web servers but actually only a few of them can be compared to Hop. Functional languages have a long standing tradition of implementing Web servers, probably pioneered by Common Lisp that, as early as 1994, was already concerned by generating dynamic HTML content [18]! Today, Haskell seems very active with HWS [19], Wash/CGI [37], and HSP [7]. HWS is a server that uses a four-stages pipeline and a one-to-one scheduler. It relies on user-threads instead of system-threads for handling each requests. User-threads work well as long as no user program can be spawn from the stages of the pipeline. This probably explains why HWS is not able to serve dynamic content. HSP is a Haskell framework for writing CGI scripts. It used to be implemented as an Apache module [20] and but it is now hosted by a dedicated server HSP(r) based on HWS. Unfortunately HSP(r), as well as Wash/CGI, is incompatible with the currently released version of GHC, the Haskell compiler. Hence we have not been able to test any of them.

Smalltalk has Seaside which is one of the precursors in using continuations for modeling Web interactions [11]. It would have been interesting to measure its performance because Smalltalk, as Hop is a dynamic programming language but unfortunately it was not possible to install it on our Linux setting.

The impact of the concurrency model on the performance of the servers has been largely studied and debated but no clear consensus prevails yet. Some pretend that an event-based model is superior to a thread model. Some pretend the contrary. A third group claims that blending the two models should be preferred [41]! Hence, the idea of proposing system independent models of the concurrency has emerged. Jaws is an adaptive Web server framework that allows programmers to implement their own Web server using on-the-shelf components [36]. This framework provides elementary blocks that can manage a pipeline, normalize URLs, support various styles of I/Os, etc. Combining these components simplifies the development of a server without penalizing its performance.

Flux [8] and Aspen [39] are two programming languages that allow programmers to choose, at compile-time, the concurrent model used at run-time. Flux consists in a set of syntactic extensions to C/C++ that are expanded, at compile-time, into regular C/C++ programs. Aspen like Erlang [3], eschews shared memory in favor of message passing. The parallel structure of an Aspen program is specified independently of its computational logic and, at run-time, Aspen dynamically allocates threads according to the dynamic workload of the server. Prototypical Web servers have been implemented in Flux and Aspen that show performance not significantly better than Apache for static and dynamic contents.

Saburo is an Aspect Oriented framework for generating concurrent programs [17]. The PhD thesis introducing Saburo focuses on the performance of Web servers. Contrary to Hop that relies on a dynamic selection of the concurrency model (implemented by means of classes and late binding), Saburo as Flux and Aspen relies on a static model. In theory these systems should then be able to perform faster than Hop because they have opportunities to optimize the implementation of the concurrency model at compile-time. In practice, the Hop implementation of the late binding used in the pipeline scheduler is fast enough not to impact the overall performance of the server.

6 Conclusion

This paper presents the Hop server that is mainly designed for running diffuse applications on the Web. The paper presents its versatile architecture that supports various concurrent programming models as well as significant parts of its implementation.

The paper shows that programming an efficient server for the diffuse Web is not only a problem of good system and network practices, although these still have a large impact on the overall performance. The new problem is to *combine*, fast network and system programming *and* fast interactions between the server main loop that deals with HTTP requests and the user helper programs that produce responses.

The solution supported by Hop consists in merging, inside a single runtime environment, the server main loop and the user programs. This can be build by using the same programming language for implementing the server itself and the user programs. Such a *bootstrapped* Web server can eliminate all communication costs between the server main loop and user programs. Hence, it can outperform traditional general purpose Web servers that handle user programs as external processes. The Hop Web server that delivers dynamic documents significantly faster than all the other tested servers shows this can achieved using high level dynamic programming languages.

References

[1] Adya, A., et al.: Cooperative Task Management without Manual Stack Management or Event-driven Programming is Not the Opposite of Tthreaded Programming. In: Proceedings of the Usenix Annual Technical Conference, Monterey, CA, USA, June 2002, pp. 289–302 (2002)

[2] Armstrong, J., et al.: Concurrent Programming in ERLANG. Prentice Hall, Englewood Cliffs (1996)

[3] Armstrong, J.: Concurrency Oriented Programming in Erlang– Invited talk of the FFG conference (2003)

[4] Banga, G., Druschel, P.: Measuring the Capacity of a Web Server. In: USENIX Symposium on Internet Technologies and Systems (1997)

[5] Bobrow, D., et al.: Common lisp object system specification– special issue, Notices (23) (September 1988)

[6] Brech, T., Pariag, D., Gammo, L.: accept()able Strategies for Improving Web Server Performance. In: Proceedings of the USENIX 2004 Annual Technical Conference, Boston, MA, USA (June 2004)

[7] Broberg, N.: Haskell Server Pages through Dynamic Loading– Haskell 2005. In: Proceedings of the 2005 ACM SIGPLAN workshop on Haskell, Tallinn, Estonia, pp. 39–48 (2005)

[8] Burns, B., et al.: Flux: A Language for Programming High-Performance Servers. In: Proceedings of USENIX Annual Technical Conference, pp. 129–142 (2006)

[9] Choi, G.S., et al.: A Multi-Threaded PIPELINED Web Server Architecture for SMP/SoC Machines. In: WWW 2005 Proceedings of the 14th international conference on World Wide Web, Chiba, Japan, pp. 730–739 (2005)

[10] Darcy, J.: Server Design (August 2002),
http://pl.atyp.us/content/tech/servers.html

[11] Ducasse, S., Lienhard, A., Renggli, L.: Seaside - a multiple control flow web application framework. In: Proceedings of the ESUG Research Track (2004)

[12] Heidemann, J.: Performance Interactions Between P-HTTP and TCP Implementations. ACM Computer Communication Review 27(2), 65–73 (1997)

[13] Joubert, P., et al.: High-Performance Memory-Based Web Servers: Kernel and User-Space Performance. In: Usenix, pp. 175–188 (2001)

[14] Krishnamurthi, S.: The CONTINUE Server (or, How I Administered PADL 2002 and 2003). In: Dahl, V., Wadler, P. (eds.) PADL 2003. LNCS, vol. 2562, pp. 2–16. Springer, Heidelberg (2002)

[15] Krishnamurthi, S., et al.: Implementation and Use of the PLT Scheme Web Server. Higher Order and Symbolic Computation 20(4), 431–460 (2007)

[16] Larus, J., Parkes, M.: Using Cohort Scheduling to Enhance Server Performance. In: Proceedings of the Usenix Annual Technical Conference, Monterey, CA, USA, June 2002, pp. 103–114 (2002)

[17] Loyaute, G.: Un modéle génératif pour le développement de serveurs internet, Univeristé Paris-Est, Paris, France (September 2008)

[18] Mallery, J.C.: A Common LISP Hypermedia Server. In: Proc. First International World-Wide Web Conference, pp. 239–247 (1994)

[19] Marlow, S.: Writing High-Performance Server Applications in Haskell, Case Study A Haskell Web Server. In: Haskell 2000: Proceedings of the ACM SIGPLAN Haskell Workshop, Montreal, Canada (September 2000)

[20] Meijer, E., Van Velzen, D.: Haskell Server Pages – Functional Programming and the Battle for the Middle Tier Abstract. In: Haskell 2000: Proceedings of the ACM SIGPLAN Haskell Workshop, Montreal, Canada (September 2000)

[21] Mogul, J.C.: The case for persistent-connection HTTP. In: SIGCOMM 1995: Proceedings of the conference on Applications, technologies, architectures, and protocols for computer communication, Cambridge, Massachusetts, United States, pp. 299–313 (1995)

[22] Mogul, J.C., Minshall, G.: Rethinking the TCP Nagle algorithm. SIGCOMM Comput. Commun. Rev. 31(1), 6–20 (2001)

[23] Mosberger, D., Jin, T.: httperf: A tool for Measuring Web Server Performance. In: First Workshop on Internet Server Performance, pp. 59–67 (1998)

[24] Nagle, J.: Congestion Control in IP/TCP Internetworks – RFC 896, Internet Engineering Task Force (January 1984)

[25] Nagpurkar, P., et al.: Workload Characterization of selected JEE-based Web 2.0 Applications. In: Proceedings of the IISWC 2008. IEEE International Symposium on Workload Characterization, September 2008, pp. 109–118 (2008)

[26] Nahum, E., Barzilai, T., Kandlur, D.D.: Performance Issues in WWW Servers. IEEE/ACM Transactions on Networking 10(1) (February 2002)

[27] Nielsen, H.F., et al.: Network Performance Eeffects of HTTP/1.1, CSS1, and PNG. In: Proceedings of the ACM SIGCOMM 1997 conference, Cannes, France (September 1997)

[28] Pai, V.S., Druschel, P., Zwaenepoel, W.: Flash: An efficient and portable Web server. In: Proceedings of the Usenix Annual Technical Conference, Monterey, CA, USA (June 1999)

[29] Pariag, D., et al.: Comparing the Performance of Web Server Architectures. SIGOPS Oper. Syst. Rev. 41(3), 231–243 (2007)

[30] Serpette, B., Serrano, M.: Compiling Scheme to JVM bytecode: a performance study. In: 7th Sigplan Int'l Conference on Functional Programming (ICFP), Pittsburgh, Pensylvanie, USA (October 2002)

[31] Serrano, M., Gallesio, E., Loitsch, F.: HOP, a language for programming the Web 2.0. In: Proceedings of the First Dynamic Languages Symposium, Portland, Oregon, USA (October 2006)

[32] Serrano, M.: The HOP Development Kit. In: Invited paper of the Seventh ACM sigplan Workshop on Scheme and Functional Programming, Portland, Oregon, USA (September 2006)

[33] Serrano, M.: Programming Web Multimedia Applications with Hop. In: Proceedings of the ACM Sigmm and ACM Siggraph conference on Multimedia, Best Open Source Software, Augsburg, Germany (September 2007)

[34] Serrano, M.: Anatomy of a Ubiquitous Media Center. In: Proceedings of the Sixteenth Annual Multimedia Computing and Networking (MMCN 2009), San Jose, CA, USA (January 2009)

[35] Shukla, A., et al.: Evaluating the Performance of User-Space and Kernel-Space Web Servers. In: CASCON 2004: Proceedings of the 2004 conference of the Centre for Advanced Studies on Collaborative research, Markham, Ontario, Canada, pp. 189–201 (2004)

[36] Smith, D.C., Hu, J.C.: Developing Flexible and High-performance Web Servers with Frameworks and Patterns. ACM Computing Surveys 30 (1998)

[37] Thiemann, P.: WASH/CGI: Server-side Web Scripting with Sessions and Typed, Compositional Forms. In: Krishnamurthi, S., Ramakrishnan, C.R. (eds.) PADL 2002. LNCS, vol. 2257, p. 192. Springer, Heidelberg (2002)

[38] Titchkosky, L., Arlitt, M., Williamson, C.: A performance comparison of dynamic Web technologies. SIGMETRICS Perform. Eval. Rev. 31(3), 2–11 (2003)

[39] Upadhyaya, G., Pai, V.S., Midkiff, S.P.: Expressing and Exploiting Concurrency in Networked Applications with Aspen. In: PPoPP 2007: Proceedings of the 12th ACM SIGPLAN symposium on Principles and practice of parallel programming, San Jose, California, USA, pp. 13–23 (2007)

[40] Von Behren, R., Condit, J., Brewer, E.: Why Events Are A Bad Idea (for higher-concurrency servers). In: Proc. of HotOSIX: the 9th Workshop on Hop Topics in Operating Systems, Lihue, Hawaii, USA (May 2003)

[41] Welsh, M., et al.: A Design Framework for Highly Concurrent Systems, Berkeley, CA, USA (2000)
[42] Welsh, M., Culler, D., Brewer, E.: SEDA: An Architecture for Well-Conditioned, Scalable Internet Services. In: Symposium on Operating Systems Principles, pp. 230–243 (2001)
[43] Welsh, N., Gurnell, D.: Experience report: Scheme in commercial Web application development. In: ICFP 2007: Proceedings of the 12th ACM SIGPLAN international conference on Functional programming, Freiburg, Germany, pp. 153–156 (2007)
[44] Yao, N., Zheng, M., Ju, J.: Pipeline: A New Architecture of High Performance Servers. SIGOPS Oper. Syst. Rev. 36(4), 55–64 (2002)
[45] Zorn, B.: The Measured Cost of Conservative Garbage Collection. Software — Practice and Experience 23(7), 733–756 (1993)

High-Performance Transactional Event Processing

Antonio Cunei[1], Rachid Guerraoui[1], Jesper Honig Spring[1],
Jean Privat[2], and Jan Vitek[3]

[1] Ecole Polytechnique Fédérale de Lausanne (EPFL)
[2] Université du Québec à Montréal (UQÀM) and Purdue University

Abstract. This paper presents a transactional framework for low-latency, high-performance, concurrent event processing in Java. At the heart of our framework lies Reflexes, a restricted programming model for highly responsive systems. A Reflex task is an event processor that can run at a higher priority and preempt any other Java thread, including the garbage collector. It runs in an obstruction-free manner with time-oblivious code. We extend Reflexes with a publish/subscribe communication system, itself based on an optimistic transactional event processing scheme, that provides efficient coordination between time-critical, low-latency tasks.We report on the comparison with a commercial JVM, and show that it is possible for tasks to achieve 50 μs response times with way less than 1% of the executions failing to meet their deadlines.

1 Introduction

Performing real-time processing in a managed language environment, such as Java, is very appealing but introduces two significant implementation challenges: memory management and inter-task communication.

Typically, garbage collectors used in commercial Java virtual machines are designed to maximize the performance of applications at the expense of predictability. Consequently, with these garbage collectors it is non-deterministic *when* and for *how long* they will run. As a consequence garbage collection introduces execution interference that can easily reach hundreds of milliseconds, preventing the timeliness requirements of the real-time systems from being satisfied. High performance real-time Java virtual machines have somewhat reduced this challenge through advances in real-time garbage collection algorithms, reducing the latency to approximately 1 ms. However, some applications have latency/throughput real-time requirements that cannot be met by current real-time garbage collection technology. For these applications, having scheduling latency requirements below a millisecond, any interference from the virtual machine is likely to result in deadline misses.

Another source of interference that can easily cause deadline misses, relates to communication between the time-critical real-time tasks, including any interaction they might have with the rest of the application. Typically, time-critical tasks only account for a fraction of the code of an entire application, the rest

J. Field and V.T. Vasconcelos (Eds.): COORDINATION 2009, LNCS 5521, pp. 27–46, 2009.

being either soft- or non-real-time code. For instance, the US Navy's DD-1000 Zumwalt class destroyer is rumored to have million lines of code in its shipboard computing system, of which only small parts have real-time constraints. Typical programming practices for sharing data would involve synchronizing access to the data. In a real-time system, this might lead to unbounded blocking of the real-time thread, so-called *priority inversion*, causing serious deadlines infringements.

One of the key design decisions of the Real-time Specification for Java (RTSJ) [9] was to address these problems with a programming model that restricts expressiveness to avoid unwanted interactions with the virtual machine and the garbage collector in particular. The RTSJ introduced the `NoHeapRealtime-Thread` for this purpose, and also proposed solutions to cope with priority inversion. As we discuss in the related work, however, experience implementing [5,13,21,2] and using [8,20,7,22,24] the RTSJ revealed a number of serious deficiencies. More recently, alternatives to `NoHeapRealtimeThread` have been proposed, such as Eventrons [26] and Exotasks [3] from IBM Research as well as Reflexes [27] and StreamFlex [28].

This work builds on our experience with Reflexes [27], a simple, statically type-safe programming model that makes it easy write and integrate simple periodic tasks observing real-time timing constraints in the sub-millisecond range, into larger time-oblivious Java applications. Reflex tasks are written in a subset of Java with special features for (1) safe region-based memory management preventing interference from the garbage collector, (2) obstruction-free atomic regions avoiding any priority inversion problems when communicating with time-oblivious code, and (3) real-time preemptive scheduling allowing the Reflex task to preempt any lower-priority Java thread, including the garbage collector. Finally, Reflexes rely on a set of safety checks, based on our previous work for Real-time Java [1,32], to ensure safety of memory operations. These checks are enforced statically by an extension of the standard Java compiler. The Reflex safe regions provide better latency than a real-time collector.

In StreamFlex [28], we extended Reflexes to support low-latency stream processing by introducing graphs of tasks that communicate through non-blocking transactional communication channels, allowing tasks to communicate in a zero-copy fashion. While these transactional channels are effective for communication, they fall short when it comes to coordination between time-critical tasks. In particular, coordinating transactions in a multi-core environment turns out to be challenging when striving for low-latency.

Publish/subscribe systems are a special case of event-based programming where a number of computational components are allowed to register, or subscribe, to events published by other components in the system [15]. This programming model has been applied in different context; in distributed systems, publish/subscribe is a convenient way to decouple producers from consumers, and to provide a simple resource discovery protocol via a registration mechanism. On a single node, publish/subscribe offers a convenient way to program dynamic systems where new rules can be added/removed dynamically and events processed in parallel. Example of applications can be found in the financial sector where events are the movement of stocks and computational elements implement trading rules. Some examples of event-based systems are Gryphon, JEDI and JavaSpaces [16,29,14].

This paper presents an extension of the original Reflex programming model with a publish/subscribe substrate that allows for coordination and communication between highly time-critical, low-latency Reflex tasks by registering for, and publishing, user-defined events. This publish/subscribe system is itself built on top of a transactional tuple space implementation that abides by the semantics described in [17] and uses the data structures described in [30]. While the original Reflex implementation used a limited form of software transactional memory based on [18] for the obstruction-free interaction with ordinary Java threads, in the extension presented in this paper, all the computation performed by a Reflex task is transactional. Thus, access to the shared space containing events and subscriptions is transactional, as are the actions performed during event processing.

Furthermore, the paper reports on a number of encouraging performance results through a comparison with equivalent executions on a commercial JVM, and documents the ability for tasks to achieve 50 μs response times with way less than 1% of the executions failing to meet their deadlines.

Finally, the focus of this paper is on the extended programming model and its performance characteristics. We explicitly do not address issues of distribution, fault-tolerance, event correlation and event lifetimes. While these are important from a usability point of view, we leave their investigation to future work.

2   Programming with Events and Reflexes

Reflexes are small time-critical tasks that are intended to execute free from interference from their environment. The task is an object of a user-defined subclass of `ReflexTask` with its own private memory area and that is executed by a real-time thread. The main responsibility of a Reflex task is to implement `execute()`, a method that will be invoked whenever the Reflex task's trigger condition evaluates to true. In this paper we extend the notion of time-triggered tasks from Reflexes [27] with registration-triggered Reflex tasks. A purely time-triggered Reflex task is one whose `execute()` method is executed according to a period specified at task instantiation. A registration-triggered Reflex task is released by the scheduler when an event that matches one of the Reflex task's registered templates is inserted in the shared space (by another Reflex task).

Fig. 1 illustrates a Reflex application consisting of a time-oblivious part and three time-critical tasks. A single transactional event space is shared by the three Reflex tasks (R1, R2, R3). The tasks can register for events, take events and write events to the shared space. Standard, time-oblivious Java code can run in the same virtual machine but has restricted ability to interact with Reflex tasks, see [27] for details.

In order to minimize latency, the Reflex programming model sports a bimodal distribution of object lifetimes for tasks. An object allocated within a Reflex task

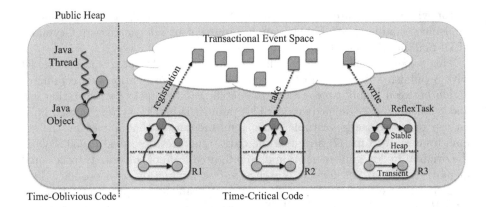

Fig. 1. Transactional Event Processing with Reflexes. Three Reflex tasks (R1, R2, R3) are concurrently using a shared event space. Reflex tasks can register for events, in which case they get to execute as soon as an event matching their registered template is put in the space (R1). Reflex task can take events from the space (R2) or put new events into it (R3). Reflex tasks execute in private memory areas and are unreachable to the public heap garbage collector. They are composed of two parts, a stable heap that is not reclaimed, and transient storage that is reclaimed after each invocation of the task.

can be either *stable*, in which case the lifetime of the object is equal to that of the task, or it can be *transient* in which case the object only lives for the duration of the invocation of the task's `execute` method after which the virtual machine will reclaim it in constant time before the next invocation of the task. Specifying whether an object is stable or transient is done at the class level. By default, data allocated by a Reflex thread is transient, while only objects of classes implementing the `Stable` marker interface will persist between invocations. Stable objects must be managed carefully by the programmer, as the size of the stable heap is fixed and the area is not garbage collected. The distinction between stable and transient objects is enforced statically by a set of static safety checks [27]. It is noteworthy that code running in transient does not require special annotations, and we can thus reuse many classes from the standard Java libraries.

Example. Fig. 2 presents a simple Reflex task. The class `StockBuyer` is declared to extend the abstract class `ReflexTask`. As such it has to implement the method `execute()`, which runs every time the task is scheduled. The state of the Reflex task consists of two fields, `maxPrice`, a double, and `handle`, a reference to a `Handle`. Being instance fields of the Reflex task, these fields persist across invocations of the task, they are the roots for its stable data. Primitive types are stable by default, and object are stable only if their defining class implement the `Stable` marker interface (as is the case for `Handle`). The role of a `Handle` is to represent a subscription that has been registered with the event space. In this case, `handle` will be notified if an event with the key `sell` is inserted in the space.

```
class StockBuyer extends ReflexTask {
    double maxPrice;
    Handle handle;

    public void initialize() {
        handle = subscribe(new Event("sell", null));
    }

    public void execute() {
        for (Event offer : handle) {
            if (isExpired(offer.get("expiry"))) return;
            double price = asDouble(offer.get("price"));
            if (price * 2 <= maxPrice)
                write(new Event("type", "buy")
                    .add("price", price));
            else
                if (price > maxPrice) maxPrice = price;
        }
    }
}
```

Fig. 2. Stock Trading with Reflexes

The `execute()` method is invoked after an event matching the subscription has been inserted in the space. By the time the Reflex task starts to execute, more matching events may have become available, or someone else may have been quicker than the Reflex task and no matching event may be present in the space any longer. Thus, `execute()` will iterate over the events that match the query and, if the price is right, it will write buy the events back to the space.

The transactional infrastructure must keep track of two kinds of events: the operations on the shared event space, and the mutations of the stable state of the Reflex task. Each iteration of the loop in `execute()` performs (1) a test to see if more data is available, then (2) it does a destructive read, and (3) in some cases a write into the space. The transactional infrastructure will record all of these operations, and manage conflict detection and rollback. On the side of the Reflex task, the only meaningful operation is the possible update to the field `maxPrice`, which will be recorded in case a rollback is necessary.

It is useful to consider the potential sources of aborts. The Reflex programming model is such that tasks 'own' all the data in both stable and transient state. Thus, all of the objects that make up a Reflex task are guaranteed to be accessed only by a single thread. This means that there can be no conflict on task data. Conflicts (and aborts) can come about in only two ways: concurrent operations on the shared event space, and explicit calls to `abort()` from a Reflex task itself.

3   Transactional Reflex API and Semantics

We present here the semantics of the shared event space (Sec. 3.1), and then explain how the shared space integrates with transactional Reflex tasks (Sec. 3.2).

3.1   Shared Event Space

An event space is a multiset of events that are shared between Reflex tasks. An event is a function from keys – represented as interned `String` objects – to values – Java objects such as boxed primitives, arrays, and certain user-defined data structures. The basic operations on a shared space are limited to three basic, non-blocking, operations: `take()`, `write()`, and `test()`, which respectively, remove and insert a deep-copied version of the provided event, and check for the availability of an event in the shared space. The arguments to all those methods are events; in the case of `take()` and `test()`, the argument is used as a template for finding matching events in the space.

The semantics of matching is the following: a template matches an event if it contains the same or fewer keys, and for each key it contains a value that is either the same of the event or null, null being a wildcard. Fig. 3 depicts a few examples on matching between templates and events.

Template		Event
['stock':'APPL', 'value':3]	matches	['stock':'APPL', 'value':3]
['stock':null, 'value':3]	matches	['stock':'APPL', 'value':3]
['stock':'APPL']	matches	['stock':'APPL', 'value':3]
['stock':'APPL', 'value':3]	!match	['stock':'APPL']

Fig. 3. Matching between templates and events

Transactional semantics of the shared space follow from [17]. Informally, a sequence of operations performed within a transaction is conflict-free if the same sequence would succeed at the time of commit.

3.2   Transactional Reflexes

An excerpt of the extended Reflex API supporting transactional event processing is given in Fig. 4. To implement a Reflex task, the programmer must provide a subclass of `ReflexTask` class. The operations available include two versions of the shared space operations, e.g. `write()` and `writeNow()`. The latter bypasses the transactional layer and updates the space directly. This is a form of open nesting [19], and is needed in combination with user-initiated `abort()` to post an event describing the reasons of the abort or containing partial results.

The semantics of `abort()` is to discard all changes to the shared space, terminate the current invocation of the `execute()` method, discard all data allocated in the transient area and finally rollback all changes in the stable heap.

In order to be notified of the insertion of an event matching some template, a Reflex task must `subscribe()` to that event. When it does, it receives an instance of `Handle` which is always allocated in stable heap of the task (and thus can be retained between invocation of `execute()`). Each handle refers to one subscription in the shared event space. A Reflex task may have multiple handles

```
public abstract class ReflexTask implements Stable {
    public ReexTask(int transientSize, int stableSize) {...}
    public abstract void execute();
    public void initialize() {};

    final void write(Event ev) {...};
    final void writeNow(Event ev) {...};
    final Event take(Event template) {...};
    final Event takeNow(Event template) {...};
    final boolean test(Event template) {...};
    final boolean testNow(Event template) {...};
    final Handle subscribe(Event template) {...};
    final void unsubscribe(Handle hndl) {...};
    final void abort() {...};
}

public final class Handle implements Stable {
    Event next();
    Event nextNow();
    boolean hasNext();
    boolean hasNextNow();
}

public class Event {
    Event();
    Event add(String key, Object value);
    Object get(String key);
}
```

Fig. 4. An excerpt of the extended Reflex API

listening on different kinds of events. When an event is inserted in the space all Reflex tasks with matching subscription will be notified. Handles support an iterator interface to query and read matching events. Invoking unsubscribe() with a provided handle causes for the Reflex task no longer to be notified when a matching event is inserted.

Reflex tasks can be active or passive. An active Reflex is time-triggered and has an associated real-time thread with a priority and a period. The semantics of an active Reflex is that every period, the implementation checks if one of the handles has witnessed insertion of a matching event. If so, the Reflex's execute() method is invoked. A Reflex with a period of 0 does not sleep between invocations of execute(). If an active Reflex has no subscriptions, the execute() method is invoked every period. A passive Reflex is event-triggered and run only when an event is available. Unlike active Reflex tasks, which has its own thread, a passive Reflex is executed by a thread taken from a thread pool and does not have any timeliness guarantees.

3.3 Legacy Reflex Communication Schemes

Besides allowing Reflex tasks to communicate and coordinate through the shared event space, as described so far, the original Reflex model also allows for tasks to communicate through static variables and for ordinary Java threads to communicate with Reflex tasks.

Communication with ordinary Java threads has to be managed carefully to avoid introducing execution interferences that could cause the Reflex task to miss its deadlines. Typical programming practices for sharing data between threads involve lock-based synchronization. In a real-time system this might lead to *priority inversion* and serious deadline misses. To encounter this, Reflexes propose a scheme based on a limited form of transactional memory in the form of obstruction-free transactional methods ensuring that the Reflex task meets its temporal requirements.

In enforcing isolation of a Reflex task, static variables pose a particular type-safety problem as references to objects allocated in different tasks or on the heap, could easily pass the isolation boundaries. To circumvent this, Reflexes restrict the use of static variables to primitive and *reference- immutable* types. Informally speaking, an object of reference-immutable type provides access to an object graph connected by references that cannot change but containing other fields that can change, i.e., primitive types.

4   Static Safety Issues

To avoid interference from the public heap garbage collector, the Reflex programming model relies on strict isolation between: (1) the Reflex tasks themselves, and (2) the Reflex tasks and the time-oblivious Java code in which the Reflex tasks have been integrated and might or might not interact with as described in [27]. The goal of the safety checks is to statically guarantee this isolation by restricting unsafe code that would violate the memory integrity and allow access to heap-allocated objects in inconsistent states, and dangling pointers to be observed. These restrictions are enforced by an extension of the standard `javac` compiler that is inherited from previous work [28] as, from checking perspective, events are similar to StreamFlex capsules. The details of the checking process are unchanged in this implementation. Note, the scope of the restrictions enforced by the checker only apply to the time-critical parts of the Reflex application, including any data shared between the Reflex tasks and time-oblivious Java code; any legacy Java code is not subject to these restrictions. The details of the simple set of restrictions that we apply to ensure this isolation are described in [27]. Fig. 5 illustrates how the isolation of Reflex tasks are preserved through static safety checks that prevent illegal references while permitting valid references.

In terms of function, events described here behave much like capsules used in StreamFlex [28] in that they are used as units of communication between tasks. Likewise, as objects they both impose similar safety risk in that references could leak between tasks and break isolation through these objects. In StreamFlex these risks are addressed by letting capsules be treated specially (i.e., they are neither transient nor stable types), and any capsule instances are allocated from a special fixed size pool. This prevents the StreamFlex task from retaining a reference to the capsule once the `execute` method has completed. Furthermore,

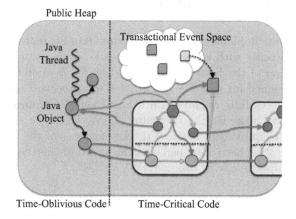

Public Heap

Fig. 5. Reflex Isolation. Illustration showing how Reflex task isolation is enforced through static safety checks that capture and prevent illegal (red) references (from other Reflex tasks or time-oblivious Java code) while permitting valid (green) references.

capsules are restricted in the types of fields that they can carry, allowing only fields of primitive or reference-immutable types. Together, the restrictions effectively prevents isolation from being violated and at the same time allow for zero-copy communication between tasks resulting in fast throughput, crucial for stream-processing applications, as demonstrated with StreamFlex [28].

In the extension described in this paper, the goal is not throughput of data processing but rather efficient and flexible coordination between time-critical, low-latency Reflex tasks. With this goal in mind, zero-copy communication is not strictly necessary, although desirable, from a performance point of view. Consequently, unlike capsules, events are not restricted in what object types they can carry. However, to ensure type safety by preventing references from leaking, when inserted into the shared space, or taken from here, the event objects (and the entire object graph they hold) are recursively deep-copied between the memory contexts of the task performing the operation and the shared event space. Furthermore, to ensure that no tasks retain a reference to an event, which could only happen if the **Event** class were to be declared stable, the **Event** class is treated as an ordinary transient type. This means that any event instances will only survive for the duration of the **execute** method (unlike the deep-copied event that following completion of the **execute** method will be present in the shared space). If events were treated as stable objects, any event ever used by the Reflex task throughout its lifetime would be allocated in its stable heap, with the probably risk of eventually running out of memory. Since, from the static safety checks of Reflexes, stable types are prohibited from referencing transient ones, an event also cannot be assigned to a field on a Reflex task (as the **ReflexTask** is declared stable, see Fig. 4). With the treatment of events as normal transient types, and the deep-copying of events into the shared space, no additional static safety checks have to be defined than those specified in [27].

5   Implementation Highlights

Reflexes have been implemented on top of the Ovm [4] real-time Java virtual machine, which comes with an optimizing ahead-of-time compiler and provides an implementation of the Real-time Specification for Java (RTSJ). The virtual machine was designed for resource constrained uni-processor embedded devices and has been successfully deployed on a ScanEagle Unmanned Aerial Vehicle in collaboration with the Boeing Company [2]. We leveraged the real-time support in the VM to implement some of the key features of the API. The virtual machine configuration here described uses the ahead-of-time compiler to achieve performance competitive with commercial VMs [24].

```
ReflexSupport.setCurrentArea(transientArea);

while (true) {
    waitForNextPeriod();
    if ((subscriptions.size() > 0) &&
        (!subscriptions.hasMatch())) continue;

    delta = new Transaction(space);
    reflex.startLogging();
    try {
        execute();
    }
    catch (Abort a) {
        reflex.undo();
        ReflexSupport.reclaimArea(transientArea);
        continue;
    }
    if (delta.validate(space)) {
        delta.commit(space);
        reflex.commit();
    } else {
        reflex.undo();
        delta.abort();
    }
    ReflexSupport.reclaimArea(transientArea);
}
```

Fig. 6. Time-triggered Reflex (pseudo code)

We outline some of the key implementation issues of Reflexes; a more detailed description appears in [27]. Reflex tasks are run by real-time threads scheduled by a priority-preemptive scheduler. For each Reflex task instance, the implementation allocates a fixed size continuous memory region for the stable heap and another region for its transient area. The `ReflexTask` object, its thread, and all other implementation specific data structures are allocated in the Reflex task's stable heap. These regions have the key property that they are not garbage collected. We are in the process of investigating using hierarchical real-time garbage collector, described in [23], to garbage collect the stable heap. This collector can collect partitions of the heap independently and, due to the special structure of the event space, we expect to have compaction with pause time bounds less than 100 microseconds. Each thread in the VM has a default allocation area. This area is the heap for ordinary Java threads and the respective transient area for all real-time threads executing Reflex tasks. The garbage collector supports pinning for objects. Pinned objects are guaranteed not to move during a garbage collection. Thus they can safely be accessed from a Reflex. The allocation policy for classes and static initializers ensures that all objects allocated at initialization time are pinned.

Our implementation also relies on a simplified version of the RTSJ region API to ensure that sub-millisecond deadlines can be met. We depart from the RTSJ by our use of static safety checks in order to ensure memory safety. That has the major advantage of avoiding the brittleness of RTSJ applications, and also brings performance benefits as we do not have to implement run-time checks, such as read and write barriers, to prevent dangling pointers.

The event space uses an event-tree data structure for fast access based on the fingerprinting scheme described in [30]. Registrations are maintained by a reverse event-tree that takes advantage of the duality between templates and events. The empty template (an event with no fields) is not allowed in a registration.

Fig. 6 shows pseudo code for the implementation of a time-triggered periodic Reflex task. The implementation of transactions is done at two levels:

- *Event space transactions* are managed by interposing a `Delta` between each Reflex task and the space. The `Delta` records all operations and will try to publish the changes when the `execute()` method returns. In Fig. 6, event space transaction code is related to the `delta` object.
- *Reflex-level transactions* are implemented by logging all memory mutations in the stable heap (as described in [18]) – transient objects can be ignored because they will be discarded when the `execute()` method returns. The log is used to undo the operations performed during an invocation of the `execute()` method. As there can be only one thread executing within a Reflex task and no other thread may observe the internals of a task (this is ensured by the static safety checks [27]), memory operations can be performed on the main memory while retaining strong atomicity. In Fig. 6, Reflex-level transactions code is related to the `ReflexTask` object.

6   Performance Evaluation

We conducted a number of empirical experiments to evaluate the performance and behavior of the proposed system. All experiments were performed on an AMD Athlon 64 X2 Dual Core processor 4400+ with 2GB of physical memory running Linux 2.6.17 extended with high resolution timer (HRT) patches [25] configured with a tick period of 1 μs. We used an Ovm build with support for POSIX high resolution timers, and configured it with an interrupt rate of 1 μs. In addition, we disabled the run-time checks of violations of memory region integrity (read/write barriers), and configured it with a heap size of 512MB. The version of the HotSpot client JVM used in our benchmarks is 1.5.0_09.

6.1   Throughput

We developed some micro-benchmarks to test the raw performance of our system.

Empty. A single Reflex task that just increments a counter. No operations are performed on the event space.

Solo. A single Reflex task subscribes and takes events it sends to itself. A `take()` and a `write()` are performed during each `execute()`.

Duo. The version of 'solo' with two Reflex tasks. Each one subscribes and takes events it sends to the other one. A `take()` and a `write()` are performed during each `execute()`.

Max. Before starting the Reflex task, the event space is filled with events containing integers. The body of the `execute()` of the Reflex task takes two integer events from the space and re-writes the one having the largest value back into the space.

Table 1 shows the performance of these micro-benchmarks.

Table 1. Execution time for 1 million iterations, and number of `take/write` operations per second

Benchmark	Time (ms)	Operations/ms
Empty	688	—
Solo	4 553	439,000
Duo	5 775	346,000
Max	6 463	464,000

6.2   Scalability

How does a system based on Reflexes scale in the presence of an increasing number of event processing elements? From a software engineering point of view, it is advantageous to represent different business rules with different Reflexes as they execute independently and can be added/removed at any time. But is it feasible to have hundreds of Reflex tasks in the same JVM? The overheads come from the memory regions and thread associated to Reflexes.

We set up a benchmark which implements a chained hand-off between Reflex tasks. Each Reflex task in the benchmark is given a unique identifier, it takes an event with its id and writes back a copy of the event with the identity of the next Reflex task. As we increase the number of tasks, the chain gets longer.

Fig. 7 shows the time it takes for an event to travel down the chain. We compare numbers for HotSpot and Ovm from one to 2,000 threads. As expected, the execution time increases with the number of Reflexes. In term of numbers of Reflex tasks, Ovm is limited only by the available memory. Thus, we were able to run with 2,000 Reflex tasks, while HotSpot fails with a Java exception if we try to create more than 1,024 threads. Interestingly, in the comparable range Reflex tasks appear more efficient on Ovm than on HotSpot. The worst case for Ovm is 1,849 microseconds while it is 2,541 for HotSpot (thus making HotSpot 27% slower for one thousand threads).

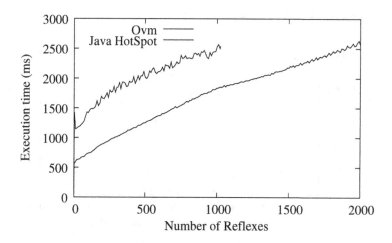

Fig. 7. Execution time as a function of the number of Reflex tasks in the hand-off chain. The x-axis is the number of executing Reflex tasks, the y-axis is the time in microseconds for one event to traverse the entire chain.

6.3 Predictability of Event Processing

Predictability is important in applications which require very low-latency responses to events. There are two challenges for a JVM here: scheduling threads periodically and preemption of non-critical threads. In this benchmark we demonstrate that Reflexes can be scheduled with sub-millisecond accuracy without interference from other concurrently running threads. To establish a worst case scenario, we consider a Reflex with a 50 μs period that performs a `take()` followed by a `write()` of the same event. Concurrently, a low-priority thread performs reads and writes to the space in a tight loop.

Fig. 8 shows the time between two invocations of the `execute()` method in a Reflex. The results are clearly concentrated around the request period with remarkably few outliers.

Fig. 9 shows that when a Reflex misses a deadline the order of magnitude is usually less than 50 μs. Interestingly, Fig. 9 also shows a few extreme deadline misses, some going as high as around 1,500 μs (not shown). We have determined these problems to be related to two timing bugs (locks being held longer than they should) that were found in the mainline Ovm code base. In terms of precision, out of 50,000 iterations only 18 periods were missed, which correspond to a deadline miss rate of 0.03%.

Fig. 10 shows the inter-arrival and processing time of the Reflex from stock trade example when executed on Ovm with a period of 80 μs. Specifically, the Reflex is responsible for generating real-time stock offers in a constant flow and writing them to the event space. As can be seen from the figure, the processing time of the stock seller Reflex lies constantly around 10 μs throughout the shown

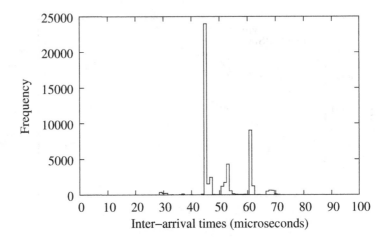

Fig. 8. Frequency of inter-arrival time for a Reflex periodically scheduled with a period of 50 μs when executed (over 50,000 iterations) concurrently with a noise maker thread. The x-axis is the inter-arrival time of two consecutive executions in microseconds. The y-axis is a frequency.

execution period. Likewise, the inter-arrival time represents a stable level of predictability – centered around the scheduled 80 μs period, and with very little variation. In fact, in our experiments covering 100,000 periodic executions, we only found 65 deadline misses (equivalent to a 99.93% met deadlines).

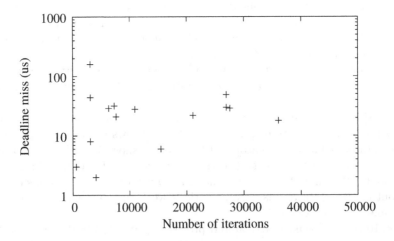

Fig. 9. Deadline misses over time for a Reflex periodically scheduled with a period of 50 μs when executed concurrently with a noise maker thread. The x-axis depicts the periodic executions over time whereas the y-axis depicts the logarithm of deadline misses in microseconds.

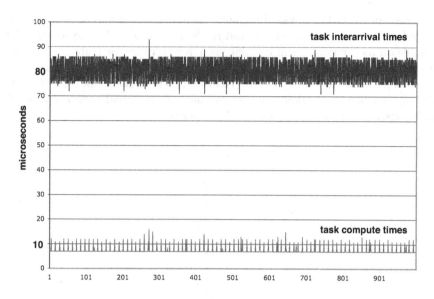

Fig. 10. Inter-arrival and processing time over time for a Reflex implementation of a stock seller scheduled with a period of 80 μs. The x-axis shows the periodic executions (only 1,000 shown) and the y-axis shows the inter-arrival and processing time (both in μs).

6.4   Reflexes on Multi-core Virtual Machine

A limitation of the Ovm implementation is that it is optimized for uni-processor systems. In order to validate applicability of our approach we ported much of the functionality of Reflexes to the IBM WebSphere Real-Time VM, a virtual machine with multi-processor support and a RTSJ-implementation. The implementation of transactions in a multiprocessor setting is significantly different. They use a roll-forward approach in which an atomic method defers all memory mutations to a local log until commit time. Having reached commit time, it is mandatory to check if the state of the Reflex has changed, and if so abort the atomic method. The entries in the log can safely be discarded, in constant time, as the mutations will not be applied. If the task state did not change, the transaction is permitted to commit its changes with the Reflex scheduler briefly locked out for a time corresponding to $\mathcal{O}(n)$, where n is the number of stable heap locations updated. We rely on a combination of program transformations and minimal native extensions to the VM to achieve this. In short, the transformations cause for all memory read and writes to be redirected to the transformation log that is allocated in the native layer on a per task basis. Other native extensions include code for switching between stable and transient memory areas.

We evaluate the impact of transactions on predictability using a synthetic benchmark on an IBM blade server with 4 dual-core AMD Opteron 64 2.4 GHz processors and 12GB of physical memory running Linux 2.6.21.4. A Reflex task is scheduled at a period of 100 μs, and reads at each periodic execute the data available on its input buffer in circular fashion into its stable state. An ordinary Java thread runs continuously and feeds the task with data by invoking an transaction on the task every 20 ms. To evaluate the influence of computational noise and garbage collection, another ordinary Java thread runs concurrently, continuously allocating at the rate of 2MB per second.

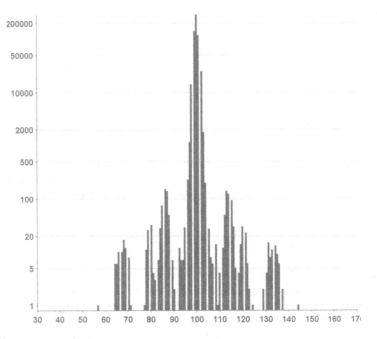

Fig. 11. Frequencies of inter-arrival times of a Reflex with a period of 100 μs continuously interrupted by an ordinary Java thread. The x-axis gives inter-arrival times in microseconds, the y-axis a logarithm of the frequency.

Fig. 11 shows a histogram of the frequencies of inter-arrival times of the Reflex. The figure contains observations covering almost 600,000 periodic executions. Out of 3,000 invocations of the atomic method, 516 of them aborted, indicating that atomic methods were exercised. As can be seen, all observations of the inter-arrival time are centered around the scheduled period of 100 μs. Overall, there are only a few microseconds of jitter. The inter-arrival times range from 57 to 144 μs.

7   Related Work

The approach presented in this paper is closely related to independent work carried out at IBM Research, namely the Eventron [26] and Exotask [3] real-time programming models. Both models have the goal of extending Java in a non-intrusive way with real-time features. They differ in the constraints they impose on programs and the real-time guarantees that can be achieved.

Eventrons provide strong responsiveness guarantees at the expense of expressiveness. In the Eventron model, a real-time task cannot allocate new objects or modify the value of reference variables. Furthermore, they are prevented, by load-time checks, from reading mutable reference variables. The stringent restriction make it safe for an Eventron task to preempt the garbage collector or any other virtual machine service, and thus make it possible to run with periods in the microseconds. Reflexes have similar responsiveness but are less restrictive due to our combination of regions and ownership types.

Exotasks extend Eventrons on a number of accounts. Most importantly, Exotasks are organized in a graph connected by non-blocking point to point communication channels. As the task are isolated, the collection is task-local and can usually be carried out in very little time. Tasks communicate by exchanging messages by deep-copy, whereas StreamFlex adopts the zero-copy communication of [28]. Whereas the message exchange used in the extension presented in this paper also is based on deep-copy, it is not limited to point-to-point communication as the shared event space also facilitates one to many communication.

An interesting question is what advantages these programming models bring compared to RTSJ's `NoHeapRealtimeThread` which is, after all, supported by all RT JVMs. Experience implementing [5,13,21,2] and using [8,20,7,22,24] the RTSJ revealed a number of serious deficiencies. In the RTSJ, interference from the garbage collection is avoided by allocating data needed by time critical real-time tasks from a part of the virtual machine's memory that is not subject to garbage collection, dynamically checked regions known as *scoped memory areas*. Individual objects allocated in a scoped memory area cannot be deallocated; instead, an entire area is torn down as soon as all threads exit it. Dynamically enforced safety rules check that a memory scope with a longer lifetime does not hold a reference to an object allocated in a memory scope with a shorter lifetime and that a `NoHeapRealtimeThread` does not attempt to dereference a pointer into the garbage collected heap.

Another issue with RTSJ is that, due to a lack of isolation, it is possible for a `NoHeapRealtimeThread` to block on a lock held by a plain Java task. If this ever occurs, all bets are off in term of real-time guarantees as the blocking time cannot be bounded. Finally, dynamic memory access checks entail a loss of compositionality. Components may work just fine when tested independently, but break when put in a particular scoped memory context. This is because for a RTSJ program to be correct, developers must deal with an added dimension: *where* a particular datum was allocated. Design patterns and idioms for programming effectively with scoped memory have been proposed [22,6,8], but anecdotal evidence suggests that programmers have a hard time dealing with `NoHeapRealtimeThread`s and that resulting programs are brittle.

The static safety checks used by Reflexes to guard against memory error, presented in [27], is an extension of the implicit ownership type system of [31], the latest in a line of research that emphasizes lightweight type systems for region-based memory [1,32]. Ownership is *implicit* because, unlike e.g. [12,10,11], no ownership parameters are needed. Instead, ownership is assumed by default by using straightforward rules.

8   Conclusion

We have presented a new transactional framework in the context of event-based programming that builds on our previous work on real-time systems. We extend Reflexes, a restricted programming model for highly responsive systems, with a shared event space, that is accessed with transactional semantics, and transactionalize the execution of the Reflexes that operate on the shared space. The resulting model ensures strong atomicity and very low performance overheads.

Our evaluation is encouraging in terms of performance, scalability and predictability when comparing to equivalent executions on a commercial JVM. Also, we have shown that it is possible to achieve 50 μs response times with way less than 1% of the executions failing to meet their deadlines.

In the future, we plan to enrich the programming model with a language for expressing complex, and temporal, patterns of events. We also plan to integrate events with the stream processing paradigm that was explored in [28]. In terms of implementation, we intend to design a customized real-time garbage collector to manage the event space and to integrate the multi-processor extensions that are currently being added to our research infrastructure.

References

1. Andreae, C., Coady, Y., Gibbs, C., Noble, J., Vitek, J., Zhao, T.: Scoped Types and Aspects for Real-Time Java. In: Thomas, D. (ed.) ECOOP 2006. LNCS, vol. 4067, pp. 124–147. Springer, Heidelberg (2006)
2. Armbuster, A., Baker, J., Cunei, A., Holmes, D., Flack, C., Pizlo, F., Pla, E., Prochazka, M., Vitek, J.: A Real-time Java virtual machine with applications in avionics. ACM Transactions in Embedded Computing Systems (TECS) 7(1), 1–49 (2007)
3. Auerbach, J., Bacon, D.F., Iercan, D.T., Kirsch, C.M., Rajan, V.T., Roeck, H., Trummer, R.: Java takes flight: time-portable real-time programming with Exotasks. In: Proceedings of the ACM SIGPLAN/SIGBED Conference on Languages, Compilers, and Tools for Embedded Systems (LCTES), vol. 42, pp. 51–62. ACM, New York (2007)
4. Baker, J., Cunei, A., Flack, C., Pizlo, F., Prochazka, M., Vitek, J., Armbruster, A., Pla, E., Holmes, D.: A real-time java virtual machine for avionics - an experience report. In: Proceedings of the 12th IEEE Real-Time and Embedded Technology and Applications Symposium (RTAS), Washington, DC, USA, pp. 384–396. IEEE Computer Society Press, Los Alamitos (2006)
5. Beebee, W.S., Rinard, M.C.: An implementation of scoped memory for real-time java. In: Henzinger, T.A., Kirsch, C.M. (eds.) EMSOFT 2001. LNCS, vol. 2211, pp. 289–305. Springer, Heidelberg (2001)

6. Benowitz, E.G., Niessner, A.: A patterns catalog for RTSJ software designs. In: Workshop on Java Technologies for Real-Time and Embedded Systems (JTRES), OTM Workshops, pp. 497–507 (2003)
7. Benowitz, E.G., Niessner, A.F.: Experiences in adopting real-time java for flight-like software. In: Proceedings of the International workshop on Java Technologies for Real-Time and Embedded Systems (JTRES), pp. 490–496 (2003)
8. Bollella, G., Canham, T., Carson, V., Champlin, V., Dvorak, D., Giovannoni, B., Indictor, M., Meyer, K., Murray, A., Reinholtz, K.: Programming with non-heap memory in the Real-time specification for Java. In: Companion of the 18th annual ACM SIGPLAN conference on Object-Oriented Programming, Systems, Languages, and Applications (OOPSLA), pp. 361–369 (2003)
9. Bollella, G., Gosling, J., Brosgol, B., Dibble, P., Furr, S., Turnbull, M.: The Real-Time Specification for Java. Addison-Wesley, Reading (2000)
10. Boyapati, C., Lee, R., Rinard, M.: Ownership types for safe programming: Preventing data races and deadlocks. In: Proceedings of the 17th Annual ACM SIGPLAN Conference on Object-Oriented Programming (OOPSLA) (November 2002)
11. Boyapati, C., Salcianu, A., Beebee Jr., W., Rinard, M.: Ownership types for safe region-based memory management in Real-Time Java. In: Proceedings of the ACM SIGPLAN Conference on Programming Language Design and Implementation (PLDI). ACM Press, New York (2003)
12. Clarke, D.G., Potter, J.M., Noble, J.: Ownership types for flexible alias protection. In: Proceedings of the 13th Annual ACM SIGPLAN Conference on Object-Oriented Programming (OOPSLA), October 1998. ACM SIGPLAN Notices, vol. 33(10), pp. 48–64. ACM, New York (1998)
13. Corsaro, A., Cytron, R.: Efficient memory reference checks for Real-time Java. In: Proceedings of Languages, Compilers, and Tools for Embedded Systems, LCTES (2003)
14. Cugola, G., Di Nitto, E., Fuggetta, A.: The JEDI event-based infrastructure and its application to the development of the OPSS WFMS. IEEE Transactions Software Engineering 27(9), 827–850 (2001)
15. Eugster, P.T., Felber, P., Guerraoui, R., Kermarrec, A.-M.: The many faces of publish/subscribe. ACM Comput. Surv. 35(2), 114–131 (2003)
16. Freeman, E., Hüpfer, S., Arnold, K.: JavaSpaces Principles, Patterns, and Practice. Addison-Wesley, Reading (1999)
17. Jagannathan, S., Vitek, J.: Optimistic concurrency semantics for transactions in coordination languages. In: De Nicola, R., Ferrari, G.-L., Meredith, G. (eds.) COORDINATION 2004. LNCS, vol. 2949, pp. 183–198. Springer, Heidelberg (2004)
18. Manson, J., Baker, J., Cunei, A., Jagannathan, S., Prochazka, M., Xin, B., Vitek, J.: Preemptible atomic regions for real-time Java. In: Proceedings of the 26th IEEE Real-Time Systems Symposium (RTSS) (December 2005)
19. Ni, Y., Menon, V.S., Adl-Tabatabai, A.-R., Hosking, A.L., Hudson, R.L., Moss, J., Saha, B., Shpeisman, T.: Open nesting in software transactional memory. In: Proceedings of the 12th ACM SIGPLAN symposium on Principles and practice of parallel programming (PPoPP), pp. 68–78 (2007)
20. Niessner, A.F., Benowitz, E.G.: Rtsj memory areas and their affects on the performance of a flight-like attitude control system. In: Proceedings of the International Workshop on Java Technologies for Real-Time and Embedded Systems (JTRES), pp. 508–519 (2003)
21. Palacz, K., Vitek, J.: Java subtype tests in real-time. In: Cardelli, L. (ed.) ECOOP 2003. LNCS, vol. 2743, pp. 378–404. Springer, Heidelberg (2003)

22. Pizlo, F., Fox, J., Holmes, D., Vitek, J.: Real-time Java scoped memory: design patterns and semantics. In: Proceedings of the IEEE International Symposium on Object-oriented Real-Time Distributed Computing (ISORC), Vienna, Austria (May 2004)
23. Pizlo, F., Hosking, A., Vitek, J.: Hiearchical real-time garbage collection. In: Proceeedings of ACM SIGPLAN/SIGBED 2007 Conference on Languages, Compilers, and Tools for Embedded Systems (LCTES), pp. 123–133 (2007)
24. Pizlo, F., Vitek, J.: An empirical evalutation of memory management alternatives for Real-time Java. In: Proceedings of the 27th IEEE Real-Time Systems Symposium (RTSS) (December 2006)
25. H. Resolution Timers, www.tglx.de/projects/hrtimers/2.6.17/
26. Spoonhower, D., Auerbach, J., Bacon, D.F., Cheng, P., Grove, D.: Eventrons: a safe programming construct for high-frequency hard real-time applications. In: Proceedings of the ACM SIGPLAN Conference on Programming Language Design and Implementation (PLDI), vol. 41, pp. 283–294. ACM, New York (2006)
27. Spring, J., Pizlo, F., Guerraoui, R., Vitek, J.: Reflexes: Abstractions for highly responsive systems. In: Proceedings of the 3rd International ACM SIGPLAN/SIGOPS Conference on Virtual Execution Environments, VEE (2007)
28. Spring, J., Privat, J., Guerraoui, R., Vitek, J.: StreamFlex: High-throughput stream programming in Java. In: Proceedings of the 22nd Annual ACM SIGPLAN Conference on Object-Oriented Programming, OOPSLA (2007)
29. Strom, R.E., Banavar, G., Chandra, T.D., Kaplan, M., Miller, K., Mukherjee, B., Sturman, D.C., Ward, M.: Gryphon: An information flow based approach to message brokering. CoRR: Distributed, Parallel, and Cluster Computing, cs.DC/9810019 (1998)
30. Vitek, J., Bryce, C., Oriol, M.: Coordinating processes with secure spaces. Science of Computer Programming 46(1-2), 163–193 (2003)
31. Zhao, T., Baker, J., Hunt, J., Noble, J., Vitek, J.: Implicit ownership types for memory management. Science of Computer Programming 71(3), 213–241 (2008)
32. Zhao, T., Noble, J., Vitek, J.: Scoped types for real-time Java. In: Proceedings of the 25th IEEE International Real-Time Systems Symposium, RTSS (2004)

Exceptionally Safe Futures

Armand Navabi and Suresh Jagannathan

Purdue University, Department of Computer Science
{anavabi,suresh}@cs.purdue.edu

Abstract. A *future* is a well-known programming construct used to introduce concurrency to sequential programs. Computations annotated as futures are executed asynchronously and run concurrently with their continuations. Typically, futures are *not* transparent annotations: a program with futures need not produce the same result as the sequential program from which it was derived. *Safe* futures guarantee a future-annotated program produce the same result as its sequential counterpart. Ensuring safety is especially challenging in the presence of constructs such as exceptions that permit the expression of non-local control-flow. For example, a future may raise an exception whose handler is in its continuation. To ensure safety, we must guarantee the continuation does not discard this handler regardless of the continuation's own internal control-flow (e.g. exceptions it raises or futures it spawns). In this paper, we present a formulation of safe futures for a higher-order functional language with first-class exceptions. Safety can be guaranteed dynamically by stalling the execution of a continuation that has an exception handler *potentially* required by its future until the future completes. To enable greater concurrency, we develop a static analysis and instrumentation and formalize the runtime behavior for instrumented programs that allows execution to discard handlers *precisely* when it is safe to do so.

1 Introduction

A *future* [3] provides a simple way for programmers to introduce concurrency to sequential programs. When executed, a computation annotated as a future yields a *placeholder* and introduces an asynchronous thread of control whose result is stored within the associated placeholder. When the computation following the future (its *continuation*) requires the future's value, it performs a *touch* or *claim* operation on the placeholder. A claim action acts as a synchronization barrier, forcing the continuation to block until the future yields a result. For programs with no side-effects, a future-annotated program exhibits the same observable behavior as the original sequential version. To preserve deterministic behavior equivalent to that of the original sequential program in the presence of side-effects requires additional machinery.

Consider the code example in Figure 1 written in an ML-like language with mutable references that has been extended with futures. Function f takes an integer argument x. If x is even, it returns the result of applying g to the value stored in reference r. If x is odd, it stores the result of g (x) in r and returns x. Variable a is bound to the result of a future-annotated computation (line 5). Thus computation f (m) is executed concurrently with its continuation. The continuation spawns future f (n) to be bound to b (line 6), which is evaluated concurrently with call f (p) (line 7). Thus, the three calls to function

J. Field and V.T. Vasconcelos (Eds.): COORDINATION 2009, LNCS 5521, pp. 47–65, 2009.

f will be executed concurrently. *Safe* futures require that concurrent execution of these calls adhere to the dependences imposed by sequential evaluation: a read of reference r performed in one call must not witness a write to r by a later one, and a write to r by one call must be witnessed by a read of r in a later call.

```
let val g = fn x => (* side-effect free computation *)      1
        val r = ref 0                                        2
        val f = fn x => if ((x mod 2) = 0) then g (!r)       3
                        else (r := g (x); x)                 4
in let val a = future (f (m))                                5
       val b = future (f (n))                                6
    in f (p)                                                 7
    end                                                      8
end                                                          9
```

Fig. 1. Safe futures in the presence of mutable references

Safety can be guaranteed using both dynamic [10] and static [9] techniques. For example, compiler inserted barriers supported by a lightweight runtime can be used to enforce dependences defined by the sequential semantics [9]. Figure 2 illustrates how function f can be rewritten based on an interprocedural control-flow analysis. The read on line 3 is preceded by barrier ALLOWED(L3), which completes only once all futures in the logical past have granted permission by performing a GRANT(L3) operation. A future can grant permission for condition L3 once it has entered a branch in which no further conflicting write access to r will be performed, or it has completed its final write to r. Thus in the true branch of function f, the future will immediately grant on L3 allowing its continuation to read r because the future will not write it. Note that the GRANT on line 3 does not notify the ALLOWED barrier on line 3; the GRANT is granting its continuation, which is in its logical future, permission to read r and the ALLOWED barrier on line 3 is waiting for permission from futures in its logical past. In the false branch, the future will only grant after it has written to r, ensuring its continuation will witness its write. Note that similar instrumentation is required to force the write on line 7 to wait for its futures (i.e. computations which execute in the logical past) to read r, but has been omitted in Figure 2 for brevity.

Given the instrumentation presented in Figure 2, consider the resulting runtime schedule for an execution where $m = 13$, $n = 4$ and $p = 2$. Since m is odd, the call f (m) will write to r. Both f (n) and f (p) will not write to r, and therefore both immediately grant on condition L3 notifying their continuations that they will not change the value of reference r. Before reading the value of r, they perform an ALLOWED operation on condition L3. The first future computation, f (m) is logically ordered before both computations, and therefore their ALLOWED barriers must wait for the future's GRANT. The future computation grants *after* it has written to r ensuring the currently executing calls to f read the value of r that is consistent with a sequential execution.

Unfortunately, the presence of mutable references is not the only means by which sequential behavior can be compromised. Exceptions and related abstractions that

```
val f =                                                          1
    fn x => if ((x mod 2) = 0)                                   2
            then let val tmp = (GRANT(L3); ALLOWED(L3); !r)     3
                 in g (tmp)                                      4
                 end                                            5
            else let val tmp = g (x)                            6
                     val _ = (r := tmp; GRANT(L3))              7
                 in x                                            8
                 end                                            9
```

Fig. 2. Barrier Instrumentation

introduce non-local control-flow introduce challenging complications. In the presence of exceptional control-flow, a future may raise an exception whose handler is defined in its continuation. Since the future and continuation are evaluated concurrently, the continuation must not be allowed to discard a handler that may be required by the future.

Consider the code example presented in Figure 3 written in an ML-like language extended with futures. The example does not have mutable references. Function f either returns the result of applying g to argument x if x is odd, or raises an exception if x is even. Under a sequential evaluation (i.e. one with futures erased), f (m) and f (n) are evaluated to completion in that order. If future f (m) raises an exception that it does not internally handle (i.e. an *escaping* exception), the continuation f (n) is not evaluated. For example if $m = 0$ then computation f (m) on line 5 raises an escaping exception and computation f (n) is not evaluated. Instead the exception raised by the future is handled by the handler on line 6 and the program evaluates to 0.

```
let val g = fn x => (* side-effect free computation *)           1
    val f = fn x => if ((x mod 2) = 1) then g (x)              2
                    else if (x = 0) then raise ZeroException   3
                         else raise NonZeroEvenException       4
in let b = future (f (m)) in f (n) end                         5
   handle ZeroException => 0                                   6
        | NonZeroEvenException => 1                            7
end                                                            8
```

Fig. 3. Safe futures in the presence of exception handling

To enforce determinism in the presence of concurrent execution, constraints must be imposed on what a future's continuation may do. In a concurrent execution, future f (m) and continuation f (n) are evaluated concurrently, but if the future raises an escaping exception the continuation should have never been evaluated. This imposes constraints on continuation f (n). For example, if $n = 2$, then f (n) will raise exception NonZeroEvenException. If continuation f (n) raises the exception before its future completes, the evaluation cannot discard the ZeroException handler and handle

NonZeroEven-Exception since the handlers may be required by f (m). Furthermore, even if the continuation does not raise an exception and instead evaluates to a value (i.e. if $n = 3$), the continuation is not free to evaluate past the exception handlers because its future still may raise an escaping exception that requires one of the handlers.

Consider enforcing the safety constraints imposed on the execution of programs that have futures and first-class exceptions, like the example below, using statically injected barriers (e.g. GRANT, ALLOWED).

```
let y = future (f (n)) in c () end handle E => ...
```

To disallow evaluation of the continuation c () from discarding the handler that may be required by future f (n), ALLOWED barriers need to be inserted at all exit points in function c. The exit points consist of program points that signify successful completion of the function and any raise statement that potentially raises an escaping exception. GRANT's would need to be inserted in function f at program points where f is guaranteed to no longer raise escaping exception E so that future f (n) will notify its continuation of when it is safe for it to proceed past the handler for E. Necessary imprecision in the static analysis to guarantee safety (especially in the presence of non-local control-flow) can lead to an overly conservative injection of ALLOWED barriers, forcing continuations to block when it may be safe to proceed, and thus limiting parallelism.

Determining the earliest point during execution for which it is safe for a continuation to cross a handler boundary (i.e. discard a handler) is the focus of this paper. The context of our investigation is a higher-order functional language with first-class exceptions. We omit mutable references from the language to focus on formulating safety for futures in the presence of non-local control-flow. The treatment of mutable references for safe futures is orthogonal to the issues raised by exception-handling, and has been studied in previous work [9,10]. We present an operational semantics that guarantees safety by stalling a continuation from discarding an exception handler before its future (or any future *it* may have created) completes. To enable greater concurrency, we formalize a flow-sensitive static analysis and instrumentation technique to annotate program points with possible escaping exceptions that may be reached from that point. We then define an operational semantics on instrumented programs that allows a continuation to cross a handler boundary before futures spawned in its try block have completed, if those futures and the futures they spawn (or may spawn) are guaranteed to not require the handler, as dictated by the results of the static analysis. Our results are the first to formalize the integration of safe (deterministic) futures within a language that supports first-class exceptions.

2   The Language

Figure 4 presents the syntax of a higher-order functional language Λ that has futures and first-class exceptions. The language is based on the language presented in [1]. It is an intermediate representation of an idealized functional language with futures. The language has been extended with first-class exceptions, an exit primitive that terminates the computation, and constructs to raise and handle exceptions. Like [1], our language does not have a touch (or claim) primitive. Instead, the parallel semantics we present

KERNEL-LANGUAGE Λ:

$$
\begin{aligned}
M \in \Lambda ::= \ & V_l \ | \ x_l \ | \ \text{exit}_l \ x \ | \ \text{raise}_l \ x \\
| \ & \text{try}_l \ M \ \text{handle} \ X \mapsto M \\
| \ & \text{let} \ x = V \ \text{in} \ M \\
| \ & \text{let} \ x = \text{if} \ y \ \text{then} \ M \ \text{else} \ M \ \text{in} \ M \\
| \ & \text{let} \ x = (y \ z) \ \text{in} \ M \\
| \ & \text{let} \ x = \text{future}(M) \ \text{in} \ M \\
V \in \text{Value} ::= \ & c \ | \ \lambda \text{x}.M \ | \ X \\
x \in \text{Vars} := \ & \{x, y, z, \ldots\} \\
c \in \text{Const} := \ & \{\text{unit}, \text{true}, \text{false}, 0, 1, \ldots\} \\
X \in \text{Exception} ::= \ & \text{Exn}_1 \ | \ \text{Exn}_2 \ | \ \ldots \ | \ \text{Exn}_n
\end{aligned}
$$

Fig. 4. Language Syntax

transparently *touch* placeholder variables. This makes future annotations truly transparent relieving the programmer of the burden of inserting touch operations based on the data flow properties of the program. Although the language does not support dynamic creation of new exception values, adding such functionality does not introduce any additional complexity to our development. We make the usual assumption that all λ- and let-bound variables are distinct. All other terms in the language (i.e. variables, values, exit statements, ...) are given unique labels so that the static analysis and instrumentation presented in Section 4 can uniquley identify program terms.

2.1 Sequential Evaluation Semantics

Figure 5 defines the sequential semantics for programs in Λ. The semantics is defined by function F_{seq} that maps a program M to a result R where R is either a constant, a procedure (i.e., λ-term), an exception value, or error. The semantics erases future annotations in a program M with a runtime term that synchronously evaluates the future computation and binds its result to a variable (resulting in program $\widetilde{M}$). The evaluation rule $N \rightarrow_{seq} N'$ reduces runtime term N to a new program term N'. Evaluating exit V causes evaluation to terminate with result V.

3 Safe (Parallel) Dynamic Evaluation

In the parallel semantics presented in this section, the result of an incomplete future computation is represented at runtime by a placeholder. The semantics specifies concurrently evaluating future computations and enforces a global logical order on computations. As demonstrated in the semantics presented in Section 3.1, this ordering is used when a computation attempts to exit the program and when a future computation invalidates its continuation by raising an escaping exception. Logically, a future computation N_f is ordered before the computation N_c associated with its continuation. Any future computations spawned during the evaluation of N_f are also ordered before

$$R \in Results ::= c \mid \lambda x.M \mid X \mid \text{error}$$

$$N \in RTTerms ::= V \mid x \mid \text{exit } V \mid \text{raise } X \mid \text{try } N \text{ handle } X \mapsto N$$

$$\mid \text{ let } x = \text{if } V \text{ then } N \text{ else } N \text{ in } N \mid \text{ let } x = (V\,V) \text{ in } N$$

$$\mid \text{ let } x = N \text{ in } N$$

$$\widetilde{M} = M[(\text{let } x = \text{future}(M') \text{ in } M'')/(\text{let } x = M' \text{ in } M'')]$$

$$F_{seq}(M) = \begin{cases} V & \text{if } \widetilde{M} \Rightarrow^*_{seq} V \\ \text{error} & \text{otherwise} \end{cases}$$

EVALUATION RULES:

$$\varepsilon \in EvalCntxt ::= [\,] \mid \text{try } \varepsilon \text{ handle } X \mapsto N \mid \text{let } x = \varepsilon \text{ in } N$$

$$\frac{N \to_{seq} N'}{\varepsilon[N] \Rightarrow_{seq} \varepsilon[N']} \qquad \varepsilon[\text{exit } V] \Rightarrow_{seq} V$$

try V handle $X \mapsto N$	$\to_{seq} V$	(try)
try raise X handle $X \mapsto N$	$\to_{seq} N$	$(handle)$
try raise X' handle $X \mapsto N$	$\to_{seq}$ raise X'	$(tryraise)$
let $x = V$ in N	$\to_{seq} N[x/V]$	$(bind)$
let $x =$ raise X in N	$\to_{seq}$ raise X	$(bindraise)$
let $x =$ if V then N_1 else N_2 in N	$\to_{seq} \begin{cases} \text{let } x = N_1 \text{ in } N & V = \text{true} \\ \text{let } x = N_2 \text{ in } N & V = \text{false} \end{cases}$	(if)
let $x = (V\,V')$ in N	$\to_{seq}$ let $x = N'[y/V']$ in $N \quad V = \lambda y.N'$	$(apply)$

Fig. 5. Sequential Evaluation

N_c. This ordering is maintained by assigning each computation an *order identifier* consisting of a real number r and integer d. A computation with order identifier (r, d) is logically ordered before a computation with (r', d') if $r < r'$. The integer d in the order identifier is used to determine how to compute new order identifiers for newly spawned computations. The primordial main computation is given order identifier $(0.0, 0)$.

Let computation N, with order identifier (r, d), evaluatee the following runtime term: $(\text{let } x = \text{future}(M) \text{ in } M')$. The semantics replaces computation N with two new computations N_f and N_c to evaluate the future computation M and its continuation M', respectively. N_f is given order identifier $(r, d + 1)$ and N_c is given $(r + 0.5^d, d + 1)$. This ordering implies that N_f is logically ordered before N_c because $(r < (r + 0.5^d))$.

Computations are evaluated in parallel, and each computation may spawn a future replacing itself with two new computations. An important property of assigning order identifiers is that all computations transitively spawned by the future computation N_f are also ordered before the continuation N_c. As explained above, if the spawning computation N has order identifier (r, d), the semantics assigns future N_f order identifier $(r, d + 1)$ and continuation N_c order identifier $(r + 0.5^d, d + 1)$. Suppose computation N_f spawns another future, $N_{f'}$ with continuation $N_{c'}$. The semantics assigns $N_{f'}$ order identifier $(\mathbf{r}, \mathbf{d} + 2)$ and $N_{c'}$ order identifier $(\mathbf{r} + 0.5^{\mathbf{d}+1}, \mathbf{d} + 2)$. Note the following relation holds: $(\mathbf{r} < (\mathbf{r} + 0.5^{\mathbf{d}+1}) < (\mathbf{r} + 0.5^{\mathbf{d}}))$. Thus $N_{f'}$ is ordered before $N_{c'}$ which is ordered before N_c. All computations transitively spawned by N_c will be given order identifiers $\mathbf{r}'$ such that $(\mathbf{r}' \geq \mathbf{r} + 0.5^{\mathbf{d}})$ and will therefore be ordered after $N_{f'}$ and $N_{c'}$. It is straightforward to see that the demonstrated relation between order identifiers holds for all futures and their continuations.

3.1 Semantics

The operational semantics (see Figure 6) is defined by function F_{sd} from program M to a result R (where R is the same as it was in the sequential semantics). The transition rule $S \Rightarrow_{sd} S'$ maps a program state to a new program state. A program state is a process S which represents a collection of concurrently evaluating runtime terms (i.e. computations). Each computation maintains a local term context which is a three-tuple consisting of the placeholder p whose value is being computed by the term, the order identifier $(\mathbf{r}', \mathbf{d}')$ of the computation that spawned the future, and the computation's own order identifier, $(\mathbf{r}, \mathbf{d})$. The original program term is the only computation that is not a future. It is evaluated with term context $\langle \mathtt{main}, (-1, -1), (0, 0)\rangle$, where $\mathtt{main}$ is a special placeholder value and $(-1, -1)$ signifies that it has no spawning parent.

Any references to a future's result in its continuation are replaced with a new placeholder variable. The semantics guarantees safety by preventing unsafe evaluation of the continuation beyond a $\varepsilon^{\bullet p}$ evaluation context. The evaluation context signifies that the term being evaluated in the hole is a continuation of the future corresponding to placeholder p. Evaluation of terms with $V^{\bullet p}$, $\mathtt{raise}\ X^{\bullet p}$, and $\mathtt{exit}\ V^{\bullet p}$ are restricted. For example, the term $(\mathtt{try}\ V^{\bullet p}\ \mathtt{handle}\ X \mapsto V')$ is stuck and cannot discard the handler because the future corresponding to p, which was spawned inside of the try body, has yet to complete and may require the handler defined by the try statement.

Runtime terms in a continuation may contain placeholder variables. The introduction of placeholder variables is discussed below as part of the *future* rule. In certain cases the result of a placeholder is required to proceed with evaluation and in other cases it is not. For example, in the term $(\mathtt{let}\ x = (p_1\ p_2)\ \mathtt{in}\ N)$ the abstraction result of p_1 is required for evaluation to proceed, but the result of argument p_2 is not required. The placeholder can simply be substituted into the λ-expression's body. Given a runtime term N with placeholder variables, the function $\mathcal{R}(N)$ annotates each placeholder variable p whose result is required with a $^+$ superscript. This distinction forces the continuation to perform a touch operation only on placeholder variables whose values are necessary to its evaluation. To guarantee that the program evaluates to a non-placeholder value, the program M is transformed to $(\mathtt{let}\ x = M\ \mathtt{in}\ \mathtt{exit}\ x)$. The exit statement forces a touch operation on variable x. This is necessary in the case that during evaluation x is replaced by a placeholder variable (e.g. if M is $(\mathtt{let}\ x = \mathtt{future}(M')\ \mathtt{in}\ x)$).

Rule *seq* states that if $N \in S$ and $N \rightarrow_{seq} N'$ then $S \Rightarrow_{sd} S'$ where in the new process state S', term N is replaced by $\mathcal{R}(N')$. Since variables may be substituted by placeholders (e.g. under *apply* rule of $\rightarrow_{seq}$), the $\mathcal{R}$ function is applied to the new term. Note that all rules, except for the *seq* rule, are on terms that contain a $^{\bullet p}$ or a placeholder variable, and that both $^{\bullet p}$ and placeholders are introduced by the *future* rule (explained below). This implies that evaluation under $\rightarrow_{seq}$ and $\Rightarrow_{sd}$ are trivially equivalent in the absence of futures. The *let* rule allows continuations to proceed past the let evaluation context. The $\varepsilon^{\bullet p}$ evaluation context is only meant to disallow unsafe evaluation (e.g. discarding of try statements).

Rule *future* defines evaluation of a future-spawning term. Given term (let $x =$ future(M) in $M') \in S$, the term is replaced in the process state with two new terms-one to evaluate the future computation M and one to evaluate the continuation M'. The continuation is evaluated in the evaluation context of the spawning term which includes any try statements that contain the spawning term. References to the variable x in M' are replaced by a fresh placeholder p' and function $\mathcal{R}$ replaces placeholders that need to be touched with p'^+. If the term context of the spawning computation is $\langle p, (\mathbf{r}, \mathbf{d}), (\mathbf{r}', \mathbf{d}') \rangle$, the term context of future computation is $\langle p', (\mathbf{r}', \mathbf{d}'), (\mathbf{r}', \mathbf{d}' + 1) \rangle$ and the term context of continuation is $\langle p, (\mathbf{r}, \mathbf{d}), (\mathbf{r}' + 0.5^{\mathbf{d}'}, \mathbf{d}' + 1) \rangle$. When the continuation requires the value of p'^+ the semantics will know which computation to synchronize with based on the term context of future computation (via the *touch* rule). The continuation term is evaluated in the $\varepsilon^{\bullet p'}$ context so as to block the continuation from discarding a handler that may be required by the future corresponding to p'. When the future evaluates to a value, it removes the blocking context from its continuation (via rule *unblock*). For a computation to evaluate to a value (rather than to $V^{\bullet p''}$, for example) all of its futures must remove their corresponding blocking contexts.

The *raise* rule defines what happens when a future raises an escaping exception. Terms in S' represent valid computations and terms in S_c represent computations that have been invalidated by this future's raise. All computations that have been spawned as a result of evaluating the continuation of the raising future are invalid. All other computations are valid. Invalidated computations are replaced with $\perp$. The term $\varepsilon^{\bullet p}$ in the continuation of the future corresponding to p is replaced with a raise of the exception from the future, propagating the future's raise to the context where it was spawned. By replacing the term and the $^{\bullet p}$, the semantics ensures that the future's raise will never be propagated again. The *exit* rule requires that all computations that are logically ordered before the exiting computation have evaluated to values and therefore cannot invalidate the exiting computation.

3.2 Example

Consider the following program:

1. let $x =$ future(M_1) in
2.   try let $y =$ future(M_2) in
3.   let $z =$ future(M_3) in M_4
4.   handle $X \mapsto c$

Evaluation begins with a single term in the process state evaluating the above let expression. The program spawns three futures M_1, M_2 and M_3 resulting in a process state with four terms. Runtime terms N_1, N_2 and N_3 correspond to program terms M_1, M_2 and M_3, respectively. The continuation of these futures is the following runtime term in the process state: $(\text{try } N_4'^{\bullet p_3 \bullet p_2} \text{ handle } X \mapsto c)^{\bullet p_1}$, where term N_4' corresponds to the evaluation of program term M_4. The bulleted evaluation context on term N_4' prevents

$$N \in RTTerms ::= \dots \mid \text{let } x = \text{future}(N) \text{ in } N \mid \perp \mid p^+ \mid N^{\bullet p}$$

$$V \in Value ::= \dots \mid p$$

$$p \in PhVars ::= \{\text{main}, p_1, p_2, \dots\}$$

$$C \in TermContext ::= \langle p \times (real \times int) \times (real \times int)\rangle$$

$$S ::= \{(N_1)_{C_1}, \dots, (N_n)_{C_n}\}$$

$$S|N_C ::= S \cup \{N_C\}$$

$$\mathcal{R}(N) = \begin{cases} V & N = V \\ x & N = x \\ \text{exit } p^+ & N = \text{exit } p \\ \text{raise } p^+ & N = \text{raise } p \\ \text{try } \mathcal{R}(N') \text{ handle } X \mapsto \mathcal{R}(N_h) & N = \text{try } N' \text{ handle } X \mapsto N_h \\ \text{let } x = \text{if } p^+ \text{ then } \mathcal{R}(N_1) \text{ else } \mathcal{R}(N_2) & N = (\text{let } x = \text{if } p \text{ then } N_1 \text{ else } N_2 \\ \quad \text{in } \mathcal{R}(N) & \quad \text{in } N) \\ \dots \end{cases}$$

$$F_{sd}(M) = \begin{cases} V & \text{if } \{(\text{let } x = M \text{ in exit } x)_{\langle \text{main}, (-1,-1),(0,0)\rangle}\} \Rightarrow^*_{sd} \\ & \quad \{(N_1)_{C_1}, \dots, (N_n)_{C_n}, (V)_{\langle \text{main}, (-1,-1),(r,d)\rangle}\} \\ \text{error} & \text{otherwise} \end{cases}$$

EVALUATION RULES:

$$\varepsilon \in EvalCntxt ::= [\,] \mid \text{try } \varepsilon \text{ handle } X \mapsto N \mid \text{let } x = \varepsilon \text{ in } N \mid \text{exit } \varepsilon \mid \text{raise } \varepsilon$$
$$\mid \text{let } x = \text{if } \varepsilon \text{ then } N_t \text{ else } N_f \text{ in } N \mid \text{let } x = (\varepsilon \, V) \text{ in } N \mid \varepsilon^{\bullet p}$$

$$\frac{N \rightarrow_{seq} N'}{S|(\varepsilon[N])_C \Rightarrow_{sd} S|(\varepsilon[\mathcal{R}(N')])_C} \quad (seq)$$

$$\frac{\text{let } x = N \text{ in } N' \rightarrow_{seq} N''}{S|(\varepsilon[\text{let } x = N^{\bullet p_1 \dots \bullet p_n} \text{ in } N'])_C \Rightarrow_{sd} S|(\varepsilon[N''^{\bullet p_1 \dots \bullet p_n}])_C} \quad (let)$$

$$\frac{\begin{array}{c} C = \langle p, (r,d), (r',d')\rangle \quad p' \text{ fresh} \\ C_f = \langle p', (r',d'), (r', d'+1)\rangle \quad C_c = \langle p, (r,d), (r'+0.5^{d'}, d'+1)\rangle \end{array}}{S|(\varepsilon[\text{let } x = \text{future}(N) \text{ in } N'])_C \Rightarrow_{sd} S|(N)_{C_f}|(\varepsilon[\mathcal{R}(N'[x/p'])^{\bullet p'}])_{C_c}} \quad (future)$$

$$\frac{(V)_{\langle p,(r,d),(r',d')\rangle} \in S}{S|(\varepsilon[p^+])_C \Rightarrow_{sd} S|(\varepsilon[V])_C} \quad \frac{(V)_{\langle p,(r,d),(r',d')\rangle} \in S}{S|(\varepsilon[N^{\bullet p}])_C \Rightarrow_{sd} S|(\varepsilon[N])_C} \quad (touch) \quad (unblock)$$

$$\frac{\begin{array}{c} C_f = \langle p, (r,d), (r',d')\rangle \\ S' = \{(N')_{\langle p_i,(r_i,d_i),(r'_i,d'_i)\rangle} \mid (N')_{\langle p_i,(r_i,d_i),(r'_i,d'_i)\rangle} \in S, \ (r'_i < r' \text{ or } r'_i \geq (r+0.5^{d-1}))\} \\ S_c = \{(\perp)_C \mid (N')_C \in S, (N')_C \notin S'\} \quad S'' = S' \cup S_c \end{array}}{S|(\text{raise } X)_{C_f}|(\varepsilon[N^{\bullet p}])_{C_c} \Rightarrow_{sd} S''|(\text{raise } X)_{C_f}|(\varepsilon[\text{raise } X])_{C_c}} \quad (raise)$$

$$\frac{\begin{array}{c} C = \langle p, (r',d'), (r,d)\rangle \\ (N_i)_{\langle p_i,(r'_i,d'_i),(r_i,d_i)\rangle} \notin S \quad r_i < r \quad N_i \neq V' \end{array}}{S|(\varepsilon[\text{exit } V])_C \Rightarrow_{sd} \{(V)_{\langle \text{main},(-1,-1),(r,d)\rangle}\}} \quad (exit)$$

Fig. 6. Safe Dynamic Evaluation

the continuation from discarding the handler, because the futures corresponding to p_2 and p_3 (i.e. N_2 and N_3) may require it.

Consider what happens if term N_2 raises exception X without handling it internally. The *raise* rule will propagate the exception into its continuation and invalidate all futures spawned by its continuation (i.e. N_3). N_3 is replaced with $\perp$, and

the term $N_4'^{\bullet p_3 \bullet p_2}$ is replaced with the raise of exception X, resulting in term
(try raise X handle $X \mapsto c)^{\bullet p_1}$.

The continuation is now free to use the handler and evaluate to c. Note that the continuation still has the blocking context for p_1 from the first future preventing it from completing with value c. This is because N_1 may exit the program or raise an escaping exception invalidating its continuation's computation. Once N_1 evaluates to a value it notifies the continuation by removing the p_1 blocking context, allowing the main thread to complete with value c.

3.3   Semantic Equivalence

In this section we provide a proof sketch proving that the result of evaluating program M under safe dynamic semantics is the same as evaluating M under sequential semantics. For the proof, we define a transform function T to map a process state S in the safe dynamic semantics to a runtime term N in the sequential semantics. We use the transform function to show that for any process state S, if $S \Rightarrow_{sd}^* V$ then $T(S) \Rightarrow_{seq}^* V$.

Given a process state S, the transform function T first identifies the computation N_f in the process state which is logically ordered before all other computations (i.e. the computation with the smallest r as its order identifier). If the continuation of N_f has not spawned any new computations, then the transform function will combine the future computation and its continuation to build runtime term (let $x = \text{future}(N_f)$ in N), where N is the continuation of N_f. If the continuation has split its computation by spawning futures, which also may have spawned other futures, then the transform function is recursively applied to all computations that have been spawned as a result of evaluating N_f's continuation to construct N_f's continuation term. The computations' order identifiers are used to identify which computations have been spawned from a given continuation. The transform function also replaces runtime terms that may appear in the safe dynamic semantics but not in the sequential semantics with equivalent terms. For example, invalidated computations represented as $\perp$ in the sequential semantics are replaced with (exit -1) which is safe because those computations will never be reached in the evaluation of the runtime term due to an exception raise. The transform function and proof details are presented in an accompanying technical report [8].

Lemma 1. *If S is a final state that evaluates to V then $T(S) \Rightarrow_{seq}^* V$.*
The lemma states that if a final process state S reached by evaluation under safe dynamic semantics evaluates to V, then the transform of the process state evaluates to V under sequential semantics.

Lemma 2. *If $S \Rightarrow_{sd} S'$, then $T(S) \Rightarrow_{seq}^* N'$ and $T(S') \Rightarrow_{seq}^* N'$.*
The lemma states that given an evaluation rule $S \Rightarrow_{sd} S'$, if the transform of S (i.e. $T(S)$) yields runtime term N_s and the transform of S' (i.e. $T(S')$) yields runtime term $N_{s'}$ then there exists a sequence of $\Rightarrow_{seq}$ rules from N_s, and a sequence of $\Rightarrow_{seq}$ rules from $N_{s'}$ that result in a common term N'. The lemma is proved by a case analysis on evaluation derivations $S \Rightarrow_{sd} S'$.

Theorem 1. *If $F_{sd}(M) = R$, then $F_{seq}(M) = R$.*
The result of evaluating program M under the safe dynamic semantics is guaranteed to

be the same as the result of evaluating M under the sequential semantics. The proof is by induction on the length of $\Rightarrow_{sd}$ evaluation sequences. The base case is demonstrated by instantiating Lemma 1 and 2 and the inductive case is demonstrated by instantiating the inductive hypothesis and Lemma 2.

4 Instrumented Evaluation

The operational semantics defined thus far prevents a continuation from executing past a `try` expression if a future spawned within the try block has yet to complete. In this section, we present a flow-sensitive static analysis, program instrumentation, and a refined operational semantics that extracts more parallelism than this conservative treatment while still guaranteeing determinism. Informally, our solution is based on the observation that if a future reaches a point in its execution where it will no longer raise escaping exception X, then its continuation can proceed past a handler for exception X.

In the instrumented semantics, the blocking evaluation context is of the form $\varepsilon^{\bullet(p,\Sigma)}$. The evaluation context signifies that the term being evaluated in the whole is a continuation of the future that corresponds to placeholder p and that the evaluation of the future may result in a raise of escaping exception $X \in \Sigma$ or may exit the program if $\texttt{exit} \in \Sigma$. A continuation evaluating runtime term $(\texttt{try}\ V^{\bullet(p,\Sigma)}\ \texttt{handle}\ X \mapsto N_h)$, where $X \notin \Sigma$ may proceed past the `try` expression (unlike in the previously presented semantics), thus discarding the handler. Static instrumentation specifies which escaping exceptions an evaluating future computation may raise and whether or not it may exit the program. We present an operational semantics that leverages the instrumentation so that a future computation notifies its continuation immediately when its computation and the futures it creates may no longer raise an escaping exception or perform an exit operation (by removing elements from Σ in the blocking context of its continuation).

4.1 Static Analysis and Program Instrumentation

Our instrumentation assumes the presence of control-flow analysis $Flow_P(x)$ [6,7] which maps variable x to all possible values it may be bound to during the evaluation of program P. Program term M is instrumented with a *grant* set Σ (represented by superscript $\triangleright\Sigma$) and a *nogrant* set Σ' (represented by subscript $\triangleleft\Sigma'$). The *grant* set Σ includes all escaping exceptions that may be raised by the instrumented term, and a special `exit` element if the term may exit the program. The *nogrant* set Σ' includes all escaping exceptions that may be raised after evaluation of the instrumented term by the enclosing term and the `exit` element if the enclosing term may exit the program after evaluation of the instrumented term. The *nogrant* set ensures a computation does not prematurely notify its continuation that it cannot reach an escaping exception or exit. Term M is transformed to the instrumented term $\widetilde{T}$ defined by the following grammar:

$$T \in InstTerms' ::= V_l \mid x_l \mid \texttt{exit}_l\ x \mid \texttt{raise}_l\ x$$
$$\mid\ \texttt{try}_l\ \widetilde{T}\ \texttt{handle}\ X \mapsto \widetilde{T} \mid \dots$$
$$\widetilde{T} \in InstTerms ::= T^{\triangleright\Sigma}_{\triangleleft\Sigma'}$$

When a future f is spawned its continuation is evaluated in context: $\varepsilon^{\bullet(p,\Sigma)}$, where Σ is initially equal to f's *grant* set. Let f be the following future computation:

$$(\texttt{let } x = \texttt{if } y \texttt{ then raise } z \texttt{ else } M_f \texttt{ in } M)$$

If $Flow_P(z) = \{X\}$ and computations M_f and M do not raise an escaping exception X (or exit), then the continuation of f may discard X's handler as soon as control enters the false branch during the evaluation of f. Static instrumentation allows the instrumented semantics to notify f's continuation when control enters the false branch. In the instrumented term below Σ and Σ_f are the *grant* sets (i.e. the sets of possible escaping exceptions and exit that may be reached) of M and M_f, respectively.

$$(\texttt{let } x = \texttt{if } y \texttt{ then } (\texttt{raise } z)^{\triangleright\{X\}}_{\triangleleft\Sigma} \texttt{ else } M_f{}^{\triangleright\Sigma_f}_{\triangleleft\Sigma'} \texttt{ in } M^{\triangleright\Sigma}_{\triangleleft\{\}})^{\triangleright\{X\}\cup\Sigma_f\cup\Sigma}_{\triangleleft\{\}}$$

As mentioned above M_f and M do not raise X (i.e. $X \notin (\Sigma_f \cup \Sigma)$). The *grant* set of the entire term captures all escaping exceptions that may be raised by the future (i.e. $\{X\} \cup \Sigma_f \cup \Sigma$). The *nogrant* set is empty; the term represents the entire future computation and therefore has no enclosing term. If f computes placeholder p, the continuation of f evaluates in context $\varepsilon^{\bullet(p,\Sigma')}$, where $\Sigma' = (\{X\} \cup \Sigma_f \cup \Sigma)$. When f's evaluation enters the false branch of the if-then-else statement, f will remove those escaping exceptions it can no longer reach from Σ' in the evaluation context of its continuation. Since both the false branch and the body of the statement do not raise X, the future will remove element X from Σ'. The result is that f's continuation will evaluate in the following evaluation context: $\varepsilon^{\bullet(p,\Sigma_f\cup\Sigma)}$.

Relation $\mathcal{I}(\widetilde{T})$ defines constraints on instrumented terms $\widetilde{T}$ (see Figure 7). Variable and value terms are uniquely labeled with their static location, and each term has its own *nogrant* set depending on its context. Of course, value and variable occurrences may not raise exceptions or exit the program so their *grant* sets are always empty. An exit state-ment obviously exits and therefore has *grant* set $\{\texttt{exit}\}$, and a raise statement clearly raises an exception. Since exceptions are first-class, the raise statement's *grant* set con-tains all exceptions it *may* raise (i.e. the *grant* set for term $(\texttt{raise}_l \ x)$ is $Flow_P(x)$). A try expression's *grant* set includes all exceptions (and exit) that escape from the try block except the handled exception, and all escaping exceptions from the handler block. Thus, the continuation of a future f will not be forced to wait for a grant on an exception that is handled internally by f. The *nogrant* set for the try expression's try block includes the try expression's *nogrant* set, all escaping exceptions raised by the handler block, and the handled exception. Computing the *grant* and *nogrant* sets for the try's handler block is straightforward, as is the case for value binding let-expressions and if-then-else expressions.

Since abstractions are first-class, the *grant* set of an application term with abstrac-tion variable y is the union of *grant* sets for $\widetilde{T}_i$ where $\lambda z.\widetilde{T}_i \in Flow_P(y)$ and the *grant* set for the body of the let-expression. An abstractions may appear in different contexts; therefore, the body of a λ-expression must be instrumented with a conserva-tive approximation for its *nogrant* set. The *nogrant* set is the union of *nogrant* sets for each context the abstraction may be applied. This is demonstrated in the instrumentation

$$\mathcal{I}(V_{l\lhd\Sigma}^{\rhd\{\}}) \qquad \mathcal{I}(x_{l\lhd\Sigma}^{\rhd\{\}}) \qquad \mathcal{I}((\mathtt{exit}_l\ x)_{\lhd\Sigma}^{\rhd\{\mathtt{exit}\}}) \qquad \frac{\Sigma = Flow_P(x)}{\mathcal{I}((\mathtt{raise}_l\ x)_{\lhd\Sigma'}^{\rhd\Sigma})}$$

$$\frac{\mathcal{I}(T_{\lhd\Sigma'\cup\Sigma_h\cup\{X\}}^{\rhd\Sigma}) \quad \mathcal{I}(Th_{\lhd\Sigma'}^{\rhd\Sigma_h})}{\mathcal{I}((\mathtt{try}_l\ T_{\lhd\Sigma'\cup\Sigma_h\cup\{X\}}^{\rhd\Sigma}\ \mathtt{handle}\ X \mapsto Th_{\lhd\Sigma'}^{\rhd\Sigma_h})_{\lhd\Sigma'}^{\rhd(\Sigma\setminus\{X\})\cup\Sigma_h})}$$

$$\frac{\mathcal{I}(T_{\lhd\Sigma'}^{\rhd\Sigma})}{\mathcal{I}(\mathtt{let}\ x = V\ \mathtt{in}\ T_{\lhd\Sigma'}^{\rhd\Sigma})_{\lhd\Sigma'}^{\rhd\Sigma}}$$

$$\frac{\mathcal{I}(Tt_{\lhd\Sigma''\cup\Sigma}^{\rhd\Sigma_t}) \quad \mathcal{I}(Tf_{\lhd\Sigma''\cup\Sigma}^{\rhd\Sigma_f}) \quad \mathcal{I}(T_{\lhd\Sigma''}^{\rhd\Sigma})}{\mathcal{I}((\mathtt{let}\ x = \mathtt{if}\ y\ \mathtt{then}\ Tt_{\lhd\Sigma''\cup\Sigma}^{\rhd\Sigma_t}\ \mathtt{else}\ Tf_{\lhd\Sigma''\cup\Sigma}^{\rhd\Sigma_f}\ \mathtt{in}\ T_{\lhd\Sigma''}^{\rhd\Sigma})_{\lhd\Sigma''}^{\rhd\Sigma_t\cup\Sigma_f\cup\Sigma})}$$

$$\frac{Flow_P(y) = \{\lambda z_1.T_1,\ldots,\lambda z_n.T_n\} \quad \mathcal{I}(T1_{\lhd\Sigma'_1}^{\rhd\Sigma_1}),\ldots,\mathcal{I}(Tn_{\lhd\Sigma'_n}^{\rhd\Sigma_n})}{\mathcal{I}(T_{\lhd\Sigma'}^{\rhd\Sigma}) \quad \Sigma'_i \subseteq (\Sigma\cup\Sigma') \quad \Sigma'' = \bigcup_{(i=1)}^{n}\Sigma_i}$$
$$\mathcal{I}((\mathtt{let}\ x = (y\ z)\ \mathtt{in}\ T_{\lhd\Sigma'}^{\rhd\Sigma})_{\lhd\Sigma'}^{\rhd\Sigma\cup\Sigma''})$$

$$\frac{\mathcal{I}(Tf_{\lhd\{\}}^{\rhd\Sigma_f}) \quad \mathcal{I}(T_{\lhd\Sigma'}^{\rhd\Sigma})}{\mathcal{I}((\mathtt{let}\ x = \mathtt{future}(Tf_{\lhd\{\}}^{\rhd\Sigma_f})\ \mathtt{in}\ T_{\lhd\Sigma'}^{\rhd\Sigma})_{\lhd\Sigma'}^{\rhd\Sigma_f\cup\Sigma})}$$

Fig. 7. Instrumentation Constraints

constraints presented in Figure 7 by requiring that the *nogrant* sets associated with the bodies of each potential abstraction is a *subset* of the set of exceptions for the current context. This overly conservative *nogrant* set disallows grants that are safe. The disallowed grants that should have been granted during evaluation of the application are applied at runtime after evaluating the application (see Figure 8). The *grant* set for a term that spawns a future consists of the *grant* set of the future term and the continuation. Thus if the term itself is spawned as a future, its continuation will need to wait for both the (sub) future and the original future to grant on exceptions and $\mathtt{exit}$. A future computation has an empty *nogrant* set because it is evaluated as a separate computation.

4.2 Semantics

Terms instrumented with *grant* and *nogrant* sets are evaluated using the semantics defined in Figures 8 and 9. In Figure 8 we omit instrumentation that is not relevant to evaluation. A local evaluation rule $\widetilde{N} \rightarrow_{is} \langle \widetilde{N}', \Sigma \rangle$ reduces an instrumented runtime term $\widetilde{N}$ to a new instrumented runtime term $\widetilde{N}'$ and a grant effect Σ. The grant effect represents the escaping exceptions (and $\mathtt{exit}$) that were reachable by $\widetilde{N}$ but not reachable by $\widetilde{N}'$.

For the $\overrightarrow{try}$ rule, the try block evaluates to a value and thus does not require the exception handler. The $\rightarrow_{is}$ evaluator will compute a grant effect consisting of those elements in the handler's *grant* set that are not in its *nogrant* set. If the body of the try statement raises the handled exception (i.e. rule $\overrightarrow{handle}$), the $\rightarrow_{is}$ evaluator grants exceptions

$$N \in RTTerms' ::= V \mid \texttt{exit } V \mid \texttt{raise } X \mid \texttt{try } \widetilde{N} \texttt{ handle } X \mapsto \widetilde{N} \mid \texttt{let } x = \texttt{if } V \texttt{ then } \widetilde{N} \texttt{ else } \widetilde{N} \texttt{ in } \widetilde{N} \mid \ldots$$

$$\widetilde{N} \in RTTerms ::= N_{\lhd \Sigma}^{\rhd \Sigma} \mid \bot \mid p^+ \mid \widetilde{N}^{\bullet(p,\Sigma)} \mid \langle \widetilde{N}, \Sigma \rangle$$

$$V \in Value ::= \ldots \mid p$$

$$p \in PhVars ::= \{\texttt{main}, p_1, p_2, \ldots\}$$

$$C \in TermContext ::= \langle p \times (real \times int) \times (real \times int) \rangle$$

$$S ::= \{(\widetilde{N_1})_{C_1}, \ldots, (\widetilde{N_n})_{C_n}\}$$

$$S | \widetilde{N}_C ::= S \cup \{\widetilde{N}_C\}$$

$$\mathcal{A}_\bullet(\widetilde{N}) = \begin{cases} \{(p,\Sigma)\} \cup \mathcal{A}_\bullet(\varepsilon[\widetilde{N'}]) & \text{if } \widetilde{N} = \varepsilon[\widetilde{N}'^{\bullet(p,\Sigma)}] \\ \phi & \text{otherwise} \end{cases}$$

$$F_{is}(M) = \begin{cases} V & \text{if } \{(\texttt{let } x = \widetilde{T} \texttt{ in exit}_l \ x)_{\langle \texttt{main},(-1,-1),(0,0)\rangle}\} \Rightarrow_{sd}^* \\ & \{(\widetilde{N_1})_{C_1}, \ldots, (\widetilde{N_n})_{C_n}, (V_{\lhd\{\}}^{\rhd\{\}})_{\langle \texttt{main},(-1,-1),(r,d)\rangle}\} \\ & \text{where } \widetilde{T} \text{ is instrumented version of } M \\ \text{error} & \text{otherwise} \end{cases}$$

EVALUATION RULES:

$$\varepsilon \in EvalCntxt ::= [\,] \mid \texttt{try } \varepsilon \texttt{ handle } X \mapsto \widetilde{N} \mid \texttt{let } x = \varepsilon \texttt{ in } \widetilde{N} \mid \texttt{exit } \varepsilon \mid \texttt{raise } \varepsilon$$
$$\mid \texttt{let } x = \texttt{if } \varepsilon \texttt{ then } \widetilde{N}_t \texttt{ else } \widetilde{N}_f \texttt{ in } \widetilde{N} \mid \texttt{let } x = (\varepsilon \ V) \texttt{ in } \widetilde{N} \mid \varepsilon^{\bullet(p,\Sigma)}$$

$$\texttt{try } V \texttt{ handle } X \mapsto N_{\lhd\Sigma'}^{\rhd\Sigma_h} \quad \to_{is} \langle V, \Sigma_h \backslash \Sigma' \rangle \qquad\qquad (\overrightarrow{try})$$

$$\texttt{try } (\texttt{raise } X)_{\lhd\Sigma'_r}^{\rhd\Sigma_r} \texttt{ handle } X \mapsto \widetilde{N} \quad \to_{is} \langle \widetilde{N}, \Sigma_r \backslash \Sigma'_r \rangle \qquad\qquad (\overrightarrow{handle})$$

$$\texttt{try } (\texttt{raise } X')_{\lhd\Sigma'_r}^{\rhd\Sigma_r} \texttt{ handle } X \mapsto N_{\lhd\Sigma'}^{\rhd\Sigma_h} \to_{is} \langle (\texttt{raise } X')_{\lhd\Sigma'_r}^{\rhd\Sigma_r}, \Sigma_h \backslash \Sigma' \rangle \qquad (\overrightarrow{tryraise})$$

$$\texttt{let } x = V \texttt{ in } N_{\lhd\Sigma'}^{\rhd\Sigma} \quad \to_{is} \langle (N[x/V])_{\lhd\Sigma'}^{\rhd\Sigma}, \phi \rangle \qquad\qquad (\overrightarrow{bind})$$

$$\texttt{let } x = (\texttt{raise } X)_{\lhd\Sigma'_r}^{\rhd\Sigma_r} \texttt{ in } N_{\lhd\Sigma'}^{\rhd\Sigma} \quad \to_{is} \langle (\texttt{raise } X)_{\lhd\Sigma'}^{\rhd\Sigma_r}, \Sigma \backslash (\Sigma' \cup \Sigma_r) \rangle \qquad (\overrightarrow{bindraise})$$

$$\texttt{let } x = \texttt{if } V \texttt{ then } N_{t\,\lhd\Sigma''_t \cup \Sigma}^{\rhd\Sigma_t} \quad \to_{is} \begin{cases} \langle (\texttt{let } x = N_{t\,\lhd\Sigma''_t}^{\rhd\Sigma_t} \texttt{ in } N_{\lhd\Sigma''}^{\rhd\Sigma})_{\lhd\Sigma''}^{\rhd\Sigma_t \cup \Sigma}, & V = \texttt{true} \\ \Sigma_f \backslash (\Sigma_t \cup \Sigma'' \cup \Sigma)) \\ \langle (\texttt{let } x = N_{f\,\lhd\Sigma''_f}^{\rhd\Sigma_f} \texttt{ in } N_{\lhd\Sigma''}^{\rhd\Sigma})_{\lhd\Sigma''}^{\rhd\Sigma_f \cup \Sigma}, & V = \texttt{false} \\ \Sigma_t \backslash (\Sigma_f \cup \Sigma'' \cup \Sigma)) \end{cases} \quad (\overrightarrow{if})$$

$$\qquad \texttt{else } N_{f\,\lhd\Sigma''_f \cup \Sigma}^{\rhd\Sigma_f} \texttt{ in } N_{\lhd\Sigma''}^{\rhd\Sigma}$$

$$(\texttt{let } x = (V \ V') \texttt{ in } N_{\lhd\Sigma'}^{\rhd\Sigma})_{\lhd\Sigma''}^{\rhd\Sigma''} \quad \to_{is} \langle (\texttt{let } x = N'^{\rhd\Sigma_1}_{\lhd\Sigma'_1}[y/V'] \qquad\qquad V = \lambda\, y.(N^{\rhd\Sigma_1}_{\lhd\Sigma'_1}) \quad (\overrightarrow{apply})$$

$$\texttt{in } \langle N_{\lhd\Sigma'}^{\rhd\Sigma}, \Sigma'_1 \backslash (\Sigma \cup \Sigma'))\rangle_{\Sigma'}^{\Sigma_1 \cup \Sigma}, \ \Sigma'' \backslash (\Sigma_1 \cup \Sigma \cup \Sigma'))\rangle$$

Fig. 8. Local Evaluation Rules for Instrumented Semantics

in the raise statement's *grant* set (i.e. the static approximation of which exceptions *may* have been raised by this statement), that are not in its *nogrant* set. Note that the instrumentation constraints ensure the exception being handled, which is clearly in the *grant* set, is also in the *nogrant* set disallowing the rule to grant on the raised exception. This is correct because the instrumentation constraints ensure that a continuation of a future does not wait for exceptions internally handled by its future. If another exception is raised in the try block (i.e. $\overrightarrow{tryraise}$ rule), the exception is propagated and since the handler is not invoked, the $\to_{is}$ evaluator will grant elements in the handler's *grant* set that are not in its *nogrant* set.

The grant effect computed by rule $\overrightarrow{bind}$ for a value-binding let-expression is empty, because the new runtime term may raise the same set of escaping exceptions as the

$$\frac{\widetilde{N} \rightarrow_{is} \langle \widetilde{N}', \Sigma \rangle}{S|(\varepsilon[\widetilde{N}])_C \Rightarrow_{is} S|(\varepsilon[\langle \mathcal{R}(\widetilde{N}'), \Sigma \rangle])_C} \quad (local)$$

$$\frac{(\text{let } x = \widetilde{N} \text{ in } N') \rightarrow_{is} \langle \widetilde{N}'', \Sigma \rangle}{S|(\varepsilon[\text{let } x = \widetilde{N}^{\bullet(p_1,\Sigma_1)...\bullet(p_n,\Sigma_n)} \text{ in } \widetilde{N}'])_C \Rightarrow_{sd} S|(\varepsilon[\langle \widetilde{N}''^{\bullet(p_1,\Sigma_1)...\bullet(p_n,\Sigma_n)}, \Sigma \rangle])_C} \quad (let)$$

$$\frac{C = \langle p,(r,d),(r',d') \rangle \quad p' \text{ fresh}}{C_f = \langle p',(r,d'),(r',d'+1) \rangle \quad C_c = \langle p,(r,d),(r'+0.5^{d'},d'+1) \rangle}{S|(\varepsilon[\text{let } x = \text{future}(N_{\lhd\{\}}^{\rhd\Sigma_f}) \text{ in } \widetilde{N}'])_C \Rightarrow_{sd} S|(N_{\lhd\{\}}^{\rhd\Sigma_f})_{C_f}|(\varepsilon[\mathcal{R}(\widetilde{N}'[x/p'])^{\bullet(p',\Sigma_f)}])_{C_c}} \quad (future)$$

$$\frac{(V_{\lhd\{\}}^{\rhd\{\}})_{\langle p,(r,d),(r',d') \rangle} \in S}{S|(\varepsilon[p^+])_C \Rightarrow_{sd} S|(\varepsilon[V])_C} \qquad \overline{S|(\varepsilon[\widetilde{N}^{\bullet(p,\phi)}])_C \Rightarrow_{is} S|(\varepsilon[\widetilde{N}])_C} \qquad (touch) \quad (unblock)$$

$$\frac{C_f = \langle p,(r,d),(r',d') \rangle}{S' = \{(\widetilde{N}')_{\langle p_i,(r_i,d_i),(r'_i,d'_i) \rangle} \mid (\widetilde{N}')_{\langle p_i,(r_i,d_i),(r'_i,d'_i) \rangle} \in S, (r'_i < r' \text{ or } r'_i \geq (r+0.5^{d-1}))\}}{S_c = \{(\bot)_C \mid (\widetilde{N}')_C \in S, (\widetilde{N}')_C \notin S'\} \quad S'' = S' \cup S_c}{S|((\text{raise } X)_{\lhd\Sigma'_f}^{\rhd\Sigma_f})_{C_f}|(\varepsilon[N_{\lhd\Sigma'_c}^{\rhd\Sigma_c}\bullet^{(p,\Sigma)}])_{C_c} \Rightarrow_{sd} S''|((\text{raise } X)_{\lhd\Sigma'_f}^{\rhd\Sigma_f})_{C_f}|(\varepsilon[(\text{raise } X)_{\lhd\Sigma'_c}^{\rhd\Sigma_f}])_{C_c}} \quad (raise)$$

$$\frac{C = \langle p,(r',d'),(r,d) \rangle}{(\widetilde{N}_i)_{\langle p_i,(r'_i,d'_i),(r_i,d_i) \rangle} \notin S \quad r_i < r \quad \widetilde{N}_i \neq V'^{\rhd\{\}}_{\lhd\{\}}}{S|(\varepsilon[(\text{exit } V)_{\lhd\Sigma'}^{\rhd\{\text{exit}\}}])_C \Rightarrow_{sd} \{(V_{\lhd\{\}}^{\rhd\{\}})_{\langle \text{main},(-1,-1),(r,d) \rangle}\}} \quad (exit)$$

$$\frac{C = \langle \text{main},(-1,-1),(r,d) \rangle}{S|(\varepsilon[\langle \widetilde{N}, \Sigma \rangle])_C \Rightarrow_{is} S|(\varepsilon[\widetilde{N}])_C} \quad (grantmain)$$

$$\frac{C_f = \langle p,(r,d),(r',d') \rangle \quad \mathcal{A}_\bullet(\varepsilon[N_{\lhd\Sigma'_f}^{\rhd\Sigma_f}]) = \{(p_1,\Sigma_1),...,(p_n,\Sigma_n)\}}{\Sigma'' = \bigcup_{(i=1)}^n \Sigma_i \quad \Sigma_g = \Sigma \backslash (\Sigma'' \cup \Sigma_f)}{S|(\varepsilon[\langle N_{\lhd\Sigma'_f}^{\rhd\Sigma_f}, \Sigma \rangle])_{C_f}|(\varepsilon[\widetilde{N}_c^{\bullet(p,\Sigma')}])_{C_c} \Rightarrow_{is} S|(\varepsilon[N_{\lhd\Sigma'_f}^{\rhd\Sigma_f}])_{C_f}|(\varepsilon[\langle \widetilde{N}_c^{\bullet(p,\Sigma'\backslash\Sigma_g)}, \Sigma_g \rangle])_{C_c}} \quad (grant)$$

$$\frac{(\text{try } \widetilde{N} \text{ handle } X \mapsto \widetilde{N}') \rightarrow_{is} \langle \widetilde{N}'', \Sigma' \rangle \quad \Sigma'' = \bigcup_{(i=1)}^n \Sigma_i \quad X \notin \Sigma''}{S|(\varepsilon[\text{try } \widetilde{N}^{\bullet(p_1,\Sigma_1)...\bullet(p_n,\Sigma_n)} \text{ handle } X \mapsto \widetilde{N}'])_C \Rightarrow_{is} S|(\varepsilon[\langle \widetilde{N}''^{\bullet(p_1,\Sigma_1)...\bullet(p_n,\Sigma_n)}, \Sigma' \rangle])_C} \quad (try)$$

Fig. 9. Global Evaluation Rules for Instrumented Semantics

reduced term. If the expression being bound results in a raise of an exception, rule $\overrightarrow{bindraise}$ will compute a grant effect that includes escaping exceptions that may be raised by the body of the let-expression, which will never be reached, (i.e. Σ) as long as those exceptions may not be raised by the raise statement (i.e. Σ_r) or by the computation following the entire term (i.e. Σ'). The rule also computes the new *nogrant* set that results from propagating the raise without evaluating the let-expression body. The new *nogrant* set is equal to the *nogrant* set of the let-expression body.

The $\overrightarrow{if}$ rule computes the grant effect resulting from taking a branch of an if-then-else statement, and recomputes the *grant* set of the entire term based on the branch taken. If the true (false) branch is taken, the *grant* set of the entire term is the union of the true (false) branch's *grant* set and the *grant* set of the let-body. The grant effect consists of exceptions raised (and exit) by the false (true) branch that cannot be raised by the true (false) branch, the let-body, or the computation that follows.

Rule $\overrightarrow{apply}$ computes the grant effect for an application term. The *nogrant* set of the abstraction body (i.e. Σ_1') may be overly conservative, not allowing the evaluation of the body to grant on certain exceptions. Thus the runtime will grant all exceptions in the *nogrant* set of the abstraction body that are not raised by the rest of the term (i.e. $\Sigma_1' \backslash (\Sigma \cup \Sigma')$) as soon as the application has completed evaluation. This is achieved by replacing the body of the let-expression with a grant effect causing the grant effect to be applied before evaluating the body. The grant effect immediately computed by the rule consists of those exceptions in the let-expression's *grant* set modulo those in the *grant* set of the abstraction's body (i.e. Σ_1), those that are reachable from the let-body (i.e. Σ) and those associated with the computation following the let-body (i.e. Σ'). Note that the grant effect will include exceptions added to the *grant* set based on the static approximation of which abstractions *may* have been bound to V as long as the exceptions may not be raised by the rest of the term or by the abstraction value actually bound to V at runtime.

The global evaluation rules are mostly analogous to the evaluation rules for the safe dynamic semantics. The *unblock* rule is worth noting because it removes the blocking evaluation for future f from a continuation as soon as f reaches a point where it has granted everything that was in its *grant* set. This allows a future computation to evaluate to a value (rather than a blocked value) before its futures complete, if they are guaranteed to not invalidate its evaluation by exiting or raising an escaping exception. Thus unlike the safe dynamic semantics, in the instrumented semantics a continuation touching a placeholder corresponding to future f does not need to block until all of f's futures complete. Three new rules are also defined: *grantmain*, *grant* and *try*. The first two deal with grant effects and the *try* allows computation within a continuation to discard an exception handler if its future indicates it is safe to do so.

The *grantmain* rule ignores grant effects from the main computation, because it is not a future of any continuation. When a local evaluation reduces to a term and grant effect $\langle \widetilde{N}, \Sigma \rangle$ the *grant* rule will grant elements in Σ that are safe to grant. An element is safe to grant if the granting computation cannot reach the element (i.e. it is not in Σ_f) and the granting future is not a continuation of another future that still may reach the element (i.e. it is not in Σ''). To compute Σ'', we use function $\mathcal{A}_\bullet$, which computes the set of futures a given term is a continuation of. The grant action is reflected in the *grant* rule by removing elements Σ_g from Σ' in the continuation's $\varepsilon^{\bullet(p,\Sigma')}$ context. The grant effect is then propagated to the continuation which may itself be a future.

The *try* rule exploits concurrency that could not be availed in the absence of instrumentation. A continuation may proceed past a try statement before its futures complete if the futures and all the futures they spawn will not require the handler defined by the try expression. This rule is similar to the *let* rule which allows evaluation of a continuation to proceed past a let term, except the *try* rule is conditional on the blocking instrumentation indicating it is safe to discard the handler.

4.3 Example

The following example shows how the instrumented semantics allows for greater parallelism than the safe dynamic semantics. For brevity we have omitted the instrumentation from the example, but we assume the program has been instrumented to satisfy the instrumentation constraints presented in Figure 7. We explain in the text any instrumentation that is relevant to the evaluation of the program.

```
1.   let x = future(T̃₁) in
2.     try let y = future(T̃₂) in
3.         let z = future(let w = if false then raise X
4.                         else T̃₃ in T̃₃')
5.         in raise X'
6.     handle X ↦ c
```

Let $\tilde{N}_1$ and $\tilde{N}_2$ be runtime terms in the process state corresponding to instrumented terms $\tilde{T}_1$ and $\tilde{T}_2$, respectively, $\tilde{N}_3$ be the runtime term for the if-then-else expression on line 3, and $\tilde{N}_4$ be the following runtime term:

$$(\texttt{try } (\texttt{raise } X')^{\bullet(p_3,\Sigma)\bullet(p_2,\Sigma_2)} \texttt{ handle } X \mapsto c)^{\bullet(p_1,\Sigma_1)}$$

In the above runtime term, Σ is the *grant* set for the if-then-else expression, Σ_1 is the *grant* set for $\tilde{N}_1$ and Σ_2 is the *grant* set for $\tilde{N}_2$. Assume that $X \notin \Sigma_2$ (i.e. $\tilde{T}_2$ may not raise escaping exception X). Since $X \in \Sigma$ due to the raise in the true branch of the future computation, the *try* rule does not hold for $\tilde{N}_4$ and the handler cannot be discarded. Once control enters the false brach during the evaluation of $\tilde{N}_3$, the $\rightarrow_{is}$ evaluator will compute a grant effect that includes elements in the *grant* set of the true branch (i.e. $\{X\}$) that are not in the *grant* and *nogrant* sets of the false branch. Let Σ_3 and Σ_3' be the *grant* and *nogrant* sets of $\tilde{T}_3$ and assume that $X \notin (\Sigma_3 \cup \Sigma_3')$ (i.e. the false branch and the body of the if expression do not raise an escaping exception X). According to the $\overrightarrow{if}$ rule, the grant effect Σ_g contains X. The *grant* rule removes X from Σ of the blocking evaluation context associated with p_3 in term $\tilde{N}_4$. The grant would be propagated but since $\tilde{N}_4$ is not a future computation (i.e. its term context is $\langle \texttt{main}, (-1, -1), (r, d) \rangle$), the *grantmain* rule applies. Since X is no longer in Σ the *try* rule applies for term $\tilde{N}_4$ allowing evaluation to proceed past the handler even though the future computations corresponding to p_2 and p_3 have yet to complete.

4.4   Semantic Equivalence

In this section we provide a proof sketch proving that evaluating program M under the instrumented semantics has the same result as evaluating M under the safe dynamic semantics. For the proof, we define a transform function $\mathcal{U}$ to map a process state S_i in the instrumented semantics to a process state S_s in the safe dynamic semantics. The transform function $\mathcal{U}$ simply erases instrumentation, replaces evaluation context $^{\bullet(p,\Sigma)}$ with $^{\bullet p}$ and replaces instrumented runtime term $\langle \tilde{N}, \Sigma \rangle$ with runtime term N. We use the transform function $\mathcal{U}$ to prove that for state S_i, if $S_i \Rightarrow^*_{is} V$ then $\mathcal{U}(S_i) \Rightarrow^*_{sd} V$. The proof details are presented in an accompanying technical report [8].

Lemma 3. *If S_i is a final state with result R then $\mathcal{U}(S_i) \Rightarrow^*_{sd} S_s$, and S_s is a final state in the safe dynamic semantics with result R.*

The proof states that if the final process state S_i reached by evaluation under instrumented semantics results in R, then the transform of the process state evaluates under safe dynamic semantics to a final state S_s with result R.

Lemma 4. *If $S_i \Rightarrow_{is} S_i'$, then $\mathcal{U}(S_i) \Rightarrow_{sd}^* S_s$ and $\mathcal{U}(S_i') \Rightarrow_{sd}^* S_s$.*

The lemma states that given an instrumented evaluation rule $S_i \Rightarrow_{is} S_i'$ the transform of S_i and S_i' are equivalent process states in the safe dynamic semantics. In other words, under $\Rightarrow_{sd}$ there exists a sequence of rules starting from $\mathcal{U}(S_i)$ and a sequence starting from $\mathcal{U}(S_i')$, such that both sequences result in a common state S_s. The proof is by case analysis on evaluation derivations $S_i \Rightarrow_{is} S_i'$. In most cases, this property is straightforward because most the rules in the safe dynamic and instrumented semantics are analogous. Thus for analogous rule $S_i \Rightarrow_{is} S_i'$, we show that applying the analogous rule in the safe dynamic semantics to the transform of S_i results in the transform of S_i' (i.e. $\mathcal{U}(S_i) \Rightarrow_{sd}^1 \mathcal{U}(S_i')$). The following rules are not analogous: *unblock, grantmain, grant, try*.

The *unblock* rule in the instrumented semantics unblocks a computation before its future completes as long as the computation's future is guaranteed not to raise an escaping exception or exit the program. Our proof leverages this guarantee. While the *unblock* rule of the safe dynamic semantics may not apply to $\mathcal{U}(S_i)$, evaluating the future computation under a sequence of $\Rightarrow_{sd}$ rules to a value will result in a state S_s, such that the *unblock* rule to applies to S_s. Rules *grantmain* and *grant* are trivial because under both rules if $S_i \Rightarrow_{is} S_i'$, then $\mathcal{U}(S_i) = \mathcal{U}(S_i')$. Proving the *try* rule is similar to the *unblock* rule. Intuitively, the proof demonstrates that runtime term (try let x = future(N) in N' handle $X \mapsto \ldots$) and runtime term (let x = future(N) in try N' handle $X \mapsto \ldots$) are equivalent as long as N and any future spawned from N do not raise escaping exception X. The instrumented semantics allows hoisting a future from a try block's evaluation context only when the static instrumentation and runtime determine it will not require the handler.

Theorem 2. *If $F_{is}(M) = R$, then $F_{sd}(M) = R$.*

Evaluating program M under the instrumented semantics will have the same result as evaluating M under the safe dynamic semantics. The proof is by induction on the length of $\Rightarrow_{is}$ evaluation sequences. The base case is demonstrated by Lemma 3 and 4. Instantiating the inductive hypothesis and Lemma 4 proves the inductive case.

5   Related Work and Conclusions

Futures were first introduced in Multilisp [3] as a high level concurrency abstraction for functional languages. Implementation of futures has been well-studied in the context of functional languages [4,5] and future-like concurrency constructs have emerged in many multithreaded languages. Recent proposals [13,14] that have future-like constructs do not guarantee safety of the kind provided by our solution.

In [10], deterministic execution of Java programs equipped with futures is enforced using a dynamic analysis that tracks accesses and updates by futures and their continuations; while this techniques deals with side-effects to shared fields, it does not enforce equivalence between a sequential and future-annotated Java program in the presence of exceptions. In [9], a static analysis and program transformation to provide coordination between futures and their continuations is given. [11] is closest in spirit to our work; their implementation is similar to the safe dynamic semantics presented here, but significantly less precise than the instrumented semantics.

The formal semantics of futures have been studied in [1,2]. Their work develops a semantic framework for an idealized language with futures, but the results do not consider how to enforce safety (i.e. determinism) in the presence of exceptions. More recently, a formal semantics for an object-oriented language with active objects, asynchronous method calls and futures was presented in [12], but this presentation does not consider enforcing determinism or deal with exceptions.

This paper presents a formulation of safe futures for a higher-order language with first-class exceptions, via a combination of a static analysis to instrument programs with information about when exceptions may or may not be raised, and an operational semantics that leverages this instrumentation to extract concurrency without violating safety. We believe our results provide a precise basis for implementations of safe futures in realistic languages that support expressive control-flow abstractions.

References

1. Flanagan, C., Felleisen, M.: The semantics of future and its use in program optimizations. In: Conference Record of POPL 1995, San Francisco, California, pp. 209–220 (1995)
2. Flanagan, C., Felleisen, M.: The semantics of future and an application. J. Funct. Program. 9(1), 1–31 (1999)
3. Halstead, R.: Multilisp: A Language for Concurrent Symbolic Computation. ACM TOPLAS 7(4), 501–538 (1985)
4. Kranz, D., Halstead Jr., R.H., Mohr, E.: Mul-T: A high-performance parallel Lisp. In: PLDI 1989, vol. 24, pp. 81–90 (July 1989)
5. Mohr, R., Kranz, D., Halstead, R.: Lazy Task Creation: A Technique for Increasing the Granularity of Parallel Programs. In: ACM LFP Programming, June 1990, pp. 185–197 (1990)
6. Shivers, O.: Control-Flow Analysis of Higher-Order Languages or Taming Lambda. Ph.D thesis, Carnegie Mellon University (May 1991)
7. Palsberg, J.: Closure analysis in constraint form. In: ACM TOPLAS, pp. 47–62 (1995)
8. Navabi, A., Jagannathan, S.: Exceptionally Safe Futures. Tech. Report CSD TR #08-027, Purdue University Department of Computer Science,
   http://www.cs.purdue.edu/homes/anavabi/tr08027.pdf
9. Navabi, A., Zhang, X., Jagannathan, S.: Quasi-static scheduling for safe futures. In: PPOPP 2008, pp. 23–32 (2008)
10. Welc, A., Jagannathan, S., Hosking, A.: Safe futures for java. In: OOPSLA 2005, pp. 439–453. ACM Press, New York (2005)
11. Zhang, L., Krintz, C., Nagpurkar, P.: Supporting Exception Handling for Futures in Java. In: PPPJ, pp. 175–184 (2007)
12. de Boer, F.S., Clarke, D., Johnsen, E.B.: A Complete Guide to the Future. In: De Nicola, R. (ed.) ESOP 2007. LNCS, vol. 4421, pp. 316–330. Springer, Heidelberg (2007)
13. Allan, E., Chase, D., Luchangco, V., Maessen, J., Ryu, S., Steele, G., Tobin-Hochstadt, S.: The Fortress Language Specification Version 1.0. Tech. report, Sun Microsystems (2008)
14. Charles, P., Grothoff, C., Saraswat, V., Donawa, C., Kielstra, A., Ebcioglu, K., von Praun, C., Sarkar, V.: X10: an object-oriented approach to non-uniform cluster computing. In: OOPSLA 2005, pp. 519–538 (2005)

Enhanced Coordination in Sensor Networks through Flexible Service Provisioning

Chien-Liang Fok, Gruia-Catalin Roman, and Chenyang Lu

Dept. of Computer Science and Engineering
Washington University in St. Louis
Saint Louis, MO, 63105, USA
{liang,roman,lu}@cse.wustl.edu

Abstract. Many applications operate in heterogeneous wireless sensor networks, which represent a challenging programming environment due to the wide range of device capabilities. Servilla addresses this difficulty in developing applications by offering a new middleware framework based on service provisioning. Using Servilla, developers can construct platform-independent applications over a dynamic and diverse set of devices. A salient feature of Servilla is its support for the discovery and binding to local and remote services, which enables flexible and energy-efficient in-network collaboration among heterogeneous devices. Furthermore, Servilla provides a modular middleware architecture that can be easily tailored to devices with a wide range of resources, allowing resource-constrained devices to provide services while leveraging the capabilities of more powerful devices. Servilla has been implemented on TinyOS for two representative hardware platforms (Imote2 and TelosB) with drastically different resources. Microbenchmarks demonstrate the efficiency of Servilla's implementation, while an application case study on structural health monitoring demonstrates the efficacy of its coordination model for integrating heterogeneous devices.

1 Introduction

Wireless sensor networks (WSNs) [17] are becoming increasingly heterogeneous due to two primary reasons. First, heterogeneity allows a network to be both computationally powerful and deployed in high densities. Powerful devices can perform complex operations, but are more expensive and power-hungry. Conversely, weak WSN devices enable higher deployment densities and increase network lifetime as they are cheaper and consume less power. By integrating devices with different resources and capabilities, a heterogeneous WSN can combine the advantages of both powerful and weak devices. Second, network heterogeneity follows from the natural evolution of WSNs. WSN devices can be embedded in the environment and remain operational for a long time. For example, due to its high deployment cost, a WSN embedded in civil infrastructure for structural health monitoring must operate over several years to be economically acceptable [24]. Similarly, many urban sensing systems [48] must also remain operational for multiple years. During the lifetime of a WSN, new devices may be developed and deployed, resulting in network heterogeneity.

Network heterogeneity presents a formidable problem for application developers. Since the target platform may consist of many different devices, the application must

J. Field and V.T. Vasconcelos (Eds.): COORDINATION 2009, LNCS 5521, pp. 66–85, 2009.

be platform-independent to avoid having to custom-tailor it to each device. Yet, the application must still be able to access platform-specific capabilities like sensing and computing to make full use of the underlying hardware. Furthermore, the application must accommodate diverse device capabilities and resources. These seemingly contradictory requirements complicate application development and motivates a new programming model.

To address the challenges of programming heterogeneous WSNs, we developed **Servilla**, a middleware framework supporting a novel coordination model. Servilla's coordination model makes three important contributions. First, applications are structured in terms of *platform-independent* tasks and expose *platform-specific* capabilities as services. This ensures that applications remain platform-independent, which is critical as WSNs become increasingly heterogeneous. It also enables applications to access resources on a device without having active processes, or agents, on the device itself. This reduces the system's minimum resource requirements, increasing the range of devices that can be supported. Second, Servilla provides a specialized service description language, which enable application tasks to selectively but flexibly access services that exploit the capabilities of the hardware available at a particular time and place. This allows better adaptation to network heterogeneity, and facilitates for the first time in-network collaboration between heterogeneous WSN devices, achieving higher levels of efficiency and flexibility. Finally, Servilla provides a modularized middleware architecture and enables asymmetry in the middleware among WSN devices. This widens the scope of hardware devices that can be integrated.

Servilla's coordination model is inspired by the concept of *Service-Oriented Computing* (SOC) [45], which provides loose and flexible coupling between application components. It is used on the Internet and has recently been explored in the context of WSNs. Two systems in particular are Tiny Web Services (TWS) [47] and PhyNet™ [6]. TWS implements an HTTP server on each device and enables applications outside of the WSN to invoke services over the Internet using HTTP requests. PhyNet™provides a central gateway that exposes WSN capabilities as web services. Unlike these systems, Servilla uniquely takes the SOC programming model *inside* a WSN. It exploits the loose coupling between service consumers and providers to separate application-level platform-independent logic from the low-level software components that exploit platform-specific capabilities. Furthermore, by allowing application logic to execute inside a WSN, higher levels of efficiency are obtainable via in-network coordination and collaboration [28]. For example, in a structural health monitoring application, a low-power device may use a simple threshold-based algorithm to detect shocks that are potentially damage-inducing, and only activate more powerful devices that perform the complex operations to localize damage when necessary [24]. Or, in a surveillance application, low-power devices may sense vibrations from an intruder and activate more powerful devices with cameras [26]. The ability to support collaboration among heterogeneous devices *inside* a WSN is a key feature that distinguishes this work from existing SOC middleware for WSNs.

The remainder of the paper is organized as follows. Section 2 presents Servilla's programming model. Section 3 presents Servilla's programming languages. Section 4

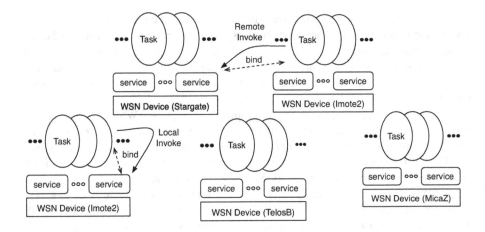

Fig. 1. Servilla targets heterogeneous WSNs in which different classes of devices provide services that are used by application tasks either locally or remotely. Services are platform-specific while tasks are platform-independent.

presents Servilla's middleware architecture and implementation. Section 5 presents an empirical evaluation on two representative sensor platforms with diverse resources. Section 6 evaluates the efficacy of Servilla by using it to implement a structural health monitoring application. Section 7 presents related work. The paper ends with conclusions in section 8.

2   Programming Model

An overview of a WSN using Servilla is shown in Figure 1. Servilla is meant for applications that run in WSNs with multiple classes of devices. It is not intended for flat WSNs composed entirely of resource-poor devices. Typical applications are long-lived, widespread, and involve many different tasks that vary in complexity and scale. They are expected to be written once, but continuously used despite hardware changes. For example, environmental monitoring or target tracking applications are long-lived and usually involve both widespread, but simple sensing tasks, and less widespread, but complex computational tasks, that process the data. By integrating both resource-poor and resource-rich devices, Servilla provides an ideal platform on which to build these types of applications. Specifically, resource-poor devices are less costly and more energy efficient, meaning they can be deployed in greater numbers at higher densities. Meanwhile, resource-rich devices are more expensive and limited in quantity, but offer computational power and advanced sensing capabilities.

Applications are implemented as tasks, which are platform-independent application processes that contain code, state, and service specifications. To ensure platform-independence, the code cannot directly access platform-specific capabilities like sensors. Instead, these capabilities are accessed as services that are provided by a *service provisioning framework*. The service provisioning framework takes a task's service specifications and finds services that match them. The service specifications describe both the service's interface and non-functional properties like energy consumption. This enables tasks, for example, to selectively use the most energy-efficient sensors.

Services expose platform-specific capabilities, are implemented natively, and can, thus, be fine-tuned for maximum efficiency. They provide a description that can be compared with a task's service specification. Services are able to maintain state, provide multiple methods, and have their own thread of control, enabling them to operate in parallel with tasks. This enables higher degrees of concurrency and efficiency. For example, in a structural health monitoring application, a service provided by a low-power device can continuously monitor an accelerometer and set a flag if the vibrations exceed a threshold. A task executing on a more powerful device can mostly remain asleep, only periodically checking for potential damage.

Tasks communicate via localized tuple spaces that are structured in the same manner as that in Agilla [19]. For brevity, they are not shown in Figure 1 since service provisioning is the focus and main contribution of this paper. Tuple space coordination facilitates decoupled communication, allowing better adaptation to a changing network. They serve as a flexible means of communication between application processes and are orthogonal to service provisioning. While service provisioning messages could be sent using tuple spaces, they are sent in an RPC-like fashion in the current implementation.

Tasks remain platform-independent by delegating all platform-specific operations to services. There are two essential steps for this to occur: *binding* and *invocation*. Binding is the process of discovering and establishing a connection to the service. Invocation is the process of accessing a service.

Service binding consists of three-steps: discovery, matching, and selection. Discovery involves finding available services. In many traditional SOC frameworks, this is done by querying a central service registry. While this is sufficient in traditional networks, it is not appropriate in WSNs for a couple reasons. First, since most WSN devices operate on batteries, accessing a distant registry is not energy efficient and can unacceptably reduce network lifetime. Second, the spatial aspect of WSNs are relevant since closer services are usually preferred, e.g., if a task wants to know the temperature, it usually wants to know the ambient temperature rather than a distant location's. For these reasons, Servilla is optimized for *localized* coordination and does not rely on a centralized service registry. Instead, each device has its own registry containing only the services that it provides.

During the service discovery process, the local registry is first checked for a match. If no match is found, neighboring devices are checked. This increases a network's flexibility by allowing tasks to run on devices that do not fully satisfy the service requirements, since missing services can be provided by neighboring devices. Furthermore, although accessing a remote service requires wireless communication, energy efficiency can be increased overall by allowing high-power devices to use low-power ones, enabling the high-power devices to remain asleep longer.

Service matching involves finding a service that fulfills a task's requirements. Recall that tasks include specifications that can be compared to descriptions provided by services. The matching process must be flexible since the service and tasks are usually developed separately. Yet, it must be semantically correct to ensure that the service behaves in a predictable manner. A service is minimally described by its interface. Ideally, the names of the methods, the order, number, and types of their parameters, and even the return types should not require an exact match for service binding for maximum flexibility. To achieve this, large amounts of meta-data must be included in the specification that describe the method names, input parameters, and return values. Unfortunately, such a specification is verbose and requires a complex parser, both of which consume sizable computational resources that are not available on many WSN devices. To account for this, Servilla compromises by dividing specifications into functional and non-functional properties. Functional properties include the interface and require an exact match. Nonfunctional properties describe attributes like power consumption and do not require an exact match. For example, suppose a FFT-calculating service has a non-functional attribute specifying that it is version 5. Such a service can be bound to a task that specifies it requires *at least* version 4. By enforcing an exact match between functional properties and an inexact match between non-functional ones, Servilla provides a degree of flexibility when binding services while still maintaining reasonable resource requirements.

Once a matching service is found, the binding process is completed by selecting it. Selection consists of informing the task of the chosen service, and is accomplished by informing the task of the provider's network address. Once done, the task can access the service by invoking it. Note that the provider's address is hidden from the application developer, who is able to invoke the service based on its name, a process that is described next.

Service invocations are analogous to remote procedure calls (RPCs). The task provides the name of the service, the method to execute, and the input parameters. After the service executes, the results are returned to the task. Since the task and service may be located on different devices, the process may fail, e.g., due to message loss. To account for this, Servilla provides a mechanism that notifies a task when and why an invocation fails. This is necessary because service invocations may fail in many ways depending on whether the service is local or remote, and tasks may want to handle various error conditions differently. For example, local invocations may fail because the service is busy, in which case the task may try again later, while remote invocations may fail due to disconnection, in which case the task may want to abort.

3   Programming Language

Servilla provides two light-weight programming languages tailored to support service provisioning in WSNs. The first, *ServillaSpec*, is used to create service specifications and descriptions that enable flexible matching between tasks and services. The second, *ServillaScript*, is used to create tasks and is compiled into bytecode that runs on a Virtual Machine. Services are implemented in NesC [21] on TinyOS [27] and compiled into native binary code for run-time efficiency. Servilla's specialized languages are now described.

```
NAME = fft
METHOD = fft-real
INPUT = {int dir, int numSamples, float[] data}
OUTPUT = float[]
ATTRIBUTE Version = 5.0
ATTRIBUTE MaxSamples = 5000
ATTRIBUTE Power = 10
```

Fig. 2. A specification describing a FFT service

```
1.  uses Temperature; // declare required service
2.
3.  void main() {
4.      int count = 0; float temp;
5.      bind(Temperature, 2); // bind service within 2 hops
6.      while(count++ < 10) {
7.          temp = invoke(Temperature, "get"); // invoke service
8.          send(temp);
9.      }
10.     unbind(Temperature);
11. }
```

Fig. 3. A task that invokes a temperature sensing service 10 times

3.1   ServillaSpec

ServillaSpec is used to describe services and is needed to match services required by tasks to those provided by devices. To support resource-constrained devices, the service specification language must be compact and should not require an overly complex matching algorithm. As such, standard specification languages used on the Internet like WSDL [49] are avoided due to their relative verboseness and highly complex parsers. ServillaSpec avoids verbose syntax and limits the types of properties that can be included in a service specification. An example is shown in Figure 2. The first line specifies the name of the service. It is followed by three-line segments each specifying the name, input parameters, and output results of a method provided by the service. The remainder of the specification is a list of attributes that specify non-functional properties of the service. They enable flexibility in matching by defining a name, relation, and value. Using attributes, a task can, for example, require a floating point FFT service that consumes *at most* 50mW. Such a specification would match a service whose description is shown in Figure 2.

By limiting the property types to be only the five shown in Figure 2 (i.e., NAME, METHOD, INPUT, OUTPUT, and ATTRIBUTE), and arranging them to always be in the same order, the specification can be greatly compressed. For example, since the service's NAME property always appears first, the property's identifier, NAME, can be omitted. Thus, the NAME property in the specification shown in Figure 2 can be compressed to just 4 bytes, "fft" followed by a null terminator. This compression saves memory and enables greater matching efficiency.

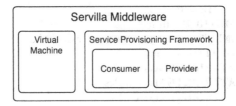

Fig. 4. Servilla's middleware consists of a virtual machine and a service provisioning framework (SPF). The SPF consists of a consumer and provider.

3.2   ServillaScript

ServillaScript is used to create application tasks. Its syntax is similar to other high level languages like JavaScript [18], but with key extensions for service provisioning. An example, shown Figure 3, implements an application that periodically takes the temperature and sends the reading to the base station. It declares the name of the file containing the specification of the required service on line 1, which in this case is a temperature sensing service. The task initiates the service binding process on line 5. The first parameter specifies which service to bind and the second specifies that registries within two hops should be searched. The task then loops ten times invoking the service on line 7 and sending the temperature to the base station on line 8. The task ends by disconnecting from the service on line 10.

The example above illustrates how ServillaScript enables tasks to 1) indicate which services are needed, 2) initiate the service discovery process, 3) invoke services, and 4) disconnect from services. Aspects not shown for brevity include checking whether a service is bound, and, if so, how far away the service is in terms of network hops. This will allow the task to throttle how often it invokes the service based on its distance. Another aspect not shown is error handling code. If an error occurs due to a service becoming unavailable, the invocation will return an error indicating the cause, as discussed in Section 2.

4   Middleware

Servilla's middleware architecture, as shown in Figure 4, consists of a virtual machine (VM) and a service provisioning framework (SPF). The VM is responsible for executing application tasks. The SPF consists of a consumer (SPF-Consumer) that discovers and accesses services, and provider (SPF-Provider) that advertises and executes services.

A VM is used because WSN devices contain processors with varying instruction sets. Application tasks are compiled into the VM's instruction set, which is uniform across all hardware platforms, ensuring that tasks are platform-independent. Furthermore, the VM enables the dynamic deployment of application tasks, justifying the need for dynamic service binding. The VM is based on Agilla [19] though with major extensions to support services and the SPF. Specifically, whenever a task performs an operation involving a service, the VM passes the task to the SPF-Consumer, which is described next.

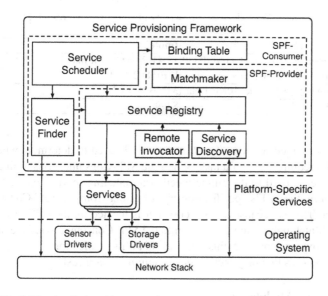

Fig. 5. The detailed architecture of the Service Provisioning Framework

4.1 SPF-Consumer

The SPF-Consumer is responsible for discovering, matching, and invoking services on behalf of tasks. As shown in Figure 5 the SPF-Consumer consists of a Service Finder, Binding Table, and Service Scheduler. The Service Finder is responsible for finding services that match a task's specifications. It first searches locally and, if no matches are found, searches one hop neighbors. Note that while this increases the likelihood of selecting a local service, it does not necessarily select the most energy efficient provider. If a task wanted to bind to an energy efficient provider, it can include an energy attribute in its service specification, thus enabling energy efficient service provisioning. When a provider is selected, its address is stored in the Binding Table. The Binding Table maps the task's service specification to the provider that will perform the service. It is updated when the Service Finder discovers a better provider and when a task explicitly unbinds from a service. A task can query a Binding Table to determine whether it has access to a particular service.

The Service Scheduler carries out the actual invocation. It takes the input parameters provided by the task, sends them to the provider, and waits for the results to arrive. Once the results arrive, it passes them to the task which can then resume executing. If the results do not arrive within a certain time, the Service Scheduler aborts the operation and notifies the task of the error.

4.2 SPF-Provider

The SPF-Provider is responsible for providing and executing services. Its architecture, shown in Figure 5, consists of a Service Registry, Matchmaker, Remote Invocator, and Service Discovery component. The Service Registry contains the specifications

Table 1. WSN devices vary widely in computational resources

	TelosB	Imote2
Processor	8MHz 16-bit TI MSP430	13-416MHz 32-bit Intel PXA271 XScale
Radio	IEEE 802.15.4	IEEE 802.15.4
Memory	48KB Code, 10KB Data	32MB Shared
Price	$99	$299

of all locally-provided services. The Matchmaker is used to determine whether a service meets the requirements of a task. When the SPF-Consumer tries to find a service, the Matchmaker is used to determine whether a matching service exists. Note that in this architecture, the task's specification must be sent from the SPF-Consumer to the SPF-Provider. This is because the Matchmaker is located on the SPF-Provider. Alternatively, the Matchmaker can be moved onto the SPF-Consumer to reduce the footprint of the SPF-Provider. However, this requires that all specifications be sent to the SPF-Consumer, a process that may incur higher communication cost.

4.3   Middleware Modularity

WSNs are becoming extremely diverse consisting of devices with resources that differ by several orders of magnitude [46,15]. This is true even as technology improves, since cost constraints ensure the continued presence of resource-limited devices. To accommodate the wide range of devices, Servilla's middleware is modularized and configurable such that a device need not implement every module to participate in the network. For example, the middleware can be configured in the following ways:

– **VM + SPF:** The full Servilla framework.
– **VM + SPF-Consumer:** Executes tasks and provides access to remote services only.
– **SPF-Provider:** Provides services for neighboring tasks to use.

A detailed analysis of the memory consumed by each configuration is given in Section 5.1. The configuration containing only the SPF-Provider is particularly interesting because it allows resource-weak, but energy efficient, devices to provide services to more powerful devices. This can result in greater overall energy efficiency and, assuming the weak devices are less costly and more numerous, increase sensing density while achieving greater sensing coverage.

The various middleware configurations are *transparent* to tasks due to the decoupled nature of the SOC model. For example, a task need not know whether there is a local SPF-Provider. If a task requires a service, it will be bound either locally or remotely depending on availability.

4.4   Implementation

Servilla has been implemented on TinyOS 1.0 and two representative hardware platforms shown in Table 1. It is divided into two levels as shown in Figure 6: a lower level consisting of shared components and a higher level consisting of Servilla's VM

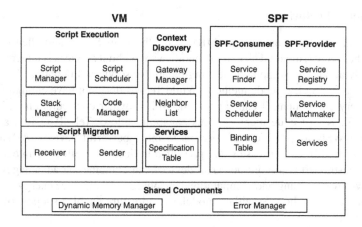

Fig. 6. Servilla's middleware components

and SPF. This section first discusses the lower level followed by the upper level. It ends with a discussion of Servilla's programming languages.

The shared components implement low-level mechanisms needed by most high-level components. The dynamic memory manager makes more efficient use of memory. This is important because Servilla has several components that require varying amounts of memory over time. The dynamic memory manager provides just enough memory for each higher-level component to complete their function and reclaims the memory when it is no longer needed. It is shared by most components in Servilla's middleware, maximizing the flexibility of memory allocation. To aid in debugging, Servilla provides an error manager that detects and sends summaries of problems to the base station. The error manager is shared by all other components in Servilla's middleware.

The SPF is implemented natively using NesC and is divided into two modules, the SPF-Consumer and SPF-Provider, as shown in Figure 6. In the SPF-Consumer, the implementation of the Service Scheduler is simplified by serializing service invocations. This has the added benefit of avoiding saturating the wireless channel. To increase energy efficiency, the Service Finder first searches the local Service Repository, if one exists, before searching one-hop neighbors. In the SPF-Provider, the Service Registry is able to support up to 256 local services.

Servilla's compiler can compile ServillaScript and ServillaSpec into a compact binary format. For example, the task shown in Figure 3 is compiled into 181 bytes of code and 30 bytes of specifications, and the specification shown in Figure 2 is compiled into just 64 bytes. Both the Servilla middleware and compiler have been released as open-source software at http://mobilab.wustl.edu/projects/servilla/.

5 Evaluation

This section presents empirical measurement of the code size and performance overhead of Servilla on both the TelosB [46] and Imote2 [15] platforms. The efficacy of the Servilla programming model is demonstrated through an application case study in the next section.

5.1   Memory Footprint

An Imote2 has sufficient memory (32MB) to hold the entire Servilla middleware. Compiled for the Imote2, the total size of the middleware without services is a mere 318KB. This is only about 1% of the total, leaving plenty for services. In contrast, TelosB devices only have 48KB of code memory. While TelosB does not have enough memory to hold every component, it can support the SPF-Provider configuration which only consumes 32 KB of code memory. This capability allows TelosB to join and contribute to a WSN as providers of services to more powerful devices. As shown in previous work [22] and our case study presented in Section 6, effective integration of resource-constrained and more powerful devices can combine the advantages of pervasive low-power sensing and computational resources, and enhance energy efficiency. This example shows how Servilla's modular architecture enables support of diverse hardware platforms.

5.2   Efficiency of Service Binding

Service binding consists of three parts: discovery, matching, and selection. This study first focuses on discovery followed by matching and selection. Recall that the current implementation requires the Service Finder to query each neighbor individually for a match. This is because Servilla uses a reliable network interface that does not support wireless broadcasts. To optimize the selection, the Service Finder first searches locally before remotely. Since the latency of a local search is negligible, we evaluate the latency of a remote search.

The latency of a remote search depends on the number of neighbors, the percentage of them that provide a matching service, and the order in which they are queried. At a minimum, one neighbor will be queried. This study evaluates only a single query, since each additional query will proportionately increase the latency. An Imote2 is used to query a TelosB to determine whether the TelosB provides a particular service. In this case, the service being queried is FFT and the specification is shown in Figure 2. It is compiled into 64 bytes, which must be sent from the Imote2 to the TelosB. Due to various bookkeeping variables, the size of the query message is 72 bytes, and the reply message is 16 bytes. The time between sending the query to receiving a reply is measured by toggling a general I/O pin before and after the query, and capturing the time between toggles using an oscilloscope. Averaged over 100 trials, the latency and 90% confidence interval is $245.6 \pm 1ms$. This latency is acceptable to many WSN applications. Moreover, it may be amortized over multiple invocations of the same service after it is bound to the task.

To evaluate the efficiency of service matching, the Matchmaker is used to compare two copies of FFT, shown in Figure 2. This incurs the worst-case latency since every property within the specification must be compared. Each experiment is repeated twenty times on both TelosB and Imote2 platforms running at all possible CPU speeds and the average latency is calculated. The results are shown in Table 2.[1] They indicate that the TelosB takes about $92ms$ to perform a match, while the Imote2 is at least ten

---

[1] The confidence intervals are negligible since the experiment runs locally and the measurements exhibit very low variance.

Table 2. Service matching latency when comparing two FFT-real service specifications

device	CPU Speed	Bus Speed	Sig.	Attr. 1	Attr. 2	Attr. 3	Other	Total	Units
TelosB	8MHz	8MHz	18	14	24	29	8	92	ms
Imote2	13MHz	13MHz	1569	1421	2642	3272	784	9688	μs
Imote2	104MHz	104MHz	198	180	330	408	94	1209	μs
Imote2	208MHz	208MHz	99	89	165	204	47	604	μs
Imote2	416MHz	208MHz	71	62	113	136	31	413	μs

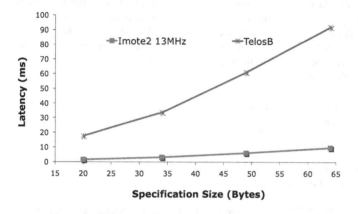

Fig. 7. The latency of comparing a specification vs. its size

times faster. The latencies are small compared to the execution times of certain VM instructions. Note that while service matchmaking does introduce overhead, it is usually done infrequently relative to service invocation.

To determine how the specification's size affects matching latency, FFT is compared to versions of itself with one, two, and all three of its attributes removed. The matching latencies is plotted against their sizes and the results are shown in Figure 7. For brevity, only the Imote2 running at 13MHz is shown. The latency when the Imote2 is running at higher frequencies is significantly lower. The results indicate that the latency is roughly proportional to its size. It is not exactly proportional because of the additional overhead incurred with the addition of each attribute, as indicated by the "other" column in Table 2.

6   Application Case Study

This section evaluates Servilla using an application case study, specifically one designed to localize damage in structures (e.g., a bridge). The application enables real-time evaluation of a structure's integrity, reducing manual inspection costs while increasing safety. WSNs have recently been used to successfully localize damage to experimental structures using a homogeneous network of Imote2 devices [24]. In this case, the algorithm, called Damage Localization Assurance Criterion (DLAC), was written using NesC specifically for the Imote2. The implementation using Servilla generalizes

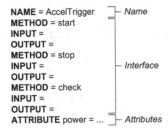

(a) The specification of service AccelTrigger provided by Imote2 and TelosB devices. The power attribute specifies the amount of power the service consumes. It is 145mW on the Imote2, and 9mW on the TelosB.

(b) The specification of a low-power version of service AccelTrigger, which is provided by the application task. Its interface is omitted since it is the same as the one in Figure 8(a). A high-power version has attribute power $\geq$ 50 mW.

```
NAME = DLAC          ⌐− Name
METHOD = find
INPUT =              − Interface
OUTPUT = float[25]   ⌐
```

(c) The specification of service DLAC provided by Imote2 devices.

Fig. 8. The services used by the damage localization application

and improves upon the original by making it platform-independent and increasing its overall energy efficiency by exploiting network heterogeneity.

The heterogeneous WSN used in this study consists of TelosB and Imote2 devices. DLAC can only run on the Imote2 due to insufficient memory on the TelosB. However, Imote2 devices consume significantly more energy than TelosB devices. Thus, using Servilla, the application can combine the advantages of both platforms by using the TelosB devices to monitor the ambient vibration levels, allowing the Imote2 devices to sleep longer. Ideally, the Imote2 devices should only be activated to perform the DLAC algorithm when the TelosB devices detect that the ambient vibration levels exceed a certain damage-inducing threshold. The dual-level nature of this configuration is common to other applications like surveillance [26], and is essential for conserving energy and increasing network lifetime.

The Servilla implementation relies on two services: AccelTrigger and DLAC. Ambient vibrations are monitored by AccelTrigger, which sets a flag when a threshold is exceeded. Its specification is shown in Figure 8(a). The service has three methods: start, stop, and check. Methods start and stop control when the service monitors the local accelerometer. The status of the flag is obtained by invoking check. Both the Imote2 and TelosB devices provide AccelTrigger. They differ in their power attribute, since the Imote2 consumes more power than the TelosB (145mW vs. 9mW).

The specification of service DLAC is shown in Figure 8(c). It contains a single method, find, that takes no parameters and returns an array of floating-point numbers that are used to localize damage to the bridge [24].

```
1.  uses AccelTiggerHP;
2.  uses AccelTiggerLP;
3.  uses DLAC;
4.
5.  void main() {
6.      bind(DLAC, 0); // bind DLAC service
7.      if(!isBound(DLAC)) exit(); // failed to bind DLAC
8.      bind(AccelTriggerLP, 1); // bind low-power AccelTrigger service
9.      if(isBound(AccelTriggerLP)) {
10.         invoke(AccelTriggerLP, "start");
11.         waitForTrigger(1);
12.     } else {
13.         bind(AccelTriggerHP);
14.         if(isBound(AccelTriggerHP)) {
15.             invoke(AccelTriggerHP, "start");
16.             waitForTrigger(0);
17.         }
18.     }
19. }
20.
21. void waitForTrigger(int useLowPower) {
22.     int vibration = 0;
23.     while(vibration == 0) {
24.         if (useLowPower)
25.             vibration = invoke(AccelTriggerLP, "check");
26.         else
27.             vibration = invoke(AccelTriggerHP, "check");
28.         if (vibration == 1) {
29.             if (useLowPower)
30.                 invoke(AccelTriggerLP, "stop");
31.             else
32.                 invoke(AccelTriggerHP, "stop");
33.             doDLAC();
34.         }
35.         sleep(1024*60*5); // sleep for 5 minutes
36.     }
37. }
38.
39. void doDLAC() {
40.     float[25] dlac_data;
41.     dlac_data = invoke(DLAC, "find");
42.     send(dlac_data); // send DLAC data to base station
43. }
```

Fig. 9. The damage localization application task

The application's task is shown in Figure 9. The first three lines specify the names of the files containing the required service specifications. The content of AccelTriggerLP is shown in Figure 8(b), and the content of DLAC is shown in Figure 8(c). Notice that AccelTriggerLP matches the TelosB version of the AccelTrigger service shown in Figure 8(a) because its power attribute is less than 50mW. AccelTriggerHP contains the same specification as AccelTriggerLP except its power attribute is $\geq$ 50 mW, which matches the service provided by the Imote2.

The application attempts to reduce energy consumption by preferentially binding to an Acceltrigger service that consumes less power. It does this by first attempting to bind using the specification within AccelTriggerLP on line 8, before using the specification within AccelTriggerHP on line 13. Once an AccelTrigger

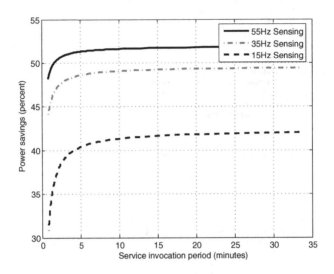

Fig. 10. Percent power savings of heterogeneous vs. homogeneous WSN

service is bound, the task periodically queries it to determine if the acceleration readings are above a certain threshold (lines 21-37). If it is, DLAC is invoked and the results are sent to the base station (lines 39-43).

To evaluate the benefit of exploiting network heterogeneity on Servilla, the task shown in Figure 9 is injected into two WSNs: a homogeneous network consisting of only Imote2 devices, and a heterogeneous network consisting of both Imote2 and TelosB devices. Since the application is written using Servilla, it is able to run on both types of networks without modification. In both cases, DLAC is executed by the Imote2, meaning the power consumption of performing damage localization is constant. However, the power consumption of AccelTrigger varies because Servilla's service provisioning framework enables an application to exploit more energy-efficient services when possible in a platform-independent and declarative fashion. Specifically, if TelosB devices are present, the service will be executed on a TelosB device since its AccelTrigger service consumes less power, otherwise it will be executed on the Imote2. We compare the power consumption of invoking AccelTrigger in different network configurations.

Since invoking AccelTrigger on the TelosB requires a remote invocation, the amount of energy saved depends on the invocation and sensing frequencies. If the service is invoked too often, more energy will be spent on wireless communication. Likewise, if the sensor is accessed very infrequently, the benefits of the TelosB is diminished since the devices will remain asleep a larger percentage of the time. To determine how much energy savings is possible, an oscilloscope is used to measure the time each platform spends computing, communicating wirelessly, and sensing, in both a homogeneous and heterogeneous network. The sensing frequency is varied between 15Hz and 55Hz (the maximum sampling frequency of the TelosB), and the service invocation frequency is varied between 50 seconds to 35 minutes. The percent savings of using a heterogeneous network relative to a homogeneous network is then calculated and the results are shown in Figure 10.

The results show that the heterogeneous implementation using Servilla achieves up to 52% power savings, and the savings increase with sensing frequency. They also show that invoking the service too frequently will reduce the amount of power saved since doing so incurs more network overhead. There is a limit to the amount of energy that can be saved as the service invocation period increases since it approaches the difference between the sensing energy consumed by the Imote2 versus the TelosB.

This case study demonstrates how Servilla enables platform-independent applications that operate over a heterogeneous WSN, and how Servilla facilitates in-network collaboration between different types of devices to attain higher energy efficiency. Moreover, it demonstrates that Servilla enables an application to bind to a more energy-efficient service through service specification.

7 Related Work

SOC has long been used on the Internet to enable independently-developed applications to interoperate. There are many SOC systems including SLP [30], Jini [31], OSGi [44], CORBA, and Web Services [2]. Servilla has three salient features that distinguish it from these SOC frameworks. First, it focuses on how service-provisioning language and middleware can be made extremely lightweight. This is necessary due to the limited resources available on many WSN devices. Many previous SOC systems have been ported to PDA-class devices, which are more powerful than the low-power sensor devices supported by Servilla. Second, Servilla is specifically designed for localized service binding which is a common case in WSNs due to limited energy resources. Finally, Servilla provides a modular middleware architecture that can be configured for devices with a wider range of resources.

SOC is a topic of interest in the coordination community. For example, new languages have been developed that enable formal reasoning about complex service interactions and compositions [8,1,38,3]. Calculi have been developed to model sessions and multi-party dynamic interactions between service users and providers [39,13]. New ways of specifying quality-of-service requirements and achieving higher levels of reliability have been proposed [4,10,12,42,9]. SOC has also been used in non-traditional environments like mobile ad hoc networks [25]. Recently, there has been increased interest in context-aware applications [43,20,16]. WSNs, being embedded and able to sense the environment, are inherently context-aware. This paper takes the natural next step of applying SOC principles to WSNs. The key distinguishing feature of Servilla lies in its capability to support both resource-constrained devices and more powerful devices, and its light-weight language and middleware tailored for in-network coordination among sensors.

Efforts to bring SOC technologies into the WSN domain include Tiny Web Services [47] and Arch Rock's PhyNet™ [6]. Both optimize existing Internet protocols to function under the severe resource constraints of WSNs. Unlike Servilla, they do not provide a mechanism for service discovery or the flexible matching of service consumers to providers *within* the WSN. Instead, they enable language-independent communication between services inside the WSN and applications outside of the WSN.

In addition to SOC, Servilla shares the common approach of using scripts in a WSN, though for different reasons. Some scripting systems, including Maté [34], ASVM [35], SwissQM [40], and Agilla [19], enable reprogramming. Other systems, including Melete [51] and SensorWare [11], enable multiple applications to share a WSN. All of these systems come with different scripting languages [33,23,37,50]. Servilla differs by focusing on challenges due to network heterogeneity and dynamics. Unlike other systems, Servilla allows scripts to remain platform-independent and dynamically find and access platform-specific services. One scripting system, DVM [7], explores the similar idea of integrating platform-independent scripts with native services. It features a dynamically extensible virtual machine in which services can register extensions. While this enables tuning the boundary between interpreted and native code, DVM does not support flexible matching between scripts and services.

Servilla introduces the idea of a modular and configurable platform in which extremely resource-poor devices only implement a fraction of the entire framework. This enables a hierarchy in which weak devices serve more powerful devices. The idea of having a hierarchy within a WSN is promoted by other systems. Tenet [22] creates a two-tired WSN in which the lower tier consists of resource-poor devices that can accept tasks from higher-tier devices. It differs from Servilla in that it does not support service discovery and dynamic binding between different devices. SONGS [36] is an architecture for WSNs that allows users to issue queries that are automatically decomposed into graphs of services which are mapped onto actual devices. SONG does not provide service binding among heterogeneous devices.

8   Conclusions

The increasing difficulty of developing applications for heterogeneous and dynamic WSNs demands a new coordination model. Servilla provides this by introducing a novel service provisioning framework that enables applications to be platform-independent while still able to access platform-specific capabilities. A salient feature of Servilla lies in its capability to support coordination and collaboration among heterogeneous devices *inside* a WSN. A specialized service description language is introduced that enables flexible matching between applications and services, which may reside on different devices. Servilla provides a modular middleware architecture to enable resource-poor devices to participate by contributing services, facilitating in-network collaboration among a wide range of devices. The efficiency of Servilla's implementation is established via microbenchmarks on two representative classes of hardware platforms. The effectiveness of Servilla's programming model is demonstrated by a structural health monitoring application case study.

Acknowledgment

This work is funded by the National Science Foundation under grants CNS-0520220, CNS-0627126, and CNS-0708460.

References

1. Abreu, J., Fiadeiro, J.L.: A coordination model for service-oriented interactions. In: Lea, Zavattaro (eds.) [32], pp. 1–16
2. Alonso, G., Casati, F., Kuno, H., Machiraju, V.: Web Services. Springer, Heidelberg (2003)
3. Ankolekar, A., Huch, F., Sycara, K.P.: Concurrent semantics for the web services specification language daml-s. In: Arbab, Talcott (eds.) [5], pp. 14–21
4. Arbab, F., Chothia, T., Meng, S., Moon, Y.-J.: Component connectors with qos guarantees. In: Murphy, Vitek (eds.) [41], pp. 286–304
5. Arbab, F., Talcott, C.L. (eds.): COORDINATION 2002. LNCS, vol. 2315. Springer, Heidelberg (2002)
6. ARCH ROCK. Arch Rock PhyNet™, http://www.archrock.com/product/
7. Balani, R., Han, C.-C., Rengaswamy, R.K., Tsigkogiannis, I., Srivastava, M.: Multi-level software reconfiguration for sensor networks. In: EMSOFT 2006: Proceedings of the 6th ACM & IEEE International conference on Embedded software, pp. 112–121. ACM, New York (2006)
8. Bettini, L., Nicola, R.D., Loreti, M.: Implementing session centered calculi. In: Lea, Zavattaro (eds.) [32], pp. 17–32
9. Bocchi, L., Ciancarini, P., Rossi, D.: Transactional aspects in semantic based discovery of services. In: Jacquet, Picco (eds.) [29], pp. 283–297
10. Bocchi, L., Lucchi, R.: Atomic commit and negotiation in service oriented computing. In: Ciancarini, Wiklicky (eds.) [14], pp. 16–27
11. Boulis, A., Han, C.-C., Srivastava, M.B.: Design and implementation of a framework for efficient and programmable sensor networks. In: MobiSys 2003: Proceedings of the 1st international conference on Mobile systems, applications and services, pp. 187–200. ACM, New York (2003)
12. Bravetti, M., Zavattaro, G.: A theory for strong service compliance. In: Murphy, Vitek (eds.) [41], pp. 96–112
13. Bruni, R., Lanese, I., Melgratti, H.C., Tuosto, E.: Multiparty sessions in soc. In: Lea, Zavattaro (eds.) [32], pp. 67–82
14. Ciancarini, P., Wiklicky, H. (eds.): COORDINATION 2006. LNCS, vol. 4038. Springer, Heidelberg (2006)
15. CROSSBOW TECHNOLOGIES. Imote2 datasheet, http://tinyurl.com/5jrw85
16. Cubo, J., Salaün, G., Cámara, J., Canal, C., Pimentel, E.: Context-based adaptation of component behavioural interfaces. In: Murphy, Vitek (eds.) [41], pp. 305–323
17. Culler, D., Estrin, D., Srivastava, M.: Overview of sensor networks. IEEE Computer 37(8), 41–49 (2004)
18. Flanagan, D.: JavaScript: The Definitive Guide, 4th edn. O'REILLY, Inc., Sebastopol (2001)
19. Fok, C.-L., Roman, G.-C., Lu, C.: Rapid development and flexible deployment of adaptive wireless sensor network applications. In: ICDCS 2005: Proceedings of the 25th IEEE International Conference on Distributed Computing Systems, Washington, DC, USA, pp. 653–662. IEEE Computer Society, Los Alamitos (2005)
20. Frey, D., Roman, G.-C.: Context-aware publish subscribe in mobile ad hoc networks. In: Murphy, Vitek (eds.) [41], pp. 37–55
21. Gay, D., Levis, P., von Behren, R., Welsh, M., Brewer, E., Culler, D.: The nesc language: A holistic approach to networked embedded systems. In: PLDI 2003: Proceedings of the ACM SIGPLAN 2003 conference on Programming language design and implementation, pp. 1–11. ACM, New York (2003)

22. Gnawali, O., Jang, K.-Y., Paek, J., Vieira, M., Govindan, R., Greenstein, B., Joki, A., Estrin, D., Kohler, E.: The tenet architecture for tiered sensor networks. In: SenSys 2006: Proceedings of the 4th international conference on Embedded networked sensor systems, pp. 153–166. ACM, New York (2006)

23. Greenstein, B., Kohler, E., Estrin, D.: A sensor network application construction kit (snack). In: SenSys 2004: Proceedings of the 2nd international conference on Embedded networked sensor systems, pp. 69–80. ACM, New York (2004)

24. Hackmann, G., Sun, F., Castaneda, N., Lu, C., Dyke, S.: A holistic approach to decentralized structural damage localization using wireless sensor networks. In: RTSS 2008: Proceedings of the 2008 Real-Time Systems Symposium, Washington, DC, USA, pp. 35–46. IEEE Computer Society, Los Alamitos (2008)

25. Handorean, R., Roman, G.-C.: Service provision in ad hoc networks. In: Arbab, Talcott (eds.) [5], pp. 207–219

26. He, T., Krishnamurthy, S., Luo, L., Yan, T., Gu, L., Stoleru, R., Zhou, G., Cao, Q., Vicaire, P., Stankovic, J.A., Abdelzaher, T.F., Hui, J., Krogh, B.: Vigilnet: An integrated sensor network system for energy-efficient surveillance. ACM Trans. Sen. Netw. 2(1), 1–38 (2006)

27. Hill, J., Szewczyk, R., Woo, A., Hollar, S., Culler, D., Pister, K.: System architecture directions for networked sensors. In: Architectural Support for Programming Languages and Operating Systems, pp. 93–104 (2000)

28. Intanagonwiwat, C., Govindan, R., Estrin, D.: Directed diffusion: a scalable and robust communication paradigm for sensor networks. In: MobiCom 2000: Proceedings of the 6th annual international conference on Mobile computing and networking, pp. 56–67. ACM, New York (2000)

29. Jacquet, J.-M., Picco, G.P. (eds.): COORDINATION 2005. LNCS, vol. 3454. Springer, Heidelberg (2005)

30. Kempf, J., Pierre, P.S.: Service location protocol for enterprise networks: implementing and deploying a dynamic service finder. John Wiley & Sons, Inc., New York (1999)

31. Kumaran, I., Kumaran, S.I.: Jini Technology: An Overview. Prentice Hall PTR, Upper Saddle River (2001)

32. Lea, D., Zavattaro, G. (eds.): COORDINATION 2008. LNCS, vol. 5052. Springer, Heidelberg (2008)

33. Levis, P.: The TinyScript Manual (July 2004), http://tinyurl.com/57kycj

34. Levis, P., Culler, D.: Maté: a tiny virtual machine for sensor networks. In: ASPLOS-X: Proceedings of the 10th international conference on Architectural support for programming languages and operating systems, pp. 85–95. ACM, New York (2002)

35. Levis, P., Gay, D., Culler, D.: Active sensor networks. In: NSDI 2005: Proceedings of the 2nd conference on Symposium on Networked Systems Design & Implementation, Berkeley, CA, USA, pp. 343–356. USENIX Association (2005)

36. Liu, J., Zhao, F.: Towards semantic services for sensor-rich information systems. In: 2nd Int. Conf. on Broadband Networks, pp. 44–51 (2005)

37. Madden, S., Franklin, M.J., Hellerstein, J.M., Hong, W.: Tag: a tiny aggregation service for ad-hoc sensor networks. SIGOPS Oper. Syst. Rev. 36(SI), 131–146 (2002)

38. Mazzara, M., Govoni, S.: A case study of web services orchestration. In: Jacquet, Picco (eds.) [29], pp. 1–16

39. Mezzina, L.G.: How to infer finite session types in a calculus of services and sessions. In: Lea, Zavattaro (eds.) [32], pp. 216–231

40. Müller, R., Alonso, G., Kossmann, D.: A virtual machine for sensor networks. SIGOPS Oper. Syst. Rev. 41(3), 145–158 (2007)

41. Murphy, A.L., Vitek, J. (eds.): COORDINATION 2007. LNCS, vol. 4467. Springer, Heidelberg (2007)

42. Nores, M.L., Duque, J.G., Arias, J.J.P.: Managing ad-hoc networks through the formal specification of service requirements. In: Ciancarini, Wiklicky (eds.) [14], pp. 164–178
43. Núñez, A., Noyé, J.: An event-based coordination model for context-aware applications. In: Lea, Zavattaro (eds.) [32], pp. 232–248
44. OSGI. Open source gateway initiative, http://www.osgi.org
45. Papazoglou, M.P., Traverso, P., Dustdar, S., Leymann, F.: Service-oriented computing: State of the art and research challenges. Computer 40(11), 38–45 (2007)
46. Polastre, J., Szewczyk, R., Culler, D.: Telos: enabling ultra-low power wireless research. In: IPSN 2005: Proceedings of the 4th international symposium on Information processing in sensor networks, Piscataway, NJ, USA, p. 48. IEEE Press, Los Alamitos (2005)
47. Priyantha, N.B., Kansal, A., Goraczko, M., Zhao, F.: Tiny web services: design and implementation of interoperable and evolvable sensor networks. In: SenSys 2008: Proceedings of the 6th ACM conference on Embedded network sensor systems, pp. 253–266. ACM, New York (2008)
48. STREELINE. Parking management, http://www.streetlinenetworks.com
49. W3C. Web services description language (wsdl), http://www.w3.org/TR/wsdl
50. Yao, Y., Gehrke, J.: The cougar approach to in-network query processing in sensor networks. SIGMOD Rec. 31(3), 9–18 (2002)
51. Yu, Y., Rittle, L.J., Bhandari, V., LeBrun, J.B.: Supporting concurrent applications in wireless sensor networks. In: SenSys 2006: Proceedings of the 4th international conference on Embedded networked sensor systems, pp. 139–152. ACM, New York (2006)

Fairness for Chorded Languages

Alexis Petrounias and Susan Eisenbach

Department of Computing, Imperial College London, United Kingdom

Abstract. Joins or chords is a concurrency construct that seems to fit well with the object oriented paradigm. Chorded languages are presented with implicit assumptions regarding the fair treatment of processes by the scheduler. We define weak and strong fairness for the Small Chorded Object-Oriented Language (^{l}SCHOOL) which allows the classification of executions as fair. We investigate the liveness behaviour of programs and establish worst-case behaviours in terms of scheduling delays.

We discover that weak fairness, although giving the scheduler implementer greater freedom in selecting the next process which is to be executed, is harder to implement than strong fairness; strong fairness benefits from a straightforward implementation, however, imposes many more constraints and limits the selection function of a scheduler.

1   Introduction

The chord construct is a concurrency mechanism inspired by the join from the Join-Calculus [1,2]. Its use should raise the level of abstraction concurrent programs are written in, making development of correct programs easier. Its simplicity is appealing and recently languages have been extended to include chords or joins: $C^\sharp$ [3], Concurrent Basic [4] an extension of Visual Basic, C_ω [5,6], JoCaml [7], and Scala [8].

Generally, programmers assume that a concurrent execution environment will benefit from a "fair" scheduler, in the sense that execution of their programs will not be arbitrarily delayed, nor that some components of their program will be treated more favourably than others. However, this assumption is not typically reflected in the formalisms which describe concurrent languages and the selection function of the scheduler is left unspecified.

Notions of *fairness* evolved from the observation that legal executions allowed lack of progress for some components of concurrent systems. We aim to determine what makes a fair chorded implementation. To achieve this we start by defining a small calculus (^{l}SCHOOL) that is object oriented with chords.

Two fundamental concepts in scheduling are *liveness* and *fairness*, here in the sense of relative allocation (fairness) of execution time and message consumption among interacting processes which are capable of executing (liveness). There are many notions of fairness depending on the kinds of guarantees one wishes to give. We investigate two primary notions of fairness, *weak* and *strong*, and describe abstract schedulers with weak and strong fairness guarantees.

The rest of the paper is organised as follows: In section 2 we introduce both chords and fairness for earlier concurrent programming languages, showing some

J. Field and V.T. Vasconcelos (Eds.): COORDINATION 2009, LNCS 5521, pp. 86–105, 2009.

of the problems that arise from non-deterministic choice in programming language constructs, and the kinds of properties schedulers handling such choice may be required to guarantee. In section 3 we introduce our calculus. Fairness is investigated in sections 4,5, and 6. Finally, we conclude in section 7.

2   Background

Chorded programs [9] consist of classes which define chords. A chord consists of a header and a body. The header consists of at most one *synchronous* method signature and zero or more *asynchronous* method signatures, while the body consists of the expressions to be executed.

The body of a chord executes when an object has received an invocation for each of the method (signatures) in its header. In general, multiple invocations are required to execute the body. The simultaneous presence of invocations for each of the methods enables the chord to *join* [1,2]. Hence a chord header can be seen as a guard for the execution of the body.

When a join occurs the participating asynchronous methods' invocations are consumed, and their arguments are passed to the body of the chord. When multiple invocations of the same method are present there is a non-deterministic choice as to which invocation is consumed.

A method can appear at most once in any chord header, but, methods can participate in multiple chord headers. If multiple chords can join by consuming the same method invocation, then the choice of which chord joins is unspecified.

The invocation of a synchronous method results in the invoking thread *blocking* until a suitable join occurs. Again, there may be a choice of which chord will join and unblock the thread if the method participates in more than one chord. Once the join occurs the invoker thread is unblocked and executes the chord body, potentially resulting in a return value.

Asynchronous methods return immediately, and their return type must be *async*, a subtype of *void*. A chord without a synchronous method is called asynchronous, and when it is capable of joining we call it *strung*; such chords will not have an invoking blocking thread. When an invocation for each of their asynchronous methods is present, the chord can join and its body is executed in a new thread. The following chord implements an unbounded buffer:

```
Object get( ) & async put( Object o ) { return o; }
```

Invoking get, which is synchronous, will result in the invoker blocking until a value is returned. The body of the chord will execute only when the chord joins, which requires an invocation of put to be present. When a join occurs, the invocation of put is consumed. Multiple invocations of put are "queued".

The primary work on fairness in concurrent programming languages was for CCS by Costa and Stirling [10] who developed weak and strong fairness for CCS. Their approach is to augment CCS with an appropriate labelling mechanism which deals with the non-deterministic choice operator +, as well as restriction and communication. The CCS operational semantics are extended so that only weakly-fair execution sequences are admitted in contrast with an approach where all executions are generated and unfair ones are then eliminated.

Weak fairness prohibits executions where a process remains enabled throughout but does not get a chance to proceed, or *remains enabled almost always*; in other words, weak fairness requires that *if a component is enabled continuously from some point onwards, then it eventually proceeds*. This implies that if a process is continuously enabled, then it proceeds infinitely often.

The resulting system allows for a "local" characterisation of weakly-fair executions, in the sense that finite sequences are shown to be weakly fair, and a continuous concatenation of such locally weakly-fair sequences produces a globally weakly-fair execution.

Strong fairness relaxes the assumption of weak fairness for a component becoming continuously enabled from some point onwards to becoming enabled infinitely often, and hence requires that *if a component is infinitely often enabled it proceeds infinitely often*. Therefore, strong fairness prohibits exactly those executions which contain components which become enabled infinitely often but proceed only a finite number of times.

Similarly to their presentation of weak fairness, a positive approach is used by which CCS is appropriately labelled and the operational semantics are extended in order to admit exactly the strongly-fair executions. In contrast with weak fairness, however, strongly-fair execution sequences cannot be characterised "locally", as there is a family of systems of processes which are strongly-fair for an indefinite number of steps, yet then become inadmissible under strong fairness.

Strong fairness implies weak fairness, and if components which become disabled never become enabled again, the two coincide [11]. An implementation of strong fairness always requiresusing queues [11].

3 ^{l}SCHOOL

^{l}SCHOOL is a small object-oriented language. The constructs of the language are limited to classes which define chords, and object instantiations of these classes which reside in a heap. Classes exist within a simple, single-inheritance hierarchy, and methods and chords can be overridden.[1]

The chord description of the previous section is based on Polyphonic $C^\sharp$, which features the *async* return type, a subtype of *void*, to indicate asynchronous methods; this is not necessary for implementing asynchronous methods, as all methods of return type *void* can be executed asynchronously. ^{l}SCHOOL does not feature the *async* type; instead, a method which has a return type of *void* can be invoked either synchronously or asynchronously. Furthermore we require exactly one argument for each method m, which we call m_x. The value of the last expression evaluated in a body becomes the return value of the chord.

The granularity level of ^{l}SCHOOL is at the individual expressions, which are either live or non-live, depending on whether they can participate in an evaluation through one of the rules. Individual expressions are annotated with

---

[1] The full set of definitions and lemmas for ^{l}SCHOOL can be found in the appendix.

Abstract Syntax

$$e \in Expr ::= null \mid this \mid x \mid new\ c \mid e.m(e) \mid e; e$$
$$MethSig ::= t\ m(c)$$
$$t \in Type ::= void \mid c$$
$$x, c, m \in Id$$

Program Representation

$$Program = (Id^c \to Id^c) \times (Id^c \times Id^m \to MethSig) \times (Id^c \to \mathcal{P}(Chord))$$
$$Chord = (Id^m \cup \{\varepsilon\}) \times \mathcal{P}(Id^m) \times Expr$$

Runtime Entities

$$Configuration = RExpr^* \times Heap$$
$$Heap = \mathbb{N} \to Id^c$$
$$re \in RExpr ::= voidValue \mid null \mid \iota \mid new\ c \mid re.m(re) \mid re; re$$
$$\iota \in \mathbb{N}$$

Labelled Runtime Entities

$$lre \in LRExpr ::= voidValue^l \mid \iota^l \mid new\ c^l \mid re.m(re)^l \mid re; re^l \mid null^l$$
$$l \in \mathcal{L}^\varepsilon$$

Fig. 1. ^{l}SCHOOL overview

unique labels, and then transitions are annotated with collections of labels which correspond to those expressions participating in an evaluation. The use of labels thus enables us to observe execution traces, and classify these as admissible or inadmissible under particular notions of fairness.

Figure 1 provides an overview of syntax and program representation. The syntax of ^{l}SCHOOL expressions, $Expr$, consists of method calls $e.m(e)$, variables x, object creation $new\ c$, sequential composition, the special receiver $this$, and the $null$ value. We use Id^m for the set of method names, Id^c for the set of class names, and Id^x for the set of variable names. ^{l}SCHOOL programs are represented using tuples of mappings. Programs consist of three mappings: inheritance, method signatures, and chords. We typically define a globally fixed variable P which contains the program, as described below.

The first component maps a class name to its direct superclass: $Id^c \to Id^c$ and the superclass of a class c is $P{\downarrow}_1(c)$. The second component maps a class name c and a method name m to the method's signature: $Id^c \times Id^m \to MethSig$ and the method signature is $P{\downarrow}_2(c,\ m)$. The signature consists of a return type, a name, and the class type of the single argument: $t\ m(c)$. The third component maps a class name to the set of chords defined in the class: $Id^c \to \mathcal{P}(Chord)$; to obtain the chords of class c we use $P{\downarrow}_3(c)$. We encode chords as triplets $(Id^m \cup \{\varepsilon\}) \times \mathcal{P}(Id^m) \times Expr$. The first element is either the name of a synchronous method, or the symbol ε if there aren't any. The second element is a set of asynchronous method names. The third is the body of the chord.

Each expression is annotated with a distinct label which is a runtime entity. Expressions which are ground values, so not considered during future evaluation steps, are each labelled with a special $empty$ label.

Evaluation Contexts

$$E[\bullet] ::= [\bullet] \mid E[\bullet].m(e) \mid \iota.m(E[\bullet]) \mid E[\bullet];e$$

Evaluation Rules

$$\frac{h(\iota) \text{ is undefined} \quad l' \text{ is fresh}}{E[new\ c]^{l}, h \xrightarrow{\{l\}} E[\iota]^{l'}, h[\iota \mapsto c]}\ \textsc{New} \qquad \frac{l' \text{ is fresh}}{E[z;e]^{l}, h \longrightarrow E[e]^{l'}, h}\ \textsc{Seq}$$

$$\frac{h(\iota){=}c \quad m \in \bigcup_{\chi \in P\downarrow_3(c)} \chi\downarrow_2 \quad E[\bullet] \neq [\bullet] \quad l', l'' \text{ are fresh}}{E[\iota.m(v)]^{l}, h \xrightarrow{\{l\}} E[voidValue]^{l'}, \iota.m(v)^{l''}, h}\ \textsc{Async}$$

$$\frac{\begin{array}{l} h(\iota){=}c \quad (m, \{m_1, \ldots, m_k\}, e) \in P\downarrow_3(c) \quad l'_0 \text{ fresh} \\ \forall\ i \in 1..k \ :\ \exists\ l'_i \in \mathcal{L}^{\varepsilon} \ :\ l'_i = \begin{cases} \varepsilon & \text{if } E_i[\bullet] = [\bullet] \\ l \in \mathcal{L}, l \text{ fresh} & \text{otherwise} \end{cases} \end{array}}{\begin{array}{l} E[\iota.m(v)]^{l_0}, E_1[\iota.m_1(v_1)]^{l_1}, \ldots, E_k[\iota.m_k(v_k)]^{l_k}, h \xrightarrow{\{l_0, l_1, \ldots, l_k\}} \\ \quad E[e[{}^{\iota}/_{this}, {}^{v}/_{m_x}, {}^{v_1}/_{m_1_x}, \ldots, {}^{v_k}/_{m_k_x}]]^{l'_0}, E_1[voidValue_1]^{l'_1}, \ldots, E_k[voidValue_k]^{l'_k}, h \end{array}}\ \textsc{Join}$$

$$\frac{\begin{array}{l} h(\iota){=}c \quad (\varepsilon, \{m_1, \ldots, m_k\}, e) \in P\downarrow_3(c) \quad l \text{ fresh} \\ \forall\ i \in 1..k \ :\ \exists\ l'_i \in \mathcal{L}^{\varepsilon} \ :\ l'_i = \begin{cases} \varepsilon & \text{if } E_i[\bullet] = [\bullet] \\ l' \in \mathcal{L}, l' \text{ fresh} & \text{otherwise} \end{cases} \end{array}}{\begin{array}{l} E_1[\iota.m_1(v_1)]^{l_1}, \ldots, E_k[\iota.m_k(v_k)]^{l_k}, h \xrightarrow{\{l_1, \ldots, l_k\}} \\ \quad E_1[voidValue_1]^{l'_1}, \ldots, E_k[voidValue_k]^{l'_k}, E[e[{}^{\iota}/_{this}, {}^{v_1}/_{m_1_x}, \ldots, {}^{v_k}/_{m_k_x}]]^{l}, h \end{array}}\ \textsc{Strung}$$

$$\frac{\overline{e^{l}} \cong \overline{e''^{l''} e''''^{l''''}} \quad \overline{e''^{l''}}, h \xrightarrow{\mu} \overline{e'''^{l''''}}, h' \quad \overline{e'''^{l'''} e''''^{l''''}} \cong \overline{e'^{l'}}}{\overline{e^{l}}, h \xrightarrow{\mu} \overline{e'^{l'}}, h'}\ \textsc{Perm}$$

Fig. 2. SCHOOL operational semantics

Only top-level run-time expressions, *RExpr*, are annotated, forming the labelled run-time expressions, *LRExpr*, and so all sub-expressions come directly from the ^{l}SCHOOL runtime expressions *RExpr* and have no labels.

Execution of ^{l}SCHOOL expressions is described by a term rewriting system in which a configuration, consisting of a collection of expressions, e_i, and a heap, h, evaluate into a new configuration:

$$e_1, \ldots, e_n, h \longrightarrow e'_1, \ldots, e'_m, h'$$

where the heap is a mapping of object addresses to their class names:

$$h : \mathbb{N} \rightarrow Id^{c}$$

and the number of expressions may change from n to m, as new expressions are *spawned* when asynchronous chords join and their bodies execute. Furthermore, threads never terminate in the sense that ground expressions are not removed from the execution, so $m \geq n$.

We also use the shorthand $\bar{e}$ for several, concurrent expressions, and thus we also have:

$$\bar{e}, h \quad \longrightarrow \quad \bar{e'}, h'$$

We describe ^{l}SCHOOL using operational semantics found in figure 2; we use the variable v to designate acceptable values for arguments to method calls, which consist of all expressions other than *voidValue*, and the variable z to designate all irreducible values (*null*, ι, *voidValue*). The evaluation rules are:

- NEW: creates a new object of a given class and allocates a previously undefined heap address which now maps to the object; returning the new address.
- SEQ: discards an irreducible value and enables the evaluation of the next expression in a sequential composition; the final value in a sequential composition cannot be discarded, and this allows the final value of a chord's body to become the return value of the chord's synchronous method.
- ASYNC: places an asynchronous invocation of a method (of *void* type and appearing in at least one asynchronous part of a chord header) into the execution, available for joining later. The invocation immediately returns *voidValue*. The condition $E[.] \neq [.]$, requiring the evaluation context to not be empty, is necessary so that we avoid infinite reductions of the form:

$$\iota.m(v), h \quad \longrightarrow \quad voidValue, \iota.m(v), h \quad \longrightarrow$$
$$voidValue, voidValue, \iota.m(v), h \quad \longrightarrow \quad \ldots$$

- JOIN: selects a chord in with a live synchronous method and *joins* this chord, consuming the corresponding asynchronous invocations (and replacing each by *voidValue*). The actual arguments are mapped to the formal arguments of the chord's body, which becomes the new evaluating expression.
- STRUNG: selects an asynchronous chord which is *strung*, i.e can join. Similar to the JOIN rule, all the asynchronous invocations are consumed, and actual arguments are mapped to the formal arguments of the chord's body, which will execute concurrently with the rest of the expressions.
- PERM enables the non-deterministic selection of expressions to evaluate and the reordering of expressions in the execution. The notation $\bar{e} \cong \bar{e'}$ means that $\bar{e'}$ is a permutation of $\bar{e}$.

The selection of which *strung* chord to join happens at two levels: multiple receiver objects may have asynchronous invocations enabling the joining of a chord, and an object may feature multiple chords which currently can join.

At each step there is a set of labels for the expressions affected by the rule used, the *participating* labels. Ground values become annotated with the empty label, and each changed or new expression gets a *fresh* label. Labels which may participate in an evaluation step are termed *active*. The freshness of a label is a property of the entire execution sequence up to the first appearance of the label. The participating labels, μ, form a set. Furthermore, the participating labels cannot be emptybecause each rule changes at least one expression from

```
1   class LabelledExample {
2     void f() & async a() { b(); }
3     void g() & async b() { print "Hi"; }
4   }
```

Listing 1.1. Example class for semantics

$$\overline{e_0^{l_0}}, h_0 \equiv \iota.f()^{l_1}, \iota.g()^{l_2}, \iota.a()^{l_3}, \iota.a()^{l_4}, h \qquad \xrightarrow[\mu_0=\{l_1,l_3\}]{\text{JOIN}}$$

$$\overline{e_1^{l_1}}, h_1 \equiv E[\iota.b()]^{l_5}, \iota.g()^{l_2}, voidValue^{\varepsilon}, \iota.a()^{l_4}, h \qquad \xrightarrow[\mu_1=\{l_5\}]{\text{ASYNC}}$$

$$\overline{e_2^{l_2}}, h_2 \equiv E[\ ]^{l_6}, \iota.g()^{l_2}, voidValue^{\varepsilon}, \iota.a()^{l_4}, \iota.b()^{l_7}, h \qquad \xrightarrow[\mu_2=\{l_2,l_7\}]{\text{JOIN}}$$

$$\overline{e_3^{l_3}}, h_3 \equiv E[\ ]^{l_6}, E[print\ ''Hi'']^{l_8}, voidValue^{\varepsilon}, \iota.h()^{l_4}, voidValue^{\varepsilon}, h$$

Fig. 3. An execution of the LabelledExample class in ^{l}SCHOOL

the initial configuration. Also, the empty label cannot be a participating label. Finally, participating labels are consumed.

Consider an example of an execution in figure 3 using the class LabelledExample from listing 1.1 with two chords: the first requires an asynchronous invocation of a in order to join with a synchronous invocation of f, while the second requires an asynchronous invocation of b in order to join with a synchronous invocation of g. Initially there exists a sole object of class LabelledExample at address ι, and four invocations of methods f, g and two of a respectively.

The first step of evaluation joins the first chord using the JOIN rule on the labels l_1 and l_3, which form the participating labels of this step, μ_0. These labels were consumed. The consuming of the asynchronous invocation of a results in its replacement with $voidValue$, and its annotation with the empty label. The body of the chord forms a new expression, and is annotated with the new label l_5. The label l_2, which did not participate in the evaluation step, appears in the resulting configuration. The next two steps of evaluation result in the second chord joining, and thus the eventual participation of l_2. The second invocation of a, labelled l_4, never participated in the execution, and so the label remains. The labels of a configuration remain finite,and there is an upper bound on the creation of new expressions, and hence new labels. The *live* labels of a configuration, $e_1^{l_1}, \ldots, e_n^{l_n}, h$, are those labels which can participate in the next evaluation step, $\xrightarrow{\mu}$. A label is live when there is at least one rule through which it can participate in the next evaluation step.

An evaluation rule may be applicable for several sets of participating labels, more than one of which may contain the live label under consideration. Also, more than one rule through which the label can participate may be applicable. The former case would hold if the label's underlying expression is a method

```
1  class LivenessExample {
2    void f() & async a() { b(); }
3    void g() & async b() { print "Hi"; }
4    void h() & async b() { print "I feel ignored"; }
5  }
```

Listing 1.2. Example class for lieveness of labels

$$\overline{e_0^{l_0}}, h_0 \equiv \iota.f()^{l_1}, \iota.g()^{l_2}, \iota.h()^{l_3}, \iota.a()^{l_4}, h \qquad\qquad \xrightarrow[\mu_0 = \{l_1, l_4\}]{\text{JOIN}}$$
$$live = \{l_1, l_4\} \qquad ignored = \emptyset$$

$$\overline{e_1^{l_1}}, h_1 \equiv E[\iota.b()]^{l_5}, \iota.g()^{l_2}, \iota.h()^{l_3}, voidValue^\varepsilon, h \qquad\qquad \xrightarrow[\mu_1 = \{l_5\}]{\text{ASYNC}}$$
$$live = \{l_5\} \qquad ignored = \emptyset$$

$$\overline{e_2^{l_2}}, h_2 \equiv E[\ ]^{l_6}, \iota.g()^{l_2}, \iota.h()^{l_3}, voidValue^\varepsilon, \iota.b()^{l_7}, h \qquad\qquad \xrightarrow[\mu_2 = \{l_2, l_7\}]{\text{JOIN}}$$
$$live = \{l_6, l_2, l_3, l_7\} \qquad ignored = \{l_6, l_3\}$$

$$\overline{e_3^{l_3}}, h_3 \equiv E[\ ]^{l_6}, E[print \ ''Hi'']^{l_8}, \iota.h()^{l_3}, voidValue^\varepsilon, voidValue^\varepsilon, h$$
$$live = \{l_6, l_8\}$$

Fig. 4. An execution of the LivenessExample class in ^{l}SCHOOL

invocation which can currently participate through the JOIN rule in two different chords. The latter case would hold if the expression can currently participate either through the JOIN rule or the STRUNG rule, again in two different chords.

At each step of an execution, if a label, l, is live, but is not in the participating labels, μ, then we say it is *ignored*. A label loses its liveness when it participates in a step of evaluation. However, a label can also lose its liveness due to another label being consumed (such as two labels competing for a sole third label in order to join). Conversely, a label may become live due to a newly created label (such as a method invocation to join).

Consider an example of liveness in figure 4 using the class LivenessExample from listing 1.2, which features three chords. The second and third chord both require an invocation of b in order to join, and hence will compete for such an invocation. Initially there exists a sole object of class LivenessExample at address ι, and four invocations: three synchronous invocations of f, g and h respectively, and an asynchronous invocation of a.

We notice that after two steps of evaluation both the second and third chords can join, as both their synchronous method invocations, g and h, respectively, can participate through the JOIN rule and consume the invocation of b; however, during the third step the invocation of g was selected to participate, and the invocation of h was ignored, resulting in loss of liveness (as there are no more asynchronous invocations of b).

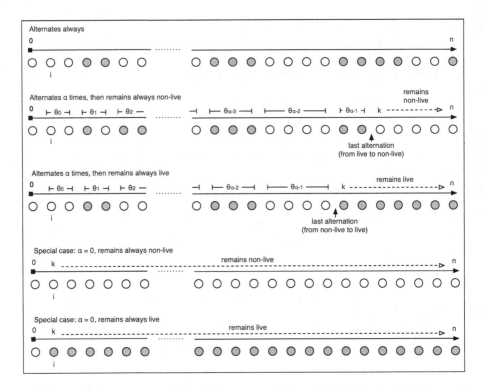

Fig. 5. Liveness behaviour of a label: alternation – label live at grey circles

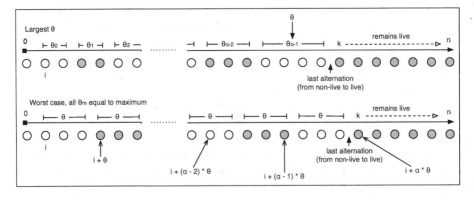

Fig. 6. Liveness behaviour of a label: worst case for the number of configurations which occur before a label alternates for the last time – label live at grey circles

The losing and regaining of liveness of a label (its *liveness behaviour*) is subject to the selection of evaluation rule applied at each step of an execution. It is possible to classify liveness behaviour in terms of patterns exhibited, and accordingly make observations on the properties of these patterns.

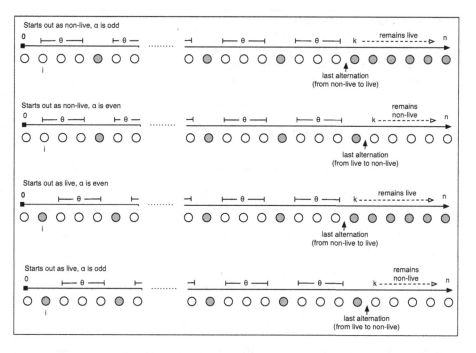

Fig. 7. Liveness behaviour of a label: maximising the number of times a label is ignored

Table 1. Summary of worst-case calculations for number of steps which occur when ignoring a label is maximised

$l \in live\left(\overline{e_i^{l_i}}\right)$	α	Worst Case Number of Steps
no	even	$i + (\alpha/2) * (\theta + 1)$
no	odd	$i + \lceil \alpha/2 \rceil * (\theta + 1) - 1$
yes	even	$i + (\alpha/2) * (\theta + 1)$
yes	odd	$i + \lfloor \alpha/2 \rfloor * (\theta + 1) + 1$

Figure 5 illustrates the possible liveness behaviours of a label: always alternating, alternating α times and then remaining always non-live or always live, and the two special cases when $\alpha = 0$.

We are interested in establishing the worst case for the number of configurations - or steps - which occur after a given number of alternations. Hence, if we assume that each θ_m is equal to θ, then we know that in the worst case, and assuming that l starts out as non-live, the last alternation will occur before the $i + \alpha * \theta$ configuration. The bottom example execution of figure 6 illustrates this pattern for l starting out as non-live and after α alternations remaining always live; the same calculation of the worst case holds for other combinations of initial and final liveness of l.

```
1   class WeakFairnessExample {
2     void f() & async a() { b(); a(); f(); }
3     void g() & async b() { print "Oh, dear..."; }
4     void h() & async a() { print "Help!"; }
5     void k() & async c() { print "Ha!"; }
6   }
```

Listing 1.3. Example class for weak fairness

$$\overline{e_0^{l_0}}, h_0 \equiv \iota.f()^{l_1}, \iota.g()^{l_2}, \iota.h()^{l_3}, \iota.k()^{l_4}, \iota.a()^{l_5}, \iota.c()^{l_6}, h$$

$$live = \{l_1, l_3, l_4, l_5, l_6\} \qquad ignored = \{l_3, l_4, l_6\}$$

$$\xrightarrow{\text{JOIN} \quad \mu_0 = \{l_1, l_5\}}$$

$$\overline{e_1^{l_1}}, h_1 \equiv E[\iota.b(); \iota.a(); \iota.f()]^{l_7}, \iota.g()^{l_2}, \iota.h()^{l_3}, \iota.k()^{l_4}, \iota.c()^{l_6}, h$$

$$live = \{l_7, l_2, l_4, l_6\} \qquad ignored = \{l_2, l_4, l_6\}$$

$$\xrightarrow{\text{ASYNC} \quad \mu_1 = \{l_7\}}$$

$$\overline{e_2^{l_2}}, h_2 \equiv E[\iota.a(); \iota.f()]^{l_9}, \iota.g()^{l_2}, \iota.h()^{l_3}, \iota.k()^{l_4}, \iota.c()^{l_6}, \iota.b()^{l_8}, h$$

$$live = \{l_9, l_2, l_3, l_4, l_6, l_8\} \qquad ignored = \{l_2, l_3, l_4, l_6, l_8\}$$

$$\xrightarrow{\text{ASYNC} \quad \mu_2 = \{l_9\}}$$

$$\overline{e_3^{l_3}}, h_3 \equiv E[\iota.f()]^{l_{11}}, \iota.g()^{l_2}, \iota.h()^{l_3}, \iota.k()^{l_4}, \iota.c()^{l_6}, \iota.b()^{l_8}, \iota.a()^{l_{10}}, h$$

$$live = \{l_{11}, l_2, l_3, l_4, l_6, l_8, l_{10}\} \qquad ignored = \{l_2, l_3, l_4, l_6, l_8\}$$

$$\xrightarrow{\text{JOIN} \quad \mu_3 = \{l_{11}, l_{10}\}}$$

$$\overline{e_4^{l_4}}, h_4 \equiv E[\iota.b(); \iota.a(); \iota.f()]^{l_{12}}, \iota.g()^{l_2}, \iota.h()^{l_3}, \iota.k()^{l_4}, \iota.c()^{l_6}, \iota.b()^{l_8}, h$$

$$live = \{l_2, l_4, l_6, l_8, l_{12}\} \qquad ignored = \{l_2, l_4, l_6, l_8\}$$

$$\xrightarrow{\text{ASYNC} \quad \mu_4 = \{l_{12}\}}$$

$$\vdots$$

Fig. 8. An execution inadmissible under weak fairness

Furthermore, we are interested in the worst case for the number of configurations - or steps - which occur when we maximise the number of times a label is ignored during finite alternating behaviour. In order for l to be ignored it must be live, and hence we consider the case where l is live for only one configuration before it alternates to non-live again, and each sequence of configurations at which l is non-live is equal to the maximum, θ. In order to consider the worst case, however, we have to take into account whether α is even or odd, and whether l starts out as live non-live. Figure 7 illustrates the four cases which arise, and table 1 summarises the calculations.

4   Definitions of Weak and Strong Fairness

Since a label is ignored only when it is live and does not participate in the current step of evaluation, and only active labels can become live, the following definitions of fairness are stated in terms of live labels, ignoring empty labels.

Definition 1 (Weak Fairness)

An execution is weakly-fair iff no process remains ignored continuously. In other words, no process remains live continuously. [10,11,12]

From this definition, every label must cease to be live after a finite number of steps. The following definition requires that for every label appearing in an execution, there exists some configuration at which the label is not live.

Definition 2 (Weakly-Fair Execution)

$$e_0^{l_0}, h_0 \xrightarrow{\mu_0} e_1^{l_1}, h_1 \xrightarrow{\mu_1} e_2^{l_2}, h_2 \xrightarrow{\mu_2} \ldots \xrightarrow{\mu_{n-1}} e_n^{l_n}, h_n \xrightarrow{\mu_n} \ldots \Longrightarrow$$
$$\forall i \in \mathbb{N} \ : \ \forall l \in labels\left(\overline{e_i^{l_i}}\right) \ : \ \exists k \geqslant i \ : \ l \notin live\left(\overline{e_k^{l_k}}\right)$$

Consider an example execution inadmissible under weak fairness using the class from listing 1.3 and the initial configuration from figure 8. The class features four chords: the first and third require the joining, respectively, of the synchronous methods f and h with the asynchronous method a, the second chord requires the joining of the synchronous method g with the asynchronous method b, and finally the fourth chord requires the synchronous method k to join with the asynchronous method c. Initially, there exists a sole object of class WeakFairnessExample at address ι, and six invocations of the methods f, g, h, k, a and c respectively (there is no invocation of b).

In the initial configuration all invocations except that of g, labelled by l_2, are live. The first invocation, labelled l_1, is selected to join with l_5, and hence the rest (l_3, l_4, l_6) are ignored. At the second configuration the sole invocation of a has been consumed, and hence the third chord cannot join any more, resulting in l_3 losing its liveness. Furthermore, the invocation of g becomes live now, as now it is possible to apply the JOIN rule with the invocation of b from within the evaluation context of l_7; instead, l_7 is selected to execute via the ASYNC rule, resulting in b entering the configuration in the next configuration with label l_8.

At this point (configuration 2) l_3 becomes live again, as it is possible to apply the JOIN rule; once again, the ASYNC is chosen with l_9 and the invocation of a enters the configuration with label l_{10}. The fourth chord is ignored for a third consecutive time. At this point, it is possible for the execution to repeat itself in this pattern indefinitely, resulting in l_4 and l_6 being ignored continuously, and hence making the execution unfair under weak fairness. Label l_2 became live in the second step and remains live; so after the second step, execution is not weakly fair for l_2. A weakly-fair execution sequence will print both "Ha!" and "Oh, dear...", although "Help!" has no guarantee of ever printing.

Definition 3 (Strong Fairness)

An execution is strongly-fair iff no process is ignored infinitely-often. In other words, no process loses and regains its liveness an infinite number of times. [10,11,12]

From definition 3 every label must cease to be live after a finite number of steps, and never regain its liveness. The following definition requires that for every label appearing in an execution, there exists some configuration such that the label is not live at that and all further configurations.

```
1  class StrongFairnessExample {
2    void f() & async a() { b(); f(); }
3    void f() & async b() { b(); f(); }
4    async b() { a(); }
5    void g() & async a() { print "Help"; }
6  }
```

Listing 1.4. Example class for strong fairness.

$$\overline{e_0^{l_0}}, h_0 \equiv \iota.f()^{l_1}, \iota.g()^{l_2}, \iota.a()^{l_3}, h$$
$$live = \{l_1, l_2, l_3\} \qquad ignored = \{l_2\}$$
$$\xrightarrow{\text{JOIN } \mu_0 = \{l_1, l_3\}}$$

$$\overline{e_1^{l_1}}, h_1 \equiv E[\iota.b(); \iota.f()]^{l_4}, \iota.g()^{l_2}, h$$
$$live = \{l_4\} \qquad ignored = \emptyset$$
$$\xrightarrow{\text{ASYNC } \mu_1 = \{l_4\}}$$

$$\overline{e_2^{l_2}}, h_2 \equiv \iota.f()^{l_5}, \iota.g()^{l_2}, \iota.b()^{l_6}, h$$
$$live = \{l_5, l_6\} \qquad ignored = \emptyset$$
$$\xrightarrow{\text{JOIN } \mu_2 = \{l_5, l_6\}}$$

$$\overline{e_3^{l_3}}, h_3 \equiv E[\iota.b(); \iota.f()]^{l_7}, \iota.g()^{l_2}, h$$
$$live = \{l_7\} \qquad ignored = \emptyset$$
$$\xrightarrow{\text{ASYNC } \mu_3 = \{l_7\}}$$

$$\overline{e_4^{l_4}}, h_4 \equiv \iota.f()^{l_8}, \iota.g()^{l_2}, \iota.b()^{l_9}, h$$
$$live = \{l_8, l_9\} \qquad ignored = \emptyset$$
$$\xrightarrow{\text{JOIN } \mu_4 = \{l_8, l_9\}}$$

$$\overline{e_5^{l_5}}, h_5 \equiv E[\iota.b(); \iota.f()]^{l_{10}}, \iota.g()^{l_2}, h$$
$$live = \{l_{10}\} \qquad ignored = \emptyset$$
$$\dots \longrightarrow$$

$$\vdots$$

$$\overline{e_6^{l_6}}, h_6 \equiv \iota.f()^{l_{11}}, \iota.g()^{l_2}, \iota.b()^{l_{12}}, h$$
$$live = \{l_{11}, l_{12}\} \qquad ignored = \{l_{11}\}$$
$$\xrightarrow{\text{STRUNG } \mu_4 = \{l_{12}\}}$$

$$\overline{e_7^{l_7}}, h_7 \equiv \iota.f()^{l_{11}}, \iota.g()^{l_2}, E[\iota.a()]^{l_{13}}, h$$
$$live = \{l_{11}, l_2, l_{13}\} \qquad ignored = \{l_2\}$$
$$\xrightarrow{\text{JOIN } \mu_4 = \{l_{11}, l_{13}\}}$$

$$\overline{e_8^{l_8}}, h_8 \equiv E[\iota.b(); \iota.f()]^{l_{14}}, \iota.g()^{l_2}, h$$
$$live = \{l_{14}\}$$

Fig. 9. An execution inadmissible under strong fairness

Definition 4 (Strongly-Fair Execution)

$$\overline{e_0^{l_0}}, h_0 \xrightarrow{\mu_0} \overline{e_1^{l_1}}, h_1 \xrightarrow{\mu_1} \overline{e_2^{l_2}}, h_2 \xrightarrow{\mu_2} \dots \xrightarrow{\mu_{n-1}} \overline{e_n^{l_n}}, h_n \xrightarrow{\mu_n} \dots \Longrightarrow$$
$$\forall\, i \in \mathbb{N}\ :\ \forall\, l \in labels\left(\overline{e_i^{l_i}}\right)\ :\ \exists\, j \geqslant i\ :\ \forall\, k \geqslant j\ :\ l \notin live\left(\overline{e_k^{l_k}}\right)$$

Consider an example execution inadmissible under strong fairness using the class from listing 1.4 and the initial configuration from figure 9. The class features four chords: the first two require the joining of the synchronous method f with the asynchronous methods a and b respectively, the third chord is asynchronous and requires only the method b, and finally the fourth chord requires the synchronous method g to join with a. Initially, there exists a sole object of class StrongFairnessExample at address ι, and three invocations of the methods f, g, and a respectively.

In the initial configuration the invocation of g, labelled l_2, is live. However, the first invocation, labelled l_1, is selected to join with l_3, and hence l_2 is ignored. In the second configuration l_2 has lost its liveness. The execution now continues for an unspecified number of steps during which the second chord joins repeatedly. Newly created labels which become live participate immediately, and since there is no availability of an invocation of a, l_2 does not regain its liveness. It is not possible, however, to claim that such an execution is strongly-fair because it is still possible for l_2 to regain its liveness. Label l_2 could lose and regain its liveness infinitely often, and hence be ignored infinitely often. Thus, a strongly-fair execution prohibits this example execution. If, however, l_2 were to participate in the step after the configuration indexed by 7 then the sequence would be admissible under strong fairness.

5   Weak Fairness

We describe a mechanism to realise weak-fairness constraints for ^{l}SCHOOL, showing how the exampleof our execution inadmissible under weak fairness needs to be constrained. Since no label remains live throughout a weakly-fair execution, starting from a configuration, each of its live labels must eventually lose its liveness. So we can consider a *localised* definition of weak fairness: a sequence is *locally weakly fair for the initially live labels* only if each of the labels is not live in at least one future configuration. Once the initial configuration's live labels have lost their liveness, we get a locally weakly-fair execution.[2]

The next locally weakly-fair execution uses the previous final configuration as the new initial configuration. The concatenation of two locally weakly-fair execution sequences is weakly fair. Also, for any locally weakly-fair execution sequence which does not result in termination, it is always possible to continue execution, and thus obtain a weakly-fair execution. Since executions can have an infinite length, a weakly-fair execution is then defined as *the maximal sequence of concatenated locally weakly-fair executions.*

One way to generate locally weakly-fair executions is to keep track of the *serviced* labels, those which have lost their liveness.Once all initially live labels are included in the set of serviced labels, we have obtained a locally weakly-fair execution sequence and begin anew. Therefore, our mechanism consists of a selection rule which allows one to freely select any applicable evaluation rule while keeping track of the serviced labels, and a concatenation mechanism which allows the construction of a weakly-fair execution sequence.

We define a weakly-fair execution as the maximal sequence of locally weakly-fair execution sequences; a locally weakly-fair execution sequence consists of weakly-fair evaluation steps, which are obtained through the WEAK selection

---

[2] Definitions, lemmas, and theorems for weak fairness can be found in the appendix.

$$\frac{\begin{array}{c}\overline{e^l}, h \xrightarrow{\mu} \overline{e'^{l'}}, h' \\ L' \text{ largest subset of } live\left(\overline{e^l}\right): \\ L \cap L' = \emptyset \quad \wedge \quad L' \cap live\left(\overline{e'^{l'}}\right) = \emptyset\end{array}}{\overline{e^l}, h, L \xRightarrow{\mu} \overline{e'^{l'}}, h', L \cup L'} \ \text{WEAK}$$

Fig. 10. Weakly-fair selection rule

$$\begin{array}{l}\overline{e_0^{l_0}}, h_0 \equiv \iota.f()^{l_1}, \iota.g()^{l_2}, \iota.h()^{l_3}, \iota.k()^{l_4}, \iota.a()^{l_5}, \iota.c()^{l_6}, h \\ \quad live = \{l_1, l_3, l_4, l_5, l_6\} \qquad ignored = \{l_3, l_4, l_6\} \\ \quad L_0 = \emptyset\end{array} \qquad \xrightarrow[\mu_0=\{l_1,l_5\}]{\text{JOIN}}$$

$$\begin{array}{l}\overline{e_1^{l_1}}, h_1 \equiv E[\iota.b(); \iota.a(); \iota.f()]^{l_7}, \iota.g()^{l_2}, \iota.h()^{l_3}, \iota.k()^{l_4}, \iota.c()^{l_6}, h \\ \quad live = \{l_7, l_2, l_4, l_6\} \qquad ignored = \{l_2, l_4, l_6\} \\ \quad L_1 = \{\underline{l_1}, \underline{l_3}, \underline{l_5}\}\end{array} \qquad \xrightarrow[\mu_1=\{l_7\}]{\text{ASYNC}}$$

$$\begin{array}{l}\overline{e_2^{l_2}}, h_2 \equiv E[\iota.a(); \iota.f()]^{l_9}, \iota.g()^{l_2}, \iota.h()^{l_3}, \iota.k()^{l_4}, \iota.c()^{l_6}, \iota.b()^{l_8}, h \\ \quad live = \{l_9, l_2, l_3, l_4, l_6, l_8\} \qquad ignored = \{l_2, l_3, l_4, l_6, l_8\} \\ \quad L_2 = \{l_1, l_3, l_5, \underline{l_7}\}\end{array} \qquad \xrightarrow[\mu_2=\{l_9\}]{\text{ASYNC}}$$

$$\begin{array}{l}\overline{e_3^{l_3}}, h_3 \equiv E[\iota.f()]^{l_{11}}, \iota.g()^{l_2}, \iota.h()^{l_3}, \iota.k()^{l_4}, \iota.c()^{l_6}, \iota.b()^{l_8}, \iota.a()^{l_{10}}, h \\ \quad live = \{l_{11}, l_2, l_3, l_4, l_6, l_8, l_{10}\} \qquad ignored = \{l_2, l_3, l_4, l_6, l_8\} \\ \quad L_3 = \{l_1, l_3, l_5, l_7, \underline{l_9}\}\end{array} \qquad \xrightarrow[\mu_3=\{l_{11},l_{10}\}]{\text{JOIN}}$$

$$\begin{array}{l}\overline{e_4^{l_4}}, h_4 \equiv E[\iota.b(); \iota.a(); \iota.f()]^{l_{12}}, \iota.g()^{l_2}, \iota.h()^{l_3}, \iota.k()^{l_4}, \iota.c()^{l_6}, \iota.b()^{l_8}, h \\ \quad live = \{l_2, l_4, l_6, l_8, l_{12}\} \qquad ignored = \{l_{12}, l_2, l_8\} \\ \quad L_4 = \{l_1, l_3, l_5, l_7, l_9, \underline{l_{10}}, \underline{l_{11}}\}\end{array} \qquad \xrightarrow[\mu_4=\{l_4,l_6\}]{\text{JOIN}}$$

$$\begin{array}{l}\overline{e_5^{l_5}}, h_5 \equiv E[\iota.b(); \iota.a(); \iota.f()]^{l_{12}}, \iota.g()^{l_2}, \iota.h()^{l_3}, print \text{“Ha!”}^{l_{13}}, \iota.b()^{l_8}, h \\ \quad live = \{l_2, l_8, l_{12}, l_{13}\} \\ \quad L_5 = \{l_1, l_3, l_5, l_7, l_9, l_{10}, l_{11}, \underline{l_4}, \underline{l_6}\}\end{array}$$

Fig. 11. A locally weakly-fair execution

rule of figure 10. The rule allows us to select any ^{l}SCHOOL evaluation rule which is applicable, while maintaining the set L of serviced labels. This set is built at each step by adding those labels which have lost their liveness; labels which have already been serviced are not placed into L again. The largest subset of live labels in the initial configuration is considered, resulting in a notion of completeness for the recording process.The WEAK is useful because it allows us to non-deterministically generate *all* weakly-fair schedules from a given initial configuration, some of which may have no finite upper bound on their length.

Each locally weakly-fair execution sequence, of some length k, begins with a finite configuration and an empty set of serviced labels L_0 and a finite set of initially live labels; at the final configuration all initially live labels are included in L_k. The sequence of participating labels is recorded in M. The size of L_i is a function of the number of labels which participate in the evaluation steps 0 through $i-1$; although there is an upper bound λ on the number of new labels

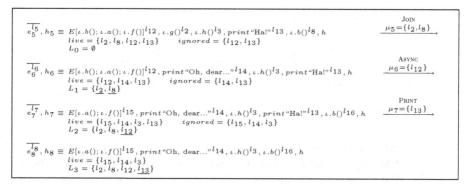

Fig. 12. Next locally weakly-fair execution to be concatenated

which can be created at each step, and hence the number of labels which be added to each L, the size of L_k has no upper bound.

We use the original example of weak fairness with the program of listing 1.3 and the initial configuration from figure 8. In figure 11 we generate a locally weakly-fair execution which is the same as the original execution up to the configuration indexed by 4; each L_i is recorded, with added labels underlined. L_0 begins empty, and L_1 contains labels l_1, l_3 and l_5, as the first and third have lost their liveness by participating in the first evaluation step, and l_3 has lost its liveness because the only label that could join with it, l_5, was consumed. The execution then continues up to configuration 4 as in the original example.

At this point we see from the set of serviced labels L_4 that all original live labels except l_4 and l_6 have been serviced; furthermore, both these labels are live, and hence we may chose to apply the JOIN rule with the labels and obtain the last configuration, indexed by 5, in the figure. Now, all original live labels are contained in L_5, and hence the execution sequence is locally weakly fair. Notice that we could have continued executing in the initial pattern an indefinite number of times before choosing to join l_4 and l_6.

Starting from the last configuration (indexed by 5) of the locally weakly-fair execution sequence from above, we can begin a new locally weakly-fair execution sequence by aiming to service the live labels $\{l_2, l_8, l_{12}, l_{13}\}$; an example such sequence is in figure 12 where the second chord joins (labels l_2 and l_8), then the invocation of **b** from the context labelled by l_{12} is placed into the configuration through the ASYNC rule, and finally the print command, labelled by l_{13}, is executed via an unspecified but obvious PRINT rule. The last set of serviced labels, L_3, is the set of original live labels, so this sequence is locally weakly-fair. The execution sequence indexed by 5 through 8 is also locally weakly-fair, and so their concatenation is weakly-fair. The message "Ha!" was printed and the message "Oh, dear..." will eventually print if we continue execution with the next locally weakly-fair sequence, however, the message "Help!" may never print.

In order to show correctness for weakly-fair executions, we first establish correctness for locally weakly-fair executions, in the sense that a locally weakly-fair execution, for each initially live label, contains at least one configuration at

$$\frac{\overline{e^l}, h \xrightarrow{\mu} \overline{e'^{l'}}, h' \\ \forall\, l \in live\left(\overline{e^l}\right)\ :\ \exists\, l \in live\left(\overline{e^l}\right)\ :\ l \leqslant_Q l \wedge l \in \mu \\ Q' = Q \upharpoonright active\left(\overline{e'^{l'}}\right) \circ active\left(\overline{e'^{l'}}\right) \setminus active\left(\overline{e^l}\right)}{\overline{e^l}, h, Q \xRightarrow{\mu} \overline{e'^{l'}}, h', Q'}\ \text{STRONG}$$

Fig. 13. Strongly-fair selection rule

which the label is not live. A weakly-fair execution sequence corresponds to a sequence of locally weakly-fair execution sequences, which in turn corresponds to an ^{l}SCHOOL execution sequence.

6   Strong Fairness

We describe a mechanism that realises ^{l}SCHOOL strong fairness constraints. The example from section 4 of an execution inadmissible under strong fairness is altered by imposing these constraints. We also present worst-case calculations for the liveness behaviour of labels under strong fairness.[3]

An execution sequence is strongly-fair when no label becomes live infinitely often. Since executions can be infinite, it is not possible to first generate all valid executions and then select those which are strongly-fair; so we employ a mechanism which *maintains* a strongly-fair execution as it is being generated.

For each application of an evaluation rule constraints are imposed on future selections, and accumulate throughout. To keep track of these constraints we introduce a *queue of labels*, which is modified at each evaluation step and passed to the next. Strong fairness is maintained by imposing constraints through the selection rule STRONG in figure 13: all new labels are appended to the queue, the order of labels remains unchanged, labels which participate in an evaluation are removed from the queue, and at each step the first live label in the queue always participates in the next evaluation step.

Starting from a finite initial configuration, a label which is repeatedly ignored will eventually reach the head of the queue. Once a label is at the head of the queue, it will be selected for participation the next time it becomes live. Since all labels are added to the queue, all labels eventually lose their liveness forever.

A queue Q is denoted by $\langle l_1 \circ \ldots \circ l_k \rangle$, and its size k is denoted by $|Q|$. The relation $l \leqslant_Q l'$ between two labels, l and l', appearing in a queue, Q, is defined either when $l = l'$, or when l appears before l' in Q.

Two operations are defined on queues: removing and appending labels – neither operation affects the order. Removal uses the *retain* operator $\upharpoonright$, which is applied to a queue Q and a set of labels S as $Q \upharpoonright S$, and results in Q', where all those labels in Q which are not in S have been removed, and the remaining labels have not changed order. Appending a queue of labels $\langle l_{k+1} \circ \ldots \circ l_{k+h} \rangle$ to Q, written as $Q \circ \langle l_{k+1} \circ \ldots \circ l_{k+h} \rangle$, results in a new queue, Q', where the

---

[3] The full set of definitions for strong fairness can be found in the appendix.

$$\overline{e_0^{l_0}}, h_0 \equiv \iota.f()^{l_1}, \iota.g()^{l_2}, \iota.a()^{l_3}, h \qquad \xrightarrow[\mu_0 = \{l_1, l_3\}]{\text{JOIN}}$$
$$live = \{l_1, l_2, l_3\} \qquad ignored = \{l_2\}$$
$$Q_0 = \langle \widehat{l_1} \circ l_2 \circ l_3 \rangle$$

$$\overline{e_1^{l_1}}, h_1 \equiv E[\iota.b(); \iota.f()]^{l_4}, \iota.g()^{l_2}, h \qquad \xrightarrow[\mu_1 = \{l_4\}]{\text{ASYNC}}$$
$$live = \{l_4\} \qquad ignored = \emptyset$$
$$Q_1 = \langle l_2 \circ \widehat{l_4} \rangle$$

$$\overline{e_2^{l_2}}, h_2 \equiv \iota.f()^{l_5}, \iota.g()^{l_2}, \iota.b()^{l_6}, h \qquad \xrightarrow[\mu_2 = \{l_5, l_6\}]{\text{JOIN}}$$
$$live = \{l_5, l_6\} \qquad ignored = \emptyset$$
$$Q_2 = \langle l_2 \circ \widehat{l_5} \circ l_6 \rangle$$

$$\overline{e_3^{l_3}}, h_3 \equiv E[\iota.b(); \iota.f()]^{l_7}, \iota.g()^{l_2}, h \qquad \xrightarrow[\mu_3 = \{l_7\}]{\text{ASYNC}}$$
$$live = \{l_7\} \qquad ignored = \emptyset$$
$$Q_3 = \langle l_2 \circ \widehat{l_7} \rangle$$

$$\overline{e_4^{l_4}}, h_4 \equiv \iota.f()^{l_8}, \iota.g()^{l_2}, \iota.b()^{l_9}, h \qquad \xrightarrow[\mu_4 = \{l_9\}]{\text{STRUNG}}$$
$$live = \{l_8, l_9\} \qquad ignored = \{l_8\}$$
$$Q_4 = \langle l_2 \circ \widehat{l_9} \circ l_8 \rangle$$

$$\overline{e_5^{l_5}}, h_5 \equiv \iota.f()^{l_8}, \iota.g()^{l_2}, E[\iota.a()]^{l_{10}}, h \qquad \xrightarrow[\mu_4 = \{l_2, l_{10}\}]{\text{JOIN}}$$
$$live = \{l_8, l_2, l_{10}\} \qquad ignored = \{l_8\}$$
$$Q_5 = \langle \widehat{l_2} \circ l_8 \circ l_{10} \rangle$$

$$\overline{e_6^{l_6}}, h_6 \equiv \iota.f()^{l_8}, E[print \text{ ``}Help\text{''}]^{l_{11}}, h$$
$$live = \{l_{11}\}$$
$$Q_6 = \langle l_8 \circ \widehat{l_{11}} \rangle$$

Fig. 14. A strongly-fair execution

appended labels appear rightmost and the existing labels have not changed order: $Q' = \langle l_1 \circ \ldots \circ l_k \circ l_{k+1} \circ \ldots \circ l_{k+h} \rangle$. Appending a set of labels, S, to a queue, Q, written as $Q \circ S$, results in the set being treated as a queue where the order of the labels is unspecified.

To establish a notion of completeness for the recording of strong fairness constraints, the definition of strongly-fair executions below requires a finite initial configuration and an initial queue which contains all initially active labels.

Consider the example of a strongly-fair execution in figure 14 using the class **StrongFairnessExample** from listing 1.4, with the same initial configuration consisting of two synchronous method invocations f and g, and an asynchronous invocation of method a. The first live label in the queue is denoted with a hat.

The first four evaluation steps coincide with the original example. At this point we assumed an indefinite repetition of the following pattern: the second chord always joins through the evaluation rule JOIN and consumes the asynchronous invocation of method b, with the latest synchronous invocation of method f participating in the join. Were this pattern to continue forever, l_2 would never regain its liveness, and each of the newly created labels would be consumed by the subsequent joining of the second chord; since no label would be ignored infinitely often, the execution would be admissible as strongly-fair.

If the execution ever involved the evaluation rule STRUNG with the current asynchronous invocation of method b, then l_2 would regain its liveness. If we were to allow l_2 to be ignored for the second time (as in the original example), the entire pattern of execution up to now could be repeated infinitely often, and thus l_2 could be ignored infinitely often, making the execution not strongly-fair.

Therefore, if after the fourth evaluation, the label l_9 is placed before the label l_8 in the queue Q_4, at the fifth evaluation step STRONG will select l_9 to participate, indeed resulting in l_2 regaining its liveness in the resulting configuration (indexed by 5). Now, however, l_2 is the earliest live label in the queue (Q_5), and thus must be selected to participate in the next evaluation step (μ_5).

Were there two invocations of the method g in the initial configuration, both could have been ignored in the first step and placed in the queue. Following a similar pattern of execution, they would both regain their liveness at the sixth configuration. The one closest to the head of the queue would be selected to participate, while the other would be ignored a second time. If the pattern were to repeat, the remaining invocation of method g would regain its liveness, but now be the first live label in the queue, participating in the next evaluation step.

Although a label can be ignored a finite number of times it is not possible to determine how many times a label will be ignored as this is a consequence of its placement in the queue and its relative order to other competing labels, which is unspecified.

7   Conclusions

From the various implementations of chords, both language-based and library-based, we noticed an implicit design assumption with regards to scheduling: the scheduler is assumed to treat processes (or threads) in a "fair" way, or to not arbitrarily delay a process capable of evaluating.

We define a small labelled calculus ^{l}SCHOOL, and then weak and strong fairness for it, enabling the creation of abstract schedulers for chorded languages which satisfy the two notions of fairness. The labelling mechanism gives us a basis for stating the aforementioned fairness notions, as well as properties such as liveness and liveness behaviours, such as worst-case and alternating liveness.

Our weakly-fair scheduler solves the problem of processes being arbitrarily ignored continuously; the mechanism consists of tracking those processes which have been given a chance to evaluate, or have been "serviced", and attempts to eliminate all outstanding non-serviced labels. Weakly-fair executions are stated in terms of local finite sequences, and such sequences, once generated, can be freely appended.

Our strongly-fair scheduler solves the problem of processes being arbitrarily infinitely-often ignored; the mechanism consists of a priority queue which records all fresh processes, and forces the selection of a process after a finite delay in such a way as to guarantee that all executions of arbitrarily large size result in processes which eventually either execute or terminate.

We observed the possible liveness behaviours of chorded programs, and obtained a notion of liveness alternation which we used to show worst-case delays of processes under strong fairness. As the underlying priority queue for strong fairness is bound by the number of concurrent processes, these worst-case calculations are also relevant to the running size of the scheduler's queue.

Our belief is that schedulers tend to be written using queues, so if fair, they are strongly-fair. Strongly-fair schedulers have a central point of control, so they are not suited to parallel or multi-core execution. As our treatment of fairness for chorded programs focussed on processes rather than something completely chord specific, it is likely that similar results would also hold true for schedulers for other concurrency constructs.

Acknowledgements

We would like to thank Neil Datta, Anastasia Niarchou, Sebastian Hunt, Maribel Fernández, and Sophia Drossopoulou for their comments.

References

1. Fournet, C., Gonthier, G.: The reflexive CHAM and the join-calculus. In: Proceedings of the 23rd ACM SIGPLAN-SIGACT Symposium on Principles of Programming Languages, St. Petersburg Beach, Florida, United States, pp. 372–385. ACM Press, New York (1996)
2. Fournet, C., Gonthier, G.: The join calculus: a language for distributed mobile programming, pp. 1–66. Applied Semantics Summer School (2008)
3. Chrysanthakopoulos, G., Singh, S.: An asynchronous messaging library for $C^\sharp$. In: Synchronization and Concurrency in Object-Oriented Languages (SCOOL) Workshop, OOPSLA (October 2005)
4. Russo, C.: Join patterns for visual basic. In: OOPSLA (2008)
5. Russo, C.: The joins concurrency library. In: Hanus, M. (ed.) PADL 2007. LNCS, vol. 4354, pp. 260–274. Springer, Heidelberg (2006)
6. Benton, N., Bierman, G., Cardelli, L., Meijer, E., Russo, C., Schulte, W.: C_ω (2004), http://research.microsoft.com/Comega/
7. Fournet, C.: The jocaml language (2008), http://jocaml.inria.fr/
8. Cremet, V.: Join definitions in scala, http://lamp.epfl.ch/~cremet/join_in_scala/
9. Benton, N., Cardelli, L., Fournet, C.: Modern concurrency abstractions for $C^\sharp$. In: Magnusson, B. (ed.) ECOOP 2002. LNCS, vol. 2374, pp. 415–440. Springer, Heidelberg (2002)
10. Costa, G., Stirling, C.: Weak and strong fairness in ccs. Information and Computation 73(3), 207–244 (1987)
11. Kwiatkowska, M.Z.: Survey of fairness notions. Information and Software Technology 31(7), 371–386 (1989)
12. Francez, N.: Fairness. ACM Press, New York (1986)

Appendix

The appendix can be found on the web at:
slurp.doc.ic.ac.uk/chords/fairness/

Mobility Models and Behavioural Equivalence for Wireless Networks

Jens Chr. Godskesen[1,*] and Sebastian Nanz[2]

[1] IT University of Copenhagen
jcg@itu.dk
[2] Technical University of Denmark
nanz@imm.dtu.dk

Abstract. In protocol development for wireless systems, the choice of appropriate mobility models describing the movement patterns of devices has long been recognised as a crucial factor for the successful evaluation of protocols. More recently, wireless protocols have also come into the focus of formal approaches to the modelling and verification of concurrent systems. While in these approaches mobility is also given a central role, the actual mobility modelling remains simplistic since arbitrary node movements are allowed. This leads to a huge behavioural overapproximation that might prevent a successful reasoning about protocol properties. In this paper we describe how to extend a process calculus by realistic mobility models in an orthogonal way. The semantics of our calculus incorporates a notion of global time passing that allows us to express a wide range of mobility models currently used in protocol development practice. Using the behavioural equivalence and pre-order of our calculus, we are furthermore able to compare the strength of these models in our approach.

1 Introduction

As a result of the availability and popularity of mobile devices with networking capabilities, the use of wireless communication has seen a tremendous increase in recent years. The applications of this technology are broad and include wireless local area networks, cellular and ad-hoc networks, and have a further growth potential in the area of ubiquitous computing.

Naturally, the interest in modelling and formal reasoning about wireless networks has risen as well, for example using process algebra as a specification formalism. Process algebra itself has proved to be a versatile formalism for modelling various kinds of concurrent systems. This versatility is needed to model wireless networks, since there are a number of key differences to other network behaviour typically modelled in process calculi. A number of works [10,7,4,11,15,8] have stressed two of the main differences: the prevalent mode of communication

---

* Supported by grant no. 272-05-0258 from the Danish Natural Science Research Council and by the VKR Centre of Excellence MT-LAB.

in wireless networks is broadcast, and the network topology can change spontaneously. The latter point implies that there is a strict separation between process actions and the mobility modelling, since changes in connectivity are influenced by environment conditions (such as node movement), but not by the actions of a protocol process.

In the works mentioned above, a simplistic view of mobility is taken by assuming that connectivity develops completely arbitrarily over time. Hence, erratic behaviour with respect to connectivity breaking and establishing is part of the model. This contrasts with the approach taken by protocol developers, where more realistic mobility models (the survey paper [2] provides a fairly comprehensive overview) are seen as a key ingredient for producing meaningful protocol evaluations using simulation. Realistic mobility models should however play an important role for formal reasoning as well because, by excluding all erratic behaviour, they can limit the size of the state space to be reasoned about, which is an important prerequisite for verification. For the same reason, stronger properties should be provable for the system.

In this paper, we provide a general model of mobility to parametrise a simple calculus with broadcast capabilities. The calculus is equipped with a notion of global time passing, such that movement trajectories of nodes can be determined explicitly via a mobility model. The general model is shown to instantiate to widely used concrete mobility models for network simulation. We develop a behavioural equivalence and pre-order that allow us to compare the strength of these mobility models in our formal setting.

The remainder of the paper is structured as follows. In Section 2 we give an introduction to a number of mobility models typically used in network simulators, and describe our general model of mobility and broadcast. We evaluate related work on modelling wireless mobility and time passing in Section 3. The syntax and semantics of our calculus are presented in Section 4. In Section 5 we develop a behavioural equivalence and apply it in order to evaluate the strength of the mobility models we have instantiated our calculus to. We give an outlook on the development of a discrete version of the semantics in Section 6 and conclude in Section 7.

2   Mobility Models for Wireless Networks

When evaluating protocols for wireless networks with respect to performance or functional correctness, a variety of assumptions has to be decided upon. Such assumptions may for example include the size and shape of the area used by the wireless devices, their transmission ranges, and their movement patterns including allowed speeds and directional changes [2]. In every case, careful choices have to be made by the analyst to ensure that the evaluation results apply in practice.

As a specific protocol may be targeted to various environment conditions, different choices of assumptions may be in order, and therefore it is important that simulation tools (such as the network simulator ns-2 [12]) or indeed verification

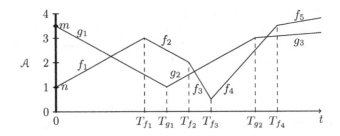

Fig. 1. Node movements described by mobility functions with timeouts

tools are parametric in these assumptions. In the following we develop such a parametric framework for use with a process algebraic approach.

We thus assume that wireless devices ("nodes") move in a *global area* $\mathcal{A}$ that is bounded and convex (this ensures that the definitions of the most commonly used mobility models are well-defined). The *boundary* of $\mathcal{A}$ is denoted by $bd(\mathcal{A})$. We assume to have a *global clock* $t \in \mathbb{R}_0^+$, such that the location $\vec{l} \in \mathcal{A}$ of a node n at time t can be determined by its associated *mobility function* $f : \mathbb{R}_0^+ \to \mathcal{A}$ as $f(t) = \vec{l}$.

We furthermore assume that each mobility function has a *timeout* $T \in \mathbb{R}_0^+ \cup \{\infty, \diamond\}$. If $T \in \mathbb{R}_0^+$, this means that f describes the trajectory of n for $t \leq T$, and has to be replaced by a new mobility function f' at time $t = T$. If $T = \infty$ the timeout never occurs and the current mobility function is always valid. We use the special symbol $\diamond$ to express that no timeout is set, i.e. the mobility function may be replaced at any time. We write a node n with mobility function f and timeout T as n_f^T.

The choice of a new mobility function is determined by a *mobility model* $\mathcal{M}$, a function that takes a pair $(\vec{l}_0, t_0)$ of a current location and a current time as input and returns, for these parameters, a set of pairs (f', T') of admissible mobility functions and their timeouts. For example, at time $t_0 = T$, node n_f^T may become $n_{f'}^{T'}$ where $(f', T') \in \mathcal{M}(f(t_0), t_0)$. It is important to note at this point that this *allows* that two nodes who happen to be at the same location at same time may take different movement trajectories: the set $\mathcal{M}(f(t_0), t_0)$ has more than one element in general, and elements (f', T') are nondeterministically chosen for each node.

Example 1. Consider the illustration in Figure 1, which describes the movement of two nodes m and n within the one-dimensional area $\mathcal{A} = [0, 4]$. We use a mobility model **Mob** defined as follows:

$$\mathbf{Mob}(\vec{l}_0, t_0) = \{(g, T) \mid g(t) = \vec{l}_0 + v \cdot (t - t_0) \cdot \alpha \wedge T \in [t_0, t_0 + 2], \text{ where } v \in [0, 2], \ \alpha \in \{1, -1\}, \ g(t) \neq bd(\mathcal{A}) \text{ for } t \in [t_0, T]\}$$

In this model, node movement is continuous in the sense that $f(T) = f'(T)$, where T is the timeout of f, and f' replaces f. Furthermore, movement takes place at constant speed $v \in [0, 2]$ and both in forward and backward direction

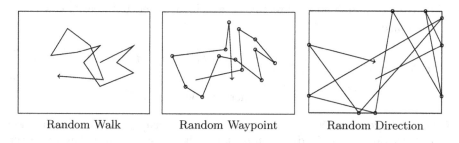

Random Walk   Random Waypoint   Random Direction

Fig. 2. Movement patterns of a node according to three mobility models

$\alpha \in \{1, -1\}$, a timeout occurs at least every 2 time units, and nodes never leave the area $\mathcal{A}$.

In Figure 1, node m moves initially according to the mobility function g_1 with timeout T_{g_1}, hence $m = m_{g_1}^{T_{g_1}}$. At time $t = 0$ node $m_{g_1}^{T_{g_1}}$ is at location $g_1(0) = 3.5 \in \mathcal{A}$ and then moves with constant speed to location $g_1(T_{g_1}) = 1$ where its mobility function g_1 is timing out, $t = T_{g_1}$. Because of the timeout, a new mobility function g_2 with new timeout T_{g_2} is chosen from $\mathbf{Mob}(g_1(T_{g_1}), T_{g_1})$ and the node thus becomes $m_{g_2}^{T_{g_2}}$. The further movements of m and those of n can be described similarly.

The proposed framework allows to describe a variety of concrete mobility models which we outline in the following.

Stationary Nodes Nodes are assumed to be stationary.

$$\mathbf{Stat}(\vec{l_0}, t_0) = \{(g, \infty) \mid g(t) = \vec{l_0}\}$$

Arbitrary Movement Nodes can change their location arbitrarily and instantaneously.

$$\mathbf{Arb}(\vec{l_0}, t_0) = \{(g, \diamond) \mid g(t) = \vec{l} \text{ where } \vec{l} \in \mathcal{A}\}$$

Random Walk Nodes choose randomly a speed $v \in \mathit{Vel}$ and a direction $\vec{\alpha} \in \mathit{Dir}$ and travel in direction $\vec{\alpha}$ at the chosen speed for a fixed time interval Δ.

$$\mathbf{RWalk}_\Delta(\vec{l_0}, t_0) = \{(g, t_0 + \Delta) \mid g(t) = \vec{l_0} + v \cdot (t - t_0) \cdot \vec{\alpha} \text{ where } v \in \mathit{Vel},$$
$$\vec{\alpha} \in \mathit{Dir}, \ g(t) \neq bd(\mathcal{A}) \text{ for } t \in [t_0, t_0 + \Delta]\}$$

(Note that in the classical model a node's trajectory is "reflected" according to $\vec{\alpha}$ when reaching the boundary of $\mathcal{A}$. While this can be expressed in our model, we modify the definition for simplicity to say that a trajectory that would reach the boundary is never chosen.)

Random Waypoint Nodes choose randomly a speed $v \in \mathit{Vel}$ and a destination $\vec{d} \in \mathcal{A}$ and travel to $\vec{d}$ at the chosen speed, where they pause for a fixed time interval p. In the following definition, t_1 is the time when the destination will be reached and $\vec{\alpha}$ is the direction in which to travel (both easily calculated from $\vec{l_0}, \vec{d}, v$).

$$\mathbf{RWay}_p(\vec{l_0}, t_0) = \{(g, t_1 + p) \mid g(t) = \begin{cases} \vec{l_0} + v \cdot (t - t_0) \cdot \vec{\alpha} & \text{if } t_0 \leq t \leq t_1 \\ \vec{d} & \text{if } t_1 < t \leq t_1 + p \end{cases}$$
$$\text{where } v \in \textit{Vel} \text{ and } \vec{d} \in \mathcal{A}\}$$

Random Direction Nodes choose randomly a speed $v \in \textit{Vel}$ and a direction $\vec{\alpha} \in \textit{Dir}$ and travel in direction $\vec{\alpha}$ at the chosen speed until they reach the boundary, where they pause for a fixed time interval p. In the following definition, t_1 is the time when the boundary will be reached and $\vec{d}$ is the point reached on the boundary (both easily calculated from $\vec{l_0}, \vec{\alpha}, v$).

$$\mathbf{RDir}_p(\vec{l_0}, t_0) = \{(g, t_1 + p) \mid g(t) = \begin{cases} \vec{l_0} + v \cdot (t - t_0) \cdot \vec{\alpha} & \text{if } t_0 \leq t \leq t_1 \\ \vec{d} & \text{if } t_1 < t \leq t_1 + p \end{cases}$$
$$\text{where } v \in \textit{Vel}, \ \vec{\alpha} \in \textit{Dir}, \ g(t_1) = \vec{d} \in bd(\mathcal{A})\}$$

The Random Walk, Random Waypoint, and Random Direction models are classical models used to realistically represent the movement of mobile nodes [2], e.g. in network simulation tools. Figure 2 depicts possible movements of a node in a two-dimensional area according to these three models, where for the Random Waypoint and Random Direction models pause times are expressed using small circles on trajectories. The Random Walk and Random Waypoint models also count as the two most commonly [2] used mobility models in research on wireless networks, and all models shown can be classified as so-called entity mobility models (where nodes move completely independent of each other). Group mobility models (where multiple nodes move together) are beyond the scope of this paper.

In contrast to the classical simulation models, the stationary model and the model of arbitrary movement have predominantly been used in formal approaches to the evaluation of wireless networks. In the next section we review these approaches.

3   Mobility and Time in Process Calculi

An important feature of the wireless medium is that all message transmissions are broadcasts, and may thus be received by several nodes. A suitable model for wireless networks must thus also determine which nodes may receive a broadcast message. In our approach, this is straightforwardly modelled by providing a function $\text{area}_n(\vec{l})$ that defines the *transmission area* of a node n at location $\vec{l}$. Hence, if a node n_f^T transmits at a time t, then nodes $m_g^{T'}$ with $g(t) \in \text{area}_n(f(t))$ may receive the transmission. Note however that transmissions may fail in reality even though nodes are within radio range, e.g. due to hidden terminal effects; this leads us later in Section 4 to an operational semantics that incorporates message loss. In all our examples we assume that area_n describes a circular

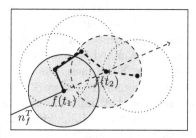

Fig. 3. Changes in the network topology due to node movement

transmission area, but differently shaped areas or even a realistic modelling of radio attenuation may be handled using a similar choice of representation.

The set of all nodes together with the transmission links between senders and receivers as edges then determines a graph, called the *network topology*, which may change over time depending on node movements. The network topology is in general given by a directed graph: unidirectional links can occur if there are different transmission radii (in our examples we assume bidirectional links to simplify presentation). An example for the change of network topology is given in Figure 3, where the moving node n_f^T with circular transmission area first establishes one connection with one of the stationary nodes at time t_1, and then breaks the connection again and has established two new links at time t_2. In the figure, the bold solid lines correspond to the node connectivity at time t_1, and the bold dashed lines to the node connectivity at time t_2.

In the following we describe related approaches to studying mobile wireless behaviour in a process algebraic setting. Process calculi with broadcast behaviour were first studied by Prasad [13] in the *Calculus of Broadcasting Systems (CBS)* and Ene and Muntean [3] in the *bπ-calculus*. These approaches are not directly suitable to describe wireless communication, since in their model all nodes in the network receive a broadcast message (*global broadcast*), whereas, as discussed above, the transmission ranges of nodes naturally introduce a kind of locality for broadcast actions (*local broadcast*). A number of process calculi that take this consideration into account have been proposed recently [10,7,4,11,15,8]. The approaches differ in the way the network topology is specified. Nanz and Hankin [10,9] have introduced $CBS^\sharp$ where the topology modelling takes place at the semantic level: every sending step in the semantics is parametrised by a directed graph that determines which nodes are connected at that moment. These connectivity graphs are nondeterministically chosen from a predefined set of graphs, hence modelling spontaneous topological changes. As node movements are otherwise unrestricted, this corresponds in our classification to the model of arbitrary movement. Based on the same principle Nanz, Nielson, and Nielson [11] have defined *bKlaim* which uses a coordination model where nodes communicate by placing message tuples into tuple spaces and retrieving them again; the same mobility model is used as in $CBS^\sharp$.

In contrast to [10,11], other approaches attempt connectivity modelling at the syntactic level. The *Calculus for Mobile Ad Hoc Networks (CMAN)* by Godskesen [4] focuses on behavioural equivalences for the purpose of security modelling. The connectivity of nodes is determined by examining the set of neighbouring nodes, associated with each node. Since these sets can change arbitrarily, node movement has no restrictions. In a more recent work [5] CMAN is equipped with a static location binding operator that limits the arbitrary mobility to happen only within the scope of the binder. Singh, Ramakrishnan, and Smolka [15] define the *ω-calculus* and use it for protocol analysis. Their connectivity modelling is based on connected groups in the connectivity graph. Each process is associated with the set of groups it belongs to, and change of group membership may be forced to comply with graph invariants. While this approach is able to restrict arbitrary movement, which we also strive to do, our model emphasizes more the importance of *realistic* transitions between connectivity graphs.

It is interesting to note that the approaches to connectivity modelling described above are just variations on traditional ways to describe ordinary graphs: using node and edge sets as in [10], adjacency lists as in [4], and maximal cliques as in [15]. One could imagine an alternative approach where connectivity and movements are coded into a distinguished process which acts as network medium. Our modelling using the *area* function for computing transmission areas strives instead to be a close model of real networks. This type of modelling can also be understood as a generalisation of the approach of Mezzetti and Sangiorgi [8], who equip each node with a location and a sending radius. Assuming a distance function, possible receivers can thus be determined from this data, together with the receivers' locations. In [8] only stationary nodes are considered, and the calculus aims at modelling MAC layer protocols (medium access control), where wireless interferences play a central role, while the other calculi mentioned here abstract from these physical complications and are suited for modelling Network layer protocols (routing). Merro [7] has used the location/radius approach in the *Calculus of Mobile Ad Hoc Networks (CMN)* with a special focus on defining appropriate behavioural equivalences in the wireless setting (again abstracting from MAC-problems). In terms of mobility modelling, CMN is restricted to the model of arbitrary movement, but introduces a switch to make selected nodes stationary.

The overview shows that current approaches to modelling mobile wireless networks have focused on stationary nodes and nodes with arbitrary movement patterns. While considering arbitrary movement seems compelling for formal verification ("all behaviour is included"), it is also limiting in many respects. For example, in security analysis one might want to establish a robustness property of a network against the influence of a single attacker. The attacker might only be able to influence nodes it can connect to, and as arbitrary movement essentially enables the attacker to be in all locations of the network simultaneously, it may be impossible to establish this property under this model. Also for properties of functional correctness the model of arbitrary movement seems inadequate, for example one would not expect a routing protocol to be able to handle completely different network topologies at every sending step. Our approach addresses this issue by offering the usage of realistic mobility models.

Lastly, we consider time passing in conjunction with wireless behaviour. While timing aspects are well-known to be essential in evaluating wireless protocols, they have not been considered for wireless calculi so far. There is however a variety of classical calculi that have been extended with time, for example TCCS [16], Timed ACP [1], TCSP [14], to mention only a few (and omitting stochastic calculi [6] where timing is determined by random variables). In [16,14], a delay action is considered to let processes idle until they can perform an action, and the maximal progress assumption is used to ensure that τ-actions cannot be delayed. In [1], time is absolute and each action is associated with a time stamp at which it should be performed. In our approach, time is also global as it is used to determine the positions of the nodes, and we consider a minimal calculus around this idea. However, our calculus is not a genuine timed calculus in that the process part does not contain operators dealing with time, only the mobility part is time dependent. Extensions of the calculus that also tag actions with delays may be considered in future work.

4   A Simple Calculus for Wireless Networks

In this section we introduce the syntax and the operational semantics of a calculus for wireless networks. The process part is deliberately chosen to be very simple and more or less standard for wireless process calculi and is not our contribution, but for the network part we add mobility functions and their timeout for individual nodes as a new feature. While we use a minimal operator set to make for a concise presentation, the process part can be extended with conditional expressions and name creation as expected, and we have proved our results for this larger set.

The labelled transition system semantics for our calculus is equipped with a notion of global time such that the mobility of nodes can be determined explicitly via a mobility function that is chosen from a mobility model parametrising the operational semantics.

4.1   Syntax

We assume to have infinite sets of *names* $\mathcal{N}$, *variables* $\mathcal{X}$, *identities* $\mathcal{I}$, as well as *process constants* (ranged over by A). The sets of *processes* and *networks* is defined as:

$$u, v \quad ::= n \mid x \quad \text{where } n \in \mathcal{N}, x \in \mathcal{X}$$

$$P, Q \quad ::= \mathbf{0} \mid \langle v \rangle.P \mid (x).P \mid A(\tilde{v})$$

$$N, M ::= a[P]_f^T \mid M \parallel N \quad \text{where } a \in \mathcal{I}$$

The terminated process is represented by $\mathbf{0}$. Output of a name v is described by the process $\langle v \rangle.P$, input and binding of the received name to the variable

x by $(x).P$. Note that the output is on a wireless channel, i.e. it has a broadcast semantics. Furthermore we are not distinguishing between multiple wireless channels (the number of these is fixed in real systems) which would be a straightforward extension if needed. We write $A(\tilde{v})$ to denote a process defined via a (possibly recursive) process definition $A(\tilde{x}) \triangleq P$. Processes are assumed to be sequential only.

Networks can be composed in parallel via $M \parallel N$, and consist of nodes of the form $a[P]_f^T$. A node consists of a process P that runs at an identified container a, where the identity a is unique in a network and represents an address of some sort. Furthermore, nodes move in a global area $\mathcal{A}$ according to their *mobility function* f, which yields a location $f(t)$ when applied to a point in time t. The *timeout* T determines until when the mobility function will be valid as spelled out in Section 2.

4.2   Operational Semantics

We equip the calculus with a parametrised operational semantics where transition rules are of the form:

$$\mathcal{M} \vdash (t, M) \xrightarrow{\lambda} (t', N) \quad \text{where} \quad \lambda ::= \tau \mid \Delta \mid \langle m \rangle @A! \mid (m)@A?$$

i.e. the parameter is $\mathcal{M}$ and configurations are pairs (t, M) of global time t and network M. Transition labels can either refer to change of mobility function (τ) or a time delay $(\Delta \in \mathbb{R}_0^+)$, or it may refer to output of a message in some area $(\langle m \rangle @A!)$ or to input of a message $((m)@A?)$ send out in some area. We always assume a configuration (t, M) to be *well-formed*, i.e. for all timeouts $T \in \mathbb{R}_0^+$ in M it must be that $t \leq T$.

The overall intuition of our semantics is that we let time proceed globally for a network and furthermore network execution not only depends on the global time but also on the mobility model $\mathcal{M}$.

We change the movement trajectories of nodes using the mobility rule:

$$\text{(mobility)} \quad \frac{(f', T') \in \mathcal{M}(f(t), t)}{\mathcal{M} \vdash (t, a[P]_f^T) \xrightarrow{\tau} (t, a[P]_{f'}^{T'})} \quad \text{if } T = \diamond \text{ or } T = t$$

The rule of time passing tells when a network may let time progress:

$$\text{(time)} \quad \mathcal{M} \vdash (t, N) \xrightarrow{\Delta} (t + \Delta, N) \quad \text{if } t + \Delta \leq T \text{ for all timeouts } T \in \mathbb{R}_0^+ \text{ in } N$$

Sending and reception is described by the following rules

$$\text{(send)} \quad \mathcal{M} \vdash (t, a[\langle m \rangle.P]_f^T) \xrightarrow{\langle m \rangle @A!} (t, a[P]_f^T) \quad \text{area}_a(f(t)) = A$$

$$\text{(receive}_1) \quad \mathcal{M} \vdash (t, a[(x).P]_f^T) \xrightarrow{(m)@A?} (t, a[P\{m/x\}]_f^T) \quad f(t) \in A$$

$$\text{(receive}_2) \quad \mathcal{M} \vdash (t, a[0]_f^T) \xrightarrow{(m)@A?} (t, a[0]_f^T) \quad f(t) \in A$$

where the operator $\mathsf{area}_a(\vec{l})$ computes the sending area of node a at location $\vec{l}$ as described in Section 3. Note that we assume that the time for transmission of messages is negligible compared to the time it takes for a node to move (for example, transmitting 100 kB with 11 Mbit/s bandwidth takes less than 0.1 s, in which a node moving at 50 km/h will move about 1 meter); therefore transmissions have no duration in our semantics.

Synchronisation of sending actions is done via the following two rules.

$$(\text{synch}_1) \quad \frac{\mathcal{M} \vdash (t, N) \xrightarrow{\langle m \rangle @ A!} (t, N') \quad \mathcal{M} \vdash (t, M) \xrightarrow{\langle m \rangle @ A?} (t, M')}{\mathcal{M} \vdash (t, N \parallel M) \xrightarrow{\langle m \rangle @ A!} (t, N' \parallel M')}$$

$$(\text{synch}_2) \quad \frac{\mathcal{M} \vdash (t, N) \xrightarrow{\langle m \rangle @ A?} (t, N') \quad \mathcal{M} \vdash (t, M) \xrightarrow{\langle m \rangle @ A?} (t, M')}{\mathcal{M} \vdash (t, N \parallel M) \xrightarrow{\langle m \rangle @ A?} (t, N' \parallel M')}$$

The rule (synch$_1$) and (synch$_2$) are similar to the rules in [13] for dealing with broadcast: a broadcast message continues to be distributed, and several nodes may agree on simultaneous reception of a message. Here we note that there are two symmetric rules to the two before, where the order of the parallel networks is switched (we do not have a structural congruence).

It is important to note that we do *not* intend that local broadcasts are actually received by *all* nodes that are located in the sending area. This is because in reality, as mentioned earlier in Section 3, message loss may occur even though nodes are within radio range. The following rule for (par) expresses this situation by allowing to be concerned with only a subset of the nodes in the network. We assume again that there is a symmetric rule available.

$$(\text{par}) \quad \frac{\mathcal{M} \vdash (t, N) \xrightarrow{\lambda} (t, N')}{\mathcal{M} \vdash (t, N \parallel M) \xrightarrow{\lambda} (t, N' \parallel M)} \quad \lambda \neq \Delta$$

The rule for recursion is standard.

$$(\text{rec}) \quad \frac{\mathcal{M} \vdash (t, a[P\{\tilde{v}/\tilde{x}\}]_f^T) \xrightarrow{\lambda} (t, a[P']_{f'}^{T'})}{\mathcal{M} \vdash (t, a[A(\tilde{v})]_f^T) \xrightarrow{\lambda} (t, a[P']_{f'}^{T'})} \quad A(\tilde{x}) \triangleq P$$

4.3 Semantic Characteristics

As pointed out in Section 3, the labelled transition semantics of our calculus differs much from the semantics of classical timed calculi: process actions are not time dependent, only the mobility part is. In the following we describe some of the semantic characteristics of change of mobility function and progress of global time, which can however be related to concepts known from timed calculi.

Like many timed calculi our calculus also gives priority to τ-actions over time delays. However, since only the mobility rule gives rise to τ-actions, this does *not* force transmitters to send instantaneously (as the "maximal progress" assumption of some timed calculi does). Instead, this condition translates to our setting in that we may only let time progress if no mobility function has timed out:

Proposition 1. *If* $\mathcal{M} \vdash (t, M) \xrightarrow{\tau} (t, M')$ *for some* M' *then* $\mathcal{M} \vdash (t, M) \xrightarrow{\Delta}\!\!\!\!\!/\,$.

Another important timed property possessed by timed calculi is *time determinism*, meaning that when time progresses the same configuration is always reached. Actually, since we have no explicit delay operators in our calculus it holds that a network does not change (syntactically) after a delay.

Proposition 2 (Time Determinism). *If* $\mathcal{M} \vdash (t, M) \xrightarrow{\Delta} (t', M')$ *and* $\mathcal{M} \vdash (t, M) \xrightarrow{\Delta} (t'', M'')$ *then* $t' = t'' = t + \Delta$ *and* $M = M' = M''$.

As corollaries we obtain that all nodes in a network must agree to let time progress (and hence all nodes must move on according to their mobility function)

Corollary 1 (Time Synchronisation). $\mathcal{M} \vdash (t, M \parallel N) \xrightarrow{\Delta} (t', M \parallel N)$ *iff* $\mathcal{M} \vdash (t, M) \xrightarrow{\Delta} (t', M)$ *and* $\mathcal{M} \vdash (t, N) \xrightarrow{\Delta} (t', N)$.

and that any delay can be divided into sub-delays:

Corollary 2 (Time Additivity). *If* $\mathcal{M} \vdash (t, M) \xrightarrow{\Delta + \Delta'} (t + \Delta + \Delta', M)$ *then* $\mathcal{M} \vdash (t, M) \xrightarrow{\Delta} (t + \Delta, M)$ *and* $\mathcal{M} \vdash (t + \Delta, M) \xrightarrow{\Delta'} (t + \Delta + \Delta', M)$

Observe that our calculus as a natural consequence does not support the property of *time persistency* i.e.

$$\text{if } \mathcal{M} \vdash (t, M) \xrightarrow{\lambda} \text{ and } \mathcal{M} \vdash (t, M) \xrightarrow{\Delta} \text{ then } \mathcal{M} \vdash (t + \Delta, M) \xrightarrow{\lambda}$$

simply because it would be unreasonable to expect due to the interplay between time and mobility that a node after some time progress will continue broadcasting in the same area.

5   A Framework for Comparing Mobility Models

In order to be able to compare the strengths of the various mobility models we provide standard behavioural pre-order and equivalences. Since we do not want to take the actual shift of mobility functions as an observable into account, these turn out to be weak simulations and bisimulations in our case.

5.1   Behavioural Pre-order and Equivalence

We consider relations $\mathcal{R}$ containing pairs $((\mathcal{M}, t, M), (\mathcal{M}', t, M'))$ consisting of two networks with identical timing information but where the networks may choose mobility functions from (in principle) different mobility models; $\mathcal{R}$ is said to be *well-formed* whenever for all such pairs (t, M) and (t, M') are well-formed.

Moreover, for ease of notation we write $(\mathcal{M}, M) \mathcal{R}_t (\mathcal{M}', M')$ if $(\mathcal{M}, t, M) \mathcal{R}$ $(\mathcal{M}', t, M')$ and $M \mathcal{R}_t^{\mathcal{M}} M'$ if $(\mathcal{M}, M) \mathcal{R}_t (\mathcal{M}, M')$.

Next we define weak simulation and bisimulation. In order to define weak labelled transitions, for each label λ, we shall write $P \overset{\lambda}{\Rightarrow} Q$ iff either $\lambda \neq \tau$ and there exist P' and Q' such that $P(\overset{\tau}{\rightarrow})^* P' \overset{\lambda}{\rightarrow} Q'(\overset{\tau}{\rightarrow})^* Q$ or $\lambda = \tau$ and $P(\overset{\tau}{\rightarrow})^* Q$.

Definition 1. *A* well-formed relation $\mathcal{R}$ *is a* weak simulation *if* $(\mathcal{M}, N) \mathcal{R}_t$ $(\mathcal{M}', M)$ *implies*

1. $\mathcal{M} \vdash (t, N) \xrightarrow{\langle m \rangle @ A!} (t, N')$ *implies* $\mathcal{M}' \vdash (t, M) \xRightarrow{\langle m \rangle @ A'!} (t, M')$ *for some* M' *and* A' *such that* $A \subseteq A'$ *and* $(\mathcal{M}, N') \mathcal{R}_t (\mathcal{M}', M')$.
2. $\mathcal{M} \vdash (t, N) \xrightarrow{(m) @ A?} (t, N')$ *implies* $\mathcal{M}' \vdash (t, M) \xRightarrow{(m) @ A'?} (t, M')$ *for some* M' *and* A' *such that* $A' \subseteq A$ *such that* $(\mathcal{M}, N') \mathcal{R}_t (\mathcal{M}', M')$.
3. $\mathcal{M} \vdash (t, N) \overset{\tau}{\rightarrow} (t, N')$ *implies* $\mathcal{M}' \vdash (t, M) \overset{\tau}{\Rightarrow} (t, M')$ *for some* N' *such that* $(\mathcal{M}, N') \mathcal{R}_t (\mathcal{M}', M')$.
4. $\mathcal{M} \vdash (t, M) \overset{\Delta}{\rightarrow} (t', M)$ *implies* $\mathcal{M}' \vdash (t, N) \overset{\Delta}{\Rightarrow} (t', N)$ *and* $(\mathcal{M}, N) \mathcal{R}_{t'}$ $(\mathcal{M}', M)$.

$\mathcal{R}$ *is a* weak bisimulation *if* $\mathcal{R}$ *and* $\mathcal{R}^{-1}$ *are weak simulations.*

We let $\sqsubseteq$ denote the largest weak simulation and $\approx$ the largest weak bisimulation. It is immediate that $\approx$ is an equivalence relation.

Notice the asymmetry in our definition of weak simulation. A network where a node may broadcast a message m within some area A is simulated by a network at least as powerful that broadcasts m in an area containing A. Dually, a network where nodes receive within some area A must be simulated by a network where nodes are capable of receiving in an area A' contained in A. Notice that a network receiving in some area can always receive in a larger area but not the other way around. The two last clauses in Definition 1 are standard.

It turns out that our bisimulations are closed by parallel composition of networks that are well-formed with respect to the current time:

Theorem 1. $N \approx_t^{\mathcal{M}} N'$ *implies* $N \parallel M \approx_t^{\mathcal{M}} N' \parallel M$ *for all* (t, M).

As we would expect our behavioural theory satisfies the following commutativity and associativity laws:

Proposition 3. $M \parallel N \approx_t^{\mathcal{M}} N \parallel M$

Proposition 4. $(M \parallel M') \parallel M'' \approx_t^{\mathcal{M}} M \parallel (M' \parallel M'')$.

Comparing a network across mobility models we can infer that

Proposition 5. $(\mathcal{M}, M) \sqsubseteq_t (\mathcal{M} \cup \mathcal{M}', M) \sqsubseteq_t (\mathbf{Arb}, M)$

because whatever M can do choosing from a mobility model $\mathcal{M}$ clearly it can do choosing from a larger set of mobility functions (and from the most powerful set of mobility functions $\mathbf{Arb}$), but not necessarily the other way around.

When comparing networks within the same mobility model, we can infer that bisimulation equivalence gets stronger if more mobility functions are available to choose from:

Proposition 6. $\approx_t^{\mathbf{Arb}} \subseteq \approx_t^{\mathcal{M} \cup \mathcal{M}'} \subseteq \approx_t^{\mathcal{M}}$

This means, if $M \approx_t^{\mathcal{M} \cup \mathcal{M}'} N$ then also $M \approx_t^{\mathcal{M}} N$ because in the former case all possible behaviours for M can be matched by N (and vice versa) when choosing mobility functions from both $\mathcal{M}$ and $\mathcal{M}'$, but then clearly with a limited choice of mobility functions M and N are still equivalent. A similar argument holds when comparing $\approx_t^{\mathbf{Arb}}$ and $\approx_t^{\mathcal{M} \cup \mathcal{M}'}$ because whatever a mobility function from $\mathcal{M} \cup \mathcal{M}'$ causes can be matched by mobility functions in **Arb**.

Finally, we observe that if a pair of networks with all timeouts being infinite belongs to $\approx_t^{\mathcal{M}}$ then it also belongs to $\approx_t^{\mathcal{M}'}$ for any $\mathcal{M}'$ because the possible choices of new mobility functions are irrelevant.

5.2 Comparing Mobility Models

Our main motivation for introducing the weak behavioural simulation and equivalence is to be able to compare mobility models, and to demonstrate formally that the choice of mobility function matters for reasoning. The latter point can be shown with the following simple example, where two networks are distinguished under the Random Walk model, but found equivalent using arbitrary movement.

Example 2. Consider the three mobility functions f, g_1, and g_2, and assume that $g_1(t_0) \in area_a(f(t_0))$ and $g_2(t_0) \notin area_a(f(t_0))$. Furthermore, let networks N_1 and N_2 be defined as follows:

$$N_i = a[A]_f^T \parallel b[B]_{g_i}^\diamond \qquad \text{where } A \triangleq \langle m \rangle.(x).A \text{ and } B \triangleq (x).\langle x \rangle.B$$

Then the following results hold:

$$N_1 \not\approx_{t_0}^{\mathbf{RWalk}_\Delta} N_2 \quad \text{and} \quad N_1 \approx_{t_0}^{\mathbf{Arb}} N_2$$

Proof. To see that the inequation holds, we have for network N_1 that

$$\mathbf{RWalk}_\Delta \vdash (t_0, N_1) \xrightarrow{\langle m \rangle @A!} (t_0, a[(x).A]_f^T \parallel b[\langle m \rangle.B]_{g_1}^\diamond) \xrightarrow{\langle m \rangle @A'!} (t_0, N_1),$$

however for network N_2, since b is not in range of a,

$$\mathbf{RWalk}_\Delta \vdash (t_0, N_2) \xrightarrow{\langle m \rangle @A!} (t_0, a[(x).A]_f^T \parallel b[(x).\langle x \rangle.B]_{g_2}^\diamond) \xrightarrow{\langle m \rangle @A'!} \not\longrightarrow.$$

In particular τ-transitions using (mobility) cannot change this situation, because in the model $\mathbf{RWalk}_\Delta$ an amount of time $\delta > 0$ would have to pass to allow for node b to move into the range of a.

To see that the equation holds, note that the two networks differ only in the initial mobility function of node b. Furthermore the model **Arb** allows every node to move instantaneously to any location $\vec{l}$:

$$\mathbf{Arb} \vdash (t_0, b[B]_{g_2}^\diamond) \xrightarrow{\tau} (t_0, b[B]_{\lambda x. \vec{l}}^\diamond)$$

Thus it is easy to establish $b[B]_{g_1}^{\diamond} \approx_t^{\mathbf{Arb}} b[B]_{g_2}^{\diamond}$ and therefore the equation holds by Theorem 1.

The next proposition is about comparing the mobility models of Section 2. As expected, the model of arbitrary movement can simulate all other models, Random Waypoint can simulate Random Direction, and all other pairs of models are incomparable.

Proposition 7. *Assume that all nodes in the network N initially have timeout t_0. Then the following results hold for $\Delta > 0$ and $p > 0$:*

1. $(\mathcal{M}, N) \sqsubseteq_t (\mathbf{Arb}, N)$ *for all* $\mathcal{M} \in \{\mathbf{Stat}, \mathbf{Arb}, \mathbf{RWalk}_\Delta, \mathbf{RWay}_p, \mathbf{RDir}_p\}$
2. $(\mathbf{RDir}_p, N) \sqsubseteq_t (\mathbf{RWay}_p, N)$
3. *All other model pairs in* $\{\mathbf{Stat}, \mathbf{Arb}, \mathbf{RWalk}_\Delta, \mathbf{RWay}_p, \mathbf{RDir}_p\}$ *are incomparable with respect to weak simulation.*

Proof (sketch). The first part of the proposition follows directly from Proposition 5. Conversely, **Arb** cannot be simulated by any other model, because it is the only model where movement does not take time. $\mathbf{RWay}_p$ can simulate $\mathbf{RDir}_p$ as it can choose the point on the boundary of $\mathcal{A}$ that a node under $\mathbf{RDir}_p$ would reach as a waypoint, and has pause times. **Stat** cannot compare with any model model except **Arb**, because it can always let time pass without movement. $\mathbf{RWalk}_\Delta$ cannot compare with either $\mathbf{RWay}_p$ or $\mathbf{RDir}_p$ because it has no notion of pause times. The remaining incomparability results can be established similarly.

6   Discretising Time Delay

The operational semantics defined in Section 4.2 is infinite state because of its real-time delay transitions, and thus there will be no hope for the immediate algorithm underlying our weak bisimulation behavioural equivalence (or weak simulation pre-order) to be decidable.

In this section we hint at future work where a finite state operational semantics and a decidable behavioural equivalence that is a sound and complete characterisation of weak bisimulation should be defined. Clearly such a decidability result relies on the process language of our calculus, but as our exposition in this paper is focused on the semantics of mobility and not on the process part we leave the discussion of an appropriate process fragment for future work.

A Discrete Time Semantics. One may observe that a time delay Δ may be safely carried out without side effects on the capability of a network configuration (t, M) if the following holds:

- No mobility function in M must *timeout* in the interval $[t, t + \Delta)$, and
- No potential receiver of a broadcast message m must *leave* the broadcasting area of the node in M broadcasting m.

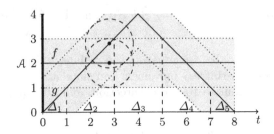

Fig. 4. Node movements and time discretisation in Example 3

To formalise these requirements let (t, M) be a well-formed network configuration, let a_i with $i \in I$ be all identifiers in M and let f_i and T_i be the mobility function and its timeout for a_i.

Then let $\Delta^t_{timeout}$ be the maximal delay Δ such that $t + \Delta \leq T_i$ for all $i \in I$ with $T_i \neq \diamond$, or if $T_i = \diamond$ for all i then $\Delta^t_{timeout} = \infty$.

Next, for all node identities a_i we need to keep track of all node identities that at time t lie within the transmission range of a_i, i.e. let

$$I^t_{a_i} = \{j \in I \mid f_j(t) \in \text{area}_{a_i}(f_i(t))\}$$

Then let Δ^t_{leave} be the smallest delay Δ such that $I^t_{a_i} \neq I^{t+\Delta}_{a_i}$, or if $I^t_{a_i} = I^{t+\Delta}_{a_i}$ for all i then $\Delta^t_{leave} = 0$.

We may now define a new time rule based on the definitions above such that:

$$\text{(time)} \quad \mathcal{M} \vdash (t, N) \xrightarrow{\Delta} (t + \Delta, N) \quad \text{if} \quad \Delta = min\{\Delta^t_{timeout}, \Delta^t_{leave}\}$$

Observe that if always $\Delta = 0$ when applying the rule above then time can be completely abstracted away in the semantics.

Example 3. To illustrate our ideas, assume for simplicity the same one-dimensional area, $\mathcal{A} = [0, 4]$, as in Example 1, and consider a network M consisting of two nodes with identities a and b respectively.

Also, suppose a mobility model $\mathcal{M}$ with just two mobility functions f and g defined by $f(t) = 2$ and by $g(t) = t$ if $t \leq 4$, and $g(t) = 8 - t$ otherwise (see 4). Suppose that the timeout for both f and g is 8.

If the two nodes initially possess the very same mobility function the network may from its initial state $(0, M)$ delay 8 time units, i.e. until the mobility functions time out.

Suppose instead that the two nodes initially contain different mobility functions, and assume for simplicity that both a and b have the same transmission radius 1. In that setting we obtain that the Δ in rule (time) defined above must be chosen according to the following sequence: $1, 2, 2, 2, 1$. That is, first delay is one time unit, then follow three delays of two time units, and finally a delay of one time unit. This situation is depicted in Figure 4.

In future research we want to identify under what restrictions the sampling points for time delays may always be precompiled from a mobility model and the broadcast area of any node. Furthermore, we aim to show that our discretised model may be preferable to models currently used as input to automatic verification tools: as our more realistic handling of connectivity change considers *fewer* possible connections, it may thus set more effective limits on the size of the state space to be considered.

7   Conclusion

In this paper we have described how to extend a simple process calculus with realistic mobility models. The semantics of our calculus incorporates a notion of global time passing that allows us to express a wide range of mobility models currently used in protocol development practice. Using the behavioural equivalence and pre-order of our calculus, we have been able to compare the strength of these models. Finally, we have briefly touched upon the issue of making the real-time semantics symbolic and finite, thereby giving hope for verification of wireless protocols modelled in our approach. In addition, our approach is a step towards bridging the gap between protocol development efforts and formal verification, since it allows to use identical mobility models for both simulation and formal reasoning.

Acknowledgements. We would like to thank the anonymous reviewers for their valuable comments on an earlier version of the paper.

References

1. Baeten, J.C.M., Bergstra, J.A.: Real time process algebra. Formal Aspects of Computing 3(2), 142–188 (1991)
2. Camp, T., Boleng, J., Davies, V.: A survey of mobility models for ad hoc network research. Wireless Communications and Mobile Computing 2(5), 483–502 (2002)
3. Ene, C., Muntean, T.: A broadcast-based calculus for communicating systems. In: Proc. FMPPTA 2003 (2001)
4. Godskesen, J.C.: A calculus for mobile ad hoc networks. In: Murphy, A.L., Vitek, J. (eds.) COORDINATION 2007. LNCS, vol. 4467, pp. 132–150. Springer, Heidelberg (2007)
5. Godskesen, J.C.: A calculus for mobile ad hoc networks with static location binding. In: Proc. EXPRESS 2008 (2008)
6. Hermanns, H., Herzog, U., Katoen, J.-P.: Process algebra for performance evaluation. Theoretical Computer Science 274(1-2), 43–87 (2002)
7. Merro, M.: An observational theory for mobile ad hoc networks. In: Proc. MFPS 2007. ENTCS, vol. 173, pp. 275–293 (2007)
8. Mezzetti, N., Sangiorgi, D.: Towards a calculus for wireless systems. In: Proc. MFPS 2006. ENTCS, vol. 158, pp. 331–353 (2006)
9. Nanz, S.: Specification and Security Analysis of Mobile Ad-Hoc Networks. Ph.D thesis, Imperial College London (2006)
10. Nanz, S., Hankin, C.: A framework for security analysis of mobile wireless networks. Theoretical Computer Science 367(1-2), 203–227 (2006)

11. Nanz, S., Nielson, F., Nielson, H.R.: Topology-dependent abstractions of broadcast networks. In: Caires, L., Vasconcelos, V.T. (eds.) CONCUR 2007. LNCS, vol. 4703, pp. 226–240. Springer, Heidelberg (2007)
12. The Network Simulator ns-2, http://www.isi.edu/nsnam/ns/
13. Prasad, K.V.S.: A calculus of broadcasting systems. Science of Computer Programming 25(2-3), 285–327 (1995)
14. Reed, G.M., Roscoe, A.W.: A timed model for communicating sequential processes. Theoretical Computer Science 58, 249–261 (1988)
15. Singh, A., Ramakrishnan, C.R., Smolka, S.A.: A process calculus for mobile ad hoc networks. In: Lea, D., Zavattaro, G. (eds.) COORDINATION 2008. LNCS, vol. 5052, pp. 296–314. Springer, Heidelberg (2008)
16. Yi, W.: Real-time behaviour of asynchronous agents. In: Baeten, J.C.M., Klop, J.W. (eds.) CONCUR 1990. LNCS, vol. 458, pp. 502–520. Springer, Heidelberg (1990)

Parametrised Constants and Replication for Spatial Mobility

Bjørn Haagensen and Hans Hüttel

Department of Computer Science, Selma Lagerlöfs Vej 300, 9220 Aalborg Øst
{bh,hans}@cs.aau.dk

Abstract. Parametrised replication and replication are common ways of expressing infinite computation in process calculi. While parametrised constants can be encoded using replication in the π-calculus, this changes in the presence of spatial mobility as found in e.g. the distributed π-calculus and the calculus of mobile ambients. Here, processes are located at sites and can migrate between them.

In this paper we say that an encoding is local if it does not introduce extra migration. We first study this property for the distributed π-calculus where locations can be dynamically created. If the set of reachable sites is static an encoding exists, but we also show that parametrised constants can not be encoded in the full calculus. The locality requirement supplements widely accepted encoding criteria. It appears to be a natural property in spatial calculi where links and locations can fail.

The versions of the distributed π-calculus with parametrised constants and replication are incomparable. On the other hand, we shall see that there exists a simple encoding of recursion in mobile ambients.

1 Introduction

Many programs are intended to run *indefinitely*. Common examples are text-editors, web-browsers, e-mail clients, and operating systems. Unless specifically instructed, such programs should not terminate. Thus, programming languages must contain constructs for such behaviour which are typically realised in terms of various loop constructs. However many times these are essentially syntactic variations of the same semantical construct.

In the setting of process calculi differences between language constructs becomes clear. Here *replication, recursion, and parametrised constants* are three common operations for expressing infinite process behaviour. We regard it as important both from a theoretical and a practical point of view to understand the *relative expressive power* of these language constructs, since this has important consequences. An example is that termination is decidable for CCS with replication, but not for CCS with parametrised constants [1]. This might occur surprising since the difference is not present in the π-calculus [2].

In this paper we study the relative expressive power of parametrised constants and replication in the Dπ-calculus [3] which extends the π-calculus by adding primitive language constructs for *locations* and *process migration*. That makes it a member of the class of process calculi for *spatial mobility*.

J. Field and V.T. Vasconcelos (Eds.): COORDINATION 2009, LNCS 5521, pp. 123–142, 2009.
© Springer-Verlag Berlin Heidelberg 2009

One of the characteristic operators in the Dπ-calculus is the process migration prefix go?$k.P$. The reduction axiom for migration is simply,

$$l[\text{go}?k.P] \longrightarrow k[P] \ , \tag{1}$$

where the redex as well as the reduct are processes located at l and k respectively. Migration is not an observable operation, i.e. it does not depend on the presence of *action* and *co-action* pairs. We consider a modified version of the axiom in (1) where migration has been made observable using actions and co-actions. The consequence is that new locations can not be spawned at runtime as in (1). We show that parametrised constants can then be encoded using replication in the modified version of the Dπ-calculus which we call D$\pi^\star$. Our encoding uses the same idea as the encoding of parametrised constants in the π-calculus [2]. Unlike the encoding of recursion in Dπ proposed in [4], our encoding avoids introducing additional migration.

However, encoding parametrised constants and recursion becomes difficult in the full Dπ-calculus (Dπ^{full}) where (1) holds. Consider the definition $A = \text{go}?l.A$ and the process $k[A]$. Now $k[A]$ can reduce to $l[A]$, and A can execute its body again, this time from l. Contrast this to a replicated process $k[\star P]$. Here we must first unfold the replication to obtain a redex, $k[P \mid \star P]$ where the process P not under $\star$ can now start executing. However in doing so we no longer have the original process, so if P is go?l the reduction sequence terminates as soon as the migration has happened since the replicated process $\star P$ is still located at k.

Despite the example given above one can not rule out that an encoding can exist. Our next section shows that we can indeed not use the encoding of parametrised constants in D$\pi^\star$ and then encode everything into Dπ^{full}. We do this by showing that there can not exists any *sensible* encoding of D$\pi^\star$ in Dπ^{full}. We also show the opposite implication, that Dπ^{full} can not be encoded in D$\pi^\star$ thus making the two calculi *incomparable*.

We then prove our main result. There is no encoding, subject to certain natural requirements, of replicated constants using replication in the Dπ^{full}-calculus. The idea is that it is not possible to ensure that the definitions of the processes are always available at arbitrary locations since locations can be created dynamically. For this purpose we introduce the notion of a *local* encoding. A local encoding is basically one which prohibits the encoded process from having more migrations than the original process.

Our locality requirement is related to the issue of *failure* in spatial networks. In [5] the authors study link and location failure in Dπ. When links or locations fail they become inert and can no longer take part in further reduction steps. Arguably failure characteristics is a fundamental property of many spatial networks that must be expressible in process calculi. It is important to note that the essence of our result is not the comparsion by encoding itself, but rather that an implementation of replicated constants by means of replication cannot be done in a decentralized way if new locations can be created dynamically.

Having identified the locality requirement in Dπ^{full} we then apply it to another calculus with spatial mobility, the calculus of mobile ambients (MA) [6]. It turns out that even though MA allows for hierarchical location structures in which ambients may move freely around, in contrast to the flat location structure of $D\pi$, we can in fact obtain a local encoding of parametrised constants using replication. The reason is that creation of new locations in MA, where recursive definitions should be placed, can be dealt with statically.

Related work: Sangiorgi and Walker show in their book on the π-calculus [2], that parametrised constants can be encoded in terms of replication. The encoding they use is similar to the one we use for encoding parametrised constants in $D\pi^\star$.

Ravara *et. al* [7] defined $lsd\pi$; a variant of $D\pi$ with lexical scoping, but without the go-operator. Channels in $lsd\pi$ are local, and migration is a consequence of triggering communication on non-local channels.

Aranda *et. al* [1] summarise known results for the π-calculus and discuss further replication vs. constants vs. parametrised constants vs. recursion in CCS. Compared to our results which relies on characteristics of spatial mobility, their results are based on subtle differences between dynamic and static name binding.

Hennessy and Hym gave an encoding of recursion using replication in the $D\pi$-calculus [4]. Their encoding uses added process migration, and hence is not local. They state that the encoding could fail if locations could fail.

The idea of enriching the semantics of unobservable reductions with actions and co-actions is due to Levi and Sangiorgi who extended MA in [8] and obtain the calculus of Safe Ambients. Their focus is on controlling interference in MA processes and in doing so obtaining a richer semantic theory.

Structure of the paper: In Section 2 we give the reduction semantics and a labelled transition semantics for $D\pi^{full}$ and show that strong and weak barbed congruence coincide with strong and weak bisimilarity. In Section 3.1 we discuss the encoding from [4]. In Section 3 we define the calculus $D\pi^\star$ and show that parametrised constants can be encoded using replication. In Section 4 we show that $D\pi^\star$ is incomparable to $D\pi^{full}$. In Section 5 we show that there is no local encoding of parametrised constants in $D\pi^{full}$. In Section 6 we encode parametrised constants in MA. Finally Section 7 concludes the paper.

2   The $D\pi$-Calculus

We give an overview of the variant of the $D\pi$-calculus we use. Details on $D\pi$ can be found in [3]. Other sources on $D\pi$ are [9,10,11,3], and [5]. (The latter deals with location and link failure in $D\pi$.)

2.1   The $D\pi^{full}$-Calculus

We define $D\pi^{full}$, a version of $D\pi$ without types or network environments, but otherwise similar to $D\pi$ in terms of its operations. Whereas the $D\pi$-calculus allows for transmission of composite values and use patterns at the receiving end for decomposing these patterns, we only allow polyadic values in communication, like in the polyadic π-calculus.

Syntax: The syntax of $D\pi^{\text{full}}$ consists of two categories, processes and networks. Let $\mathcal{N}$ be an infinite countable set of names. Let $a, b, c, \ldots, k, l, m, \ldots, x, y, z, \ldots$ range over $\mathcal{N}$. We write $\widetilde{u}$ for a possibly empty sequence of names. The syntax is given by the following grammar.

Definition 1 ($D\pi^{\text{full}}$-syntax). *Processes and networks are defined by:*

$$P, Q ::= a!\langle\widetilde{v}\rangle.P \quad | \quad a?(\widetilde{x}).P \quad | \quad [a = b].P, Q \quad | \quad \text{rec}\,X.P \quad | \quad P \,|\, Q$$
$$\text{go}?k.P \quad | \quad \text{STOP} \quad | \quad \star P \quad | \quad A\langle\widetilde{v}\rangle \quad | \quad X \quad | \quad (\nu u)P$$
$$M, N ::= k[P] \quad | \quad N \,|\, M \quad | \quad (\nu u)N \quad | \quad \mathbf{0}$$

At the process level the constructs are in order: input– and output prefixing, if-then-else, recursion, parallel composition, migration, the nil-process, replication, parametrised constants, recursion variables, and restriction. Specific to the $D\pi^{\text{full}}$-calculus, and of particular interest for us, is the migration operator $\text{go}?k.P$. When the $\text{go}?k$-capability is exercised the process P moves from its present location to the location k. Networks are located process $l[P]$, parallel compositions of networks, and restriction.

Names are bound by restriction and input-prefixing and recursion variables are bound by the operator $\text{rec}\,X.P$. The sets of *free* and *bound* names and recursion variables are defined accordingly. Given a process P and network N, $\text{fn}(P)$ and $\text{fn}(N)$ denote the set of free names and $\text{bn}(P)$ and $\text{bn}(N)$ the set of bound names. We assume that α-conversion on names and recursion variables holds.

For parametrised constants we suppose that each $A\langle v_1, \ldots, v_k\rangle$ has a corresponding defining equation $A(x_1, \ldots, x_k) = P$ given such that $\{x_1, \ldots, x_k\} \subseteq \text{fn}(P)$ and whenever we speak of processes and networks we assume that these equations can be looked up in a set denoted Δ.

The following syntactic conventions are assumed. Input $a?(\widetilde{x})$, output $a!\langle\widetilde{v}\rangle$, restriction (νv), and recursion $\text{rec}\,X$ binds stronger than parallel composition. E.g. $\text{go}?k.P \,|\, Q$ means $(\text{go}?k.P) \,|\, Q$ and similarly for the other constructs. Moreover trailing occurrences of STOP are omitted, $(\nu v_1) \ldots (\nu v_k)P$ is written $(\nu\widetilde{v})P$ and we sometimes write $a!.P$ for $a!\langle\widetilde{v}\rangle.P$ and $a?.P$ for $a?(\widetilde{x}).P$ if $\widetilde{v}$, respectively $\widetilde{x}$ are empty sequences.

Definition 2 ($D\pi^{\text{full}}$ network contexts). *Network contexts are defined by:*

$$\mathscr{N} ::= (\nu n)\mathscr{N} \quad | \quad (-) \,|\, \mathscr{N} \quad | \quad \mathscr{N} \,|\, (-) \quad | \quad l[P] \quad | \quad (-) \;.$$

As usual different networks can be defined by e.g. changing the ordering of parallel components. Structural equivalence abstracts from such differences.

Definition 3. *Structural equivalence is the least equivalence relation on networks closed under $\mathscr{N}$ and satisfying the abelian monoid laws with respect to $|$ and following axioms:*

$$
\begin{array}{ll}
\text{(S-SCOPE)} & (\nu n)(N \,|\, M) \equiv N \,|\, (\nu n)M, n \notin \text{fn}(N) \\
\text{(S-RES-NIL)} & (\nu n)\mathbf{0} \equiv \mathbf{0} \\
\text{(S-FLIP)} & (\nu n)(\nu m)N \equiv (\nu m)(\nu n)N \;.
\end{array}
$$

Reduction semantics and barbed bisimulation:

Definition 4. *The reduction relation is a binary relation over networks defined by the rules in Table 1 and axioms in Table 2.*

Table 1. Contextual rules

$$(\text{R-STRUCT}) \quad \frac{N' \equiv N \quad N \longrightarrow M \quad M \equiv M'}{N' \longrightarrow M'}$$

$$(\text{R-RES}) \quad \frac{N \longrightarrow N'}{(\nu n)N \longrightarrow (\nu n)N'} \qquad (\text{R-PAR}) \quad \frac{N \longrightarrow N'}{N \mid M \longrightarrow N' \mid M}$$

Table 2. $D\pi^{\text{full}}$ reduction axioms

$(\text{R-COM}) \quad l[a!\langle \widetilde{v}\rangle.P] \mid l[a?(\widetilde{x}).Q] \longrightarrow l[P] \mid l[Q\{\widetilde{v}/\widetilde{x}\}]$

$(\text{R-REP}) \quad l[\star P] \longrightarrow l[P] \mid l[\star P]$

$(\text{R-REC}) \quad l[\text{rec } X.P] \longrightarrow l[P\{\text{rec } X.P\}/X]$

$(\text{R-CONST}) \; l[A\langle v_1,\dots,v_n\rangle] \longrightarrow l[P\{v_1,\dots,v_n/x_1,\dots,x_n\}]$
$\qquad \qquad \text{if } A(x_1,\dots,x_n) = P \in \Delta$

$(\text{R-EQ}) \quad l[[u = u]P, Q] \longrightarrow l[P]$

$(\text{R-NEQ}) \quad l[[u = v]P, Q] \longrightarrow l[Q] \text{ if } v \neq u$

$(\text{R-SPLIT}) \quad l[P \mid Q] \longrightarrow l[P] \mid l[Q]$

$(\text{R-GO}) \quad l[\text{go}?k.P] \longrightarrow k[P]$

$(\text{R-NEW}) \quad l[(\nu n)P] \longrightarrow (\nu n)l[P] \text{ if } n \neq l$

The rules in Table 1 are standard contextual rules yielding reductions in various contexts and closure under $\equiv$. Table 2 shows the axioms that defines the behaviour of located processes. The (R-COM) axiom expresses communication. Its characterising property is that in addition to the names of the communication channels, the names of the locations must also be equal. In the reduct $Q\{\widetilde{v}/\widetilde{x}\}$ denote the process Q with all free occurrences of $\widetilde{x}$ replaced by $\widetilde{v}$ using α-conversion to avoid capturing names. (R-REP), (R-REC), and (R-CONST) activates, or *unfolds* the three different operators for infinite behaviour. These axioms together with (R-SPLIT) and (R-NEW) are sometimes included as part of the $\equiv$-relation. We represent them by a reduction step as this gives a simpler correspondence with the transition relation.

The (R-SPLIT) axiom is worth pointing out. It implies that $l[P \mid Q]$ and $l[P] \mid l[Q]$ are identified up to weak process equivalence. The (R-GO)-axiom expresses process mobility. Some of its properties are relevant for our work. Firstly the location l from which P moves disappears after the reduction has taken place. Moreover the target location k is dynamically created by the reduction. This happens independently of whether k and l already exist as in e.g.

$$l[\mathsf{go}?k.P] \mid l[R] \mid k[R'] \longrightarrow k[P] \mid l[R] \mid k[R'] \ .$$

Let $\longrightarrow^*$ denote the reflexive and transitive closure of $\longrightarrow$.

Next we define strong and weak barbed bisimulation and congruence.

Definition 5 (Strong and weak barbs). *Define strong and weak barbs on networks as follows.*

- *A network N has a strong barb on channel a at location l, denoted $N \downarrow_{a@l}$, if $N \equiv (\tilde{n})(M \mid l[a!\langle \tilde{v} \rangle.Q])$ for some $M, Q, a, \tilde{n},$ and $\tilde{v}$ such that $l, a \notin \tilde{n}$.*
- *A network N is said to have a weak barb on channel a at location l, denoted $N \Downarrow_{a@l}$, if there is some N' such that $N \longrightarrow^* N'$ and $N' \downarrow_{a@l}$.*

The definition of barbs captures the idea that a communication requires the observable presence of a location as well as a channel. For instance if

$$P = (\nu a)(l[a?(x).Q]) \mid k[a?(x).Q] \mid k[a!\langle v \rangle.b!\langle v \rangle.Q] \ .$$

Then $P \downarrow_{a@k}$, $P \Downarrow_{b@k}$, but $P \not\downarrow_{a@l}$.

Definition 6 (Strong barbed bisimulation and congruence). *A binary symmetric relation $\mathcal{R}$ is called a* barbed bisimulation *if whenever $(N, M) \in \mathcal{R}$ the following holds.*

(i) $N \downarrow_{a@l}$ implies $M \downarrow_{a@l}$.
(ii) $N \longrightarrow N'$ implies that $M \longrightarrow M'$ such that $(N', M') \in \mathcal{R}$.

Networks M and N are called barbed bisimilar, *denoted $N \sim_b M$ if they are related by some barbed bisimulation. Networks N and M are called* barbed congruent, *denoted $M \sim_b N$ if for all network contexts $\mathcal{N}$, $\mathcal{N}(M) \sim_b \mathcal{N}(N)$.*

Definition 7 (Weak barbed bisimulation and congruence). *A binary symmetric relation $\mathcal{R}$ is called a* barbed bisimulation *if whenever $(N, M) \in \mathcal{R}$ the following holds.*

(i) $N \Downarrow_{a@l}$ implies $M \Downarrow_{a@l}$.
(ii) $N \longrightarrow N'$ implies that $M \longrightarrow^* M'$ such that $(N', M') \in \mathcal{R}$.

Networks M and N are weak barbed bisimilar, *denoted $N \cong_b M$, if they are related by some barbed bisimulation. Networks N and M are* weak barbed congruent, *denoted $M \cong_b N$ if for all network contexts $\mathcal{N}$, $\mathcal{N}(M) \cong_b \mathcal{N}(N)$.*

Transition semantics and bisimulation: We define the labelled transition semantics in terms of an early-style semantics. The labelled transition relation is a ternary relation over networks N and M and labels. Labels are on the form $(\tilde{m})l : a!\langle \tilde{v} \rangle$, $a?(\tilde{x})$, or τ. We let μ range over labels.

Definition 8 (Labelled transition system). *The labelled transition relation is the smallest binary relation over networks satisfying the axioms and rules in Table 3 below in addition to the rules in Table 1 and* (R-REP), (R-REC), (R-CONST), (R-EQ), (R-NEQ), (R-SPLIT), (R-GO), *and* (R-NEW) *with* $\longrightarrow$ *replaced by* $\xrightarrow{\tau}$ *and renamed by using the* (LT-) *prefix instead of* (R-).

Table 3. $D\pi^{\text{full}}$-specific transition rules

$$(\text{LT-OUT}) \qquad l[a!\langle \widetilde{v}\rangle.P] \xrightarrow{l:a!\langle \widetilde{v}\rangle} l[P]$$

$$(\text{LT-IN}) \qquad l[a?(\widetilde{v}).P] \xrightarrow{l:a?(\widetilde{v})} l[P\{\widetilde{v}/\widetilde{x}\}]$$

$$(\text{LT-OPEN}) \qquad \dfrac{N \xrightarrow{(\widetilde{m})l:a!\langle \widetilde{v}\rangle} N'}{(\nu n)N \xrightarrow{(n\widetilde{m})l:a!\langle \widetilde{v}\rangle} N'} \quad \text{where } n \notin \{l,a\} \text{ and } n \in \widetilde{v}$$

$$(\text{LT-COMM-L}) \qquad \dfrac{M \xrightarrow{l:a?(\widetilde{v})} M' \quad N \xrightarrow{(\widetilde{n})l:a!\langle \widetilde{v}\rangle} N'}{M \mid N \xrightarrow{\tau} (\nu\widetilde{n})(M' \mid N')}$$

$$(\text{LT-COMM-R}) \qquad \dfrac{N \xrightarrow{(\widetilde{n})l:a!\langle \widetilde{v}\rangle} N' \quad M \xrightarrow{l:a?(\widetilde{v})} M'}{N \mid M \xrightarrow{\tau} (\nu\widetilde{n})(N' \mid M')}$$

The rules in Table 3 are straightforward extensions of the transition rules for the π-calculus [2] accounting for the presence of locations.

Let $\xrightarrow{\tau}^{*}$ denote the reflexive and transitive closure of $\xrightarrow{\tau}$. Moreover $\xRightarrow{\epsilon}$ is defined as $\xrightarrow{\tau}^{*}$, and we write $\xRightarrow{\mu}$ for $\xRightarrow{\epsilon}$ if $\mu = \tau$ and $\xRightarrow{\epsilon} \circ \xrightarrow{\mu} \circ \xRightarrow{\epsilon}$ otherwise.

Definition 9 (Early strong bisimulation). *A binary symmetric relation $\mathcal{R}$ is called a (early) strong bisimulation if whenever $(N, M) \in \mathcal{R}$ the following holds.*

- *$N \xrightarrow{\mu} N'$ implies that there is some M' such that $M \xrightarrow{\mu} M'$ and such that $(N', M') \in \mathcal{R}$*

Networks N and M are called strong bisimilar, *denoted $N \sim M$, if there is some strong bisimulation $\mathcal{R}$ such that $(N, M) \in \mathcal{R}$.*

Definition 10 (Early weak bisimulation). *A binary symmetric relation $\mathcal{R}$ is called a (early) weak bisimulation if whenever $(N, M) \in \mathcal{R}$ the following holds.*

- *$N \xrightarrow{\mu} N'$ implies that there is some M' such that $M \xRightarrow{\widehat{\mu}} M'$ and such that $(N', M') \in \mathcal{R}$*

Networks N and M are called weak bisimilar, *denoted $N \approx M$, if there is some weak bisimulation $\mathcal{R}$ such that $(N, M) \in \mathcal{R}$.*

Some properties of $D\pi^{full}$-calculus: Bisimulation in the π-calculus is not a congruence [12]. The reason is that bisimulation is not closed with respect to arbitrary name-substitutions. This in turn means that bisimulation is not closed with respect to input contexts. However in $D\pi^{full}$ we only require closure under application of network contexts, which we recall from Definition 2 does not include input prefixing. It is therefore easy to show that strong and weak bisimulation as defined in Definition 9 and Definition 10 are in fact congruences.

Proposition 1. *We have $N \longrightarrow N'$ iff $N \xrightarrow{\tau}\equiv N'$*

Theorem 1. *We have $\sim_b=\sim$ and $\cong_b=\approx$.*

3   A Migration Preserving Encoding

In preparation of presenting the encoding of parametrised constants we start by recalling the encoding in the π-calculus [2]. Our encoding is a natural extension of this encoding. We nevertheless preffer to give it in full details since it has not, to our knowledge, previously been done in calculi with spatial mobility.

3.1   On Encoding Parametrised Constants

We refrain from defining the formal semantics of the polyadic π-calculus, but recall that the process-terms are essentially the same as the process-terms in $D\pi^{full}$ without the go?-prefix. The main reduction axiom is similar to the (R-COM)-axiom but without the location,

$$a?(\widetilde{x}).P \mid a!\langle\widetilde{v}\rangle.Q \longrightarrow P\{\widetilde{v}/\widetilde{x}\} \mid Q .$$

In the π-calculus parametrised constants are encoded using replication in the following manner. A mapping $\kappa : \mathcal{P} \longrightarrow \mathcal{P}$ is said to act *homomorphic* on an n-ary operator $\times$ if $\kappa(\times(P_1,\ldots,P_n)) = \times(\kappa(P_1),\ldots,\kappa(P_n))$. E.g. if $\kappa(\ )$ is homomorphic on $\mid$, then $\kappa(P \mid Q) = \kappa(P) \mid \kappa(Q)$. Define a mapping $[\![\ ]\!]'$ from process-terms to process-terms which is homomorphic in all except the following case. Let $[\![A\langle\widetilde{v}\rangle]\!]' = a!\langle\widetilde{v}\rangle$. Then extend $[\![\ ]\!]'$ to the equations defining the constants by letting $[\![A(\widetilde{x}) = P]\!]' = \star a?(\widetilde{x}).[\![P]\!]'$ for each defining equation $A(\widetilde{x}) = P$. The full encoding is given by placing the encoding of the equations and processes in parallel. Consider the equation $A(\widetilde{x}) = P$ and a simple call, $A\langle\widetilde{v}\rangle \longrightarrow P\{\widetilde{v}/\widetilde{x}\}$. The encoding is,

$$[\![A\langle\widetilde{v}\rangle]\!]' \stackrel{def}{=} (\nu a)(a!\langle\widetilde{v}\rangle \mid \star a?(\widetilde{x}).[\![P]\!]') .$$

In the encoded process we can unfold the replication once and perform the recursive call by sending the parameters $\widetilde{v}$ on the channel a. I.e.

$$(\nu a)(a!\langle\widetilde{v}\rangle \mid a?(\widetilde{x}).[\![P]\!] \mid \star a?(x_1,\ldots,x_k).[\![P]\!]) \longrightarrow (\nu a)([\![P]\!]\{\widetilde{v}/\widetilde{x}\} \mid \star a?(\widetilde{x}).[\![P]\!]).$$

Full details of this encoding as well as the π-calculus can be found in e.g. [2].

Consider what would happen if we attempted to apply the same approach on the following $D\pi^{full}$-network.

$$N_1 = l_1[A \mid s!.b!\langle l_2\rangle] \mid l_2[s!.b!\langle l_3\rangle] \mid l_3[s!.b!\langle l_4\rangle] \mid \cdots ,$$

where $A = s?.b?(x).\,go?x.A$. The network N_1 synchronises on s, gets the name of a neighboring location l_2 and migrates to l_2. At l_2 the protocol starts over again, by synchronising on s, and getting the name of l_2's neighboring location l_3. Thus N_1 reduces to $l_k[A] \mid l_k[s!.\overline{b}!\langle l_{k+1}\rangle]$.

Suppose we wanted to use the encoding outlined above to express N_1 using replication in place of parametrised constants. We get

$$[\![N_1]\!]' = l_1[a! \mid \star a?.s?.b?(x).\,go?x.a! \mid s!.b!\langle l_2\rangle] \mid l_2[s!.b!\langle l_3\rangle] \mid l_3[s!.b!\langle l_4\rangle] \mid \cdots .$$

$[\![N_1]\!]'$ can reduce to $l_2[a!] \mid l_2[s!.a!\langle l_3\rangle] \mid l_3[s!.a!\langle l_4\rangle] \mid \cdots$. But now the network is stuck since the encoding of the equation $A(\widetilde{x}) = P$ is not accessible, but remains at the location where the initial recursive call was made.

A solution to this problem is proposed by Hennessy and Hym [4] who encode *recursion* in terms of replication. The idea is that whenever a recursive call is made, a process migrates to a special *home*-location where the body is fetched. This encoding is proven correct in [4], but relies on introducing extra migrations.

3.2   The $D\pi^\star$-Calculus

We now define the $D\pi^\star$-calculus in which we encode parametrised constants. Compared to $D\pi^{full}$, $D\pi^\star$ is a rather restricted calculus. The restriction we impose is that the target location of a migration must exist, and moreover it must also accept entry by the migrating process. This restriction in fact renders the location structure in $D\pi^\star$ *static* (see Lemma 5).

Definition 11 ($D\pi^\star$-syntax). *The processes and networks of the $D\pi^\star$-calculus are given by the following two grammars*

$$P ::= \text{as in Definition 1} \ldots \quad | \quad go!v.P \quad | \quad go?v.P .$$

The grammar for networks is identical to the one in Definition 1.

Structural equivalence is defined as in Definition 3. The reduction semantics is essentially obtained from that of $D\pi^{full}$ with a few modifications.

Definition 12 (Reduction relation for $D\pi^\star$). *The reduction relation, $\longrightarrow\!\!\!\!\rightarrow$, is a binary relation over networks satisfying the rules in Table 1 and Table 2 with the following modifications.*

- *Replace all occurrences of $\longrightarrow$ with $\longrightarrow\!\!\!\!\rightarrow$.*
- *Replace the rule (R-GO) with*

$$(\text{LT-GO}) \ l[go?k.P] \mid k[go!k.Q] \longrightarrow\!\!\!\!\rightarrow k[P] \mid k[Q] .$$

We leave the names of the rules unchanged; it should be clear from the use of either $\longrightarrow$ or $\longrightarrow$ whether we are speaking of $D\pi^{full}$ or $D\pi^\star$. Early strong and weak barbed bisimulation and congruence is defined as in Definition 6 and Definition 7 by replacing $\longrightarrow$ with $\longrightarrow$.

The labels are as in $D\pi^{full}$ in addition to labels for migration actions– and co-actions, $(\tilde{n})\,\mathsf{go?}k, P$, where $\tilde{n} \subseteq \mathrm{fn}(P)$ and $\mathsf{go!}k, P$ respectively. The former means that P is being sent to the destination k while exporting the private names $\tilde{n}$. The latter means that the location k can receive P.

Definition 13 (Labelled transition relation for $D\pi^\star$). *The labelled transition relation,* $\overset{\mu}{\longrightarrow}$*, is defined in the same way as for* $D\pi^{full}$*, with the following modifications to the SOS-rules.*

- *Replace all occurrences of* $\overset{\mu}{\longrightarrow}$ *with* $\overset{\mu}{\longrightarrow}$*.*
- *Replace the rule* (LT-GO) *with the following two rules.*

$$(\text{LT-GO?})\ l[\mathsf{go?}k.P] \xrightarrow{\mathsf{go?}k,P} l[\text{STOP}]$$

$$(\text{LT-GO!})\ k[\mathsf{go!}k.Q] \xrightarrow{\mathsf{go!}k,P} k[P] \mid k[Q]\ .$$

- *Add the rules*

$$(\text{LT-MIGOPEN})\ \frac{N \xrightarrow{(\tilde{n})\,\mathsf{go?}k,P} N'}{(\nu n)N \xrightarrow{(n\tilde{n})\,\mathsf{go?}k.P} N'}$$
$$where\ n \in \mathrm{fn}(P)$$

$$(\text{LT-GO})\ \frac{M \xrightarrow{(\tilde{n})\,\mathsf{go?}k,P} M' \quad N \xrightarrow{\mathsf{go!}k,P} N'}{N \mid M \xrightarrow{\tau} (\nu\tilde{n})(N' \mid M')}\ .$$

The transition semantics makes explicit that migration is in essence a higher-order operation. Thus the definitions of strong and weak barbed bisimilarity are not as simples as for $D\pi^{full}$. The challenges with higher-order communication are discussed in [13] and we follow [13] and use a notion of *contextual* bisimulation. Despite the added complexity following with contextual bisimulation the semantic theory for $D\pi^\star$ remains quite manageable. The reason is that we do not have full higher-order communication where process variables can occur as arbitrary subprocesses and multiple times. In fact, a received process always occurs exactly once as a parallel network in the receiving context. Due to space constraints the definitions are omitted, but it is relatively straightforward to prove that the results stated in Section 2.1 also hold in $D\pi^\star$.

3.3   Encoding Parametrised Constants in $D\pi^\star$

The encoding is defined for finite sets of constants. The main encoding function is given in terms of auxiliary encodings; $\mathcal{P}\,[\![\cdot]\!]$ encodes processes and $\mathcal{N}\,[\![\cdot]\!]$ encodes networks. Let I be an index set for Δ and $\tilde{a}$ a set of fresh names (wrt. to the encoded network) such that the set $\tilde{a}$ is in one-to-one correspondence with I.

Definition 14 (Encoding of processes). *Let a mapping* $\mathcal{P}\,[\![\,]\!]$ *from process terms to process terms be given by the following clauses*

$$\mathcal{P}\,[\![\text{STOP}]\!]_{\tilde{a}} = \text{STOP}$$
$$\mathcal{P}\,[\![A_i\langle\tilde{y}_i\rangle]\!]_{\tilde{a}} = a_i!\langle\tilde{y}_i\rangle \text{ for } a_i \in \tilde{a}\ ,$$

and by asserting that $\mathcal{P}\,[\![\,]\!]$ *is a homomorphism on all other operators.*

The names $\tilde{a}$ on which the encoding depends are the names on which recursive calls are invoked, similar to what we saw in Section 3.1.

Definition 15 (Encoding of networks). *The encoding of networks is homomorphic on restriction and parallel composition and defined as follows on locations,*

$$\mathcal{N}\,[\![l[P]]\!]_{\tilde{a}} = l[\mathcal{P}\,[\![P]\!]_{\tilde{a}}] \mid \prod_{a_i, i \in I} l[\mathcal{P}\,[\![A_i]\!]_{a_i}]\ .$$

The full encoding, $[\![\,]\!]$, is defined as: $[\![N]\!] = (\nu\tilde{a})\,\mathcal{N}\,[\![N]\!]_{\tilde{a}}$, where $\tilde{a}$ is restricted at the top-level to prevent contexts from interfering with the protocol. Note that this encoding does not introduce extra migration. In the sequel we write $l[\mathcal{P}\,[\![\Delta]\!]_{\tilde{a}}]$ in place of $\prod_{a_i, i \in I} l[\mathcal{P}\,[\![A_i]\!]_{a_i}]$. With these definitions we can show operational correspondence and full abstraction with respect to barbed congruence.

Before stating these results we make a few remarks on some characteristics of the encoding. The encoding in the π-calculus is not compositional up to $=$ but it is compositional up to $\cong_b$. By compositional we mean that $[\![M \mid N]\!] \bowtie [\![M]\!] \mid [\![N]\!]$ for some equivalence relation $\bowtie$. Our encoding is not compositional up to $=$ or $\equiv$. Consider the encoding of the network $l\lfloor P\rfloor \mid l\lfloor Q\rfloor$

$$[\![l\lfloor P\rfloor \mid m\lfloor Q\rfloor]\!] = (\nu\tilde{a})\big(l\lfloor\mathcal{P}\,[\![P]\!]_{\tilde{a}}\rfloor \mid l[\mathcal{P}\,[\![\Delta]\!]_{\tilde{a}}] \mid m\lfloor\mathcal{P}\,[\![Q]\!]_{\tilde{a}}\rfloor \mid m[\mathcal{P}\,[\![\Delta]\!]_{\tilde{a}}]\big)\ .$$

On the other hand

$$[\![l\lfloor P\rfloor]\!] \mid [\![m\lfloor Q\rfloor]\!] = (\nu\tilde{a})\big(l\lfloor\mathcal{P}\,[\![P]\!]_{\tilde{a}}\rfloor \mid l[\mathcal{P}\,[\![\Delta]\!]_{\tilde{a}}]\big)\,(\nu\tilde{a}')\big(m\lfloor\mathcal{P}\,[\![Q]\!]_{\tilde{a}'}\rfloor \mid l[\mathcal{P}\,[\![\Delta]\!]_{\tilde{a}'}]\big).$$

Thus $[\![l\lfloor P\rfloor \mid m\lfloor Q\rfloor]\!] \not\equiv [\![l\lfloor P\rfloor]\!] \mid [\![m\lfloor Q\rfloor]\!]$. However our encoding is not even compositional up to $\cong_b$. Suppose in the example above that $P = \text{go}?m.B$, $Q = \text{go}!m.\text{STOP}$, and $B \stackrel{\text{def}}{=} b!$. Now $[\![(l[P] \mid m[Q])]\!] \Downarrow_{b@m}$, but $([\![l[P]]\!] \mid [\![m[Q]]\!]) \not\Downarrow_{b@m}$. In particular this means that the encoding can not be applied to subnetworks and subsequently assembled to form a larger network.

Theorem 2 (Full abstraction). *We have that* $N \cong_b M$ *iff* $[\![N]\!] \cong_b [\![M]\!]$.

By looking at the encoding a tempting alternative, which also avoids introducing extra migration, could be to use the following as the defining clause for migration, $[\![\text{go}?k.P]\!] = \text{go}?k.([\![\Delta]\!] \mid P)$. However, this is not a well-defined encoding since there can be occurrences of go in definitions in Δ.

4 $D\pi^\star$ Is Incomparable to $D\pi^{full}$

In this section we show that $D\pi^\star$ is incomparable to $D\pi^{full}$. We use Gorla's observations in [14] and [15] in order to establish parts of this result. The following lemmas are immediate.

Lemma 1. *Let $N \mid M$ be a $D\pi^{full}$-term and suppose $N \mid M \xrightarrow{\tau}$. Then one of the following conditions holds.*

- $N \xrightarrow{\tau}$ *or* $M \xrightarrow{\tau}$
- $N \xrightarrow{(\widetilde{n})l!a\langle\widetilde{v}\rangle}$ *and* $M \xrightarrow{l?a\langle\widetilde{v}\rangle}$ *(or the roles of N and M are switched)*

Lemma 2. *Let $N \mid M$ be a $D\pi^\star$-term and suppose $N \mid M \xrightarrow{\tau}$. Then the following holds.*

- $N \xrightarrow{(\widetilde{n})\, go?k,P}$ *and* $M \xrightarrow{go!k,P}$ *(or the roles of N and M are switched),*

together with the assertions in Lemma 1.

Lemma 3. *If $N \xrightarrow{\mu}$, then $fn(\mu) \subseteq fn(N)$.*

Let $\mathcal{L}$ be a calculus defined using names from $\mathcal{N}$. A permutation σ is a bijective mapping from $\mathcal{N}$ to itself. In the following Definition 16, Proposition 2, and Definition 17 are adapted from [15].

Definition 16 (Sensible encoding). *Let A and B be calculi and $[\![\cdot]\!]$ an encoding from A to B. Then $[\![\cdot]\!]$ is a sensible encoding if the following holds:*

1. *Permutation preserving: $[\![N\sigma]\!] = [\![N]\!]\,\sigma$ for every permutation σ.*
2. *Homomorphic: $[\![N \mid M]\!] = [\![N]\!] \mid [\![M]\!]$ and $[\![(\nu n)N)]\!] = (\nu n)\,[\![N]\!]$.*
3. *Barb preserving: $N \Downarrow_\alpha$ implies $[\![N]\!] \Downarrow_\alpha$.*
4. *Operational correspondence: If $N \xrightarrow{\tau} N'$ then there is N'' such that $[\![N]\!] \xrightarrow{\tau}{}^* N''$ and $[\![N']\!] \approx N''$. Conversely if $[\![N]\!] \xrightarrow{\tau} N'$ then there is N'' such that $N \xrightarrow{\tau}{}^* N''$ and $N' \approx [\![N'']\!]$.*
5. *Termination preserving: N terminates iff $[\![N]\!]$ terminates.*

Proposition 2. *Let A and B be calculi, and let $[\![\cdot]\!]$ be a sensible encoding from A to B. Assume there is some term N in A such that $N \not\xrightarrow{}$, while $[\![N]\!] \xrightarrow{\tau}$. Then $[\![\cdot]\!]$ introduces divergence.*

Lemma 4. *The $D\pi^\star$-calculus can not be encoded in $D\pi^{full}$.*

Proof. Let $n[go!n] \mid n[go?n]$ be a $D\pi^\star$-network and assume $[\![\cdot]\!]$ is an encoding into $D\pi^{full}$. If $[\![\cdot]\!]$ is a sensible encoding, its encoding is

$$[\![n[go!n] \mid n[go?n]]\!] = [\![n[go!n]]\!] \mid [\![n[go?n]]\!]$$

Since the original network can reduce and by operational correspondence, the encoding must also reduce. This implies, by Lemma 1, that one of the following must hold

(i) $[\![n[\text{go}!n]]\!] \xrightarrow{\tau}$ or $[\![n[\text{go}?n]]\!] \xrightarrow{\tau}$ or

(ii) $[\![n[\text{go}!n]]\!] \xrightarrow{(\widetilde{n})l:a!\langle\widetilde{v}\rangle}$ and $[\![n[\text{go}?n]]\!] \xrightarrow{l:a?\langle\widetilde{v}\rangle}$ for some $a, l, \widetilde{n}$ and $\widetilde{v}$.

The third case where the roles are switched is handled in the same way as (ii) and therefore omitted. Now if either reduction in (i) is the case, then clearly the encoding diverges by Proposition 2. The cases (ii) and (iii) all fails for the same reason. Consider the transition $[\![n[(\widetilde{n})\,\text{go}!n]]\!] \xrightarrow{l:a!\langle v\rangle}$. By Lemma 3, l and a must be free in $[\![n[\text{go}!n]]\!]$. Let σ permute a and l. Then $[\![n[\text{go}!n]]\!]\,\sigma \xrightarrow{(\widetilde{n})a:l!\langle v'\rangle}$ for some v'. If $n = l$ or $n = a$ then $[\![n[\text{go}!n]\sigma]\!] \xrightarrow{(\widetilde{n})l:l!\langle v'\rangle}$ or $[\![n[\text{go}!n]\sigma]\!] \xrightarrow{(\widetilde{n})a:a!\langle v'\rangle}$. In either case $[\![n[\text{go}!n]\sigma]\!] \neq [\![n[\text{go}!n]]\!]\,\sigma$. If $n \neq l \neq a$, then $[\![n[\text{go}!n]\sigma]\!] = [\![n[\text{go}!n]]\!]$ for all σ, which contradicts the fact that $[\![\cdot]\!]$ is permutation preserving.   □

In order to prove the opposite direction we argue by contradiction using that new locations can not be dynamically created $D\pi^\star$. In addition to being sensible we shall in the following require the encoding to be *location preserving* in the sense that $[\![l[P]]\!] = l[[\![P]\!]]$. This is part of our notion of a local encoding which discuss in more detail in Section 5.

Lemma 5. *Let N be a $D\pi^\star$-network and assume the set of locations in N is $\mathcal{L}$. Then whenever $N \xrightarrow{\tau}{}^* N'$ we have that the set of locations in N' is $\mathcal{L}$.*

In Lemma 5 $\mathcal{L}$ contains all all names l such that $l[P]$ is a subnetwork of N.

Lemma 6. *The calculus $D\pi^{full}$ can not be encoded in $D\pi^\star$.*

Proof. Suppose $[\![\ ]\!]$ is an encoding from $D\pi^{full}$ to $D\pi^\star$ and consider the network $N = l[\text{go}?n.a! \mid a!]$. This N can now reduce to $N' = n[a!] \mid l[a!]$. The set of locations in N is the singleton $\{l\}$. Since the encoding is location preserving we then have that the set of locations in $[\![N]\!]$ must be $\{l\}$. Moreover by operational correspondence we know that there is M such that $[\![N]\!]$ reduces to M and $M \approx [\![N']\!]$. Finally the encoding must preserve barbs, in particular $[\![N']\!]$ has a $a@n$-barb and hence so must M. But this contradicts Lemma 5 as the set of locations in M must be $\{l\}$.   □

Definition 17. *Two calculi A an B are incomparable if there is no sensible location preserving encoding from A to B and vice versa.*

5   There Is No Local Encoding in $D\pi^{full}$

A better encoding would be one that avoided the need for the requirements introduced by our encoding and by the encoding of Hennessy and Hym [4]. We call an encoding with this property a *local encoding*.

In the discussion in Section 3.1 we gave an example of a parametrised process which can not be encoded in $D\pi^{full}$ using the same idea as in the π-calculus. The problem is that we need access to the definitions at all locations. This is possible if the set of locations is static. However in $D\pi^{full}$ we can easily define a process that creates arbitrarily many locations.

$$A = (\nu b)a!\langle b\rangle.c!\langle b\rangle \mid a?(x).\,\mathrm{go}?x.A \tag{2}$$

Now

$$\begin{aligned}
l[A] &\longrightarrow^* (\nu b)l[a!\langle b\rangle.c!\langle b\rangle \mid a?(x).\,\mathrm{go}?x.A]\\
&\longrightarrow^* (\nu b)(l[c!\langle b\rangle] \mid b[A])\\
&\longrightarrow^* (\nu b)(l[c!\langle b\rangle] \mid (\nu b')(b[c!\langle b'\rangle] \mid b'[A]))
\end{aligned}$$

$$\vdots$$

For proof technical reasons we need to keep track of migration. We do this by annotating reductions that are migrations. Formally the reduction relation becomes either $\longrightarrow^\emptyset$ or $\longrightarrow^{\mathrm{go}?k}$ for some $\mathrm{go}?k$ and depending on whether the (R-Go) axiom has been used in the derivation. Then replace the (R-Go) axiom in Section 2.1 with the axiom $l[\mathrm{go}?k.P] \longrightarrow^{\mathrm{go}?k} k[P]$ and all other axioms with $N \longrightarrow^\emptyset N'$. Moreover the contextual rules and rule for structural congruence are adapted to allow for the information in the annotation to flow from the premise to the conclusion. If in an annotated reduction $\longrightarrow^{\mathrm{go}?k}$ the name k is α-converted in the corresponding process we must also update the annotation. Note that (R-Res)-rule is replaced by the rule

$$\frac{N \longrightarrow^{\mathrm{go}?k} N'}{(\nu n)N \longrightarrow^{\mathrm{go}?k} (\nu n)N'},$$

regardless of whether $k = n$ thus $\mathrm{go}?k$-marked reductions behave like τ-transitions.

Lemma 7. $N \longrightarrow N'$ iff $N \longrightarrow^\emptyset N'$ or $N \longrightarrow^{\mathrm{go}?k} N'$ for some $\mathrm{go}?k$.

In the rest of this section we simply write $\longrightarrow$ for $\longrightarrow^\emptyset$.

Definition 18 (Local encoding). *An encoding is* local *if it satisfies the following properties:*

1. *The encoding respects locations, i.e.* $[\![l[P]]\!] = l[[\![P]\!]]$.
2. *Homomorphic with respect to* $\mid$.
3. *If* $[\![l[P]]\!] \longrightarrow^{\mathrm{go}?k} N$, *then* $l[P] \longrightarrow^* \longrightarrow^{\mathrm{go}?k} N'$ *for some* N' *such that* $[\![N']\!] \cong_b N$. *If* $l[P] \longrightarrow^{\mathrm{go}?k} N'$, *then* $[\![l[P]]\!] \longrightarrow^* \longrightarrow^{\mathrm{go}?k} N$ *for some* N' *such that* $[\![N']\!] \cong_b N$.
4. *Property 4 of Definition 16.*

Property 2 says that the encoding is homomorphic with respect to parallel composition. Here we emphasise that no new parallel components are added. Properties 1 and 3 are new and deserve some explanation.

Property 1 asserts that we can not add processes when encoding locations. Note that it does not ensure that new locations and migrations are not added.

For instance the encoding $[\![l[0]]\!] = l[\text{go}?k]$ satisfies property 1. Property 1 is related to property 2, i.e. we can not add something in parallel with neither P inside l or in parallel with l itself. The latter is not strictly necessary. In $D\pi$, $l[P \mid Q]$ is weakly barbed bisimilar to $l[P] \mid l[Q]$ so we could have allowed some $l[R]$ to be added in parallel. The proof of the negative result still works. The encoding in Section 3.3 fails to be local on exactly this account. However it seems more general to keep it this way since not all calculi identify parallel compositions of equal location names. Moreover allowing for an extra parallel component implies some technical difficulties since we must also handle the case when such a process is *not* added.

One half of Property 3 prevents the encoding from introducing extra migrations involving dynamically created locations (recall that by property 1 the encoding can not itself introduce new locations). The other half of Property 3 requires the encoding to have at least the same migrations as the original process.

We have already seen that the encoding in Section 3.1 is not local. We now show that there cannot exist a local encoding of parametrised constants in terms of replication in $D\pi^{\text{full}}$.

Definition 19. *Let $r(P)$ denote the replication depth of a process P defined inductively by the following clauses*

$$r(\text{STOP}) = 0 \qquad r(P_1 \mid P_2) = \max(r(P_1), r(P_2))$$
$$r(\star P) = 1 + r(P) \quad r(N \mid M) = \max(r(N), r(M)) \quad ,$$

and by asserting that $r(\ )$ is a homomorphism on all other operators.

Definition 19 simply enables us to count the nesting depth of the $\star$-operator in a process. We are not interested in the global total, but the maximum number in any parallel component. Hence we take the maximum in the clauses for parallel composition and if-then-else. E.g. if $P = \star Q$, where $Q = \star Q' \mid \star Q''$ and $Q'' = \star Q'''$, then $r(P) = 3$. First we note that any process which does not use replication must indeed terminate. This does not in general hold in higher-order calculi and is therefore a point which needs to be checked in $D\pi$ because of the higher-order flavour of the migration operation.

Lemma 8. *Let P be a $D\pi^{\text{full}}$-process such that $r(P) = 0$*

$$\{P' \mid P \longrightarrow^* P'\}/_\equiv \text{ is finite } .$$

Corollary 1. *Let P be a $D\pi^{\text{full}}$-process such that $r(P) = 0$. Then any reduction sequence starting from P can only contain finitely many go?k labelled reductions (up to $\equiv$).*

Next, we characterise those migrations that appear within a replicated process. Let Q^n denote Q composed n times by $\mid$.

Definition 20. *A reduction $N \longrightarrow^* \longrightarrow^{\text{go}?k} (\nu\tilde{n}')(k[Q'] \mid l[P'] \mid M')$ is $\star$-released if there is some $\tilde{n}$, and P such that*

$$N \longrightarrow^* (\nu\tilde{n})(l[P] \mid M) \longrightarrow^* \longrightarrow^{\text{go}?k} (\nu\tilde{n}')(k[Q'] \mid l[P'] \mid M') .$$

and the following holds. $P = \star Q$ and for some $n \geq 1$ we have

$$(\nu\widetilde{n})(l[Q^n] \mid M) \longrightarrow^* \longrightarrow^{\mathsf{go?}k} (\nu\widetilde{n}')(k[Q'] \mid M') \ .$$

where $P' = \star Q$ and the go?k-marked reduction came from Q^n. We call P the $\star$-source of N.

The idea with $\star$-released reductions is to identify those go?k-reductions that are generated by replicated go?k-prefixed processes. An example of a network with $\star$-released reductions is $N = l[(\nu k) \star (a?(x).\,\mathsf{go?}k \mid a!\langle v\rangle)) \mid P]$.

$$
\begin{aligned}
N \longrightarrow &l[(\nu k) \star (a?(x).\,\mathsf{go?}k \mid a!\langle v\rangle))] \mid l[P] \\
\longrightarrow &(\nu k)(l[\star(a(x).\,\mathsf{go?}k \mid a!\langle v\rangle)] \mid l[P]) \\
\longrightarrow^* &(\nu k)(l[\mathsf{go?}k] \mid l[\star(a?(x).\,\mathsf{go?}k \mid a!\langle v\rangle)] \mid l[P]) \\
\longrightarrow^{\mathsf{go?}k} &(\nu k)(k[\text{STOP}] \mid l[\star(a?(x).\,\mathsf{go?}k \mid a!\langle v\rangle)] \mid l[P])
\end{aligned}
$$

The $\star$-source is the replicated process on the l-location in the second reduct. On the other hand there are no $\star$-released reductions from $l[\mathsf{go?}k.\star a(x).P]$.

Lemma 9. *If $N \longrightarrow^* \longrightarrow^{\mathsf{go?}k} (\nu\widetilde{n}')(k[Q'] \mid l[P'] \mid M')$ such that the reduction is $\star$-released and P is the $\star$-source of N, then $r(Q') < r(P)$.*

Proof. (Sketch) By definition there is $\widetilde{n}$ and P such that

$$N \longrightarrow^* (\nu\widetilde{n})(l[P] \mid M) \longrightarrow^* \longrightarrow^{\mathsf{go?}k} (\nu\widetilde{n}')(k[Q'] \mid l[P'] \mid M') \ .$$

If $r(M) > r(P)$ the assertion clearly holds. If $M \leq r(P)$ we also see that the assertion holds since Q' is a subprocess of P with a go?k-prefix consumed $\square$

A process must have a finite description. Hence a direct consequence of Lemma 9 is that no reduction sequence can containing infinitely many $\star$-released reductions. On the other hand we have the following lemma.

Lemma 10. *A reduction sequence with infinitely many go?k reductions must also contain infinitely many $\star$-released reductions.*

Proof. Suppose for a contradiction that the reduction sequence contains only finitely many $\star$-released reductions. Then there must be a last such reduction. Since by assumption there are infinitely many go?k reductions there must be more go?k reductions following the last $\star$-released. This reduction must have been caused by a go?k prefix not under $\star$ (because otherwise the reduction would be $\star$-released). If the reduction was caused by some go?k.P and $r(P) = 0$, then the reduction sequence would terminate by Lemma 8. On the other hand it might be the case that $r(P) > 0$ but none of the go?k reductions can come from unfolding, because then they would be $\star$-released. $\square$

Theorem 3. *There is no local encoding of parametrised constants using replication in $D\pi^{full}$.*

Proof. Assume that an encoding satisfying the properties of Definition 18 exists. We are going to show that if the encoding of a parametrised constant $A\langle\widetilde{x}\rangle$ admits an infinite sequence of migrations satisfying certain conditions, then every newly created sublocation will have lower replication depth. This then means these locations cannot contain a copy of the recursive definition. This then leads to a contradiction of Property (2) of Definition 18.

We consider a process $A\langle\widetilde{x}\rangle$ with a definition, $A(\widetilde{y}) = P$ satisfying the following properties:

1. The body P does not contain more than one occurrence of $A\langle\widetilde{x}\rangle$.
2. There are no subprocesses on the form $B(\widetilde{z})$ in P.
3. There exists a R such that the only reduction sequence involving migration is an infinite reduction sequence with initial segments on the form

$$l[A\langle\widetilde{x}\rangle] \longrightarrow^* \longrightarrow^{\mathsf{go}?k_1} \longrightarrow^* \cdots \longrightarrow^{\mathsf{go}?k_n} (\nu\widetilde{k})\big(l[P'] \mid \prod_{i=1}^{n-1} k_i[P_1] \mid k_n[R]\big) \ . \quad (3)$$

where neither P_1 nor P' calls on parametrised constants and $\widetilde{k} = k_1, \ldots, k_n$.

We know from Equation (2) that such a process exists.

Now consider the encoding of the defining process for $A\langle\widetilde{x}\rangle$, $[\![P]\!]$. By our assumptions about the encoding, we must have that the encoding permits a reduction sequence with initial segments on the form

$$[\![l[A\langle\widetilde{x}\rangle]]\!] \longrightarrow^* \longrightarrow^{\mathsf{go}?k_1} \longrightarrow^* \cdots \longrightarrow^{\mathsf{go}?k_n} \left[\!\!\left[(\nu\widetilde{k})\big(l[P'] \mid \prod_{i=1}^{n-1} k_i[P_1] \mid k[R]\big) \right]\!\!\right] \ . \quad (4)$$

This process must contain instances of replication, for otherwise $[\![l[A\langle\widetilde{x}\rangle]]\!]$ would terminate. Let $d = r([\![P]\!])$. Moreover, it is the case that infinitely many $\mathsf{go}?k_i$-reductions in the infinite reduction sequence (4) must be $\star$-released.

Since P does not contain parallel occurrences of $A\langle\widetilde{x}\rangle$, at most one call of $A(\widetilde{y})$ can exist in R. $A\langle\widetilde{x}\rangle$ must appear in R, if the reduction sequence is to be infinite. However, by Lemma 9, the replication depth of $[\![R]\!]$ is strictly smaller than that $[\![P]\!]$. If we choose $n = d$, we see that $[\![R]\!]$ will have replication depth 0. But then $[\![R]\!]$ cannot contain an encoding of $[\![P]\!]$ as a subprocess.   □

6   Encoding in Mobile Ambients

An interesting question is what it is that makes local encodings of parametrised constants impossible in $D\pi^{\mathrm{full}}$? We can obtain some insight into this by a comparison with MA. We shall show that parametrised constants can in fact be encoded using replication in MA. The complete MA calculus is defined in [6]. In this section ! denotes replication as usual in MA.

Definition 21. *The terms of the MA-calculus are given as follows:*

$$P ::= \mathbf{0} \ \mid \ P \mid Q \ \mid \ (\nu x)P \ \mid \ !P \ \mid \ x[P] \ \mid \ A\langle\widetilde{x}\rangle \ \mid \ M.P \ \mid \ \langle\widetilde{M}\rangle$$
$$M ::= \mathsf{in}\, x \ \mid \ \mathsf{out}\, x \ \mid \ \mathsf{open}\, x \ \mid \ (\widetilde{x}) \ .$$

Definition 22 (Partial). *Redution axioms:*

$$x[\text{in } y.P \mid Q] \mid y[R] \longrightarrow y[x[P \mid Q] \mid R] \quad \text{open } x.P \mid x[Q] \longrightarrow P \mid Q$$

$$y[x[\text{out } y.P \mid Q] \mid R] \longrightarrow x[P \mid Q] \mid y[R] \quad \langle \widetilde{M} \rangle \mid (\widetilde{x}).P \longrightarrow P\{\widetilde{M}/\widetilde{x}\}$$

There are contextual rules and closure under $\equiv$ [6] on MA terms. $\equiv$ is basically defined in the same way as in the π-calculus with the addition of scope extrusion on locations. Locations in MA [6] can be nested and form hierarchical structures. On the other hand in MA a single ambient can not non-deterministically spawn new locations as in $D\pi$. Rather the ambient targeted by the migration must already exist. Recall that Δ denotes the set of parametric constant definitions and define an encoding as following:

Definition 23. *The encoding of parametrised constants is homomorphic on all except the following operators:*

$$\mathcal{A}[\![\Delta]\!] = \prod_{i \in I} a_i[!\text{open } b_i.(\widetilde{x}).start[\text{out } a_i. \mathcal{A}[\![P]\!]]]$$

$$\mathcal{A}[\![x[P]]\!] = x[\Delta \mid \mathcal{A}[\![P]\!]] , \text{ where } \Delta = \mathcal{A}[\![\Delta]\!] \mid !\text{open } start.0$$

$$\mathcal{A}[\![A\langle\widetilde{x}\rangle]\!] = b_i[\text{in } a_i.\langle\widetilde{x}\rangle]$$

The full encoding is: $[\![P]\!] = (\nu\widetilde{a}, \widetilde{b}, start)(\mathcal{A}[\![P]\!])$, where $\widetilde{a}, \widetilde{b}$ and $start$ are fresh.

Proposition 3. *Operational corresondence holds as follows:*

- *Suppose $P \longrightarrow P'$. Then $[\![P]\!] \longrightarrow^* [\![P']\!]$.*
- *If $[\![P]\!] \longrightarrow P'$, then either*
  - *$P \longrightarrow P''$, and $[\![P'']\!] = P'$*
  - *$P \longrightarrow P''$ and for some P''', $P' \longrightarrow P'''$ such that $[\![P'']\!] = P'''$.*

7   Conclusion

In this paper we discussed the expressiveness of parametrised constants versus replication in a version of the $D\pi$-calculus we called $D\pi^{\text{full}}$ and the MA-calculus. $D\pi^{\text{full}}$ as well as MA are spatial calculi with process migration. It has been shown that an encoding of parametrised constants using replication exists in $D\pi^\star$, a restricted version of $D\pi^{\text{full}}$ in which the location structure is static. We introduced the notion of a local encoding and showed that there is no local encoding of parametrised constants using replication in the $D\pi^{\text{full}}$-calculus. On the other hand a simple encoding of the same constructs is possible in MA.

A possible interpretation of our results is that the granularity of migration is governing for the implementability of parametrised constants. In MA entire ambients move, thus bringing along the encoding of the defining equations. This in contrast to $D\pi^{\text{full}}$ where only processes move.

Moreover, whereas the location structure in $D\pi^{\text{full}}$ is flat, the MA calculus allows for nesting of locations and is in that respect more expressive than $D\pi^{\text{full}}$.

The positive result can then be interpreted as an indication that the complexity of the spatial location structure does not affect implementability of parametrised constants. Conversely the negative results may indicate that even in the presence of a simple flat spatial structure, the ability to spawn new locations dynamically prevents distributed implementations of parametrised constants. We believe this is useful knowledge in e.g. distributed implementations spatial process calculi.

We also showed that $D\pi^\star$ can not be encoded in $D\pi^{\text{full}}$ and vice versa, rendering the calculi incomparable. In the introduction we mentioned that the first result can be thought of as a confirmation that it is not possible to encode parametrised constants in $D\pi^{\text{full}}$ by first encoding into $D\pi^\star$ and then encode the resulting processes in $D\pi^{\text{full}}$. On the other hand the opposite assertion, that $D\pi^{\text{full}}$ can not be encoded in $D\pi^\star$, can be viewed as a indication that imposing a static location structure indeed implies a loss in expressive power.

Another aspect we believe is important, is our new notion of a local encoding. The incomparability result relies on a number of requirements defining a sensible encoding. Most of them are widely accepted as reasonable in the process calculi community. Many date back to work relating to the notion of *syntactic sugar* in the λ-calculus and can be found in[16] albeit in more general formulations and primarily discussed in the context of functional languages.

We believe that the locality requirement could be a candidate for addition to the existing set of widely accepted encoding criteria. Firstly it is simple and can be formulated without using complicated difficult to understand techniques. In fact the formulation on surface resembles e.g. the criteria for homomorphism with respect to parallel composition. This has the benefit that it does not rely on too many specifics of the calculi, but rather just on the existence of the location primitive (which is present in many spatial calculi). Secondly it is motivated by issues related to failures in distributed networks. I.e. it seems natural for an encoding intended to work in a spatial network in the presence of failures to require that it can not rely on migrating between possibly remote locations. Again we believe that the locality principle captures this idea nicely. One criticism is that it is not very fine grained. I.e. one could envision parts of the network such as the LAN being more reliable than the WAN. This is not currently possible to express. Moreover although the idea appears intuitively easy to understand, we have not developed any formal framework for evaluating its applicability.

In future work it would be highly relevant to investigate how recursion fits into this picture. The results in Section 3 and Section 6 are established in terms of parametrised constants. It is plausible that they hold for recursion as well. Assume $\widetilde{x} \overset{\text{def}}{=} \text{fn}(P)$. There is then a simple encoding of recursion.

$$[\![\text{rec}\, X.P]\!] \overset{\text{def}}{=} [\![P]\!] \ , \ \Delta \overset{\text{def}}{=} \Delta \cup \{A_X(\widetilde{x}) = P\} \ , \text{ and } [\![X]\!] \overset{\text{def}}{=} A_X(x_1, \ldots, x_n) \ .$$

At least this encoding is not sensitive to the issue of localeness since Δ is globally available. Another highly relevant direction is to apply our notion of local encoding in other process calculi with spatial mobility. Finally this is initial work using local encodings. It could be interesting to see if the encoding criteria could be reffined. A concrete refinement could be to adopt the work of Gorla in [14] which for instance could enable us to encompass the top-level restrictions used in the encoding in Section 3.3.

Acknowledgments. We deeply thank the anonymous reviewers for useful advice.

References

1. Aranda, J., Di Giusto, C., Palamidessi, C., Valencia, F.D.: On Recursion, Replication and Scope Mechanisms in Process Calculi. In: de Boer, F.S., Bonsangue, M.M., Graf, S., de Roever, W.-P. (eds.) FMCO 2006. LNCS, vol. 4709, pp. 185–206. Springer, Heidelberg (2007)
2. Sangiorgi, D., Walker, D.: The π-calculus: A Theory of Mobile Processes. Cambridge University Press, Cambridge (2001)
3. Hennessy, M.: A Distributed Pi-Calculus, 1st edn. Cambridge University Press, Cambridge (2007)
4. Hym, S., Hennessy, M.: Adding Recursion to Dpi. Theoretical Computer Science 373(3), 182–212 (2007)
5. Francalanza, A., Hennessy, M.: Location and Link Failure in a Distributed π-calculus. Sussex Technical Report 2005:01, University of Sussex (January 2005)
6. Cardelli, L., Gordon, A.D.: Mobile Ambients. Theoretical Computer Science 240(1), 177–213 (2000)
7. Ravara, A., Matos, A.G., Vasconcelos, V.T., Lopes, L.: Lexically scoped distribution: what you see is what you get. Electronic Notes in Theoretical Computer Science 85(1), 61–79 (2003)
8. Levi, F., Sangiorgi, D.: Controlling Interference in Ambients. In: Symposium on Principles of Programming Languages, pp. 352–364 (2000)
9. Hennessy, M., Riely, J.: Resource Access Control in Systems of Mobile Agents. Information and Computation 173, 82–120 (2002)
10. Ciaffaglione, A., Hennessy, M., Rathke, J.: Proof Methodologies for Behavioural Equivalence in DPI. In: Wang, F. (ed.) FORTE 2005. LNCS, vol. 3731, pp. 335–350. Springer, Heidelberg (2005)
11. Hennessy, M., Merro, M., Rathke, J.: Towards a Behavioural Theory of Access and Mobility Control in Distributed Systems. Theoretical Computer Science 322(3), 615–669 (2004)
12. Milner, R., Parrow, J., Walker, D.: A Calculus of Mobile Processes, Part I/II. Information and Computation 100, 1–77 (1992)
13. Sangiorgi, D.: Expressing Mobility in Process Algebras: First-Order and Higher-Order Paradigms. Ph.D thesis, University of Edinburgh, Dept. of Computer Science (1993)
14. Gorla, D.: Towards a Unified Approach to Encodability and Separation Results for Process Calculi. In: van Breugel, F., Chechik, M. (eds.) CONCUR 2008. LNCS, vol. 5201, pp. 492–507. Springer, Heidelberg (2008)
15. Gorla, D.: On the Relative Expressive Power of Asynchronous Communication Primitives. In: Aceto, L., Ingólfsdóttir, A. (eds.) FOSSACS 2006. LNCS, vol. 3921, pp. 47–62. Springer, Heidelberg (2006)
16. Felleisen, M.: On the Expressive Power of Programming Languages. Science of Computer Programming 17(1-3), 35–75 (1991)

Biochemical Tuple Spaces for Self-organising Coordination

Mirko Viroli and Matteo Casadei

Alma Mater Studiorum – Università di Bologna
via Venazia 52, 47023 Cesena, FC, Italy
{mirko.viroli,m.casadei}@unibo.it

Abstract. Inspired by recent works in computational systems biology and existing literature proposing nature-inspired approaches for the coordination of today complex distributed systems, this paper proposes a mechanism to leverage exact computational modelling of chemical reactions for achieving self-organisation in system coordination.

We conceive the notion of biochemical tuple spaces. In this model: a tuple resembles a chemical substance, a notion of activity/pertinency value for tuples is used to model chemical concentration, coordination rules are structured as chemical reactions evolving tuple concentration over time, a tuple space resembles a single-compartment solution, and finally a network of tuple spaces resembles a tissue-like biological system.

The proposed model is formalised as a process algebra with stochastic semantics, and several examples are described up to an ecology-inspired scenario of system coordination, which emphasises the self-organisation features of the proposed model.

1 Introduction

The characteristics of the ICT landscape – yet notably changed by the advent of ubiquitous wireless connectivity – will further re-shape due to the increasing deployment of computing technologies like pervasive services and social networks: new devices with increasing interaction capabilities will be exploited to create services that inject and retrieve data from any location of the very dynamic and dense network that will pervade our everyday environments. Addressing this scenario calls for finding infrastructures promoting a concept of eternality, namely, changes in topology, device technology, and continuous creation of new services, have to be dynamically tolerated as much as possible, and incorporated with no significant re-engineering costs at the middleware level [30]. As far as coordination is concerned, this means that coordination models will increasingly be required to tackle self-adaptation, self-management, self-optimisation – in one word, full *self-organisation* – as inherent system properties rather than peculiar aspects of individual coordinated components.

The concept of self-organising coordination then enters the picture, which is based on the idea of structuring local coordination rules – which are possibly stochastic and timed – so as to make interesting global properties appear

J. Field and V.T. Vasconcelos (Eds.): COORDINATION 2009, LNCS 5521, pp. 143–162, 2009.

by emergence [28]. As typical in self-organising computational mechanisms, the most promising direction so far to design such coordination behaviour is to take inspiration from natural systems, where self-organisation is intrinsic to the basic "rules of the game". Nature-inspired solutions have already been studied in the area of distributed computing in general [1], and also in coordination models like e.g. Tota [19] (in which tuples model computational fields distributed in the network) and SwarmLinda [20] (where tuples act like ants in a colony to diffuse in the system).

Among the others, the chemical metaphor appears particularly interesting for the simplicity of its foundation. Chemistry has been proposed as a source of inspiration for works in distributed computing and coordination since many years, like in the Gamma language [5] and the chemical abstract machine [3]. The basic idea of these models is to coordinate components (programs and data) like they were molecules floating in the distributed system, with chemical rules (that consume and produce sets of components) driving the coordination process— also framed as *transactions* as in the Swarm language in [14]. Although this metaphor of coordination is enlightening, we observe that this is not brought to its full realisation, since it does not capture a key issue of chemistry that is responsible of its intrinsic self-organisation properties, namely, the concept of chemical rate and its underlying impact on chemical system dynamics. As many chemical reactions can occur at a given time, system evolution is driven by their chemical rate, probabilistically discharging unlikely behaviour paths while promoting those actually observed in practice. Not by chance, quantitative aspects like probability recently entered the picture of computational models [6], and coordination in particular [7,12,24], as a way of providing a more refined view of non-determinism so as to better model (and simulate) the behaviour of highly dynamic and open systems.

Following results developed in the context of computational systems biology [15], where exact modelling of chemical reactions – given in [16] – is the corner-stone for applying computer models to the analysis of biological systems, in this paper we aim at evolving existing chemical metaphors for coordination, so as to leverage the self-organisation character of exact chemical behaviours.

The concept of biochemical tuple spaces is introduced. In this model, tuples are always associated with an activity/pertinency value (related to tuple weights in the probabilistic extension of LINDA introduced in [7]), which resembles chemical concentration and measures the extent to which the tuple can influence the coordination state—e.g., a tuple with low concentration would be rather inert, hence taking part in coordination with very low frequency. Chemical-like laws, properly installed into the tuple space, evolve concentration of tuples over time *exactly* in the same way chemical substances would behave into a solution [16], hence promoting the exploitation of chemical patterns that make interesting self-organisation properties emerge. Additionally, such laws are extended with a mechanism of tuple diffusion that models chemical substances crossing the boundary of biological compartments. Accordingly, our model allows us to draw a conceptual bridge between a network of tuple spaces and a whole biological system—a multi-compartment system, a tissue of cells, up to envisioning connections with full organs, embryos, or organisms. Studying how biological patterns can be usefully exploited to build computing systems is a subject of ongoing and future investigations (see e.g. [8]): still, we show that simple artificial laws make interesting properties of self-adaptation, self-optimisation, and openness uniformly emerge into tuple space systems, like (to the best of our knowledge) in no other existing coordination models.

The remainder of this paper is organised as follows. Section 2 provides a background discussion for this paper clarifying related approaches. Section 3 describes the proposed model informally first, and then formally by relying on a process-algebraic approach in the standard style of several coordination models languages [29]. Section 4 provides a number of examples that show the behaviour of the introduced coordination primitives and of the chemical reactions model. Section 5 goes into the details of the self-organisation character of our framework, illustrating a case study of "service ecosystems" [30], where the coordination space is shown to intrinsically support spatial competition of services implemented by external agents. Finally Section 6 concludes providing final remarks.

2 Background and Related Work

Our work focusses on a stochastic extension of the basic LINDA framework, likewise e.g. [7,24]: this is motivated by the need of reifying the state of system components into a space (and evolving such a state chemically), hence the tuple space model provides a simple and coherent foundation. In [7] a probabilistic extension of LINDA is introduced where tuples are equipped with weights that affect the probability of their retrieval: in our work we have a similar notion of tuple concentration, though it is used not only for stored tuples, but also in templates to be searched. In [24] an extension of KLAIM is described in which choices and parallel composition can have probabilities, and nodes have rates that model their activity. While we could have adopted some of these features more systematically, the focus of this paper is elsewhere, namely, in the idea of evolving the weight/concentration of tuples over time by chemical-like laws.

The techniques used to realise this mechanism are inherited from works in Computational Systems Biology (CSB) and other related areas [15], like e.g. the well-known stochastic π-calculus [25]. In this language, molecules are modelled as protocol-based processes, while instead we directly model them as atomic data structures (tuples) that change state by rewriting transition rules as in [13]—interestingly, and as will be clarified later, we could use a tuple space as a real-time chemical simulator, observed/affected by coordinated components. Similarly to mobile ambients [9], we model a system as a network of compartments that may allow molecules to cross their boundaries—in future works, also dynamic and mobile networks can be devised as studied in [9]. Tuple diffusion is achieved by an enhanced form of chemical law, which on the right-hand side can also have "actions" that send a tuple/molecule in a neighbouring compartment—such an approach is typical in contexts like membrane computing [23].

Likewise most works in CSB, our model is based on the framework of CTMC (Continuous-Time Markov Chains). A CTMC is basically a graph where nodes represent system states, and edges represent system transitions and are tagged with positive real numbers called *rates*. A rate represents the average frequency of the transition, assuming that the temporal distance between two occurrences of the transition follows a negative exponential probability distribution. This model is a variation/extension of DTMC (Discrete-Time Markov Chains), where edges are labelled with probabilities instead of rates, and transitions do not require a continuous time to occur but are rather discrete—in this model the sum of exit probabilities from a node should be 1.

The motivation for using this particular stochastic meta-model comes from the work of Gillespie in [16], which argued that a stiff solution of chemical reactions can be simulated as a CTMC computational system. Suppose a solution of substances X, Y and Z, with n_x, n_y and n_z molecules each, and a chemical law of kind $X+Y \xrightarrow{r} Z$, meaning that with chemical rate r one molecule of X binds with one of Y, transforming into a single new molecule of Z. The effect of the transition is to decrease n_x and n_y and increase n_z; moreover, the transition dynamics is as in CTMC with rate equals to $r * n_x * n_y$, i.e., the chemical rate multiplied by the number of possible combinations of molecules that cause the reaction— this number would be n_x for rule $X \xrightarrow{r} Z$, $n_x * n_y * n_z$ for rule $X + Y + Z \xrightarrow{r} W$, $n_x * (n_x{-}1)/2$ for rule $X + X \xrightarrow{r} Z$ (since the order of molecules when colliding is not relevant), and so on. In [16], an algorithm for simulating chemical reactions – and hence CTMCs – has been proposed, that is commonly used in CSB. At each step, compute the markovian rate of all chemical laws as seen above, let them be $r_1, \ldots, r_n$ and their sum be S, and apply one of them probabilistically, namely, the probability of picking law i is r_i/S. The whole process is executed again and simulation time is increased by Δt time-units (i.e., seconds), computed as $log(1/\tau)/R$ where τ is a random number in between 0 and 1.

This algorithm is typically used to perform experiments, namely, to find actual instances of system behaviour by simulation. In this paper we propose a different approach, where this algorithm defines an on-line behaviour of the coordination "machine" that runs tuple spaces—it would be the program of a programmable tuple space, e.g., in TuCSoN [21]. Observing a tuple space equipped with chemical rules reveals exactly a chemical solution spontaneously evolving, or when broadly observing a network, a biochemical-like system dynamics. Hence, we are promoting here a view of *coordination through a biochemical-like medium*, envisioning the possibility of enjoying the typical self-organisation patterns of biochemistry—self-regulation, self-adaptiveness, and so on.

For instance a law of the kind $X+Y \xrightarrow{r} X+X$ can be used to model a predator X that eats a prey Y, and accordingly generates a son. As a result, programming coordination rules in terms of chemical-like reactions can also be viewed as describing the behaviour of an "ecology" of tuples, from which we might expect behaviours like partial/global diffusion, competition, extinction, survival, and the like, that can find interesting applications in the context of pervasive computing as suggested in [30]. In a sense, the proposed model could also be named "ecological tuple spaces"—depending on whether transformation laws are designed based on ecological considerations rather than biochemical ones— but when describing our model we mostly refer to biochemistry due to the above background in CSB.

Finally, it is worth noting that our work belongs to a research thread trying to use exact biochemical behaviours to design computing systems, like the study of expressiveness and termination in [10,31], the calculus of nano devices in [13], and the identification of biochemical computing patterns in [8]—in our work however some of our chemical laws are synthetic for they have no natural counterpart.

3   The Coordination Model

Informal description. The proposed model of chemical tuple spaces is an extension of standard LINDA settings with multiple tuple spaces. In LINDA a tuple space acts as a repository of tuples (structured data chunks like records), which is used as a coordination medium provided to external "agents": such agents coordinate their behaviour by accessing tuple spaces through primitives *out*, *rd* and *in*, used to insert, read, and remove a tuple, respectively. Operations *rd* and *in* can specify a tuple template – a tuple with wildcards in place of some of its arguments –, and their execution blocks until a matching tuple is found. This model is used in distributed systems to provide agents with mediated interaction, supporting spatial and temporal uncoupling, and is the basic model upon which full-featured coordination infrastructures have been introduced: industrial-oriented ones like JavaSpaces and GigaSpaces, and research-oriented ones like TuCSoN [21] and Tota [19] just to mention a few.

The basic idea of the proposed model is to attach to each tuple an integer value called "concentration", which can be seen as a measure of the pertinency/activity of the tuple—the higher it is, the more likely and frequently the tuple will influence system coordination. Concentration of tuples is dynamic (as pertinency/activity typically is), and evolves using a chemical-like behaviour, namely, chemical rules can be installed into the tuple space which affect concentrations over time precisely in the same way chemical substances evolve into chemical solutions. This will ultimately allows us to inject self-organising behaviour in the tuple space.

Primive *out* can now be used to inject a tuple with any initial concentration: if the same tuple was already occurring in the space, the two tuples will join and their concentrations summed—chemically speaking, *out* amounts to injecting a chemical substance into a solution. Primitive *in* can be either used to entirely remove a tuple (if no concentration is specified), or to decrease the concentration of an existing tuple—*in* amounts to removing (partially or entirely) a chemical substance from a solution. Primitive *rd* is similar to *in* but it just reads tuples instead of removing them—*rd* amounts to observing a chemical substance in a solution, in order to know its concentration. Note that, if t is a tuple specified by *in* or *rd* operations, a tuple existing in the space is looked that match t as in LINDA: differently from LINDA, matching function is here application-dependent and can be continuous as in [20,27]—stronger matching implies higher probability of finding a certain tuple.

A coordination system is deployed as a set of tuple spaces, with a concept of topological structure—each tuple space has a set of tuple spaces in its neighborhoud. Interaction between tuple spaces follows the *linkability* model [26], and is achieved through a special kind of chemical law that, other than just changing tuple concentration, fires some tuples to a tuple space in the neighbourhood picked probabilistically. This mechanism mimics the concept of biological compartment (i.e. ambient as in [9]), whose boundary can be crossed by chemical substances, and allows us to conceive systems as biological-like networks of nodes—ultimately justifying the term "*biochemical* tuple spaces".

Syntax. We present the biochemical tuple space model by means of a calculus with operational semantics in the style of other works in coordination [29]. Let meta-variable σ range over tuple space identifiers, τ over first-order terms, v over logic variables, r over positive real numbers including 0, and n, m over natural numbers; real and natural numbers, as well as literals, can be used as constants for building terms. A substitution of variables $v_1, \ldots, v_n$ to terms $\tau_1, \ldots, \tau_n$ is expressed by notation $\{v_1/\tau_1, \ldots, v_n/\tau_n\}$, and is applied to a term τ by syntax $\tau\{v_1/\tau_1, \ldots, v_n/\tau_n\}$, e.g., $a(v, 1)\{v/2\}$ evaluates to $a(2, 1)$. The notation is then abused writing $\{\tau/\tau'\}$ for a minimal substitution such that $\tau\{\tau/\tau'\} = \tau'$. If τ' is not a logic instance of τ, i.e., it cannot be obtained from τ by any substitution, then $\{\tau/\tau'\} = \perp$—i.e. the result makes no sense as in partial functions, hence it cannot be used to make substitutions.

The syntax of the model is expressed by the following grammar:

$$
\begin{aligned}
t &::= \tau\langle n\rangle & &\text{Tuple} \\
T &::= 0 \mid t \mid t^{\leadsto} \mid (T \mid T) & &\text{Tuple set} \\
L &::= [T_i \overset{r}{\mapsto} T_o] & &\text{Chemical Law} \\
S &::= 0 \mid T \mid L \mid (S \mid S) & &\text{Space} \\
A &::= wait(r) \mid out(\sigma, t) \mid in(\sigma, t) \mid rd(\sigma, t) & &\text{Actions} \\
P &::= 0 \mid A.P \mid call\, D(\tau_1, \ldots, \tau_n) & &\text{Process} \\
C &::= 0 \mid [\![S]\!]_\sigma \mid \sigma \overset{r}{\leadsto} \sigma \mid P \mid (C \mid C) & &\text{Configuration}
\end{aligned}
$$

Term $\tau\langle n\rangle$ represents a tuple with content τ and concentration value n. Syntax $\langle 1\rangle$ is considered optional, so that tuple τ actually means $\tau\langle 1\rangle$. Note that to represent tuples we rely on first-order terms rather than mere lists of values and wildcards as in LINDA—similarly to [21].

T is a composition (by operator "$\mid$") of tuples residing in the space (t) and tuples to be sent outside the tuple space ($t^{\leadsto}$), called *firing tuples*. L is a chemical-like law, expressing transformation of tuple set T_i (reactants) into T_o (effects) with chemical rate r; note that although not explicitly prevented here, laws whose reactants include firing tuples seem not useful—and hence they might be excluded from a surface language for chemical laws. A is the set of agent actions, including a primitive to wait a delay time with markovian rate r, as well as the set of primitive LINDA operations for inserting (out), removing (in) and reading (rd) tuples to/from a given tuple space with identifier σ. P defines protocols of agents in a process-algebraic style: 0 is the completed process, $A.P$ means executing action A and then behaving like P, and finally $call\, D(\tau_1, \ldots, \tau_n)$ is invocation of a process definition as in π-calculus, namely, a definition of the kind "$def\, D(v_1, \ldots, v_n) := P$" should be provided to give semantics to symbol D. Finally, C is a system configuration, which is modelled as a flat composition of processes P, tuple spaces $[\![S]\!]_\sigma$ (σ is the space identifier), and links between tuple spaces $\sigma \overset{r}{\rightsquigarrow} \sigma'$ (markovian rate r here represents the average frequency at which tuples can move from σ to σ').

Note that all the above elements are considered as terms, e.g., ".$\langle.\rangle$" is considered as a binary functor, and similarly for all the other constructs: hence, substitutions can be applied to any of them.

We assume the existence of a matching function for terms, $\mu(.,.)$, that is not fixed in our model, but can be application-specific. Matching function μ should be such that $\mu(\tau, \tau') \in [0, 1]$: intuitively, matching gives 0 if τ and τ' do not match, 1 if they completely match, and any value in between to represent partial matching. Matching function is in principle orthogonal to the concepts of logic instance and substitution: though, in our calculus the result of $\mu(\tau, \tau')$ is used only if notation $\{\tau/\tau'\}$ makes sense. This abstraction over μ is meant to take into account different matching scenarios that can occur in practice: purely structural ones as in LINDA where there is no concept of partial match, those providing partial matching [18] (as envisioned e.g. for SwarmLinda [20,11]), or semantic matching [2] as would be proper in the domain of pervasive computing.

As typical in process algebras, we find it useful to introduce a congruence relation "$\equiv$", stating when two configurations are to be considered syntactically equal, and hence can be used one in place of the other:

$$0 \mid S \equiv S \quad S \mid S' \equiv S' \mid S \quad (S \mid S') \mid S'' \equiv S \mid (S' \mid S'')$$
$$0 \mid C \equiv C \quad C \mid C' \equiv C' \mid C \quad (C \mid C') \mid C'' \equiv C \mid (C' \mid C'')$$
$$call\, D(\tau_1, \ldots, \tau_n) \equiv P\{v_1/\tau_1, \ldots, v_n/\tau_n\} \quad \text{if } def\, D(v_1, \ldots, v_n) := P$$
$$\tau\langle n \rangle \mid \tau\langle m \rangle \equiv \tau\langle n+m \rangle \quad \tau\langle 0 \rangle \equiv 0 \quad \tau\langle n \rangle^{\rightsquigarrow} \mid \tau\langle m \rangle^{\rightsquigarrow} \equiv \tau\langle n+m \rangle^{\rightsquigarrow} \quad \tau\langle 0 \rangle^{\rightsquigarrow} \equiv 0$$

The former two lines state that operator "$\mid$" is associative, commutative, and absorbs 0 (both in tuple sets and in system configurations): this is used to mean that tuple sets and system configurations are actually multisets. Third line contains the classical rule for process definitions as in π-calculus. Fourth line states that a tuple (even a firing one) can be either seen as joined into a single term, representing the whole substance in the solution, or splitted in two (or recursively more) terms down to tuples with concentration 1. Accordingly, to actually read the overall concentration of a tuple in a system, a partial operator "$\oplus$" is introduced, which takes a tuple t and a space S, and yields a space as follows

$$\tau\langle n \rangle \oplus S = \begin{cases} \tau\langle n \rangle \mid S & \text{if } \tau\langle m \rangle \notin S \\ \bot & \text{otherwise} \end{cases}$$

namely, when a space S is unified with $\tau\langle n\rangle \oplus S'$ it means that tuple τ has overall concentration n in S, since we are sure that S' does not include any tuple with content τ.

Operational semantics. The operational semantics of this calculus is given as an hybrid CTMC/DTMC model, since we need to specify probabilities that should not involve duration as in DTMC, other than a CTMC model for chemical rules. A transition system $(C, \rightarrow, \lambda)$ is defined where transitions are of the kind $C \xrightarrow{\lambda} C'$, meaning that system configuration C moves to C' with dynamics/likelihood expressed by label λ; a label is either *(i)* of kind r, modelling a continuous-time transition with markovian rate r, or *(ii)* of kind $r\star$, modelling a discrete (immediate) transition with likelihood r—namely, the former is continuous as in CTMC, the latter is discrete as in DTMC. More precisely, given a system state C_0, let $\{(\lambda_1, C_1), \ldots, (\lambda_n, C_n)\}$ be the set of distinct couples (λ_i, C_i) such that $C_0 \xrightarrow{\lambda_i} C_i$, then we have three different cases:

- if all λ_i are of kind r_i, then the transition at C_0 is given a CTMC model;
- if all λ_i are of kind $r_i\star$, then the transition at C_0 is given a DTMC model where probabilities are obtained by normalising rates, namely, $p_i = r_i / \sum_{i=1}^n r_i$;
- otherwise, elements of kind r_i are ignored, hence second case applies.

Essentially, this is a CTMC model where labels $r\star$ actually have priority: they define instantaneous transitions that might be in critical race with each other, in which case they are chosen probabilistically. Practically, this model can be approximated as a pure CTMC model where $\star$ represents a very high multiplicative factor—a programming pattern typically used in stochastic languages such as stochastic π-calculus—and hence standard analysis tools can be used.

Transition relation is defined by the rules in Figure 1. Rule (PAR) gives semantics to parallel composition: any subsequent rule is actually local, since any

(PAR)	$C \mid C'$	$\xrightarrow{\lambda}$	$C \mid C''$ if $C' \xrightarrow{\lambda} C''$
(OUT)	$out(\sigma, \tau\langle n\rangle).P \mid [\![S]\!]_\sigma$	$\xrightarrow{1\star}$	$P \mid [\![\tau\langle n\rangle \mid S]\!]_\sigma$
(RDV)	$rd(\sigma, \tau\langle v\rangle).P \mid [\![\tau'\langle n\rangle \oplus S]\!]_\sigma$	$\xrightarrow{\mu(\tau,\tau')\star}$	$P\{\tau/\tau'\}\{v/n\} \mid [\![\tau'\langle n\rangle \mid S]\!]_\sigma$
(RD)	$rd(\sigma, \tau\langle n\rangle).P \mid [\![\tau'\langle n{+}m\rangle \oplus S]\!]_\sigma$	$\xrightarrow{\frac{n+m}{n}\mu(\tau,\tau')\star}$	$P\{\tau/\tau'\} \mid [\![\tau'\langle n{+}m\rangle \oplus S]\!]_\sigma$
(INV)	$in(\sigma, \tau\langle v\rangle).P \mid [\![\tau'\langle n\rangle \oplus S]\!]_\sigma$	$\xrightarrow{\mu(\tau,\tau')\star}$	$P\{\tau/\tau'\}\{v/n\} \mid [\![S]\!]_\sigma$
(IN)	$in(\sigma, \tau\langle n\rangle).P \mid [\![\tau'\langle n{+}m\rangle \oplus S]\!]_\sigma$	$\xrightarrow{\frac{n+m}{n}\mu(\tau,\tau')\star}$	$P\{\tau/\tau'\} \mid [\![\tau'\langle m\rangle \oplus S]\!]_\sigma$
(W)	$wait(r).P$	$\xrightarrow{r}$	P
(LNK)	$[\![\tau\langle n{+}1\rangle^\frown \oplus S]\!]_\sigma \mid [\![S']\!]_{\sigma'} \mid \sigma \overset{r}{\leadsto} \sigma'$	$\xrightarrow{r(n+1)}$	$[\![\tau\langle n\rangle^\frown \mid S]\!]_\sigma \mid [\![\tau'\langle 1\rangle \mid S']\!]_{\sigma'} \mid \sigma \overset{r}{\leadsto} \sigma'$
(CHM)	$[\![[T_i \overset{r}{\mapsto} T_o] \mid T \mid S]\!]_\sigma$	$\xrightarrow{\mu(T_i,T)\,G(r,T,T\mid S)}$	$[\![[T_i \overset{r}{\mapsto} T_o] \mid T_o\{T_i/T\} \mid S]\!]_\sigma$

Fig. 1. Operational Semantics

subsystem C' is allowed to move to a subsystem C''. Rule (OUT) states that as long as a process wants to perform an *out* over space σ, the tuple is immediately inserted in that space, and the process continuation P can carry on.

Rule (RDV) handles *rd* operations that specify a variable v as concentration, which reads any matching tuple τ' with concentration n: the process continuation P carries on after applying substitution $\{\tau/\tau'\}$ and $\{v/n\}$. This transition is discrete and its likelihood is given by $\mu(\tau, \tau')$—in particular, the transition is impossible if τ and τ' do not match, hence the *rd* operation is blocked until a matching tuple is found. Rule (RD) defines an alternative reading style, where tuple concentration is actually specified: in this case, any matching tuple with greater concentration can be read, and the likelihood also depends on the ratio between concentrations of τ' and τ—in particular, the higher the concentration of the searched tuple, thehigher the probability for the tuple to be retrieved. Rules (INV) and (IN) are similar to (RDV) and (RD), but they extract tuples instead of just reading them, namely, they decrease their concentration. Rule (W) states that an agent executing a *wait(r)* simply waits a timeout with markovian rate r, that is, with an average $1/r$ elapsed time according to negative exponential probability distribution.

Rule (LNK) is used when a firing tuple exists in a space σ, in which case this tuple can be sent to any space σ' in the neighbourhood, using the link's rate as markovian rate of the transition, multiplied by the firing tuple concentration. Finally, rule (CHM) transforms tuple concentrations by a chemical law: roughly, if the precondition T_i is found in the space, then the rule can be applied that removes T_i and replaces it with T_o. In the general case where a tuple set T is found that is not equal to T_i, but it rather matches T_i, note that $\{T/T_i\}$ could provide more solutions. For instance $\{t(X)|t(Y) / t(1)|t(2)\}$ could yield substitutions $\{X/1, Y/2\}$ or $\{X/2, Y/1\}$. Note that in rule (CHM) one transition is allowed for each different solution of substitution $\{T_i/T\}$, hence one will be chosen probabilistically depending on the matching function. The markovian rate of rule (CHM) is given by $\mu(T_i, T) * G(r, T, T|S)$, which computes the transition rate according to Gillespie's algorithm. The right factor is obtained by $r * count(T, T|S)$, where function $count(T, S)$ counts how many different combinations of tuples in T actually occur in S, namely:

$$count(0, S) = 1, \quad count(\tau\langle n\rangle \oplus T, \tau\langle m\rangle \oplus S) = \frac{m(m-1)\ldots(m-n+1)}{n!} * count(T, S)$$

4 Examples

Here we discuss some basic examples of interactions between agents and tuple spaces, with the goal of showing some basic features of the model as well as explaining design choices applied in operational semantics. In the following examples, tuples are written using typetext font, and literals starting with an uppercase are supposed to be variables.

Linda default behaviour. First of all, it is interesting to notice that the model presented in this paper is indeed an extension of LINDA. By applying the following constraints we obtain a model that is comparable to standard tuple space models: *(i)* no chemical laws are to be installed into the tuple space; *(ii)* agents execute primitives *out*, *rd*, and *in* by specifying tuples with concentration 1; *(iii)* matching and substitution comply with LINDA template mechanism; and *(iv)* probabilistic information about likelihood of transitions is neglected. As a simple example, consider a system configuration of the kind

$$out(\sigma, \mathtt{t(a)}).out(\sigma, \mathtt{t(b)}).0 \mid in(\sigma, \mathtt{t(X)}).in(\sigma, \mathtt{t(X)}).0 \mid [\![0]\!]_\sigma$$

and remember that when concentration is not specified, 1 is assumed—e.g. $out(\sigma, \mathtt{t(a)})$ would mean $out(\sigma, \mathtt{t(a)}\langle 1 \rangle)$. This configuration models an initially empty tuple space σ and two processes: one willing to insert tuples $\mathtt{t(a)}$ and then $\mathtt{t(b)}$, the other willing to remove two tuples matching template $\mathtt{t(X)}$. By rule (OUT), tuple $\mathtt{t(a)}$ is inserted in the space moving configuration to:

$$out(\sigma, \mathtt{t(b)}).0 \mid in(\sigma, \mathtt{t(X)}).in(\sigma, \mathtt{t(X)}).0 \mid [\![\mathtt{t(a)}]\!]_\sigma$$

Next, either (OUT) fires again or (IN)—(INV) cannot fire since here concentration is 1 by default, it is not a variable. If (IN) fires first, system configuration moves to

$$out(\sigma, \mathtt{t(b)}).0 \mid in(\sigma, \mathtt{t(a)}).0 \mid [\![0]\!]_\sigma$$

since substitution $\{\mathtt{X/a}\}$ propagates to the continuation of the second process. Now, by an (OUT) even tuple $\mathtt{t(b)}$ is inserted in the space: first process is terminated, while second one gets stuck for there is no match for its *in* operation.

According to our semantics, all transitions in this example are labelled 1⋆, but this information is neglected in this initial view. The resulting behaviour is hence comparable to LINDA model—though formally proving equivalence is out of the scope of this paper.

Probabilistic observation. If we relax fourth constraint above, our model turns into the description of a probabilistic version of LINDA, where reading and removing tuples is performed taking into account the concentration of tuples similarly to [7]. Consider system configuration:

$$[\![\mathtt{t(a)}\langle 2 \rangle \mid \mathtt{t(b)}\langle 1 \rangle]\!]_\sigma \mid in(\sigma, \mathtt{t(X)}).0$$

Only rule (IN) applies and two transitions are accordingly allowed, one moving configuration to $\mathtt{t(a)}\langle 1 \rangle \mid \mathtt{t(b)}\langle 1 \rangle$ with label 2⋆, the other to $\mathtt{t(a)}\langle 2 \rangle$ with label 1⋆: this means that the probability of the two transitions is 2/3 and 1/3, respectively.

Differently from [7], in our model *in* and *rd* operations can even specify a concentration greater than 1, which can be used to extract a whole set of identical tuples. In the case of system configuration

$$[\![\mathtt{t(a)}\langle 20 \rangle \mid \mathtt{t(b)}\langle 10 \rangle \mid \mathtt{t(c)}\langle 5 \rangle]\!]_\sigma \mid in(\sigma, \mathtt{t(X)}\langle 10 \rangle).0$$

two transitions are allowed, one decreasing by 10 concentration of t(a) with label 2⋆, the other decreasing by 10 concentration of t(b) with label 1⋆—there is not sufficient concentration of t(c) to match the request.

A final observation style is the one where an agent wants to know the concentration of a tuple (RDV), or wants to entirely remove a tuple by moving its concentration to 0 (INV), which is achieved specifying a tuple whose concentration is a variable. The second case for instance is exemplified in this configuration

$$[\![t(a)\langle 20\rangle \mid t(b)\langle 5\rangle]\!]_\sigma \mid in(\sigma, t(X)\langle v\rangle).0$$

where it is equally probable to entirely remove t(a) unifying v with 20 and X with a, or to remove t(b) unifying v with 5 and X with b.

Alternative matching mechanisms. We now suppose that, for the application at hand, a more complex matching function is provided—the details on how a matching function can be imposed/changed into a tuple space are not discussed here. Finding a general-purpose matching function in the domain of open systems (e.g. in the Web) is the subject of many ongoing research efforts in different contexts [27,22,2,17]: we here consider a simplified example for the sake of clarity. Consider a matching function such that $\mu(\tau, \tau')$ still yields 0 if τ' is not an instance of τ, but in the opposite way it does not just yield 1 as in previous cases, but rather a number in between 0 and 1. The matching function could be based on the idea that each variable more suitably binds with a subset of terms, namely, $\mu(X, \tau)$ measures the extent to which τ corresponds to the concept that variable X means to represent—this mechanism would resemble *is-of* concept in ontology-based matching [2]. As an example, suppose configuration

$$[\![t(a)\langle 20\rangle \mid t(b)\langle 10\rangle \mid t(c)\langle 10\rangle]\!]_\sigma \mid in(\sigma, t(X\_a\text{-otherwise-b})).0$$

and suppose that matching t(X_a-otherwise-b) with t(a) gives 1, with t(b) gives 0.5, and with t(c) gives 0. Then, formula $\frac{n+m}{n}\mu(\tau, \tau')$ associates label 20⋆ to removal of t(a), 5⋆ to removal of t(b), and 0⋆ to t(c)—hence resulting probabilities would be 0.8, 0.2 and 0.

Matching is quite orthogonal to the definition of our coordination model, yet it enables interesting application scenarios based on semantic coordination [27].

Observing a chemical reaction. It is now time to describe what happens when chemical reactions are installed into the tuple space. The idea is that, though all coordination primitives seen above are still supported, the concentration of tuples does not only depend on agent interactions, but it varies "spontaneously" due to an inner behaviour of the tuple space—as typical in self-organising coordination [28], like e.g. in [12]. Suppose an agent is defined in terms of the following protocol

$$def\, D(vt, vn) := out(\sigma, vt\langle vn\rangle).call\, D'(vt)$$
$$def\, D'(vt) := wait(1).rd(\sigma, vt\langle vn\rangle).call\, D'(vt)$$

and let the initial system state be:

$$call\, D(t(a), 1000) \mid [\![0]\!]_\sigma$$

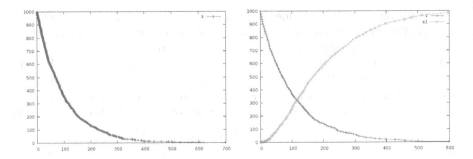

Fig. 2. (a) Example of tuple decay, with initial concentration 1000 and decay rate 0.01; (b) Example of tuple diffusion, from one space (s) to another (s1), with initial concentration 1000, diffusion rate 0.01, and link rate 0.01

Process $call\,D(\texttt{t(a)}, 1000)$ is equivalent to $out(\sigma, \texttt{t(a)}\langle 1000\rangle).call\,D'(\texttt{t(a)})$, hence the agent first inserts tuple $\texttt{t(a)}\langle 1000\rangle$ and then, at an average of 1 time per time unit, it reads the concentration of $\texttt{t(a)}$, recursively and indefinitely—how it uses the result of observations is not modelled. Without any other agent existing in the system, and any chemical law installed, the agent will perceive such a concentration as being fixed to 1000.

We now repeat the experiment by first installing in σ the most simple case of chemical system as described in [16], namely the single chemical reaction $[\texttt{t(X)} \xmapsto{0.01} 0]$, which makes any tuple $\texttt{t(X)}$ decay like in radioactivity. As tuple $\texttt{t(a)}\langle 1000\rangle$ is inserted in the space, two transitions can fire: the former is (W) with markovian rate 1, the latter is (CHM) that has markovian rate $0.01 * 1000 = 10$ and that leads to a system state where concentration of $\texttt{t(a)}$ decreases to 999. According to the Markov memoryless property, the agent and tuple space activities proceed in parallel without influencing each other. On the one hand, tuple concentration fades with negative exponential distribution, up to completely vanishing; on the other hand, the agent keeps cyclically reading such a concentration value, observing its decreasing dynamics. For instance, in the simulation of Figure 2 (a), tuple $\texttt{t(a)}$ disappears after about 700 time units[1].

This basic example finds applications in enhancing tuples with a time-pertinency, namely, they exist in the space only for limited time—depending on initial concentration and decay rate. Note that this idea is a fundamental brick of typical nature-inspired self-organisation mechanisms, like digital pheromones and computational fields [19]—others examples will be shown in Section 5.

Multiple tuple spaces and tuple diffusion. In our approach, the distributed system is dipped with tuple spaces, each residing in a (physical or virtual) node and connected to others according to the topological structure of the network;

---

[1] A tuple space evolution can in principle be simulated using any of the available frameworks for continuous-time Markov chains. For the sake of our explorations we developed a prototype ad-hoc simulator directly implementing Gillespie's algorithm, and charted results using **gnuplot** (2D) and **Matlab** (3D).

agents interact with tuple spaces specifying their unique identifier—the actual position of the agent is of no interest here for we focus on the coordination side. Interaction between tuple spaces in our model is achieved with chemical laws that produce firing tuples. Consider a very simple example of system configuration:

$$[\![t(a)\langle 1000\rangle \mid [t(X) \xmapsto{0.01} t(X)^{\rightsquigarrow}]\!]\!]_\sigma \mid [\![0]\!]_{\sigma'} \mid \sigma \xrightarrow{rl} \sigma'$$

Two tuple spaces σ and σ' exist and are interconnected with link rate rl, the former has tuple $t(a)$ with concentration 1000 and a law to diffuse such a tuple, the latter is empty. One transition here is allowed which, with rate 10, applies the chemical law turning the system in:

$$[\![t(a)\langle 999\rangle \mid t(a)\langle 1\rangle^{\rightsquigarrow} \mid [t(X) \xmapsto{0.01} t(X)^{\rightsquigarrow}]\!]\!]_\sigma \mid [\![0]\!]_{\sigma'} \mid \sigma \xrightarrow{rl} \sigma'$$

Now another transition is also enabled (due to rule LNK) which transfers the firing tuple to σ' with rate rl. This would lead to:

$$[\![t(a)\langle 999\rangle \mid [t(X) \xmapsto{0.01} t(X)^{\rightsquigarrow}]\!]\!]_\sigma \mid [\![t(a)\langle 1\rangle]\!]_{\sigma'} \mid \sigma \xrightarrow{rl} \sigma'$$

Note that in case more connected spaces would exist, one is chosen probabilistically based on link rates.

The overall observed behaviour, e.g. from the simulation in Figure 2 (b), shows that the concentration of the tuple in σ decreases as in decay: all tuples get transferred to σ', though with a small time delay due to the link. When more articulated topologies are set up, it is possible to leverage spatial diffusion of tuples—as in self-organisation patterns of the Tota middleware.

5   A Case Study of Service Ecosystems

As discussed in Introduction, nature-inspired metaphors are promising approaches to tackle the characteristics of modern computer systems, and in particular, self-organisation. Independently of the abstraction level considered in nature (physical, chemical, biological, or social), one can always recognize that above a spatial environmental substrate, individual "components" of different kinds interact, compete, and combine with each other according to complex patterns, but in respect of very basic laws: what is eventually perceived is always a sort of natural "ecosystem" (of particles, molecules, cells, animals, and so on). A similar schema could be used to enact computing systems, through an infrastructure substrate conceived as the space in which bringing to life a sort of "ecosystem of services", intended as spatially-situated individuals whose computational activities, while serving to own specific purposes, are subject to a limited set of basic laws of the ecosystem. The dynamics of the ecosystem, as determined by the enactment of proper laws, will provide for spontaneously enforcing features of self-organisation as endogenous properties of the ecosystem.

Turned in our context, this amounts to disseminate the network with biochemical tuple spaces with proper, general-purpose chemical rules. Services, users, and devices – seen as the individuals of the ecosystem – interact with each other through such distributed coordination medium. Each of them, located in a region of the network, will reify its relevant information through proper tuples placed into the local tuple space, and which will be subject to an evolution of concentration (i.e. activity/pertinency level) that will ultimately result in the survival/extinction of certain services – but also composition, aggregation, diffusion, and evolution can be envisioned – and in general to the enactment of an ecological dynamics to the overall system.

Although deeply discussing and evaluating this idea is out of the scope of this paper, we here present a simple scenario of service spatial competition, which will provide a further contribution to understanding the expressiveness and opportunities of the proposed coordination model.

An example scenario. We start considering a simple scenario in which a single tuple space mediates the interactions between services and users in an open and highly-dynamic system—this examples will later be evolved to multiple tuple spaces. In this context there is no knowledge about which services will be deployed and how much they will be used – i.e. whether and how much they will successfully attract client needs or not – hence semantic matching will be needed to dynamically bind services and clients—following e.g. the approaches in [2,27] based on ontological reasoning.

We aim at building a system manifesting an ecological behaviour, namely: *(i)* services that do not attract clients fade until eventually disappearing from the system, *(ii)* successful services will more and more attract new clients, and accordingly, *(iii)* overlapping services compete with each other for survival, some of them eventually extinguishing. Example protocols for services and clients are as follows:

$$def\,D_s := out(\sigma, \texttt{publish(service(ids,desc))}).call\,D'_s$$
$$def\,D'_s := in(\sigma, \texttt{toserve(service(ids,desc),request(Idc,Req))}).$$
$$out(\sigma, \texttt{reply(Idc,Rep)}).call\,D'_s$$

$$def\,D_c := out(\sigma, \texttt{request(idc,req)}).in(\sigma, \texttt{reply(idc,Rep)})$$

A service agent *call* D_s first declares its role by publishing its service description through an *out*; from then on, cyclically, it will consume requests for its service and then insert a tuple representing a reply. Dually, a client *call* D_c inserts a request as a tuple `request(idc,req)`, and accordingly retrieves a reply. Note that the tuple space is charged with the role of binding a request with a reply, creating tuple `toserve` where the request is matched with the service that is chosen to serve it—much like in service matchmaking [22]. Most notably, the outcome of such matching will ultimately determine successfull services—some services might end up being never exploited, some others may become intensively used.

This behaviour can be automatically enacted by installing in the tuple space the rules shown in Figure 3 and by a proper matching function that – other than binding requests and replies – properly tunes chemical rates. Such rules are described in the following by examples.

(DECAY)	$\text{DECAY} \overset{r_{dec}}{\longmapsto} 0$
(FEED)	$\text{publish(SERVICE)} \overset{r_{feed}}{\longmapsto} \text{SERVICE} \mid \text{publish(SERVICE)}$
(USE)	$\text{SERVICE} \mid \text{REQUEST} \overset{r_{use}}{\longmapsto} \text{SERVICE}\langle 2\rangle \mid \text{toserve(SERVICE,REQUEST)}$
(DIFFUSE)	$\text{SERVICE} \overset{r_{diff}}{\longmapsto} \text{SERVICE}^{\rightsquigarrow}$

Fig. 3. Chemical-like Laws for Ecological Services

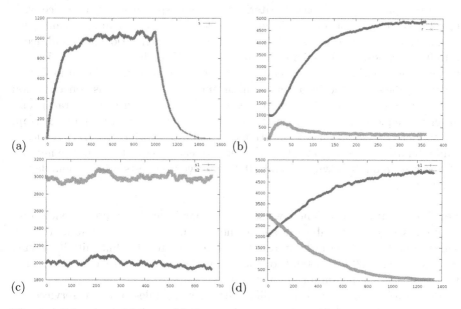

Fig. 4. (a) Service publishing, (b) Service permanent use, (c) Service symmetric competition, (d) Service asymmetric competition

Publishing services. Chemical rule (DECAY) states that any tuple τ will possibly fade with negative exponential dynamics (since DECAY is a variable): the idea is that μ should tune the overall *decay rate*, which is $\mu(\text{DECAY}, \tau) * r_{dec}$—it can give perfect match to tuples that should more quickly decade like those of services, or give no match as in the case, e.g., of requests or replies.

Chemical rule (FEED) is used to insert a service(ids,desc) tuple in the space, and to keep increasing its concentration: this process will stop when the publish tuple decays. Again, the rate will depend on the matching function, and accordingly we denote as *feed rate* of a service s the chemical rate of the (FEED) rule when applied to s. Figure 4 (a) shows an example run with a service inserted into a system with decay rate 0.01 and feed rate 10 (note the concentration shortly finds an equilibrium around the ratio value 1000), and where the decay rate of feeding tuple is 0.001 (feeding ends at about 1000 time units). As feeding completes, and without clients around as seen later, the service inevitably fades until vanishing.

Decay/Service equilibrium. While the publishing mechanism can be useful to bootstrap a service, it is later necessary that clients start exploiting the service, providing a positive feedback that increases and then sustains service concentration. Rule (USE) provides this mechanism along with service-client binding [2]: it takes a `service` and `request` tuple that match, and provides a `toserve` tuple as well as increasing service concentration by one—this rule resembles prey-predator system of Lotka-Volterra equations [4,16]. Function μ can be built to give this rule higher rates if service and request strongly match based on some semantic-based criterion, e.g. how specialised is a service with respect to the request, or which portion of an articulated request it can serve. As an example, suppose that while a service has concentration 1000 and decay rate 0.01, requests keep arriving at rate 50, and (USE) law matches service and request with markovian rate 0.00005: a resulting behaviour is shown in Figure 4 (b). The system reaches a new equilibrium, where service has concentration 5000 (the ratio between rate of requests arrival and service decay rate), and unserved requests stabilise to few hundreds. Namely, after an initial bootstrap, the service concentration is proportional to the rate at which it serves requests, while the use rate is responsible of the service reactiveness, hence of the number of unserved requests—with use rate 0.05 unserved requests remain bounded to few units.

Service competition. The laws seen so far intrinsically support service competition. Consider the above scenario, now with two services that match the same requests: both with decay rate 0.01 and use rate 0.05, but initially having concentration 2000 and 3000. From the example run in Figure 4 (c) we can see that they remain in equilibrium at the initial state.

This equilibrium is however unlikely in practice, unless the two services are really identical, namely, two instances of the same service. In fact, if the services have even a slightly different use rate, then one of the two will loose competition and fade until vanishing, as show in Figure 4 (d) where the two use rates are 0.06 and 0.04.

Competition in a spatial system. Now suppose that instead of a single tuple space, we actually have a network of tuple spaces, all programmed with the chemical laws in Figure 4, namely, laws for competition as seen above as well as a diffusion law for tuples (DIFFUSE). We also suppose that such a law diffuses only service tuples, which is achieved by a matching function such that $\mu(\texttt{SERVICE}, \tau)$ yields 1 for service tuples, and 0 for other tuples. The resulting system can be used to support a pervasive computing scenario in which the infrastructure coordinates users and services, and such that when a service is injected into one node of the network (i.e. the node in which the developer resides), it starts diffusing around on a step-by-step basis, until possibly covering the whole network—hence moving from a local to a global service. Such diffusion would resemble e.g. how chemical substances diffuse into tissues of cells.

We consider as a reference a torus-like network of 15 × 15 nodes—namely, a grid where nodes on the boundary are actually connected with nodes on the other

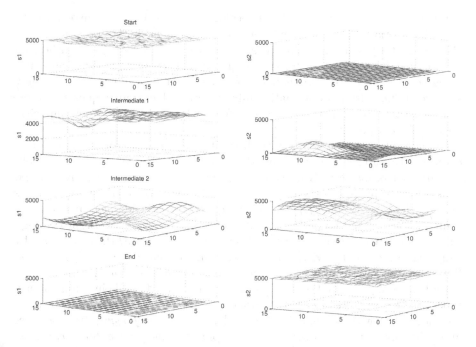

Fig. 5. Spatial competition between two services in a torus-like network: 4 snapshots

side, so that all nodes have 4 neighbouring nodes. In all nodes, requests for using a service arrive at fixed rate, and a service called s1 is the only one available that match them. Hence, in all nodes we have the situation exemplified in Figure 4 (b) where s1 has approximately concentration 5000, in spite of diffusion – we use a high link rate equal to 10^6.

Another service s2 is at some point developed that can serve requests with use rate 0.1 instead of 0.05 like s1 does, namely, it is a service developed to more effectively serve those requests. This service is injected into a random node of the network with very low concentration (10 in our experiments). The situation is depicted in the first row of Figure 5, where on left we have concentration of s1 in all nodes, and on right concentration of s2. As shown in the second row, service s2 starts diffusing, and where it diffuses concentration of s1 decreases— we could expect this behaviour from the experiment in Figure 4 (d), showing that the best service tends to win in spite of initial concentration. After about 1500 time units, s2 is prevailing on s1 as shown in third row, until in fourth row (time 3900) the situation is completely inverted with respect to the initial state: service s2 completely faded away and was replaced by s1.

Discussion. This example emphasises the fact that tuples in our model are used to reify the interaction state of each individual (e.g. service tuples are used as a reification of the service state), and more generally, the set of tuples in the network represents the current "ecological" state of the system, evolved by agent interactions, but also by chemical stochastic behaviour. This state highly affects agent behaviour: for instance, as soon as a service tuple vanishes, its service would be allowed to process requests with decreasing frequency, until being completely unused. Although a service might be willing to increasingly serve requests, it is our coordination infrastructure that binds requests and services, possibly preventing such a service from achieving its goal when implicitly selected for extinction.

In particular, compared to a traditional solution based on standard non-deterministic tuple spaces, we support a significant extent of the following self-organisation properties: *(self-adaptation)* the best service is actually selected for survival, though this choice depends on the dynamics of incoming requests and can change over time; *(spatial-sensitiveness)* the diffusion mechanism makes competition be a spatial notion, possibly regionalising the network into ecological niches where different services develop; *(self-optimisation)* the mechanism by which not all injected services remain active can be seen as a sort of garbage collection that is key to support long-term evolution; and *(openness)* the same set of basic laws are expected to work in spite of the unpredictable incoming of new types of services and request. Other properties that we expect to support by more advanced laws, without changing the model, include: *(self-aggregation)* services automatically compose to better serve incoming requests; *(context-awareness)* services automatically match local contextual information to provide a more specific (context-aware) service; and (*self-healing*) specialised services can be injected in the system with the goal of protecting/repairing the ecology, e.g., to quickly extinguish a malevolent service. To the best of our knowledge, no existing coordination model can tackle these properties in a uniform and coherent way as the biochemical tuple space model does.

6   Conclusions

The coordination model described in this paper can be the basis for building coordination infrastructures for open service systems, where self-organisation policies can be enacted through eco-inspired chemical laws. This infrastructure can be seen as a distributed virtual machine playing the role of an exact biochemical simulator [16], which enacts chemical-laws as if they were a "declarative program" to be executed.

Future work will be devoted to provide a prototype implementation first: a candidate underlying infrastructure is TuCSoN [21], featuring tuple centres that can be programmed so as to handle *(i)* the notion of concentration, *(ii)* the new coordination primitives, and *(iii)* the inner behaviour driven by chemical laws [28]. Other than implementation, we will study the introduction of new self-organisation patterns, like the possibility for services to autonomously compose, aggregate and evolve to win competition, getting inspiration from both the biochemical and ecological metaphors, with the goal of finding applications in pervasive service ecosystems as envisioned in [30]. It is worth noting that in our model designing chemical rules and their rates is a quite critical task, since a slightly wrong design could end up in unusable systems: this is why extensive simulations of selected use scenarios are in general to be conducted at design-time, possibly coupled by some form of automatic adjustment of chemical rates depending e.g. on the system load, which will be subject of our future investigations.

References

1. Babaoglu, O., Canright, G., Deutsch, A., Caro, G.A.D., Ducatelle, F., Gambardella, L.M., Ganguly, N., Jelasity, M., Montemanni, R., Montresor, A., Urnes, T.: Design patterns from biology for distributed computing. ACM Trans. Auton. Adapt. Syst. 1(1), 26–66 (2006)
2. Bandara, A., Payne, T.R., Roure, D.D., Gibbins, N., Lewis, T.: A pragmatic approach for the semantic description and matching of pervasive resources. In: Wu, S., Yang, L.T., Xu, T.L. (eds.) GPC 2008. LNCS, vol. 5036, pp. 434–446. Springer, Heidelberg (2008)
3. Berry, G., Boudol, G.: The chemical abstract machine. Theoretical Computer Science 96(1), 217–248 (1992)
4. Berryman, A.A.: The origins and evolution of predator-prey theory. Ecology 73(5), 1530–1535 (1992)
5. Bonâtre, J.-P., Le Métayer, D.: Gamma and the chemical reaction model: Ten years after. In: Coordination Programming, pp. 3–41. Imperial College Press, London (1996)
6. Bravetti, M.: Stochastic and real time in process algebra: A conceptual overview. Electr. Notes Theor. Comput. Sci. 162, 113–119 (2006)
7. Bravetti, M., Gorrieri, R., Lucchi, R., Zavattaro, G.: Quantitative information in the tuple space coordination model. Theor. Comput. Sci. 346(1), 28–57 (2005)
8. Cardelli, L.: Artificial biochemistry. Technical Report TR-08-2006, University of Trento Centre for Computational and Systems Biology (2006)
9. Cardelli, L., Gordon, A.D.: Mobile ambients. Theoretical Computer Science 240(1), 177–213 (2000)
10. Cardelli, L., Zavattaro, G.: On the computational power of biochemistry. In: Horimoto, K., Regensburger, G., Rosenkranz, M., Yoshida, H. (eds.) AB 2008. LNCS, vol. 5147, pp. 65–80. Springer, Heidelberg (2008)
11. Casadei, M., Menezes, R., Viroli, M., Tolksdorf, R.: Using ant's brood sorting to increase fault tolerance in Linda's tuple distribution mechanism. In: Klusch, M., Hindriks, K.V., Papazoglou, M.P., Sterling, L. (eds.) CIA 2007. LNCS, vol. 4676, pp. 255–269. Springer, Heidelberg (2007)
12. Casadei, M., Viroli, M., Gardelli, L.: On the collective sort problem for distributed tuple spaces. Science of Computer Programming (2009) (in press), doi:10.1016/j.scico.2008.09.018
13. Credi, A., Garavelli, M., Laneve, C., Pradalier, S., Silvi, S., Zavattaro, G.: nanok: A calculus for the modeling and simulation of nano devices. Theor. Comput. Sci. 408(1), 17–30 (2008)
14. Cunningham, H.C., Roman, G.-C.: A unity-style programming logic for shared dataspace programs. IEEE Trans. Parallel Distrib. Syst. 1(3), 365–376 (1990)
15. Fisher, J., Henzinger, T.A.: Executable cell biology. Nature Biotechnology 25, 1239–1249 (2007)

16. Gillespie, D.T.: Exact stochastic simulation of coupled chemical reactions. The Journal of Physical Chemistry 81(25), 2340–2361 (1977)
17. Giunchiglia, F., Yatskevich, M., Shvaiko, P.: Semantic matching: Algorithms and implementation. J. Data Semantics 4601, 1–38 (2007)
18. Madhavan, J., Bernstein, P.A., Rahm, E.: Generic schema matching with cupid. In: VLDB, pp. 49–58. Morgan Kaufmann, San Francisco (2001)
19. Mamei, M., Zambonelli, F.: Programming pervasive and mobile computing applications with the TOTA middleware. In: Pervasive Computing and Communications, March 2004, pp. 263–273. IEEE, Los Alamitos (2004)
20. Menezes, R., Tolksdorf, R.: Adaptiveness in linda-based coordination models. In: Di Marzo Serugendo, G., Karageorgos, A., Rana, O.F., Zambonelli, F. (eds.) ESOA 2003. LNCS (LNAI), vol. 2977, pp. 212–232. Springer, Heidelberg (2004)
21. Omicini, A., Zambonelli, F.: Coordination for Internet application development. Autonomous Agents and Multi-Agent Systems 2(3), 251–269 (1999)
22. Paolucci, M., Kawamura, T., Payne, T.R., Sycara, K.P.: Semantic matching of web services capabilities. In: Horrocks, I., Hendler, J. (eds.) ISWC 2002. LNCS, vol. 2342, pp. 333–347. Springer, Heidelberg (2002)
23. Paun, G.: Membrane Computing: An Introduction. Springer, New York (2002)
24. Pierro, A.D., Hankin, C., Wiklicky, H.: Continuous-time probabilistic klaim. Electr. Notes Theor. Comput. Sci. 128(5), 27–38 (2005)
25. Priami, C.: Stochastic pi-calculus. The Computer Journal 38(7), 578–589 (1995)
26. Ricci, A., Omicini, A., Viroli, M.: Extending ReSpecT for multiple coordination flows. In: Arabnia, H.R. (ed.) International Conference on Parallel and Distributed Processing Techniques and Applications (PDPTA 2002), Las Vegas, NV, USA, July 2002, vol. III, pp. 1407–1413. CSREA Press (2002)
27. Tolksdorf, R., Nixon, L.J.B., Simperl, E.P.B.: Towards a tuplespace-based middleware for the Semantic Web. Web Intelligence and Agent Systems 6(3), 235–251 (2008)
28. Viroli, M., Casadei, M., Omicini, A.: A framework for modelling and implementing self-organising coordination. In: 24th Annual ACM Symposium on Applied Computing (SAC 2009), March 8-12, vol. III, pp. 1353–1360. ACM, New York (2009)
29. Viroli, M., Omicini, A.: Coordination as a service. Fundamenta Informaticae 73(4), 507–534 (2006)
30. Zambonelli, F., Viroli, M.: Architecture and metaphors for eternally adaptive service ecosystems. In: IDC 2008, September 2008. Studies in Computational Intelligence, vol. 162, pp. 23–32. Springer, Heidelberg (2008)
31. Zavattaro, G.: Reachability analysis in bioambients. Electr. Notes Theor. Comput. Sci. 227, 179–193 (2009)

Multicore Scheduling for Lightweight Communicating Processes

Carl G. Ritson, Adam T. Sampson, and Frederick R.M. Barnes

Computing Laboratory, University of Kent, Canterbury, Kent, UK
cgr@kent.ac.uk, ats@offog.org, frmb@kent.ac.uk

Abstract. Process-oriented programming is a design methodology in which software applications are constructed from communicating concurrent processes. A process-oriented design is typically composed of a large number of small isolated concurrent components. These components allow for the scalable parallel execution of the resulting application on both shared-memory and distributed-memory architectures. In this paper we present a runtime designed to support process-oriented programming by providing lightweight processes and communication primitives. Our runtime scheduler, implemented using lock-free algorithms, automatically executes concurrent components in parallel on multicore systems. Runtime heuristics dynamically group processes into cache-affine work units based on communication patterns. Work units are then distributed via wait-free work-stealing. Initial performance analysis shows that, using the algorithms presented in this paper, process-oriented software can execute with an efficiency approaching that of optimised sequential and coarse-grain threaded designs.

1 Introduction

Interest in concurrent programming techniques is growing as a result of the increasing ubiquity of multicore systems on the desktop, and in mobile and embedded systems. Designing applications which can scale to not only the current generation of multicore systems, but also the next, is an important research topic. Process-oriented programming is one concurrency paradigm available for creating such scalable software.

Process-oriented programming employs concurrency as a design tool for constructing software applications. Small independent concurrent processes are composed to form larger components, which through continued composition form the application as a whole. The developer is dissuaded from using forms of sharing which may introduce race-hazards and aliasing errors; they may even be prevented from doing so by the compiler [44]. Instead interaction between processes takes place via explicit communication and synchronisation primitives. These expose dependencies at the design level and permit diagrammatic representations such as Figure 12. While in the past message-passing concurrency mapped processes one-to-one to processors [21, 42], process-oriented designs are intended to be architecture independent [9, 17, 25, 32].

J. Field and V.T. Vasconcelos (Eds.): COORDINATION 2009, LNCS 5521, pp. 163–183, 2009.
© Springer-Verlag Berlin Heidelberg 2009

Parallel execution potential is inherent in a process-oriented design, and is bounded only by the number of ready processes. While the size of components varies with the design style chosen, a typical process-oriented design can have thousands of processes. Furthermore, as processes are created and connections between them made at runtime, truly dynamic systems can be modelled directly as process networks [34, 45]. The explicit transfer of state using communication allows unmodified designs to be serialised for a single processor [39], and parallelised across shared-memory and distributed-memory multiprocessor systems [41, 43].

We would like process-oriented software to execute with comparable performance to a sequential implementation in the absence of hardware parallelism, and automatically scale when multiple processors are available. To make this possible, scheduling and communication overheads must be minimised. Communication between processes must have an overhead comparable to calling a procedure, or invoking a method on an object. Runtime implementations which build communication upon common locking and operating system synchronisation primitives do not provide sufficient performance. Process-oriented software also requires functionality not provided by many lightweight threading frameworks (see section 6).

In this paper we present implementation details of our runtime kernel for realising scalable process-oriented programming on multicore systems. Specifically we contribute:

- Wait-free algorithms for process migration via work stealing [12, 14].
- Automatically grouping communicating processes into cache-affine work units at runtime.
- Multiprocessor-aware interprocess communication with an average overhead of only 140 cycles on modern commodity hardware.
- A mechanism for choice over a set of communication channels inspired by that available on the INMOS Transputer [11, 27], but made multiprocessor-safe.

Our runtime is a C library and provides a C API. It can also be used through occam-π, a concurrent programming language which supports process-oriented design. The occam-π language extends original occam [32] with channel, process and data mobility. It is rooted in the formalisms of Hoare's CSP [26, 39], and Milner's π-calculus [34].

occam-π is being used as an implementation language for complex systems research [7]. A complex system can be modelled as agents, each of which is a composition of concurrent processes. Agents move through and interact with their environment by communicating with it. The environment itself is also a composition of concurrently executing processes. Simulations can scale up to hundreds of thousands of processes [38]. Using the runtime presented in this paper, these simulations can be executed in real time on commodity workstations, utilising all processing resources available.

The rest of the paper is as follows. In section 2 we introduce our lightweight processes and a system for scheduling them across multiprocessors while attempting to enhance cache utilisation. Section 3 describes communication channels, which can be used to pass information between processes executing on the same processor or separate processors in a shared-memory system. Primitives for choice, protecting shared resources and synchronising large numbers of processes are discussed in section 4. Finally an evaluation of performance comparing a sample set of applications implemented using other concurrency frameworks is presented in section 5. Related work is presented in section 6. Our conclusions and details of possible future work are in sections 7 and 8.

2   Processes

In this section we describe our runtime's cooperative scheduling model for concurrent processes. As the fundamental building blocks of process-oriented software, processes must be lightweight. Our design is intended to minimise context-switch times and memory usage, as well as exploit cache affinity and hardware parallelism.

For reference in later sections we must first describe how processes are represented by the scheduler kernel. Each process has a *process descriptor* used to store state when descheduled or performing certain kernel calls. The descriptor can be allocated statically on the process stack, or when state does not need to persist across kernel calls it may be allocated dynamically at the point of call. In either case, the size of the process descriptor is eight machine words (32 bytes on a 32-bit machine). This minimal memory overhead makes the creation of very large numbers of processes practical.

The process descriptor contains the following elements:

Alternation State	Priority and Affinity Mask
Communication Data Pointer	Stored Instruction Pointer
Queue Link Pointer	Stored Stack Pointer

2.1   Scheduling

Our scheduling model is divided into uniprocessor and multiprocessor components. In the next three sections we focus on uniprocessor scheduling. We also explain how processes can be grouped to enhance cache-affinity.

For each physical processor in the host system a scheduler instance, a *logical processor*, is started. The logical processor contains a *run queue*, which is a linked list of *batches*. Batches are in turn linked lists of process descriptors, linked using the `Queue Link Pointer` field. An overview of this structure can be seen in Figure 1.

The scheduler executes each batch by moving the processes it contains to its *active queue*. A *dispatch count* is calculated based on the number of processes in the batch (multiplied by a constant) and bounded by the *batch dispatch limit*. The dispatch count is decremented each time a process is taken from the active queue and executed. When the dispatch count reaches zero, and the active queue is not empty, the current active queue is stored in to a new batch which is added to the end of the run queue.

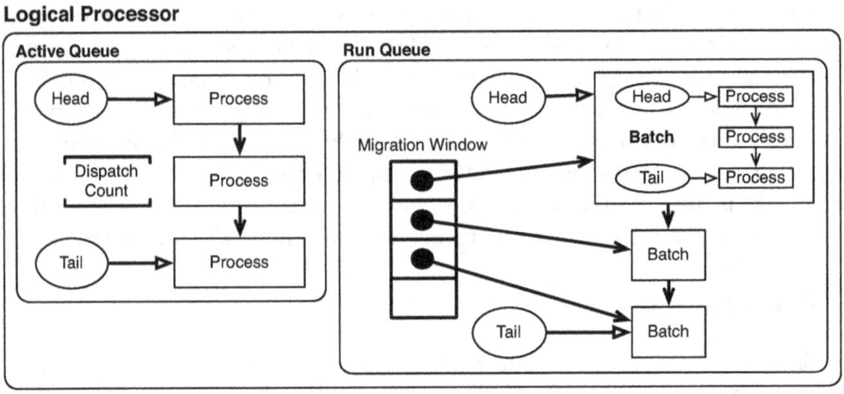

Logical Processor

Fig. 1. A logical processor instance schedules batches of processes on each physical processor. Batches in the migration window can be stolen by other logical processors.

Batching. As outlined above, batches are the base unit of work stored in scheduler data structures, and also for migration (see section 2.2). Batches address the issue of cache thrashing which can occur with process-oriented designs. It is highly probable that with a large number of processes switched frequently, the working set will exceed the processor's cache size. Processes and their data will be drawn into cache only to be rapidly evicted again, serving few or no hits. Modern processor architectures rely on cache to compensate for the high-latency of system memory, so sidelining the cache will severely restrict performance. The solution is to reduce the size of the working set by minimising the memory overheads on processes and partitioning the run queue. Vella proposed and experimented with dividing the run queue into batches of processes [14, 43]. Each batch is executed multiple times before moving on to the next. Relatively small batches fit well within the processor cache. Successive executions permit cache utilisation, thus improving performance.

Our scheduler attempts to group processes into the same batch when they communicate or synchronise with each other. By forming batches in this way, processes which communicate frequently are scheduled on the same processor, reducing interprocessor traffic. This is an improvement to Vella's techniques which used fixed-size batches determined by the developer and compile-time analysis. Our variable-size batches are formed and split automatically using runtime heuristics.

Following a context switch, if the dispatch count is not zero, then the next process on the active queue is dispatched. If not, then the scheduler restarts with a new batch. Context switches occur under two conditions. Most commonly, the current process blocks on a communication or synchronisation primitive and is descheduled. Alternatively, a process may cooperatively yield to the scheduler, in which case it is placed at the end of the active queue. With the exception noted below, processes rescheduled by the currently executing process, for example by the completion of communication, are also placed on the end of the active queue. It is this action which draws related processes into the same batch.

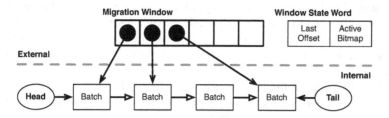

Fig. 2. A fixed-size migration window array allows one logical processor to "steal" batches from another

Batch Size. If processes are always drawn into a batch during creation and communication, then one batch will eventually grow to encompass all processes in the system. This will prevent batching from having caching benefits as the working set will contain all active processes. Therefore a mechanism is required to prevent batches growing too large and to separate processes which lose association.

We observe that in high valency subgraphs of a process-oriented program network, there will be points when only one process in the subgraph is active. This process reschedules other processes in the subgraph which may then in turn become the only active process. Based on this observation we state that if while executing a batch there is a point at which only one process is active then that batch is probably optimal, i.e. contains only one subgraph. Conversely batches which never meet this condition during execution should be *split*. Batches are split by placing the head process of the active queue in one batch, and the remainder in another. This is a unit-time operation, and so can be carried out frequently. Repeated execution and split cycles quickly reduce large and unrelated batches to small related process subgraphs. Erroneous splits will quickly reform based on the other scheduling rules.

Additional mechanisms to control batch size can be introduced by modifying the dispatch count in response to specific events. Process creation is one example. During process creation the new process is placed on the end of the active queue. Process creation does not cause a context switch; however, the runtime kernel decrements and tests the dispatch count. This prevents the batch size exceeding the dispatch count. Furthermore, if the dispatch count reaches zero and the aforementioned conditions for batch splitting are met, then the process creating new processes will be split into a separate batch from the newly created processes. The newly created batch is then free to migrate. Thus a process spawning a large number of children may continue to execute while its children begin execution on other logical processors in the system.

2.2   Process Migration

In this section we describe how logical processors interact as part of a multiprocessor system. In particular, we give details of our algorithms for wait-free work stealing.

Amdahl's law [6] states that for a *fixed* problem size, the total parallel speed up is limited by the sequential overhead. Hence when scheduling large numbers of processes on a multicore system, a single locked run queue represents a scalability bottleneck [28]. For this reason we do not use a global run queue in our runtime design.

Work is distributed between logical processors via migration. Processes are free to migrate between logical processors, except where restricted by an explicit affinity setting. Migration occurs in two circumstances:

1. A process which blocks during communication or synchronisation and is descheduled on one logical processor can be rescheduled by a process executing on a different logical processor. Unless prohibited by affinity settings, the rescheduled process continues execution on the rescheduling logical processor.
2. A logical processor which runs out of batches to execute may *steal* batches from other logical processors [12, 14].

The first case occurs as part of the communication and synchronisation algorithms outlined in sections 3 and 4. The second case is the mechanism by which work is spread across the system. It is further underpinned by the observation that independent long-running subgraphs of processes will tend to be split into separate batches, which can be stolen by idle logical processors.

The run queue of each logical processor is private and cannot be accessed by other scheduler instances. To allow batch migration, a fixed-size window onto the end of each run queue provides access to other logical processors. The fixed size of the window allows it to be manipulated using wait-free algorithms [23, 24]. These provide freedom from starvation and bounded completion when contention arises, improving scalability over locks.

Lock-free and wait-free algorithms are often complex to implement and rely on expensive atomic memory operations such as *compare-and-swap* [10]. Despite this, efficient lock-free algorithms are more scalable than their lock-based counterparts [18]. Hence our decision to refine existing wait-free work-stealing for using in our scheduler [12, 14].

Figure 2 shows the relationship of the migration window to the run queue. There are three algorithms for accessing the migration window: local enqueue, local dequeue, and remote dequeue.

Local Enqueue. Figure 3 shows the algorithm used to place a batch onto the run queue of a logical processor and make it visible in the migration window.

Typically, internal operations on the window will be more common than external operations, therefore we decided to optimise for this case rather than the contended case. The effect of this optimisation is that the final step of the algorithm can produce corruption of the window state word. In the event of corruption the window will appear to external logical processors to contain more batches than it does; however, this does not affect correct operation of the external dequeue algorithm (only its operating efficiency). The result is an algorithm with a deterministic execution time and only one expensive atomic operation.

1. Link the batch into the run queue linked list.
2. Load the window state word (see Figure 2).
3. Generate a new offset by incrementing the last offset, handling roll over where appropriate.
4. Record the generated offset into the batch data structure.
5. Atomically swap the batch pointer with the window entry at the generated offset.
6. If the result of the swap is not null, then a batch has been knocked out of the window; clear its stored offset to indicate it is no longer part of the window.
7. Update the window state word with the generated offset and active bitmap. This update is done with a blind write, and thus may overwrite updates from external dequeues.

Fig. 3. Migration window local enqueue algorithm

1. Remove the head batch from the run queue linked list.
2. If the batch has no stored window offset then the dequeue is complete (the batch is not in the window).
3. Atomically swap null with the migration window entry associated with the batch.
4. If the result is null then the batch has been *stolen* by an external scheduler. It is placed on a *laundry queue* on the logical processor for later cleanup. Dequeue of this batch fails, and we must restart the algorithm at step 1.
5. The bitmap in the window state word is updated to clear the associated bit. As with the enqueue algorithm, this occurs via a blind write.

Fig. 4. Migration window local dequeue algorithm

Local Dequeue. To dequeue a batch from its run queue, a logical processor uses the algorithm in Figure 4.

While the dequeue algorithm may fail and have to restart, it is bounded by the number of batches enqueued on the logical processor. In the worst case, every batch may have been stolen and the scheduler must scan every batch to discover this. Local scanning does not, however, create contention with other logical processors, except for underlying system resources such as the memory bus.

Remote Dequeue. When one logical processor attempts to steal work from the migration window of another, it does so using the algorithm in Figure 5. This algorithm requires only two atomic operations in the optimal case.

Having migrated a batch the logical processor copies the contents to a new local batch data structure and marks the original batch as clean and discards the pointer to it. The originating logical processor will later collect the original batch structure and reuse it. This allows each logical processor to maintain its own pool of batch structures, and minimises cache ping-pong (inverting the scheme creates higher cache traffic).

1. Load the window state word, creating a local copy.
2. Rotate the active bitmap by the last offset.
3. Scan the bitmap to select an entry to steal. If the bitmap is empty, migration fails.
4. Atomically swap the window entry with null.
5. If the result is null, clear the associated bitmap bit and restart at step 3.
6. Atomically clear the window state word bitmap bit; dequeue succeeds and the result of the atomic swap is the stolen batch.
7. A local copy of the stolen batch is created, and the original batch marked clean and its reference discarded.

Fig. 5. Migration window remote dequeue (theft) algorithm

3   Communication

Interprocess communication is central to process-oriented programming, for sharing state and synchronising computation. The efficiency of communication therefore directly affects the performance of process-oriented designs.

Our runtime kernel provides a single basic communication primitive for processes to exchange data: point-to-point synchronised channels. Synchronised channels require no buffers and data is copied or moved (depending on the mode of operation) directly between the source and destination processes. Buffered channels can be constructed efficiently by placing buffer processes between communicating processes. Transactions involving may parties sharing a channel are implemented by associating the channel with a mutual exclusion lock (see section 4).

1. Read the channel word.
2. If it is null or the alternation bit is set (the other party is waiting on multiple channels):
   (a) Store the process state in the process descriptor (instruction pointer, etc.).
   (b) Store the destination or source buffer pointer in the process descriptor (`Communication Data Pointer`).
   (c) Atomically swap the process descriptor with the channel word.
   (d) If the result is not null, and the alternation bit is not set, then the read at step 1 was stale; jump to step 3.
   (e) If the alternation bit is set on the result, then trigger the event (using algorithm in Figure 10).
   (f) A context switch occurs and a new process to execute is selected as described in section 2.
3. The channel word is not null, hence a process is blocked on it.
4. Load the destination or source buffer pointer from the blocked process descriptor.
5. Copy data or move references and ownership.
6. Reset the channel word to null.
7. Reschedule the process blocked on the channel.

Fig. 6. Channel communication algorithm

Operations for channel input and output take a source or destination buffer and a size in bytes to copy. Alternatively the source and destination may be a reference to a memory object allocated through the runtime kernel, in which case the reference is moved between the processes together with ownership of the object.

A channel is represented by a single machine word. The word stores a pointer to the process descriptor (section 2), a structure guaranteed to be word-aligned. The lowest order bits of the word also carry state information about the process descriptor. For the algorithm which follows only the *alternation bit* is relevant. It indicates whether the process descriptor stored in the channel is *blocked* on this channel or *waiting* on a number of channels and events (see section 4.1).

Basic channel communication, regardless of direction, is performed using the algorithm in Figure 6. Using this algorithm the second process to reach the channel completes the synchronisation and thus the communication. This results in, typically, only one of the two processes performing an expensive atomic operation.

4   Synchronisation

In addition to communication, processes often need to synchronise in ways which do not involve data exchange. This section describes additional synchronisation primitives supported by our runtime.

4.1   Alternation

For many purposes, blocking channel communication is sufficient; however, processes often need to choose between a number of channels and other events. Our runtime kernel supports choice over a number of channels and timer events: we call this *alternation*. occam-π supports this via an ALT language construct.

Alternation allows a process to wait for one or more of a set of channels to become ready. When an element of the waited set becomes ready, the process is rescheduled and can make a choice as to which channel to communicate with. This is similar to the POSIX select system call.

In this section we present algorithms designed for one process waiting on a set of channels, while other processes sharing those channels commit. This constraint is enforced by the present version of the occam-π language and inherited from the original occam language. More general synchronisation algorithms are part of our ongoing research.

Alternation consists of the following steps:

Initialisation. The Alternation State field of the process descriptor is initialised. The alternation state consists of:

- *flags* indicating what stage of alternation the process is in. The initial flags are enabling and not ready.

1. Read the channel word.
2. If the channel word is not null, then atomically clear the **not ready** flag of the alternation state. The enable operation completes indicating the channel is ready.
3. Atomically swap a pointer to the process descriptor with the *alternation bit* set into the channel word.
4. If the result is not null, then the value in step 1 was stale. Write the result back to the channel word and continue as in step 2.
5. Atomically increment the alternation state reference count.

Fig. 7. Channel enable algorithm

1. Read the channel word.
2. If it does not contain a pointer to the process descriptor of the alternating process, then the channel is ready. The operation returns indicating the channel is ready.
3. Atomically compare-and-swap null to the channel, if this fails then the channel just became ready; the algorithm completes as in step 2.
4. Channel is not ready, decrement the reference count in the **Alternation State**.
5. Return value indicates channel not ready.

Fig. 8. Channel disable algorithm

1. Read the reference count of the **Alternation State**.
2. If the reference count is one then alternation is finalised; leave algorithm.
3. Save the process state as if to context switch.
4. Atomically decrement and test the reference count.
5. If the reference count does not reach zero then context switch.

Fig. 9. Alternation finalisation algorithm

1. Read the **Alternation State** of the process descriptor to trigger.
2. Generate a new state with the **not ready** and **waiting** flags cleared, and the reference count decremented by one.
3. Use a compare-and-swap operation to replace the **Alternation State**.
4. If the operation fails restart at step 1.
5. If the original state had the **waiting** flag set, or the *new* reference count is zero, then reschedule the process.

Fig. 10. Event trigger algorithm

- a *reference count* which tracks the number of pointers to the process descriptor, initially one. When a logical processor triggers an event which is part of an alternation it takes one of these references. The alternation only completes when all references have been counted back through the disable algorithm or via event triggers.

Channel Enabling. Each channel a process alternates over is enabled using the algorithm in Figure 7.

Waiting for Events. Once the process has enabled all the events it makes a kernel call to wait. An atomic compare-and-swap is used to clear the `enabling` and `not ready` flags, and set the `waiting` flag. If the compare-and-swap succeeds then the process is descheduled and a context switch occurs. Failure indicates that an event has become ready, in which case the `enabling` flag is atomically cleared and execution of the process continues.

Channel Disabling. Having been woken up, the process disables channels using the algorithm in Figure 8.

Finalisation. Having disabled all channels, the alternation is finalised using the algorithm in Figure 9. This completes the alternation and communication with any ready channels may take place.

Event Trigger Algorithm. Whenever a logical processor needs to signal an alternating process that an event has become ready, it executes the *event trigger algorithm* in Figure 10. This is the algorithm referenced at step 2(e) of the basic channel communication algorithm in Figure 6.

4.2   Mutual Exclusion

Section 3 describes communication channels capable of synchronous point-to-point exchanges involving a pairs of processes. As developers, we often need to have multiple communication peers using the same channel. This is particularly useful for implementing the deadlock-free client-server design pattern [47], in which a number of clients communicate with a single server over channels.

To support this functionality our runtime provides mutual exclusion locks, which can be associated with the channel directions. This allows ordered multi-access channels to be constructed. The lock *claim* and *release* algorithms are non-blocking and prevent starvation using FIFO queuing. Importantly, the occam-π compiler enforces claim and release semantics on these locks, so that an application developer cannot forget to release the channel lock.

4.3   Barriers

Our runtime also supports a barrier synchronisation type. Processes can *enroll*, *resign* and *synchronise* on such barriers. Processes synchronising on a barrier are blocked until all other processes enrolled on the barrier are also synchronising. Barriers may also be communicated by reference over channels, atomically enrolling the receiver as part of the communication; this permits semantics such as those described by Welch and Barnes [46].

Barriers of this type are useful in implementing agent simulations. Each agent is enrolled on a barrier and synchronises on it to maintain time-step with the other agents in the simulation. With many thousands of agents synchronising, the performance of barrier operations is critical. It is also important to minimise the time between barrier completion and returning to the state where all enrolled processes are scheduled for execution across available logical processors.

5   Performance

In this section we present preliminary results from a number of benchmarks we have developed to test and compare the performance of our runtime. The source codes for these benchmarks are publicly available [2].

All our benchmarks were performed on an eight core Intel Xeon workstation composed of two E5320 quad-core processors running at 1.86GHz. Pairs of cores share 4MiB of L2 cache, giving a total of 16MiB L2 cache across eight cores. For all tests the workstation ran Linux 2.6.25 (with Gentoo r7 patches). Where appropriate, the maxcpus boot time flag was used to control the number of available processor cores.

Comparison of our results was performed by close reimplementation of our benchmarks using multiple languages and concurrency frameworks:

- *CCSP C* - our runtime programmed using its C API.
- *CCSP occam-π* - our runtime programmed using the occam-π.
- *Erlang* - a functional programming language with asynchronous message passing [1]. We used version 5.6.3 with HiPE [35].
- *Haskell* - a functional programming language with lightweight threads and one-place buffered channels provided by the MVar primitive. We used GHC version 6.8.2 [22].
- *pthread C* - POSIX threads accessed via the GNU C library. Mutual exclusion (pthread_mutex_t) and condition variables (pthread_cond_t) are use to construct one-place buffered communication channels.

5.1   Process Ring

To examine communication overheads, we construct a ring of n *element* processes, and one *initiator* process. Element processes loop: they receive an integer token from the previous process in the ring, increment it, then send it on to the next process. The initiator, adds tokens, counts them passing and after a given count removes them from the ring. By increasing the number of tokens "in flight" around the ring, we increase the number of potentially concurrently executing processes.

Given the time taken for a single token to circulate the ring we can estimate the average communication time of each language runtime as $time \div ((elements + 1) \times roundtrips)$. For all our examples, there are 255 element processes and tokens

---

[1] We have not forced synchronised communications, but instead we coerced our designs to function with asynchronous messaging. This should be a performance benefit for Erlang.

Table 1. Communication times, calculated using process ring results

Implementation	1-core (ns)	8-core (ns)
CCSP C	73	75
CCSP occam-π	46	39
Erlang	1697	1675
Haskell	269	9892
pthread C	5013	3485

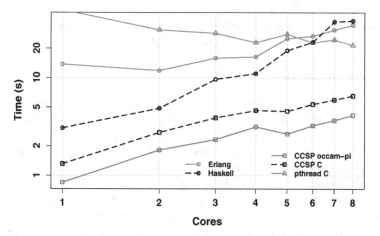

Fig. 11. With 64 tokens in the process ring, we increase the number of processor cores

make 1024 round trips. With 255 elements it is likely that all processes will fit within the processor caches, allowing us to examine the best-case communication time.

Table 1 shows communication times in nanoseconds. These are based on the circulation of a single token when one core or eight cores enabled.

The communication time for Erlang and our runtime are relatively unaffected by the number of processor cores. While both CCSP C and CCSP occam-π implementations use the same runtime, the occam-π compiler caches scheduling pointers in registers, reducing the kernel call overhead. This explains the 30ns difference in the results.

POSIX threads performance is noticeably improved by more cores. We speculate that threads are being given processor affinity by the Linux scheduler. This then improves performance as interprocessor communication via processor caches is faster than Linux's context-switch.

Haskell performance degrades significantly with the addition of cores. We suspect this reflect internal contention exposed by multiple processors accessing the Haskell runtime in parallel.

The plot in Figure 11 shows the time taken for 1024 circulations of 64 concurrent tokens as the number of processor cores is increased. With the exception of POSIX threads, all the implementations show decreased performance with increasing numbers of cores. This reflects the fact that, for user processes, communicating between processor cores is more expensive than simulated communication on the same core. As the number of concurrent processes increases, they are scheduled on to separate cores, increasing the communication costs.

Our runtime, while not performing as in the optimal case (single-core execution), does control the slow down with increasing numbers of cores. We would not expect performance to degrade below interprocessor communication time.

Erlang and Haskell performance also degrades with increasing numbers of cores, Haskell more notably so. POSIX threads performance improves, again we suspect this is for the reasons previously stated.

5.2   Agent Simulation

As previously mentioned, occam-π is being used for complex systems modelling as part of the CoSMoS project [1]. The investigators are exploring using process-oriented methodologies for building models of emergent behaviour, and creating a generic toolkit for doing so. One of the early models investigated by the group was a process-oriented implementation of Craig Reynolds' *boids*, a simulation of flocking behaviour [37]. The CoSMoS project's implementation, *occoids*, employs *agent* processes with internal concurrency to implement the boids and their behaviour rules [7]. Agent processes move through a grid of *location* processes, connecting and reconnecting as they go. The topology of space can be modified by adjusting the underlying network connections, and this technique has been exploited to build an implementation which spans a network of computers with only minor changes to the code base.

We have constructed a benchmark based on occoids. Our benchmark is designed to be easy to implement in other languages, and produces results which allow the verification of an implementation's correctness. The simulated space is a two-dimensional torus, and agent positions are represented as integers relative to the centre of their present location. The occoids simulation uses floating-point variables so as not to unduly quantise space; however, integers allow us to easily verify the simulation output and avoid any associated variations in floating point support.

With reference to the process diagram in Figure 12. Location processes, acting as servers, maintain a data structure containing all agents presently in their grid area. View processes act as servers to clients, but also clients to the location processes, building aggregate lists of all agents within nine adjacent locations each simulation step. Agent processes query a view process, and calculate a repulsive force from other visible agents, applying an internal *bias*. Having determined the force, the agent signals movement to its location, reconnecting to a new location if appropriate. Agents maintain a consistent sense of time using barrier synchronisations between activity phases.

The bias is updated based on the position of the agent and the number of other agents seen. In effect the bias produces randomised behaviour in the agents. The

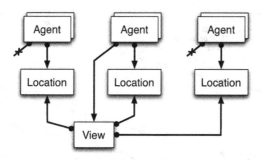

Fig. 12. Simplified occoids process diagram. Boxes represent concurrent processes. Arrows represent two-way client-server channel connections, with the arrow pointing at the server. Agent processes connect to their present location, and "see" other agents via the location's view.

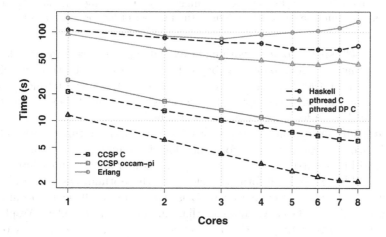

Fig. 13. Increasing the number of cores applied to the agent simulation. The simulation is a 10x10 grid and 1200 agent processes.

initial position of all other agents in the simulation acts as the seed, and hence can be easily reproduced.

As a comparison to the process-oriented design, we implemented a hand-optimised data parallel version using POSIX threads. Only one thread is used per processor core, and each thread executes a fixed number of agents. Data updates are performed in parallel using fine-grain locking of location data structures. This version represents the optimal case and appears as *pthread DP C* in Figures 13 and 14.

Figure 13 shows comparative results as we increase the number of available processor cores with a fixed-size world grid and number of agents. With reference to the process-oriented implementations, our runtime provides a marked improvement in performance and scalability. Erlang and Haskell fail to achieve

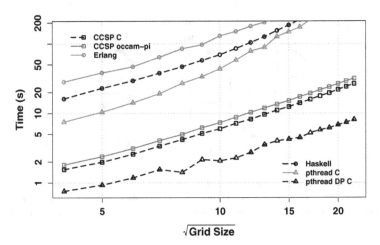

Fig. 14. Simulation time for agents benchmark with increasing grid size. Each grid location has 12 initial agents. The x-axis is the number of locations in each axis.

more than 50% speed up, even with eight available processors. In particular Erlang performance begins to degrade beyond three cores. POSIX threads achieve approximately a 100% speed up over eight cores, while our runtime achieves 350%. Comparing with the optimal case, which has a 575% speed up, there clearly is still room for improvement in our scheduler.

The overall performance of the C version using our runtime is 50% of the optimal case. Assuming this performance loss is communication and scheduling overhead then further refinements of our scheduler and compiler integration should be able to bring performance closer to the optimal case. The reduced performance of occam-π compared to C is due to more efficient optimisation of serial code by the GNU C compiler than the occam-π compiler. We plan to overcome this by targeting GNU C as part of a new compiler we are developing.

Figure 14 shows results when scaling the simulation size with eight cores. Simulation size is controlled by increasing the grid size and number of agents. In this test our runtime also outperforms other process-oriented implementations. The other process-oriented implementations increasingly diverge from the optimal case with increasing problem size. The similarity of our runtime's scaling curve to the optimal suggests that refining of our existing runtime may be sufficient to achieve near optimal performance.

6   Related Work

Many frameworks and languages provide concurrency primitives beyond those supported by OS threads and locks. This stems from a desire make concurrent programming easier, and to avoid common errors associated with locks and shared-memory [40]. For example message-passing frameworks such as PVM [19] and MPI [21] provide primitives similar to those presented in this paper, but do so for a course-grain network environment.

It is also desirable to provide lightweight concurrency primitives when the number of concurrent elements is high [15], or the application has more complete information on how they interact and should be scheduled. Of particular relevance to our work are lightweight runtimes for task parallelism such as Cilk [13], OpenMP [4] and Intel's Thread Building Blocks (TBB) [3]. These runtimes employ modern work-stealing scheduler designs similar to our own, but do not provide primitives suitable for implementing process-oriented designs.

OpenMP and Intel's TBB emphasize the data parallelism of tasks, and only provide for communication of data asynchronously via shared memory. Neither framework provides constructs for communicating data with synchronisation. OpenMP's mutual exclusion locks can be used to implement communication channels. However, unlike POSIX threads, there is no conditional variable which can be used to efficiently implement resume on data or buffer space availability. While TBB's `concurrent_queue` provides a communication channel like interface, TBB only permits parallel tasks over ranges of data and does not support the spawning of continuously running tasks.

Programming environments such as Cilk [13] and Java's Fork/Join framework [30] focus on scheduling finite tasks with well-structured computational dependencies (directed acyclic graphs). Within these frameworks the dependency graph provides the scheduling scope and the depth of the graph can be used to bound the number of active tasks and memory utilisation. These bounding guarantees are based on the space requirements of the serial execution of the same program. Our process-oriented programs do not necessarily have a serial execution, so this model of space bounding is not applicable. Furthermore, as the lifetime of individual tasks is bounded, a LIFO scheduling order is appropriate. Lock-free operations on LIFO stacks are simpler than those on a FIFO queue. The processes we define in this paper have unbounded lifetimes and hence FIFO scheduling ensures all processes are serviced. A FIFO scheduling order distinguishes the scheduling algorithms presented in this paper from those of other work-stealing schedulers.

Process-oriented programming is very similar to the stream programming paradigm. Stream programs consist of graphs of concurrent communicating elements which transform input to output. Process-oriented programming is distinguished from stream programming in that it permits the dynamic creation of processes and their runtime reconnection, whereas a stream program's data graph is fixed which allows compile-time and instruction-level scheduling strategies [29].

In the benchmarks presented in this paper (section 5) we have focused on languages with clear support for implementing process-oriented designs, examining both Erlang and Haskell. Erlang provides asynchronous message passing, which can simulate communication channels, and has a shared-memory multiprocessor runtime [8]. Haskell as a pure functional language focuses on deterministic parallel graph reduction rather than task interaction, but does provide a `MVar` primitive akin to a one-place buffered communication channel [22]. However, while both Erlang and Haskell provide support for lightweight concurrency, neither runtime (as tested), employs a work-stealing scheduler or lock-free algorithms between communicating concurrent elements.

Concurrent ML (CML) is another functional language which provides lightweight concurrency primitives [36]. It implements channels and message passing using continuations on top of Standard ML. We excluded it from our comparisons as CML was not originally intended for multiprocessor execution. A successor language to CML, Manticore, attempts to address heterogeneous parallelism [16]. Manticore is still in the design and implementation phases and this prevented us making any performance comparisons.

In summary, the runtime presented in this paper provides multi-core scheduling for lightweight concurrent communicating processes which can be defined and reconnected at program run time. In doing so it provides support for process-oriented programming multi-core systems not provided by other frameworks for lightweight concurrency.

7   Conclusions

We have implemented a multicore scheduler for fine-grain concurrent software developed using process-oriented programming. Process-oriented designs have a high degree of inter-process communication, and involve many more processes than physical processors. We address this in our runtime design by ensuring that:

- The serialisation bottleneck of a global run queue is avoided by scheduling processes independently on each core.
- Cache utilisation is improved by batching communicating processes.
- No programmer intervention is required to achieve multicore execution of process-oriented designs. Processes and batches are automatically distributed and migrated between processor cores.
- Contention within the scheduler is reduced using lock-free algorithms.
- Lock-free algorithm performance is optimised by minimising the number of atomic instructions, particularly in hot paths.

The performance results presented in this paper show that by addressing these points our runtime has significantly better performance than a number of other frameworks for implementing process-oriented designs. Specially, our runtime brings the performance of process-oriented software close to that of optimised multithreaded implementations.

Using the runtime presented in this paper, process-oriented design can be applied to develop software for multicore systems without the associated complexities and hazards of threads, locks and shared-memory. Furthermore, we expect refinements of our runtime design to be able to allow unmodified process-oriented software to fully utilise hardware parallelism in future generations of multicore processors [5, 31, 33, 43].

8 Future Work

As presented, our runtime does not provide any asynchronous communication mechanism. Instead, we implement asynchronous messaging using buffer processes on synchronous channels. While this design decision was influenced by the target occam-π, a language with no asynchronous communication primitives, it may be that asynchronous communication warrants direct implementation. An investigation of the impact of asynchronous communication on the performance and expressibility of complex systems simulations is required. It should also be noted that there is an argument for synchronous channels being easier for developers to reason about and formally verify.

Further benchmark comparisons of our work are required to provide a comprehensive picture of performance. In particular, research into process-oriented implementations of other common benchmark suites is part of our future work. One possibility is to reimplement benchmarks developed for stream programs, such as the StreamIt benchmark suite [20, 29] - although, as noted in section 6, these do not deal with the dynamic nature of process creation and communication in process-oriented programs.

Acknowledgements. We thank Richard Jones for his feedback on this research. We would also like to thank the anonymous referees for their detailed comments. This work was funded by EPSRC grant EP/D061822/1.

References

1. Complex Systems Modelling and Simulation infrastructure (CoSMoS), http://www.cosmos-research.org
2. http://projects.cs.kent.ac.uk/projects/kroc/svn/ kroc/trunk/tests/ccsp-comparisons/
3. Intel. Threading Building Blocks 2.1, http://www.intel.com/software/products/tbb/
4. OpenMP Application Program Interface, Version 3.0 (May 2008)
5. Acharya, A., Tambe, M., Gupta, A.: Implementation of production systems on message-passing computers. IEEE Transactions on Parallel and Distributed Systems 3(4), 477–487 (1992)
6. Amdahl, G.M.: Validity of the single processor approach to achieving large-scale computing capabilities. In: AFIPS Conference Proceedings, pp. 483–485 (1967)
7. Andrews, P., Sampson, A.T., Bjørndalen, J.M., Stepney, S., Timmis, J., Warren, D., Welch, P.H.: Investigating patterns for process-oriented modelling and simulation of space in complex systems. In: Proceedings of the Eleventh International Conference on Artificial Life. MIT Press, Cambridge (2008)
8. Armstrong, J., Virding, R., Wikström, C., Williams, M.: Concurrent Programming in Erlang, 2nd edn. Prentice-Hall, Englewood Cliffs (1996)
9. Athas, W.C., Seitz, C.L.: Multicomputers: message-passing concurrent computers. Computer 21(8), 9–24 (1988)
10. Attiya, H., Lynch, N., Shavit, N.: Are wait-free algorithms fast? J. ACM 41(4), 725–763 (1994)

11. Barron, I.M.: The transputer. In: MiniMicro West 83, San Francisco, CA, November 1983, pp. 1–8 (1983)
12. Blumofe, R.D., Leiserson, C.E.: Scheduling multithreaded computations by work stealing. J. ACM 46(5), 720–748 (1999)
13. Blumofe, R.D., Joerg, C.F., Kuszmaul, B.C., Leiserson, C.E., Randall, K.H., Zhou, Y.: Cilk: an efficient multithreaded runtime system. In: PPOPP 1995, pp. 207–216. ACM, New York (1995)
14. Debattista, K., Vella, K., Cordina, J.: Wait-free cache-affinity thread scheduling. IEE Proceedings Software 150(2), 137–146 (2003)
15. Von Eicken, T., Culler, D.E., Copen Goldstein, S., Erik Schauser, K.: Active messages: a mechanism for integrated communication and computation. In: Proceedings of the 19th Annual International Symposium on Computer Architecture, pp. 256–266 (1992)
16. Fluet, M., Rainey, M., Reppy, J., Shaw, A., Xiao, Y.: Manticore: a heterogeneous parallel language. In: DAMP 2007, pp. 37–44. ACM, New York (2007)
17. Foster, I.: Compositional parallel programming languages. ACM Trans. Program. Lang. Syst. 18(4), 454–476 (1996)
18. Fraser, K., Harris, T.: Concurrent programming without locks. ACM Trans. Comput. Syst. 25(2), 5 (2007)
19. Geist, A., Beguelin, A., Dongarra, J., Jiang, W., Manchek, R., Sunderam, V.: Parallel Virtual Machine: A Users' Guide and Tutorial for Networked Parallel Computing. MIT Press, Cambridge (1994)
20. Gordon, M.I., Thies, W., Amarasinghe, S.: Exploiting coarse-grained task, data, and pipeline parallelism in stream programs. SIGARCH Comput. Archit. News 34(5), 151–162 (2006)
21. Gropp, W., Lusk, E., Thakur, R.: Using MPI: Portable Parallel Programming With the Message-Passing Interface. MIT Press, Cambridge (1994)
22. Harris, T., Marlow, S., Peyton Jones, S.: Haskell on a shared-memory multiprocessor. In: Haskell 2005: ACM SIGPLAN workshop on Haskell, pp. 49–61. ACM, New York (2005)
23. Herlihy, M.: Wait-free synchronization. ACM Trans. Program. Lang. Syst. 13(1), 124–149 (1991)
24. Herlihy, M.: A methodology for implementing highly concurrent data objects. ACM Trans. Program. Lang. Syst. 15(5), 745–770 (1993)
25. Hill, M.D., Larus, J.R., Wood, D.A.: Tempest: a substrate for portable parallel programs. In: Compcon 1995, March 1995, pp. 327–333 (1995)
26. Hoare, C.A.R.: Communicating Sequential Processes. Communications of the ACM 21(8), 666–677 (1978)
27. INMOS Limited. The T9000 Transputer Instruction Set Manual. SGS-Thompson Microelectronics, Document number: 72 TRN 240 01 (1993)
28. Kaieda, A., Nakayama, Y., Tanaka, A., Horikawa, T., Kurasugi, T., Kino, I.: Analysis and measurement of the effect of kernel locks in SMP systems. Concurrency and Computation: Practice and Experience 13(2), 141–152 (2001)
29. Kudlur, M., Mahlke, S.: Orchestrating the execution of stream programs on multicore platforms. SIGPLAN Not. 43(6), 114–124 (2008)
30. Lea, D.: A Java Fork/Join Framework. In: JAVA 2000, pp. 36–43. ACM, New York (2000)
31. Lu, H., Dwarkadas, S., Cox, A.L., Zwaenepoel, W.: Message passing versus distributed shared memory on networks of workstations. In: Supercomputing, 1995. Proceedings of the IEEE/ACM SC 1995, p. 37 (1995)

32. May, D.: OCCAM. ACM SIGPLAN Notices 18(4), 69–79 (1983)
33. May, M.D., Thompson, P.W., Welch, P.H.: Networks, Routers and Transputers. IOS Press, Amsterdam (1993)
34. Milner, R.: Communicating and Mobile Systems: the Pi-Calculus. Cambridge University Press, Cambridge (1999)
35. Pettersson, M., Sagonas, K., Johansson, E.: The HiPE/x86 Erlang Compiler. In: Hu, Z., Rodríguez-Artalejo, M. (eds.) FLOPS 2002. LNCS, vol. 2441, pp. 228–244. Springer, Heidelberg (2002)
36. Reppy, J.H.: Concurrent programming in ML. Cambridge University Press, Cambridge (1999)
37. Reynolds, C.W.: Flocks, herds and schools: A distributed behavioral model. In: SIGGRAPH 1987, pp. 25–34. ACM, New York (1987)
38. Ritson, C.G., Welch, P.H.: A process-oriented architecture for complex system modelling. In: Communicating Process Architectures 2007, pp. 249–266. IOS Press, Amsterdam (2007)
39. Roscoe, A.W., Hoare, C.A.R., Bird, R.: The Theory and Practice of Concurrency. Prentice Hall PTR, Englewood Cliffs (2005)
40. Savage, S., Burrows, M., Nelson, G., Sobalvarro, P., Anderson, T.: Eraser: a dynamic data race detector for multithreaded programs. ACM Trans. Comput. Syst. 15(4), 391–411 (1997)
41. Schweigler, M.: A Unified Model for Inter- and Intra-processor Concurrency. Ph.D thesis, University of Kent (August 2006)
42. Sodan, A.C.: Message-passing and shared-data programming models - wish vs. reality. In: HPCS 2005, May 2005, pp. 131–139 (2005)
43. Vella, K.: Seamless Parallel Computing on Heterogeneous Networks of Multiprocessor Workstations. Ph.D thesis, University of Kent (December 1998)
44. Welch, P.H., Barnes, F.R.M.: Mobile Data Types for Communicating Processes. In: Proceedings of the International Conference on Parallel and Distributed Processing Techniques and Applications 2001, June 2001, pp. 20–26. CSREA Press (2001)
45. Welch, P.H., Barnes, F.R.M.: Communicating mobile processes: introducing occam-pi. In: Abdallah, A.E., Jones, C.B., Sanders, J.W. (eds.) Communicating Sequential Processes. LNCS, vol. 3525, pp. 175–210. Springer, Heidelberg (2005)
46. Welch, P.H., Barnes, F.R.M.: Mobile Barriers for occam-pi: Semantics, Implementation and Application. In: Communicating Process Architectures 2005, pp. 289–316. IOS Press, Amsterdam (2005)
47. Welch, P.H., Justo, G.R.R., Willcock, C.J.: Higher-Level Paradigms for Deadlock-Free High-Performance Systems. In: Transputer Applications and Systems 1993, Proceedings of the 1993 World Transputer Congress, pp. 981–1004. IOS Press, Amsterdam (1993)

Automata for Context-Dependent Connectors

Marcello Bonsangue[1,3], Dave Clarke[2], and Alexandra Silva[3]

[1] LIACS, Leiden University, The Netherlands
[2] Dept. Computer Science, Katholieke Universiteit Leuven, Belgium
[3] CWI, The Netherlands

Abstract. Recent approaches to component-based software engineering employ coordinating *connectors* to compose components into software systems. For maximum flexibility and reuse, such connectors can themselves be composed, resulting in an expressive calculus of connectors whose semantics encompasses complex combinations of synchronisation, mutual exclusion, non-deterministic choice and state-dependent behaviour. A more expressive notion of connector includes also context-dependent behaviour, namely, whenever the choices the connector can take change non-monotonically as the context, given by the pending activity on its ports, changes. Context dependency can express notions of priority and inhibition. Capturing context-dependent behaviour in formal models is non-trivial, as it is unclear how to propagate context information through composition. In this paper we present an intuitive automata-based formal model of context-dependent connectors, and argue that it is superior to previous attempts at such a model for the coordination language Reo.

1 Introduction

The holy grail of component-based software engineering is to develop truly reusable software components which can be sold off-the-shelf and reused to build software systems [31]. Research on software composition plays a key role in this quest, as it offers flexible ways of plugging together components. Some approaches to software composition use textual *glue code* [15,26,28], usually in a scripting language, whereas others offer a more visual approach, where 'channels' or 'connectors' are used to compose components into a system [1,9,14,17].

Connectors play the role of coordinating software systems, yet their functionality is traditionally more limited than scripting languages. This trend has been reversed with investigation into the notion of compositional connectors [1,26]. In such a setting, connectors are formed by composing simpler connectors such as channels together. These 'languages' express various coordination patterns exhibiting combinations of synchronisation, mutual exclusion, non-deterministic choice, and state-dependent behaviour. A number of component connector models exist, including Reo [1], Ptolemy [23], Ptolemy II [24], MoCha [17], Manifold [5], pipe and filter architectures [30]. Although these overlap in philosophy and functionality, Reo is the only one that enables synchrony and mutual exclusion to propagate through connectors.

J. Field and V.T. Vasconcelos (Eds.): COORDINATION 2009, LNCS 5521, pp. 184–203, 2009.
© Springer-Verlag Berlin Heidelberg 2009

The trend is to increase (or improve) the expressiveness of such coordination models by investigating features such as dynamic reconfiguration [21], data sensitive operations such as data filtering and transformation [10], and context-dependent behaviour [11]. The latter feature is characterised by behaviours which depend upon both the positive and negative occurrences of I/O requests on the boundary ports of the connector. This paper follows this trend, by investigating the notion of context dependency in the setting of the coordination language Reo [1]. Context dependency enables connectors to be more responsive to changes in their environment, and thus increases the expressiveness of connectors enabling them to express, for example, priority and inhibition. Our primary goal is twofold, namely to produce a model of context-dependent connectors which avoids a number of the problems of previous such models for Reo, in a manner which can be implemented efficiently.

Context-dependent behaviour has already been studied in the context of non-monotonic concurrent constraint programming [13] and generative communication [16], where operators are defined with the ability of observing the absence of data. The extra difficulty present in connector-based models is how to propagate context-dependent behaviour properly.

Contributions. This paper presents a compositional automata model for expressing context-dependent connectors. Following intensional automata [12], the model expresses context dependency by modelling both the I/O *requests* from the environment and the *firings* of the connector. It is a simple and intuitive model, in the sense that automata corresponding to basic connectors have a small number of states and transitions, compared to intensional automata. Moreover, because our automata are partial, the model overcomes a problem with *totality preservation* present in connector colouring [11].

Connector plugging is achieved by a novel two-step composition operation consisting of a product, modelling the independent execution of distinct connectors, plus a synchronisation operation. Composition propagates context information, which contains both positive and negative information. Using this we define a previously elusive notion of *enabledness* and show that it is also appropriately propagated through composition. We also formally define the notion of *context dependency*, which had never been formalized for any of the other existing models of Reo. The presented automata model also enables an efficient implementation of context dependent Reo connectors, combining the benefit of previous automata-based implementations [25] with the context dependency originally developed in the connector colouring model [11].

Organisation. Section 2 describes the Reo coordination language and highlights problems with its models with regard to context dependency. Section 3 describes *guarded strings*, the formal basis for traces of context dependent connectors. Section 4 describes *guarded automata*, the basis of our formalism, along with its product and synchronisation operations, and the additional conditions required for modelling Reo connectors. Section 5 describes and justifies various technical conditions present in our model, including giving properties. Section 6 concludes.

2 The Coordination Language Reo and Its Models

Reo [1] is a model of component coordination wherein component *connectors* are constructed by composing more primitive connectors, such as channels, data replicators, stream mergers and routers. Primitives express state-dependent synchronisation and mutual exclusion constraints on their ports, along with the data flow between the ports that synchronise. Primitives can exhibit different behaviours in terms of synchronisation and mutual exclusion of their ports, the direction of data flow, the presence of buffering, state, and whether or not data can be lost. Composition of connectors is achieved by plugging ports together (one-to-one, in the direction of data flow, is sufficient). Composition imposes the constraint that the two ports plugged together synchronise, and hereby synchronisation and mutual exclusion constraints propagate through a connector.

A number of Reo's primitive connectors are depicted in Fig. 1. These form quite an expressive set of connectors (most connectors appearing in the literature use these or their close relatives). Their semantics are presented later in Fig. 3.

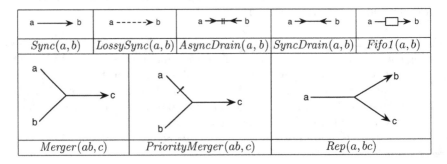

Fig. 1. Basic Reo channels

The interaction model presupposed by Reo is that components try to write or take data from the ports it is connected to. The connector then determines when the write or take 'fires', together with passing data along through the channels of the connector. The notion of synchrony is equated with the ports that fire together, and mutual exclusion is when ports cannot fire together. Most existing formal models of Reo express only the sets of write/take actions which can fire together, dubbed as *firing*. Context-dependent behaviour goes beyond this: such behaviour differs depending upon both the positive and negative occurrences of I/O requests on the boundary ports of the connector. Using this *request* information as well, connectors can express a notion of priority, when two or more choices are possible, and a notion of inhibition wherein attempts by the components to perform operations blocks (certain) firings from occurring.

Informal accounts of Reo give a localised description of the context-dependent nature of certain connectors. For instance, the LossySync channel (with ports a and b) has the behaviour that if a write request and a take request are present on a and b, respectively, then data flows from a to b (synchronously). If, however, no take on b is present, then data may flow at a, but it is lost in the channel. In contrast, the Sync channel (with ports a and b) is not context dependent: data must only flow synchronously. In fact, we will show in the sequel that this channel behaves as identity when composed with other channels. Notions of priority can also be described in this fashion, by using the context (boundary I/O requests) to break any non-determinism.

The problem with this kind of description, first identified by Clarke et al. [11], is that it relies on the presence of requests on the ports of primitives, but after composition these ports are generally no longer on the boundary of a connector, but made internal, and informal accounts do not provide a precise enough description of how context-dependent behaviour propagates through composition. This is a consequence of the impedance mismatch resulting from the plugging together two ports: both ports are expecting some environment to initiate interaction, but the environment (some component) is not present at the point where two ports are joined. Arbab [1] describes how *offers* of data (writes) and willingness to *accept* data (takes) propagate through channels, but unfortunately, this description is incomplete and imprecise, in particular with regard to how context propagation interacts with non-deterministic choice. Clarke et al. [10] goes as far as arguing that there are no natural intuitive models for Reo, hence no natural or obvious way of implementing it, as our intuition about data flow networks is insufficient to determine how connectors behave. Two consequences of this are, firstly, that the semantics of any Reo connector can only be understood in terms of a specific semantic model and appropriate translation into the model, and, secondly, that the only effective implementations of Reo have been direct implementations of some semantic model; no reference model exists.

2.1   Formal Models of Reo

Numerous models have been proposed in the literature to capture the state-dependent, synchronisation and mutual exclusion constraints imposed by a Reo connector over its ports. Providing a semantic model which captures the desired context-dependent nature of Reo connectors in a compositional manner has, however, been a challenge. Models either express no context dependency or are inadequate at doing so.

Constraint automata [7] have transitions whose labels capture the synchronisation (and data flow) between ports, implicitly expressing mutual exclusion, by describing the sets of ports that fire together (the 'firing set') at the exclusion of the ports not mentioned in the set. In their basic form, however, constraint automata cannot express context dependency.

A coalgebraic model of Reo [6] was provided in terms of relations on timed data streams (so-called Abstract Behaviour Types [2]). These were shown to be more or less equivalent to constraint automata, and thus unable to express context dependency. Moreover, the underlying time streams are infinite, so the model excludes not only finite behaviour, but also connectors which exhibit finite behaviour on any of their ports.

Connector colouring [11] describes the behaviour of a connector in a compositional fashion by colouring the parts where data flows and where it does not flow with different colours, requiring simply that colours match at connected ports. The model also captures context-dependent behaviour by propagating negative information about the absence of data flow through the connector. This model was extended to cover both state changes and the passing of data using tile logic [3]. Nonetheless, this model and its extension suffer from a number of problems. The first is that some colourings are non-causal, but this can easily be fixed by tracking the causality relation [12].[1] The second problem is that degenerate behaviour can arise in certain circumstances (see Section 5). Colouring tables normally are defined to give a colouring for all possible boundary conditions. However, this *totality* property is not preserved by composition. Furthermore, composition with a non-total colouring table can result in no behavioural description for connectors, whereas often the semantics should be that no flow is possible. (By analogy, this is the difference between $\emptyset$ and $\{\emptyset\}$.) When composed with any other connector (even when the two parts are not connected), the resulting composite has no behaviour.

Intentional automata [12] express context dependency by labelling transitions with a request set and a firing set, where the request set models the context and the firing set models the subsequent behaviour. In addition, states record pending requests—namely, requests that have arrived but have not fired. This means that there are quite a large number of states in the automata managing the buffering and firing of such requests, and automata rapidly become difficult to manipulate and not suitable for model checking purposes. For example, one Sync channel requires 3 states, and 2 disconnected Sync channels require 9 states. In constraint automata and our model, only 1 state is required in both cases.

The Büchi automata model of Reo [18,19] assigns to connectors infinite fair behaviours. In this model, τ-transitions capture the arrival of requests, which are recorded in states. In this model, there are two different non-equivalent ways of modelling something as simple as a Sync channel. Thus the model differs significantly from other approaches.

Mousavi *et al.* [27] describe Reo's semantics using structural operational semantics. To capture context-dependent behaviour (of lossy synchronous channels) a global *maximal progress* rule is employed to remove undesired behaviours. This was subsequently encoded into Alloy [20]. The kind of context-dependent behaviour which can be captured by this rule is limited, as it cannot express the preference between two unrelated behaviours.

Barbosa *et al.* [8] present models of Reo-like connectors. The semantics is given by process algebra expressions, where both the presence and absence of signals can be specified. Complex connectors are then built from simpler ones using one of five combinators: parallel composition, interleaving, hook, right and left join. However, these composition operations increases the complexity of the model without gaining any expressiveness.

---

[1] Our model also does not deal with causality issues; Costa's fix is applicable here [12].

Unlike constraint automata, our model can express context dependency using a request and firing set, as in intentional automata. We abstract away from data flow constraints, but indicate how to add them back into the model in Section 6. Our model is significantly more compact than intentional automata, in terms of both the number of states and transitions, as information about pending requests is not stored in states—it can easily be calculated. In contrast to the Büchi model, our model expresses only finite behaviours and records request sets in transition labels along with the firing sets, instead of in the states, resulting in more intuitive models. Furthermore, our model expresses only the positive behaviour, and does not rely crucially on the Büchi acceptance criteria to rule out unwanted 'paths' in automata. The semantics of our model is based on finite strings, which are much simpler than relations on timed data streams underlying the coalgebraic model. Our model also overcomes the totality problem of connector colouring by, ironically, not insisting that the transition relation is total, and by interpreting the absence of a transition simply as no behaviour for the given context. In contrast to Mousavi *et al.*'s model, our approach achieves an expressive notion of context dependency in a compositional manner without recourse to a global rule. Our composition operation is a compact two-step operation, much simpler than the five operations proposed by Barbosa *et al.*. As far as we can tell, merely just adding information recording the absence of signals is insufficient to adequately deal with context dependent behaviour.

Overall, we claim that our automata are simpler and more intuitive than existing models of context dependent connectors. In addition, we prove numerous relevant properties about our model, not even considered by others.

3   Preliminaries: Guarded Strings

Let $\Sigma = \{\sigma_1, \ldots, \sigma_k\}$ and $\mathcal{B}_\Sigma$ be the free Boolean algebra generated by the following grammar:

$$ g ::= \sigma \in \Sigma \mid \top \mid \bot \mid g \vee g \mid g \wedge g \mid \overline{g} $$

We refer to the elements of the above grammar as *guards* and in its representation we frequently omit $\wedge$ and write $g_1 g_2$ instead of $g_1 \wedge g_2$. Given two guards $g_1, g_2 \in \mathcal{B}_\Sigma$, we define a (natural) order $\leq$ by putting $g_1 \leq g_2 \iff g_1 \wedge g_2 = g_1$. The intended interpretation of $\leq$ is logical implication—g_1 implies g_2.

Given a guard g there exists an equivalent guard $norm(g) = \bigvee \bigwedge a$, where $a \in \Sigma \cup \overline{\Sigma}$, with $\overline{\Sigma} = \{\overline{\sigma} \mid \sigma \in \Sigma\}$, and $\bigvee$ and $\bigwedge$ the extensions of $\vee$ and $\wedge$, respectively, to sets of guards. The guard $norm(g)$ is usually called the disjunctive normal form of g. Since $norm(g)$ can be written as a disjunction, we use the notation $g' \in norm(g)$ to refer to an arbitrary disjunct of $norm(g)$.

An *atom* of $\mathcal{B}_\Sigma$ is a guard $a_1 \ldots a_k$ such that $a_i \in \{\sigma_i, \overline{\sigma}_i\}$, $1 \leq i \leq k$. We can think of an atom as a truth assignment. We denote atoms by Greek letters $\alpha, \beta, \ldots$ and the set of all atoms of $\mathcal{B}_\Sigma$ by $\mathbf{At}_\Sigma$. Every element of a finite Boolean algebra can be written as a disjunction of atoms. Given $S \subseteq \Sigma$, we define $\widehat{S} \in \mathcal{B}_\Sigma$ as the conjunction of all elements of S. For instance, for $S = \{a, b, c\}$ one has

$\widehat{S} = abc$. We define the atom associated with a set S in the expected way —
$\alpha_S = \widehat{S} \wedge \widehat{\Sigma \setminus S}$. For example, if $\Sigma = \{a, b, c\}$, then $\alpha_{\{a,b\}} = ab\bar{c}$. Conversely, the
set associated with an atom α is defined as $\alpha^+ = \{\sigma \in \Sigma \mid \alpha \le \sigma\}$.

A guarded string over Σ is a sequence $x = \langle \alpha_1, f_1 \rangle \langle \alpha_2, f_2 \rangle \ldots \langle \alpha_n, f_n \rangle$, where
$n \ge 0$ and each $\alpha_i \in \mathbf{At}_\Sigma$ and $f_i \subseteq \Sigma$. Thus, a guarded string is an el-
ement of $(\mathbf{At}_\Sigma \times 2^\Sigma)^*$. For simplicity, we drop the brackets and write $x = \alpha_1 f_1 \alpha_2 f_2 \cdots \alpha_n f_n$.

To understand the intuition behind guarded strings, imagine that Σ contains
the names of all doctors in a hospital. Every hour there is a meeting to distribute
the incoming patients. Each atom α_i describes the definite presence or absence
of every doctor in the meeting at hour i and f contains the doctors that got
a patient. Thus, the guarded string $\langle \alpha_1, f_1 \rangle \langle \alpha_2, f_2 \rangle \ldots \langle \alpha_n, f_n \rangle$ will contain the
activity of the doctors from hours 1 to n.

4   Guarded Automata

In this section, we define a new automata model for context-dependent connectors. We start by introducing a generic automata, acceptor of guarded strings
and we define a product operation. Then, suitable restrictions are introduced
to single out the class of Reo automata, *i.e.*, automata that are valid models of
context-dependent connectors, for which a synchronization operation is defined.

Definition 1 (Guarded automaton). *A* guarded automaton *over an alphabet
of ports* Σ *is a non-deterministic (and possibly partial) automaton with transition
labels* $\mathcal{B}_\Sigma \times 2^\Sigma$. *Formally, a guarded automaton is a triple* (Σ, Q, δ) *where* Q *is
a (finite) set of states and* $\delta \subseteq Q \times \mathcal{B}_\Sigma \times 2^\Sigma \times Q$ *is the transition relation.*

We use the following notation in the representation of guarded automata:

$$q \xrightarrow{g|f} q' \iff \langle q, g, f, q' \rangle \in \delta$$

If there is more than one transition from state q to q' we often just draw one
arrow and separate the labels by commas. Intuitively, a transition $q \xrightarrow{g|f} q'$
denotes that the actions in f will occur if the guard g is true.

Example guarded automata over the alphabet $\{a, b\}$ are depicted in Fig. 2.

A guarded automaton can be seen as an acceptor of guarded strings as follows.
Given a guarded string $\alpha_1 f_1 \alpha_2 f_2 \cdots \alpha_n f_n$ and a state q in the automaton the

Fig. 2. Examples of guarded automata over the alphabet $\{a, b\}$

string is *accepted* in state q if there exists $q \xrightarrow{g|f_1} q' \in \delta$ such that $\alpha_1 \leq g$ and $\alpha_2 f_2 \cdots \alpha_n f_n$ is accepted in q'. The empty string ε is accepted in any state. We denote by $\mathcal{L}_q$ the set of guarded strings accepted in a state q. Note that our definition of acceptance implies that $\mathcal{L}_q$ is always non-empty and prefix-closed.

Another way to compute the language $\mathcal{L}_q$ would be to first write every guard g as a disjunction of atoms $\bigvee_I \alpha_i$ (for instance $a = a\bar{b} \vee ab$), replace the transition $q \xrightarrow{g|f_1} q' \in \delta$ by the transitions $q \xrightarrow{\alpha_i|f_1} q'$ and then compute the accepted language of the automata in the standard way. An interesting remark is that if one writes the automaton only using atoms, as described above, and then determinizes it using a subset construction, the resulting automata will have a transition function of type $Q \to (1 + Q)^{\mathbf{At}_\Sigma \times 2^\Sigma}$ [22]. It is then well-known [29] that such automata have as final semantics precisely the non empty and prefix closed languages $\mathcal{L} \subseteq 2^{(\mathbf{At}_\Sigma \times 2^\Sigma)^*}$.

Two automata are equivalent if they accept the same language. We also introduce a novel notion of bisimulation, which implies language equivalence.

Definition 2 (Bisimulation). *Given guarded automata $\mathcal{A}_1 = (\Sigma, Q_1, \delta_1)$ and $\mathcal{A}_2 = (\Sigma, Q_2, \delta_2)$. We call $R \subseteq Q_1 \times Q_2$ a bisimulation iff for all $\langle q_1, q_2 \rangle \in R$:*

1. *For all $q_1 \xrightarrow{g|f} q_1' \in \delta_1$ and $\alpha \in \mathbf{At}_\Sigma$ such that $\alpha \leq g$, there exists a*

   $q_2 \xrightarrow{g'|f} q_2' \in \delta_2$ *such that $\alpha \leq g'$ and $\langle q_1', q_2' \rangle \in R$;*

2. *For all $q_2 \xrightarrow{g|f} q_2' \in \delta_2$ and $\alpha \in \mathbf{At}_\Sigma$ such that $\alpha \leq g$, there exists a*

   $q_1 \xrightarrow{g'|f} q_1' \in \delta_1$ *such that $\alpha \leq g'$ and $\langle q_1', q_2' \rangle \in R$.*

We say that two states $q_1 \in Q_1$ and $q_2 \in Q_2$ are bisimilar if there exists a bisimulation relation containing the pair $\langle q_1, q_2 \rangle$ and we write $q_1 \sim q_2$. Two automata $\mathcal{A}_1$ and $\mathcal{A}_2$ are bisimilar if there exists a bisimulation relation such that every state of one automata is related to some state of the other automata and we write $\mathcal{A}_1 \sim \mathcal{A}_2$. The automata depicted in the following figure are bisimilar.

Theorem 1. *Let $\mathcal{A}_1 = (\Sigma, Q_1, \delta_1)$ and $\mathcal{A}_2 = (\Sigma, Q_2, \delta_2)$ be guarded automata and $q_1 \in Q_1, q_2 \in Q_1$. Then, $q_1 \sim q_2 \Rightarrow \mathcal{L}_{q_1} = \mathcal{L}_{q_2}$.*

4.1 Product

In this section we define a product operation for guarded automata. This definition differs from the classical definition of product for automata: the automata have disjoint alphabets and they can either take steps together or independently. In the latter case the transition explicitly encodes that the other automaton cannot perform a step in the current state, using the following notion:

Definition 3. *Given a guarded automaton* $\mathcal{A} = (\Sigma, Q, \delta)$ *and* $q \in Q$ *we define*

$$q^\sharp = \neg \bigvee \{g \mid q \xrightarrow{g|f} q' \in \delta\}.$$

This captures precisely the conditions in which $\mathcal{A}$ cannot fire in state q. Note that if q has no outgoing transitions then $q^\sharp = \top$ and if q has a transition defined for every $g \in \mathcal{B}_\Sigma$ then $q^\sharp = \bot$. Intuitively, if $q^\sharp = \top$ (resp. $q^\sharp = \bot$) then the state can never (resp. always) inhibit the step of a state in another automaton, in the context of the product, defined below. For instance, in the automata

one has $q_1^\sharp = \bar{a} \vee \bar{b}$ and $q_2^\sharp = \bar{a}$.

Definition 4 (Product). *Given two guarded automata* $\mathcal{A}_1 = (\Sigma_1, Q_1, \delta_1)$ *and* $\mathcal{A}_2 = (\Sigma_2, Q_2, \delta_2)$ *such that* $\Sigma_1 \cap \Sigma_2 = \emptyset$, *we define the* product *of* $\mathcal{A}_1$ *and* $\mathcal{A}_2$ *as* $\mathcal{A}_1 \times \mathcal{A}_2 = (\Sigma_1 \cup \Sigma_2, Q_1 \times Q_2, \delta)$ *where*

$$\delta = \{ (q,p) \xrightarrow{gg'|ff'} (q',p') \mid q \xrightarrow{g|f} q' \in \delta_1 \text{ and } p \xrightarrow{g'|f'} p' \in \delta_2 \} \tag{1}$$

$$\cup \{ (q,p) \xrightarrow{gp^\sharp|f} (q',p) \mid q \xrightarrow{g|f} q' \in \delta_1 \text{ and } p \in Q_2 \} \tag{2}$$

$$\cup \{ (q,p) \xrightarrow{gq^\sharp|f} (q,p') \mid p \xrightarrow{g|f} p' \in \delta_2 \text{ and } q \in Q_1 \} \tag{3}$$

Here and throughout, we use ff' as a shorthand for $f \cup f'$. Case (1) accounts for when both automata fire in parallel. Cases (2) and (3) account for when one automata fires and the other is unable to (given by $p^\sharp$ and $q^\sharp$, respectively).

The following is an example of the product of two automata.

Observe that the automaton $1 = (\emptyset, \{\cdot\}, \emptyset)$ is a neutral element for product. The product operator satisfies expected properties such as commutativity and associativity. The first property follows directly from the definition. The second one follows from the definition and the fact that $(q_1, q_2)^\sharp = q_1^\sharp \wedge q_2^\sharp$.

4.2   Reo Automata

In this section we focus on a subclass of guarded automata that constitutes an operational model for context dependency. Intuitively, every transition $q \xrightarrow{g|f} q'$

in an automaton corresponding to some Reo connector represents that, if the connector is in state q and the boundary requests present at the moment, encoded as an atom α, are such that $\alpha \leq g$, then the ports f will fire and the connector will evolve to state q'. Not all guarded automata correspond to valid Reo connectors. We are interested only in automata where each guard $g|f$ satisfies two criteria: *reactivity*—data flows only on ports where a request is made, capturing Reo's interaction model; and *uniformity*—which captures two properties, firstly, that the request set corresponding precisely to the firing set is sufficient to cause firing, and secondly, that removing additional unfired requests from a transition will not affect the (firing) behaviour of the connector. These two properties are captured in the following definition.

Definition 5 (Reo automaton). *A* Reo automaton *over an alphabet Σ is a guarded automaton (Σ, Q, δ) such that for each $q \xrightarrow{g|f} q' \in \delta$:*

$$- \; g \leq \widehat{f} \qquad\qquad\qquad\qquad\qquad\qquad \text{(reactivity)}$$

$$- \; \forall g \leq g' \leq \widehat{f} \cdot \forall \alpha \leq g' \cdot \exists \, q \xrightarrow{g''|f} q' \in \delta \cdot \alpha \leq g'' \qquad \text{(uniformity)}$$

Among the guarded automata depicted in Fig. 2 only the third one is a Reo automaton (in fact, it models a FIFO1 channel). The first automaton is not uniform, because $ab \leq a \leq a$ and there is no transition whose guard g is such that $a\overline{b} \leq g$. The second automaton in not reactive: $a\overline{b} \not\leq ab$.

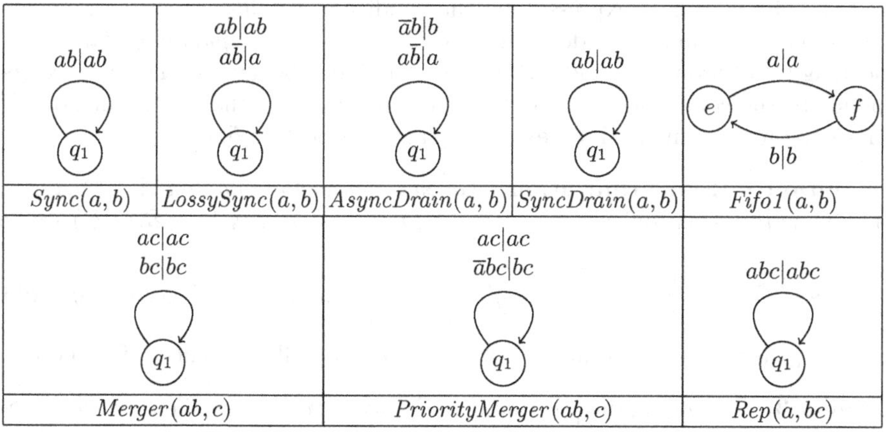

$ab\|ab$	$ab\|ab$ $a\overline{b}\|a$	$\overline{a}b\|b$ $a\overline{b}\|a$	$ab\|ab$	$a\|a$
q_1	q_1	q_1	q_1	$e \quad f$ $b\|b$
$Sync(a,b)$	$LossySync(a,b)$	$AsyncDrain(a,b)$	$SyncDrain(a,b)$	$Fifo1(a,b)$
$ac\|ac$ $bc\|bc$		$ac\|ac$ $\overline{a}bc\|bc$		$abc\|abc$
q_1		q_1		q_1
$Merger(ab,c)$		$PriorityMerger(ab,c)$		$Rep(a,bc)$

Fig. 3. Guarded automata for basic Reo channels

In Fig. 3 we depict the guarded automata for the basic channel types listed in Fig. 1. Here it is worth remarking that the automata for LossySync, AsyncDrain and PriorityMerger contain negative information in some of their guards. As we will show later this is the key to represent and propagate context-dependent behaviour, which all these channels exhibit.

Lemma 1. *Reo automata are closed under product, i.e., product preserves reactivity and uniformity.*

4.3 Synchronization

We now define a synchronization operation which corresponds to connecting two ports in a Reo connector. In order for this operation to be well-defined we need that the transition labels in the automata are normalized (the formal justification for this is presented in Section 5.1). More precisely, we need each guard in a label to be a conjunction of literals. Note that in the automata presented in Figure 3 for basic Reo channels this is already the case.

Definition 6. *Given a guarded automaton* $\mathcal{A} = (\Sigma, Q, \delta)$ *we define the normalization of* $\mathcal{A}$ *as* $norm(\mathcal{A}) = (\Sigma, Q, norm(\delta))$ *where*

$$norm(\delta) = \{\ q \xrightarrow{g'|f} q' \ \mid \ q \xrightarrow{g|f} q' \ \in \delta \text{ and } g' \in norm(g)\}$$

Lemma 2. *Reo automata are closed under normalization, i.e., normalization preserves reactivity and uniformity. Moreover,* $\mathcal{A} \sim norm(\mathcal{A})$.

Now we are ready to define the synchronization operation of two ports a and b (that are then made internal). In the new automaton only transitions where either both a and b or neither a nor b fire are kept—that is, a and b synchronize. In order to propagate context information (requests), we require that the guard contains either a or b, expressed by the condition $g \not\leq \overline{a}\overline{b}$, which more or less corresponds an internal node acting like a *self-contained pumping station* [1], meaning that an internal node cannot actively block behaviour. This also corresponds to the condition in connector colouring [11] that the reason for no flow on a node must come from an external place (see Section 5.5).

Definition 7 (Synchronization). *Given a guarded automaton* $\mathcal{A} = (\Sigma, Q, \delta)$. *We define the* synchronization *of* a *and* b *(*$a, b \in \Sigma$*) as* $\partial_{a,b}\mathcal{A} = (\Sigma, Q, \delta')$ *where*

$$\delta' = \{\ q \xrightarrow{g\backslash ab|f\backslash\{a,b\}} q' \ \mid \ q \xrightarrow{g|f} q' \ \in norm(\delta) \text{ s.t. } a \in f \Leftrightarrow b \in f \text{ and } g \not\leq \overline{a}\overline{b}\}$$

Here, $g\backslash ab$ is the guard obtained from g by deleting all ocurrences of a and b.

Lemma 3. *Reo automata are closed under synchronization, i.e., synchronization preserves reactivity and uniformity.*

The product and synchronization operations can be used to obtain, in a compositional way, the guarded automaton of a Reo connector built from primitive connectors for which the automata are known. Given two Reo automata $\mathcal{A}_1$ and $\mathcal{A}_2$ over disjoint alphabets Σ_1 and Σ_2, $\{a_1, \ldots, a_k\} \subseteq \Sigma_1$ and $\{b_1, \ldots, b_k\} \subseteq \Sigma_2$ we construct $\partial_{a_1,b_1}\partial_{a_2,b_2} \cdots \partial_{a_k,b_k}(\mathcal{A}_1 \times \mathcal{A}_2)$ as the automaton corresponding to a connector where port a_i of the first connector is connected to port b_i of the second connector, for all $i \in \{1, \ldots, k\}$. Note that the 'plugging' order does not matter because of ∂ is commutative and it interacts well with product. In addition, the sync channel $Sync(a, b)$ acts as identity (modulo renaming). These properties are captured in the following lemma.

Lemma 4. *Given Reo automata $\mathcal{A}_1 = (\Sigma_1, Q_1, \delta_1)$ and $\mathcal{A}_2 = (\Sigma_2, Q_2, \delta_2)$. Then:*

1. $\partial_{a,b}\partial_{c,d}\mathcal{A}_1 = \partial_{c,d}\partial_{a,b}\mathcal{A}_1$, *if* $a, b, c, d \in \Sigma_1$.
2. $(\partial_{a,b}\mathcal{A}_1) \times \mathcal{A}_2 \sim \partial_{a,b}(\mathcal{A}_1 \times \mathcal{A}_2)$, *if* $a, b \in \Sigma_1$ *and* $\Sigma_1 \cap \Sigma_2 = \emptyset$.
3. $\partial_{a,c}(\mathcal{A}_1 \times Sync(a, b)) \sim \mathcal{A}_1[b/c]$, *if* $a, b \notin \Sigma_1$ *and* $c \in \Sigma_1$.

where $\mathcal{A}[b/c]$ is $\mathcal{A}$ with all occurrences of c replaced by b.

Moreover, we remark that $\sim$ is a congruence with respect to the product and synchronisation operations.

5 Discussion

The model presented above contains many technical details. In order to justify them, we present a theorem and/or counter-example to illustrate their purpose. In the examples we mark in **bold** transitions in the product automaton which are deleted in the synchronization step because the condition $b \in f \Leftrightarrow c \in f$ fails, and we mark in gray the transitions that are removed because $g \leq \overline{bc}$.

The following definition will come in handy.

Definition 8 (Firings). *Let $\mathcal{A} = (\Sigma, Q, \delta)$ be a guarded automaton. Given $q \in Q$ and $\alpha \in \mathbf{At}_\Sigma$ define the set of possible firings in q induced by α as*

$$\mathbf{firings}_\mathcal{A}(q, \alpha) = \{(f, q') \mid q \xrightarrow{g|f} q' \in \delta \ \land \ \alpha \leq g\}.$$

We will drop the subscript $\mathcal{A}$ whenever the automaton is clear from the context.

5.1 Uniformity, Normalization and the Sync Channel

A desirable property of a model of (context-dependent) connectors is that the Sync channel acts like an identity (modulo port renaming) whenever plugged into another connector (Lemma 4). The following example demonstrates that this property fails to hold without the uniformity property of Definition 5. Consider a channel $Loser(a, b)$ which fires port a only if a request of port b is also present. Its guarded automaton is non-uniform, as it should have transition $a|a$. Composing with a synchronous channel gives an automaton which should be $Loser(a, d)$ if Sync behaved like the identity:

$$Loser(a,b) = \boxed{q_1} \circlearrowright ab|a \qquad \partial_{b,c}(Loser(a,b) \times Sync(c,d)) = \boxed{(q_1, q_1)} \circlearrowright a|a$$

A similar reason justifies the fact that we have to normalize the automaton before applying the synchronization operator. Suppose we want to compose a lossy synchronous channel with a synchronous channel. The automaton for the product $LossySync(a, b) \times Sync(c, d)$ is:

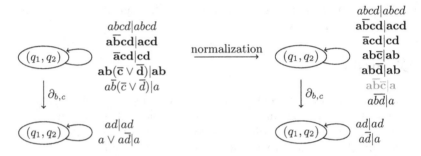

Now applying $\partial_{b,c}$ with and without normalizing results in different automata:

The Sync channel behaves like an identity only in the second case.

5.2   Totality and Inhibition

Two notions of totality can be defined for connectors. We phrase them in terms of guarded automata, although they apply to other models too.

Definition 9 (Totality). *A guarded automaton* $\mathcal{A} = (\Sigma, Q, \delta)$ *is said to be total if and only if for all states* $q \in Q$ *and for all* $\alpha \in \mathbf{At}_\Sigma$, $\mathbf{firings}(q, \alpha) \neq \emptyset$.

The presentation of connector colouring [11] requires that the colouring tables are total. Unfortunately, composition does not preserve totality. Consider the Rep-AsyncDrain in Fig. 4. In the connector colouring model its colouring table is not total, which might lead to unexpected behaviours during composition. For example, when a FullFifo$_1$ is plugged into the Rep-AsyncDrain, the composite has an empty colouring table, corresponding to "no behaviour possible." If this is further composed with other connectors, the colouring table remains empty, even if no connection is made with the FullFifo$_1$-Rep-AsyncDrain composite.

We do not require totality, and due to the use of negative information in the product, composition with Rep-AsyncDrain causes no problems, as its automata is one with no transitions (Fig. 4), which behaves neutrally in the composition (since $(q_1, q_2)^\sharp = \top$).

We also find it unnecessary to specify any behaviour that does not result in a firing (though we do permit τ-transitions, represented by $\top | \emptyset$). The following

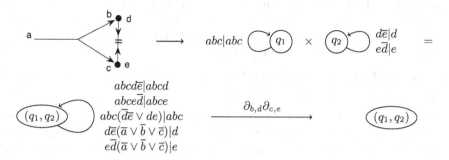

Fig. 4. Guarded automaton for $\partial_{b,d}\partial_{c,e}(Rep(a,bc) \times ASyncDrain(d,e))$

definition captures a sensible notion, which is weaker than totality. It states that if some request set α causes a firing, then all larger request sets also cause a firing (though not necessarily the same one).

Definition 10 (Firing upclosed). *A guarded automaton* $\mathcal{A} = (\Sigma, Q, \delta)$ *is said to be firing upclosed if and only if for all states* $q \in Q$ *and for all* $\alpha \in \mathbf{At}_\Sigma$, *if* **firings**$(q, \alpha) \neq \emptyset$, *then for all* α_1 *such that* $\alpha^+ \subseteq \alpha_1^+$ *we have* **firings**$(q, \alpha_1) \neq \emptyset$.

This is a nice property, but it turns out that, in general, composing Reo automata does not preserve firing upclosure. Consider the following example connector $\partial_{b,b'}\partial_{c,c'}PriorityMerger(ab,c) \times Rep(c',b'd)$ and its accompanying automaton, where a is the higher priority port: [2]

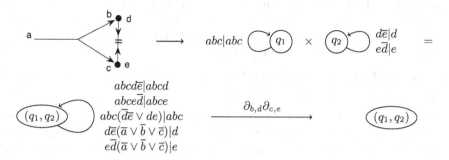

$$\bar{a}d|d \ \circlearrowright \ q$$

This automaton is not firing upclosed, as although $d|d$ produces a firing, ad does not. In fact, a request on a acts to inhibit the firing of d, without itself being fired. This kind of behaviour was not considered in previous models of Reo. We tried to find an alternative definition of synchronisation, $\hat{\partial}$, which preserved Firing upclosed. Unfortunately, all our attempts failed to satisfy the required equivalence $\hat{\partial}_{a,b}\hat{\partial}_{c,d}\mathcal{A} \sim \hat{\partial}_{c,d}\hat{\partial}_{a,b}\mathcal{A}$. Embracing partiality—that is, the absence of firing upclosure—open the door to connectors which act as request-based *inhibitors*, as in the previous example.

5.3   Context Dependency and Negative Guards

We now formally define the notion context-dependency. This has never been formalized for any of the other existing models of Reo.

---

[2] Note that this connector contains a causal loop, which should produce no data. A more complex variant without the causality problem can be easily produced, by inserting a $SyncSpout(a,b)$ plugged to a $SyncDrain(b',c)$ between b and b'.

Definition 11 (Firing Monotonic). *Let $\mathcal{A} = (\Sigma, Q, \delta)$ be a guarded automaton. $\mathcal{A}$ is firing monotonic if and only if for all states $q \in Q$ and for all $\alpha_1, \alpha_2 \in \mathbf{At}_\Sigma$ if $\alpha_1^+ \subseteq \alpha_2^+$, then $\mathbf{firings}(q, \alpha_1) \subseteq \mathbf{firings}(q, \alpha_2)$. That is, $\mathbf{firings}(q, \_)$ is monotonic for all $q \in Q$.*

Definition 12 (Context Dependent). *A guarded automaton $\mathcal{A}$ is context dependent if and only if it is not firing monotonic.*

Thus an automaton exhibits context dependent behaviour in state q whenever there exist $\alpha_1, \alpha_2 \in \mathbf{At}_\Sigma$ such that $\alpha_1^+ \subseteq \alpha_2^+$ and $\mathbf{firings}(q, \alpha_1) \not\subseteq \mathbf{firings}(q, \alpha_2)$. Intuitively, this means that the state q has a transition that will be blocked in the presence of certain additional requests. In the following automata, the state q exhibits context dependent behaviour, because $\mathbf{firings}(q, a\bar{b}) = \{(q, a)\} \not\subseteq \{(q, ab)\} = \mathbf{firings}(q, ab)$, whereas the state p does not.

The following lemmas show that negative information in guards is required to express context dependency.

Lemma 5. *Let $\mathcal{A}$ be a guarded automaton for which no negative atoms appear in the guards. Then $\mathcal{A}$ is firing monotonic.*

Lemma 6. *Firing monotonicity is preserved by product and synchronisation.*

Constraint automata [7] can be embedded in a natural way into our model by transforming every transition labelled by F into a transition labelled by $\hat{F}|F$. As a consequence of the previous lemmas, this makes explicit the fact that constraint automata do not exhibit context dependent behaviour.

In addition we have, for Reo automata:

Lemma 7. *A firing monotonic Reo automaton is firing upclosed.*

The LossySync channel is not firing monotonic, yet it is firing upclosed.

5.4   Enabledness and Product

We now formally define the notion of enabledness, which captures that a port can fire whenever a request is made on that port (in a given state). This property has not been previously formalised for existing models of Reo. We also show that this property is propagated through product, though this would not be the case if negative information were not included in the definition of product.

Definition 13 (Enabledness). *Let $\mathcal{A} = (\Sigma, Q, \delta)$ be a guarded automaton. A port $a \in \Sigma$ is enabled in a state q if for all $\alpha \in \mathbf{At}_\Sigma$ such that $\alpha \leq a$, (1) $\mathbf{firings}(q, \alpha) \neq \emptyset$ and (2) for all $(f, \_) \in \mathbf{firings}(q, \alpha)$ we have $a \in f$.*

Intuitively, a port a is enabled whenever all request sets containing a match some guard g and a subsequently fires. Including negative information in the definition of product (using $q^\sharp$) preserves *enabledness* through product.

Lemma 8. *Let $\mathcal{A}_1 = (\Sigma_1, Q_1, \delta_1)$ and $\mathcal{A}_2 = (\Sigma_2, Q_2, \delta_2)$ be guarded automata with $\Sigma_1 \cap \Sigma_2 = \emptyset$. Assume that in $\mathcal{A}_1$ the port $a \in \Sigma_1$ is enabled in state $q \in Q_1$. Then in $\mathcal{A}_1 \times \mathcal{A}_2$, the port a is enabled in all states (q, q'), where $q' \in Q_2$.*

Without negative information in the product, enabledness is not preserved, as the following counter-example demonstrates. Port a of $LossySync(a, b)$ is enabled. If we remove the $q^{\sharp}$ from the definition of product, thus taking the naive definition of product ($\hat{\times}$) following the definition in constraint automata directly, then a is no longer enabled in $LossySync(a, b) \hat{\times} Sync(c, d)$, because a transition with guard $cd|cd$ is present in the resulting automaton. This transition matches request set acd, but a does not fire.

5.5   Justification of the $g \not\leq \overline{a}\overline{b}$ Condition in $\partial_{a,b}$

The LossySync-Fifo1 example (Fig. 5) alone motivated the research into context-dependent models. When the Fifo buffer is empty, data must flow through the LossySync into the buffer, as the buffer's port c is enabled. Our product and synchronisation operations ensure this. What existing research lacks is a general and formal characterisation of the requirements underlying this example. We believe that until now, the required technical machinery was missing.

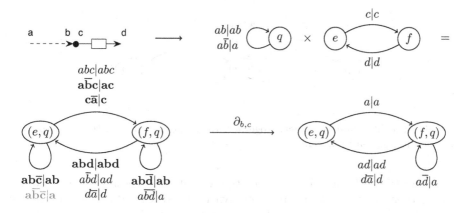

Fig. 5. LossySync-Fifo1

Definition 14. *Let $\mathcal{A} = (\Sigma, Q, \delta)$ be a guarded automaton. We say that a port $a \in \Sigma$ is (q, R)-sensitive for state $q \in Q$ and request set $R \subseteq \Sigma$ whenever $a \in f$ for all $(f, \_) \in \mathbf{firings}(q, \alpha_{R \cup \{a\}})$.*

This property holds for port b in $LossySync(a, b)$ in the request set $\{a\}$, and for port c in $Fifo1(c, d)$ in state empty for all request sets. In contrast, port a of $Merge(ab, c)$ is not sensitive for request set $\{b, c\}$.

The following lemma captures the property underlying the LossySync-Fifo1 example:

Lemma 9. *Let $\mathcal{A} = (\Sigma, Q, \delta)$ be a Reo automaton, $a, b \in \Sigma$, $q \in Q$, and $R \subseteq \Sigma$ a request such that $a, b \notin R$. If a is $(q, R \cup \{b\})$-sensitive and b is $(q, R \cup \{a\})$-sensitive, then $\mathbf{firings}_{\partial_{a,b}\mathcal{A}}(q, \alpha_R) = \{(f \setminus \{a, b\}, q') \mid (f, q') \in \mathbf{firings}_{\mathcal{A}}(q, \alpha_{R \cup \{a,b\}})\}$.*

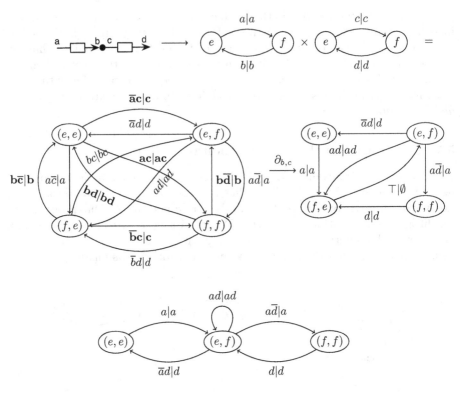

Fig. 6. Two Fifo1 buffers plugged together, their automaton, and the result of performing 'hiding'—a Fifo2 buffer

This says that if both a and b are mutually enabled in the presence of request set R, then they will both fire when synchronised, excluding the alternative possibility that both do not fire. Constraint automata [7] would include both.

We believe that this kind of analysis is only the beginning in the key issue of more deeply understanding the interaction between synchronisation and context dependency [11,19,12].

5.6   Choice of Operations

The original model of constraint automata [7] included one operation for composing automata, namely a *join*, which played a similar role to both of our operations combined. Having a separate product and synchronisation operation enables a more fine grained analysis, which we believe was required to obtain the results presented here. Barbosa *et al.* [8] go even further, presenting 5 operations (*parallel*, *interleaving*, *hook*, *left join* and *right join*). Our product merely places two connectors next to each other, without restricting their behaviour, whereas Barbosa *et al.*'s model forces a choice between parallel or interleaving composition. Left join and right join (approximately the counterpart of replicator and merger) are modelled by primitive automata in our model, not as operations. Their hook operation is the same as our synchronisation.

5.7 'Hiding'

Constraint automata [7] models of Reo include a 'hiding' operation, which compresses τ transitions in the automata, which are transitions labelled by $\top|\emptyset$ in our model. See Figure 6. This can be used to obtain an automaton for a FIFO2 channel from the composite of two FIFO1 channels. The alternative variant defined by Costa [12] is equally applicable, and perhaps more robust.

6   Conclusion and Future Work

We have presented a new semantic model for context-dependent Reo connectors. The automata corresponding to primitive channels are very compact and intuitive. As a novelty, when compared to previous approaches, our model takes negative information into account in the composition operations. This has allowed us to provide a 'correct' behavioural description of connectors (such as the Repl-AsyncDrain example) which were not possible in other models. Moreover, we provided a detailed justification for the various properties of our model. We hope that our research will contribute to a more axiomatic description of Reo connectors.

In this paper, we have not taken into account the actual data flowing through the connectors. This was in order to not distract the reader from the actual novelty of the paper. In fact, data constraints form a boolean algebra and can be added exactly in the same way as we have dealt with guards. Moreover, our model can be used to give a significantly simpler account of quantitative Reo [4]. At present, we are incorporating our automata model into CWI's *Eclipse Coordination Tools*[3] This will enable the generation of Java implementations of our automata for composing components and services.

Kleene algebra with tests [22] (KAT) are to guarded automata what regular expressions are to ordinary finite automata. Therefore, we want to explore how KAT expressions can be used to specify and synthesize Reo connectors. This will give us an algebraic description of Reo connectors, for which reasoning can be automated. More generally, since our automata can be seen as ordinary labelled transition systems with structured labels, we are interested in the connection with temporal logic and model checking.

References

1. Arbab, F.: Reo: a channel-based coordination model for component composition. Mathematical Structures in Computer Science 14(3), 329–366 (2004)
2. Arbab, F.: Abstract behavior types: a foundation model for components and their composition. Sci. Comput. Program. 55(1-3), 3–52 (2005)

---

[3] http://reo.project.cwi.nl/

3. Arbab, F., Bruni, R., Clarke, D., Lanese, I., Montanari, U.: Tiles for Reo. In: WADT (2009) (to appear)
4. Arbab, F., Chothia, T., van der Mei, R., Meng, S., Moon, Y., Verhoef, C.: From Coordination to Stochastic Models of QoS. In: Field, J., Vasconcelos, V.T. (eds.) COORDINATION 2009. LNCS, vol. 5521, pp. 268–287. Springer, Heidelberg (2009)
5. Arbab, F., Herman, I., Spilling, P.: An overview of Manifold and its implementation. Concurrency - Practice and Experience 5(1), 23–70 (1993)
6. Arbab, F., Rutten, J.: A coinductive calculus of component connectors. In: Wirsing, M., Pattinson, D., Hennicker, R. (eds.) WADT 2003. LNCS, vol. 2755, pp. 34–55. Springer, Heidelberg (2003)
7. Baier, C., Sirjani, M., Arbab, F., Rutten, J.: Modeling component connectors in Reo by constraint automata. Sci. Comput. Program. 61(2), 75–113 (2006)
8. Barbosa, L., Barbosa, M.: A perspective on service orchestration. In: Science of Computer Programming (2008) (accepted for publication)
9. Barbosa, M., Barbosa, L., Campos, J.: Towards a coordination model for interactive systems. Electr. Notes Theor. Comput. Sci. 183, 89–103 (2007)
10. Clarke, D., Proença, J., Lazovik, A., Arbab, F.: Deconstructing Reo. In: FOCLASA 2008 (2008) (to appear)
11. Clarke, D., Costa, D., Arbab, F.: Connector colouring I: Synchronisation and context dependency. Sci. Comput. Program. 66(3), 205–225 (2007)
12. Costa, D.: Formal Models for Context Dependent Connectors for Distributed Software Components and Services. Ph.D thesis (2009) (to appear)
13. de Boer, F., Kok, J., Palamidessi, C., Rutten, J.: Non-monotonic concurrent constraint programming. In: ILPS, pp. 315–334 (1993)
14. Fiadeiro, J., Lopes, A.: Community on the move: Architectures for distribution and mobility. In: de Boer, F.S., Bonsangue, M.M., Graf, S., de Roever, W.-P. (eds.) FMCO 2003. LNCS, vol. 3188, pp. 177–196. Springer, Heidelberg (2004)
15. Fournet, C., Gonthier, G.: The join calculus: A language for distributed mobile programming. In: Barthe, G., Dybjer, P., Pinto, L., Saraiva, J. (eds.) APPSEM 2000. LNCS, vol. 2395, pp. 268–332. Springer, Heidelberg (2002)
16. Gelernter, D.: Generative communication in Linda. ACM Trans. Program. Lang. Syst. 7(1), 80–112 (1985)
17. Scholten, J.: Mobile channels for exogenous coordination of distributed systems: semantics, implementation and composition. Ph.D thesis, LIACS, Faculty of Mathematics and Natural Sciences, Leiden University (January 2007)
18. Izadi, M., Bonsangue, M.: Recasting constraint automata into Büchi automata. In: Fitzgerald, J.S., Haxthausen, A.E., Yenigun, H. (eds.) ICTAC 2008. LNCS, vol. 5160, pp. 156–170. Springer, Heidelberg (2008)
19. Izadi, M., Bonsangue, M., Clarke, D.: Modelling component connectors: Synchronisation and context-dependency. In: Proceedings of SEFM 2008. IEEE Computer Society Press, Los Alamitos (2008) (to appear)
20. Khosravi, R., Sirjani, M., Asoudeh, N., Sahebi, S., Iravanchi, H.: Modeling and analysis of Reo connectors using Alloy. In: Lea, D., Zavattaro, G. (eds.) COORDINATION 2008. LNCS, vol. 5052, pp. 169–183. Springer, Heidelberg (2008)
21. Koehler, C., Arbab, F., de Vink, E.: Reconfiguring distributed Reo connectors. In: WADT (2009) (to appear)
22. Kozen, D.: On the coalgebraic theory of Kleene algebra with tests. TR 10173, Computing and Information Science, Cornell University (March 2008)

23. Lee, B., Lee, E.: Hierarchical concurrent finite state machines in Ptolemy. In: ACSD, pp. 34–40. IEEE Computer Society, Los Alamitos (1998)
24. Liu, X., Xiong, Y., Lee, E.: The Ptolemy ii framework for visual languages. In: HCC, p. 50. IEEE Computer Society, Los Alamitos (2001)
25. Maraikar, Z., Lazovik, A., Arbab, F.: Building mashups for the enterprise with SABRE. In: Bouguettaya, A., Krüger, I., Margaria, T. (eds.) ICSOC 2008. LNCS, vol. 5364, pp. 70–83. Springer, Heidelberg (2008)
26. Misra, J., Cook, W.: Computation orchestration: A basis for wide-area computing. Journal of Software and Systems Modeling (May 2006)
27. Mousavi, M., Sirjani, M., Arbab, F.: Formal semantics and analysis of component connectors in Reo. Electr. Notes Theor. Comput. Sci. 154(1), 83–99 (2006)
28. Nierstrasz, O.: Piccola - a small compositional language (invited talk). In: Ciancarini, P., Fantechi, A., Gorrieri, R. (eds.) FMOODS. IFIP Conference Proceedings, vol. 139. Kluwer, Dordrecht (1999)
29. Rutten, J.: Coalgebra, concurrency, and control. In: Boel, R., Stremersch, G. (eds.) Discrete Event Systems (analysis and control), Proceedings of WODES 2000, pp. 31–38. Kluwer, Dordrecht (2000)
30. Shaw, M., Garlan, D.: Software Architecture. Prentice Hall, Englewood Cliffs (1996)
31. Szyperski, C.: Component Software: Beyond Object-Oriented Programming, 2nd edn. Addison-Wesley Professional, Reading (2002)

Contract-Based Coordination
of Hardware Components
for the Development of Embedded Software

Tayeb Bouhadiba and Florence Maraninchi

Verimag*, Centre équation - 2, avenue de Vignate, 38610 GIÈRES — France
{tayeb.bouhadiba,florence.maraninchi}@imag.fr

Abstract. Embedded software is intrinsically concurrent, because an embedded system has several computing units. The way the software pieces communicate and synchronize depends on the hardware architecture. If the architecture is regular and fixed, there often exists a *programming model* that allows software developers to use it. If the architecture is ad hoc, heterogeneous, or changing, such a programming model does not exist, and the software developer has to be provided with a sufficient view of the hardware behavior. We propose a notion of *contract* associated with a component-based description framework, to help defining such views. The contracts are used to describe and simulate the potentially complex behaviors of the hardware execution platform, but only the situations the embedded software should be aware of. In some sense, the "semantics" of concurrency between the software pieces is given by the structure of the hardware platform, the interface it exposes to the software, and its contract behavior.

Keywords: Executable Contracts, Components, Embedded Systems, Hardware/Software Interface, Simulation Models.

1 Introduction

1.1 Development of Hardware/Software Embedded Systems

Embedded hardware/software systems (ranging from systems-on-a-chip to distributed fault-tolerant avionics systems) involve several software components, running on the various computing units, with or without operating systems. The way they synchronize and exchange information depends on the architecture and properties of the hardware platform.

Programming Models. When the architecture is sufficiently regular and fixed (e.g., arrays of identical processors connected with a network-on-chip), there usually exists a corresponding high level *programming model*; it allows to describe

---

* Verimag is an academic research laboratory affiliated with: the University Joseph Fourier (UJF), the National Research Center (CNRS) and Grenoble Institute of Technology.

the software with abstractions like "SMP" or "dataflow", etc. Then, automatic tools can *map* the software pieces onto the computing units, guaranteeing that the synchronizations on the actual hardware happen as they were described in the high level programming model.

When Programming Models Do Not Exist. When the architecture is heterogeneous, ad hoc, and/or subject to changes during the design of the system, there does not exist such a *programming model*. In this case, the hardware architecture has to be described in such a way that the software developer knows how to use it. This view of the hardware, for the software developer, is much more abstract than the descriptions needed to build the actual hardware. The model of the hardware should also be efficiently executable, and available early, to serve as a virtual prototype.

Systems-on-a-chip are a typical domain in which the hardware and the software may be designed together. Transaction-level modeling (TLM) [8] has been proposed, abstracting away the details of register-transfer level models (RTL). The standard language of the domain in the industry is SystemC/TLM, which has been quite successful in providing virtual prototypes of complex hardware platforms, so that software developers can start developing the embedded software long before the chip is available. The definition of what is a good TL model is still the subject of many discussions. Abstractions are needed because of simulation speed, of course, but it is also a very good idea to write the software without being allowed to take fine hardware details into account. This make it more robust, in the sense that it is less sensitive to small variations of the hardware behavior. This is mainly why a TL model is essentially *untimed* and *asynchronous*. A certain amount of *non-determinism* is also present in the model. For instance, in SystemC, the behavior of hardware components is simulated with C++ threads, which are scheduled by a non-deterministic scheduler. A difficulty with TLM in SystemC is that it is not always obvious to separate the model from the execution engine. An advantage is that SystemC modeling encourages a component-based approach. Initiatives like IPXact[1] try to define standard specifications for the components, but this is quite informal for the moment.

1.2 Components and Contracts for Embedded Systems

There has been a lot of work, in recent years, on component models for embedded systems, formalized or not, focused on refinement, or concurrency models, or expressivity, etc. See, for instance, logical contracts for Lustre [16], reactive modules [2], interface automata [6], conditional dependencies in Signal [13], etc. The purpose of this paper is not to discuss the advantages, drawbacks and relative expressivity of all these proposals, because this would deserve a whole paper.

We concentrate on the problem of defining contracts for the simulation of hardware platforms. We will use a very simple model inspired by Ptolemy [3].

---

[1] See www.eclipse.org/dsdp/dd/ipxact/toc.html

In Ptolemy, systems are made of *actors* (in the sense of [1]) connected to each other, and coordinated by a *director* that implements a given MoCC (model of computation and communication). Ptolemy proposes a quite large catalog of discrete and continuous MoCCs. Our model inspired by Ptolemy is called 42 [15,17]. It is restricted to discrete systems, and the main difference with Ptolemy is that the various directors corresponding to MoCCs are expressed as small programs in terms of more basic notions like the activation of the components, the transmission of data from one component to another, etc. Section 2 will briefly present this model.

The other important notion for this paper is that of a *contract*. *Contracts* were proposed originally by B. Meyer for the programming language Eiffel, and have proven very useful for (object-oriented) software design. A lot of tools, like JML [12] allow to obtain defensive code automatically from the expression of contracts. Some extensions like JASS (Java with Assertions) [5] of the original proposition allow to express *logical-time contracts* (one can express an assumption like: "*the inputs to method* m, *during the whole execution of a program, are increasing*", which could not be expressed with pre and post conditions associated with methods). Such logical-time contracts have also been proposed in a synchronous framework for concurrent software, as shown in [16], and are very similar to the *sequential don't cares* used by hardware designers [21], or to the *circular assume-guarantee reasoning* described in [18].

The notion of a contract, extended with logical-time, seems to be appropriate for hardware/software systems, and for our purpose of designing abstract models of the hardware. The hardware components have to respect *synchronization* contracts between each other, because of bus protocols, and various constraints on the possible connections; the hardware platform seen as a whole, and the embedded software, also have to respect contracts between each other.

1.3   Contributions and Structure of the Paper

The contributions of this paper are the following:

1. A notion of *control contract* for the 42 components, rich enough to express complex synchronizations between components. An assemblage of components can be simulated given the contracts only, before the detailed behavior of the components is known.
2. An extension of the 42 implementation to allow the execution of a hardware model, together with some embedded software.
3. An illustration of this early execution mechanism for building high-level models of hardware platforms inspired by TLM; these platforms can be simulated together with the actual embedded software. The contribution is the definition of TL-like modeling for hardware platforms, independent of a particular language and simulation engine.

Section 2 briefly presents the model 42; Section 3 presents the contracts for 42; Section 4 shows how to use these contracts for the simulation of hardware platforms together with some embedded software. Section 5 and 6 describe a case-study, for which we demonstrate the benefits of early simulation. Section 7 is a list of related work, and Section 8 is the conclusion.

2   An Overview of the Component Model 42

The original definition of 42, and examples, can be found in [15,17].

Basic Components. Figure 1 shows a 42 component. It is a black-box that has input and output *data* ports, and input and output *control* ports. The input control ports are used to ask it to perform a computation *step*. A step corresponds to a terminating (non-necessarily deterministic) piece of code. A component has some internal memory. The input and output data ports are used to communicate data between the components. The output control ports will be used by the components to send information to the controller (see below).

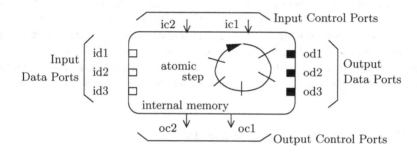

Fig. 1. A Basic 42 Component

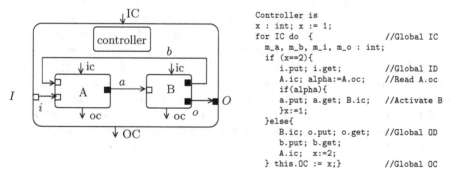

Fig. 2. Assembling Components

```
Controller is
x : int; x := 1;
for IC do  {                    //Global IC
    m_a, m_b, m_i, m_o : int;
    if (x==2){
        i.put; i.get;           //Global ID
        A.ic; alpha:=A.oc;      //Read A.oc
        if(alpha){
            a.put; a.get; B.ic; //Activate B
        }x:=1;
    }else{
        B.ic; o.put; o.get;     //Global OD
        b.put; b.get;
        A.ic;  x:=2;
    } this.OC := x;}            //Global OC
```

Fig. 3. Controller Code of Figure 2

Assembling Components. Components are connected by directed *wires*. An input data port can be connected to an output data port of the same type (we will assume this is always true in the sequel). The control ports are connected to the *controller*, not directly to each other. A wire does not mean a priori any synchronization, nor memorization.

In the sense of Ptolemy [3], a *system* (see Fig. 2) is made of components connected by wires (the *architecture*) plus a *controller* that activates the components and decides what happens on the wires. The model is hierarchic: an architecture plus a controller form a new *component*. It exposes new input and output data and control ports. The global output data ports (e.g., O) are connected to output data ports of subcomponents (e.g., o), and the global input data ports (e.g., I) are connected to input data ports of the subcomponents (e.g., i).

The Controller. Figure 3 is an example, given in some simple imperative style. The controller defines how the components behave together. It is in charge of *translating* an activation request on one global control input port (e.g., IC, also referred to as a *macro-step* in the sequel), into a sequence of activations of the subcomponents, and data exchanges between them (also called *micro-steps*). It defines what the *MoCC* is, at this level. To achieve this, the controller may use some temporary variables explicitly associated with the wires (e.g., m_a), whose lifetime is limited to the macro-step. It uses simple primitives of two forms: activation of subcomponents (e.g., A.ic) and data management: a.put moves the value from the port A.a to the memory associated with the wire a, whereas a.get moves the value stored from the wire to the right port B.a. The controller also reports on the activity of subcomponents through global output control ports (e.g., OC).

3   Rich Control Contracts for 42

In this section, we propose a definition of *control contracts* for 42. The formal definition can be found in [17]. In 42, contracts are similar to the *protocols* widely used in object-oriented designs (see, for instance [22,20]). When specifying a class in an object-oriented framework, a protocol can be used to specify, for instance, that method m1 should always be called before method m2, unless method m3 has been called at least twice. The idea in 42 is similar: contracts will be used to specify sequential constraints between the control inputs and outputs by a finite state machine. Moreover, the contract will specify which of the inputs are needed for each control input (the "assume" part of a contract), and which of the data and control outputs are produced (the "guarantee" part). We restrict to *control contracts*: they express how the components should be activated, but tell nothing on the values that may be accepted or delivered, except for particular data ports (see below).

3.1   Definition

Figure 4 shows a protocol for the component C of Figure 1. Each transition has a label of the form:

```
[condition] (data req) control input / control output (data prod).
```

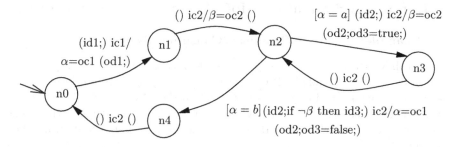

Fig. 4. Example Contract for the Component of Fig. 1

The variables denoted by Greek letters are used to store the value of control outputs. A control output is of some enumerated type. They may be used later on in the protocol itself; let us note the set of such variables V. The [condition] part is built from the variables in V. The (data req) part expresses conditional data dependencies; the conditions are built on V too. For instance (id2,if $\neg\beta$ then id3) means that the transition needs id2 and, if the value stored in variable β is false, it also needs id3. The (data prod) is built similarly, and expresses which outputs are indeed produced. For some of the data ports, which are used for synchronizations (e.g., an interrupt) the contract may also express which value is indeed produced (e.g., od3 = true). This can be done only if the type of the port is finite (some enumeration, usually). The control input is a single control input. the control outputs gives the control outputs that are indeed produced, and may indicate that their values are stored in variables of V. Initially, the protocol is in its initial state (n0), and then it evolves according to the sequence of activations produced by the controller in response to a sequence of macro-steps. Each macro-step is considered to start in the state where the protocol was at the end of the previous macro-step.

3.2   Compatibility Issues

The code of a component should be *compatible* with its contract: for instance, if the contract declares that only input id is required for a given step, the component should not make use of the other inputs. If the contract declares that a given data output is produced for a given step, then the actual component should indeed produce it. The complete definition is given in [17].

Checking this kind of property statically, in the general case, is a complex program analysis problem. For instance, in most programming languages, determining which variables are read by a particular piece of code is undecidable. On the contrary, if the component is a piece of hardware, described in a language like VHDL, then the use of inputs and the actual production of outputs might be analyzable by model-checking techniques in some cases. The purpose of this paper is not to check statically that components conform with their contracts. We will see in sections 4.5, 6.3 below that the compatibility property can be checked dynamically if the contract is executed together with the actual component.

4   Defining a Simulation MoCC as a Contract Interpreter

4.1   Example: A Simple Producer/Consumer System

Figure 5 shows the structure of a system made of three components: a producer, a consumer, and a bounded FIFO used to store the elements produced before they are consumed. The intended behavior is that the producer and the consumer perform cyclic jobs, writing to or reading from the FIFO from time to time. The producer should wait when the FIFO is full, and the consumer should wait when it is empty.

In the 42 model, the data ports and connections are representative of the real hardware system. For instance, there is a protocol between the FIFO and the consumer: the latter should send a request to the FIFO to know whether it may deliver an element, and it is blocked until the FIFO answers this request by a grant signal. Similarly, the producer should send a request to know whether the FIFO still has some room available, and it is blocked until the FIFO accepts the WRITE operation by sending a grant signal.

In the 42 model, the control ports are connected (implicitly) to the controller, and are used to obtain a simulation model. Each component has a single control input called op, meaning: *perform a single atomic execution step*. The model is sufficiently abstract to represent systems in which the consumer and the producer are dedicated hardware components, or two CPUs with embedded software.

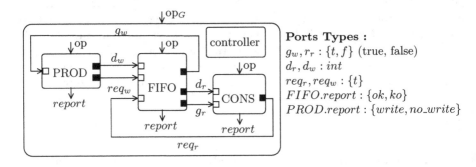

Ports Types :
$g_w, r_r : \{t, f\}$ (true, false)
$d_r, d_w : int$
$req_r, req_w : \{t\}$
$FIFO.report : \{ok, ko\}$
$PROD.report : \{write, no\_write\}$

Fig. 5. The Producer/Consumer Example in 42

4.2   What Do We Want to Observe?

Before defining the simulation model, let us define precisely what we want to observe in such a simulation; remember that the idea is to show "all" possible behaviors of the hardware platform to the software developer. In the example, the producer could be implemented as embedded software running on a CPU.

A lot of real behaviors of the hardware are similar, from the point of view of the software, hence we define an abstract view, keeping only the behaviors that *matter.* Since the three components could be running in true physical parallelism, with or without a common clock, the most abstract view imposes to consider them as purely *asynchronous.*

Figure 6 recalls the importance of atomicity in such asynchronous models, based on interleaving semantics. Consider two entities running in parallel, described by the automata (1) and (2). Associating a label a to a single transition means that the part of the behavior of the entity 1 described by a can be considered as *atomic* with respect to their parallel behaviors. In other words, nobody running in parallel can observe the internal states of entity 1 during action a. The set of all possible global behaviors is given by automaton (4). Now, if automaton (2) is replaced by automaton (3), meaning that b should not be considered as atomic, then the global behaviors are those of automaton (5), in which new states appear. The a transition from state X means that in entity 2, the intermediate state between b' and b'' is observable by entity 1.

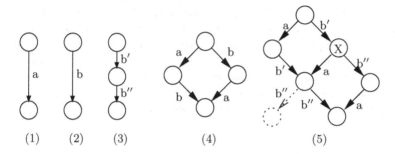

(1)   (2)   (3)   (4)   (5)

Fig. 6. Asynchronous Models

Choosing the granularity of atomic transitions is an intrinsic modeling problem. When modeling the behaviors of two threads on a mono-processor with a preemptive scheduler, the only possible choice is to consider the atomicity as given by the execution platform: instructions in the processor are atomic (non interruptible by the scheduler). Hence a thread is described by a detailed automaton, with explicit states between machine instructions. The model is appropriate for checking parallel programs that use low-level synchronization mechanisms like semaphores of atomic read-write machine instructions.

However, in higher level models, the notion of atomicity may be of a coarser granularity. In transaction-level models, typically, the granularity reflects the fact that we do not need to observe the precise interleavings of the components' behaviors. We only need to observe the interleavings at a granularity given by the explicit synchronizations between the components.

4.3   Contracts, and Interpreting Contracts

Principles. In 42 simulation models like the one of Figure 5, the atomicity is expressed by the op control input. Each activation of the component with input op makes it execute a (potentially long but terminating) piece of its behavior.

In a 42 model made of two components C1 and C2, we can consider each of the components to be an automaton, whose transitions are labeled by op. The simulation produces the paths of the asynchronous interleaving product of these two automata. The contracts of the components contain all the information needed to understand the explicit synchronizations between them. The simulation MoCC — and the corresponding 42 controller — can be obtained automatically. In fact, the simulation MoCC is simply an *non-deterministic interpreter* of the components' contracts.

Example. Let us illustrate all this with the example. The contracts of the producer, the consumer, and the FIFO, are given by Figures 7, 8 and 9 respectively. Paragraph 4.5 will explain the `assert` statement attached to state p3 of Figure 7. The types of the ports are given in Figure 5. Figure 10 gives a small part of the graph whose paths are explored by the non-deterministic contract interpreter. The simulation starts with all the components' contracts in their initial state. At each simulation step, the choice of the component to consider is non-deterministic, among the components whose contract shows that at least one transition is possible (all data required are present in the set *Available*). Activating a component consists in choosing a transition in its contract, from the current state. After the activation, the required data are removed from the set *Available*, the provided ones are added to it. The control outputs are given non-deterministic values (in their finite domain).

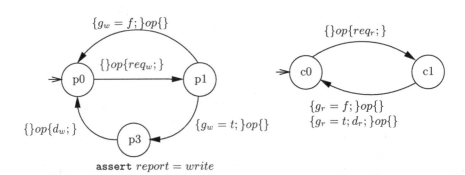

Fig. 7. Contract of The Producer. It sends a request to write to the FIFO, via its port req_w. If it receives $g_w = f$, it is not allowed to write, and returns to its initial state (it will have to issue another request later). Otherwise, it will receive $g_w = t$. At this point, it may send a data via its port d_w and return to the initial state.

Fig. 8. Contract of The Consumer. It sends a request to read from the FIFO, via its port req_r, and waits for a response. If it receives $g_r = f$, it is not allowed to read, and returns to its initial state (it will have to issue another request later). If it receives $g_r = t$, it is granted access to read; it also needs the data read, via its port d_r, and returns to its initial state.

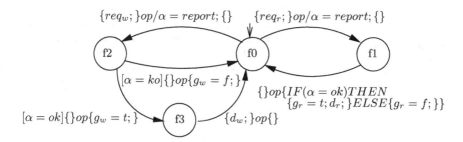

Fig. 9. Contract of The FIFO. The FIFO receives a request for a read via its port req_r and puts a value on the *report* output control port which is stored in variable α. This value tells the controller whether the FIFO is empty. If it is not empty ($\alpha = ok$), it grants access, providing $g_r = t$ together with the data read (via port d_r). Otherwise, if it is empty, it does not grant access and provides $g_r = f$. Similarly, the FIFO responds to a write request when it receives req_w. It provides a value on *report* stored in α telling whether the FIFO is full. If $\alpha = ko$ (the FIFO is full), it will not grant access for a write, and sends $g_w = f$. If $\alpha = ok$, the FIFO grants access for the write request (it sends $g_w = t$) and waits for the value to be written on its d_w input data port.

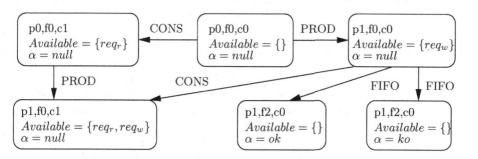

Fig. 10. Interleaving components executions

4.4   Executing Embedded Software on the Hardware Model

Assume the producer component is actually a processor that executes some embedded code. An example software code is given by Figure 12. On the real hardware, the functions like **send_req()** will be implemented by accesses to the drivers' registers. To make the same software run together with the simulation of the hardware platform, these functions are implemented as a *wrapper* of the embedded software, whose code is given in Figure 11. The wrapped software corresponds to the 42 component called **PROD** on Figure 5. **send_req()** and **write_v(data)** are used to send a write request, and to write on the d_r data port. The wrapper functions produce the *report* control outputs.

Technically, the software is run as a thread that may suspend itself with **pause**. The simulation of the hardware platform is the main program; it may reactivate the software thread with the **resume()** function. Consider a case when the

```
                         int send_req(){         int main(...) {
                           reqr.write(t);          int val, g;
write_v(int val){          report.write("no_write");  while(1) {
  report.write("write");   pause();                  val = ...
  pause();                 return gw.read();         // some value
  dw.write(val);         }                           g = send_req();
  pause();               op(){                       if(g==1)
}                          resume();                   write_v(val);
                         }                         }}
```

Fig. 11. Wrapper Primitives in Some Imperative Style.   **Fig. 12.** Software C-code
p.write(val) writes val on port p; p.read() reads the
port p.

simulation controller transforms a global activation opG into an activation of the
producer component (PROD.op). This resumes the thread of the software, which
runs until the next pause in a communication primitive (e.g., send_req). The
software thread being suspended, the simulation controller considers PROD.op
to be terminated. Next time it will be activated, the software thread will start
execution from where it had paused. An execution from one pause to the next
one is the *atomic* step of the producer component.

4.5   Introducing Assertions in Contracts

Assertions are introduced to be able to check the compatibility between a component and its contract, dynamically. An assertion is a logical property associated
with a state of a contract, and expressing conditions on the control outputs of
the component. In figure 7, if the contract is in state p3, the assertion tells that
the value of the *report* output control port should be write.

When executing the contracts alone, the values of the control outputs are
non-deterministic, and the assertions are not checked. When running actual embedded software, the production of the control outputs is done by the wrapper
functions. Hence checking the control output of the wrapper component is a way
of checking that the software has indeed made a call to the write_v() function.
If the software does not call write_v(), the control output is no_write, and the
assertion is violated. This mechanism makes it possible to run the software and
to check the compatibility with the contract, even if it is given as object code.
The only constraint is that it uses the interface functions to access the hardware.

5   A Hardware/Software Case-Study

5.1   Structure of the System, Intended Behavior and Potential Bugs

Figure 13 is the structure of the system under study. It is made of a CPU, a
LCD display, a bus, and a memory. The LCD is a component that may be programmed by the CPU, in order to perform repetitive transfers from the memory

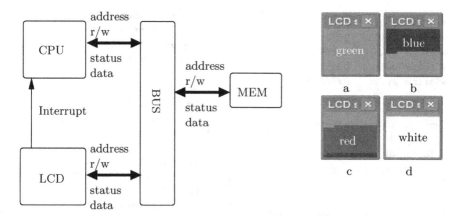

Fig. 13. An Example System-on-a-Chip   **Fig. 14.** LCD ScreenShots

(like a DMA, Direct Memory Access Component). There is a need for some communication between the LCD and the CPU, to inform it that the transfers that were programmed are finished. This is done with an interrupt. In order to display something on the LCD, the software writes an image in some dedicated place of the memory; then it programs the LCD so that it now transfers from the memory to the screen; then it waits for the interrupt from the LCD, meaning the transfer is finished. Figure 15 gives the software that will be run on the CPU (more details below).

Intended Behavior. In our example, the software repeatedly displays a full green screen, then a blue one, then a red one, and so on. On Figure 14, (a) and (b) show normal states of the display. (b) is possible because the LCD may take some time to replace a full green screen by a full blue one. (b) corresponds to the following situation: the CPU had written a green image before, it has just written a blue one; it is waiting for the interrupt telling it that the blue transfer is finished. The LCD is transferring the blue image, part of the green one is still visible. When the transfer is finished, and the screen is totally blue, it will send the interrupt to the CPU.

On the contrary, (c) should not be possible. The only way of obtaining such a state is when the software starts reprogramming the LCD (writing the red image, for instance) without waiting for the last programming to finish.

Typical Bugs. A typical misconception of the hardware platform is to forget the interrupt wire between the LCD and the CPU. If this wire does not exist, the only way for the software to know that a transfer is finished would be to have a precise knowledge of the *time* it can take. In high level models like TL models, this is prohibited. Synchronizations should be made explicit, so as to get robust software, able to run correctly on various hardware platforms, with different timings. A typical synchronization bug in the software is to forget to

```
#define WIDTH    20
#define HEIGHT   20
#define blue     0xff0000ff
#define red      0xffff0000
#define green    0xff00ff00


void lcd_print
(unsigned long int pattern ) {
  int y;
  for (y=0; y<HEIGHT*WIDTH; y++)
    write_mem(y, pattern);
}


int main(int argc, char **argv) {
    while(1) {
        lcd_print(green);
        write_lcd(0x01,0x1);
        wait_interrupt();
        lcd_print(blue);
        write_lcd(0x01,0x1);
        wait_interrupt();
        lcd_print(red);
        write_lcd(0x01,0x1);
        wait_interrupt();
    }
}
```

```
interrupt : bool;
write_lcd(int a, int d){
  report.write("LT");
  report'.write("NoIT");
  pause();
  acd_c.write(a,"W",d);
  target.write("L");
  pause(); resp_c.read();
}
write_mem(int a, int d){
  report.write("MT");
  report'.write("NoIT");
  pause();
  acd_c.write(a,"W",d);
  target.write("M");
  pause(); resp_c.read();
}
wait_interrupt(){
  report'.write("IT");
  pause();
  interrupt=0;// clear interrupt
}
op(){
  if(intr.read()!=null)
    interrupt=1;// set interrupt
  else  resume();
}
```

Fig. 15. Software Code and Wrapper

wait for the interrupt from the LCD. Another kind of bug would be due to pure *data* errors, like writing to an erroneous part of the memory, or writing only a part of the image, or using the wrong color, etc.

6 Designing and Exploiting a Model in 42

The benefits of a 42 model for the system described above are the following. First, the whole system can be described by its architecture and the contracts of the components, without knowing the details of the components. Then, the system can be simulated following the principles of section 4.3. In this first step, the contract of the CPU is in fact the contract of: the CPU plus the software that will run on it; but the part of the behavior which is due to the software is very abstract, as we will see on the example.

Second, when the architecture and the contracts have been simulated so that early synchronization problems (like forgetting the interrupt wire, or forgetting to wait for the interrupt in the CPU+SW contract) have been discovered and corrected, the same model can be simulated together with the execution of the

Ports Type:
CPU.report : $\{MT, LT\}$ **acd$_X$** : $[a : int, c : \{R, W\}, d : int]$ **intr** : $\{t, f\}$
CPU.report$'$: $\{IT, NoIT\}$ **resp$_X$** : $[status : bool, data : int]$ **target** : $\{L, M\}$
LCD.report : $\{ok, ko\}$

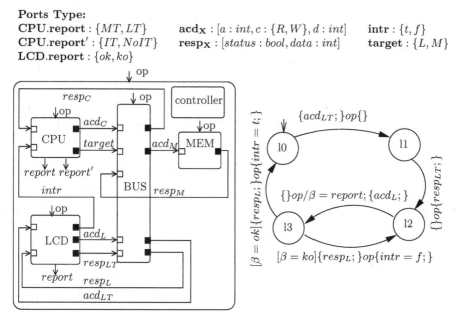

Fig. 16. 42 Model of the Example in Fig. 13   **Fig. 17.** The Contract of the LCD

real software. This allows to see more bugs, typically the data bugs (wrong color, etc.). But the interesting part is that it allows to check the compatibility between the contract of the CPU component (which includes some information on the software) and the actual piece of software, written in C or other languages.

6.1   The 42 Model

Figure 16 is the structure of the model in 42. Each wire between two components models a communication in the real hardware platform. The types of the wires may be Boolean (e.g., for *intr*) or records (e.g., *acd$_X$* encapsulates the address, the control R/W, and the data to be written). Each component is equipped with its local contract where the output control values may be used. LCD.report may take the value ok (resp. ko) which states that the transfer of the image from the memory is finished (resp. not finished).

The contract of the CPU (Figure 18) is in fact the contract of the embedded software, plus some hardware mechanisms like the memorization of the interrupts until they are taken into account (variable interrupt in Fig. 15). The CPU contract reports on the state of the software, which may end an atomic step in three cases: either it stops just before an access to the memory or the LCD, or it is waiting for an interrupt. These three situations are encoded with the two control outputs *report* and *report$'$*. *report* may take its value in { MT, LT } (memory or LCD access, respectively). *report$'$* may take its value in { IT, NoIT }. IT indicates that the software is waiting for an interrupt.

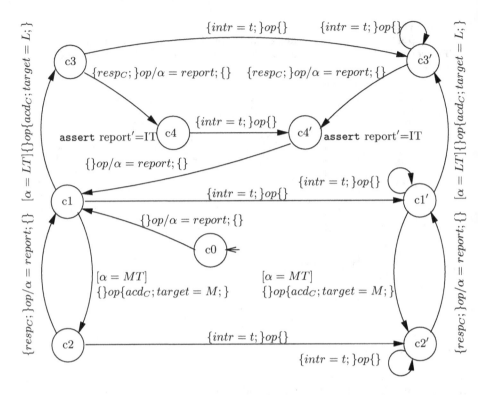

Fig. 18. Contract of The CPU Component (Software + interrupt bit). see Fig. 16 for Ports Types.

The LCD contract (Figure 17) describes the following behavior: in state 10 the LCD waits until it is programmed by the CPU (this comes as a data on input acd_{LT}, transition to 11). Then it acknowledges this by writing to its port $resp_{LT}$ and it reaches state 12. The loop between 12 and 13 corresponds to a sequence of read actions from the memory (acd_L), each of them being acknowledged ($resp_L$). For each read the contract stores the control output *report* in variable β. In state 13, if β is ok it means this was the last read, and the LCD returns to state 11 and writes a **true** value to its interrupt port (**intr=t**), for the CPU. If β is ko, it writes a **false** value (**intr=f**) and continues.

The contract of the memory (Figure 19) is quite simple: it accepts read or write requests on its input port acd_M and acknowledges them by $resp_M$ (which encapsulates the request status, and potentially a data delivered for a read request).

The contract of the bus (Figure 20) is more complex, because it describes the correct transportation of read and write accesses, and their corresponding acknowledgments. The possible transfers are: the CPU writes to the memory; the LCD reads from the memory. We do not consider the case of parallel software running on the CPU and issuing several accesses to the bus in parallel. The contract of the bus shows that an access to the bus can be memorized until the

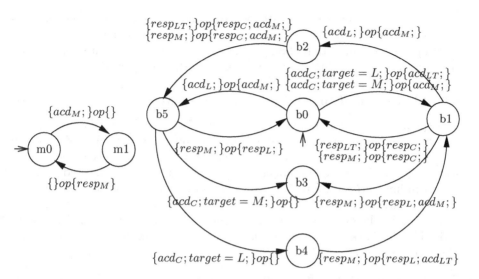

Fig. 19. Contract of the
memory

Fig. 20. Contract of the bus

current transfer is terminated, but only two parallel transfers are considered. In a real bus, this is far more complex, but the contract is of the same form (we would need a better language than flat explicit automata to describe it, though).

The contract of the CPU is as follows. The unprimed states (resp. the primed ones) correspond to cases when there is no memorized interrupt (resp. there is a memorized interrupt). When the interrupt arrives (transitions labeled by $\{intr = t\}op\{\}$), the contract changes from an unprimed state to a primed one (e.g., c4 to c4'). When the interrupt is taken into account, the contract changes from a primed state to an unprimed one (the only one is from c4' to c1, the **interrupt bit** may not be cleared before receiving the acknowledgment corresponding to the last **LCD programming**).

From the initial state c0, the initial activation op goes to state c1 and corresponds to the first part of the software, before it stops for a memory or LCD access (at this point, it *should not* stop because it is waiting for an interrupt). The *report* output stored in α indicates the target (MT or LT).

From c1, the interrupt can be taken, and the contract goes to c1'. Otherwise, the software starts the memory or LCD access, by sending relevant information on its output data ports (acd_C, $target$). It goes to c2 or c3.

In c2 and c3, the CPU is waiting for the acknowledgment from the target component ($resp_C$). From c2 it goes back to c1 for potential new memory accesses; from c3 it goes to c4: the LCD has been programmed, and the software should now wait for the interrupt stating that the LCD has finished.

From c4, the only possible change is that the interrupt arrives, and is stored. The contract goes to state c4'. Then the software can take it into account, and go to state c1 again.

The `assert` statement associated with `c4` and `c4'` tells that, when the contract is in these states, the actual implementation should be waiting for the interrupt. This information about the implementation comes through the control output *report'* , which will be produced by the wrapper (Fig. 15).

6.2   Simulation of the Hardware Platform Alone

As explained in section 4.3, the hardware platform can be simulated alone. In fact we use a very abstract view of the embedded software, included in the contract of the CPU. An exhaustive simulation would build the complete interleaving graph (for applying model-checking), but it can also be used as input for a runtime verification tool (in the sense of a tool like Verisoft [9], or using dynamic partial orders adapted to SystemC/TLM [11]). Even if we do not use a specification language for temporal properties, we can observe *generic* properties like deadlocks, and some livelocks. The two following simulation results, obtained for the case study, illustrate two bugs that can be found early.

The Interrupt Bug. After writing an image, the processor waits for an interrupt coming from the LCD to start writing a new image. If the interrupt never occurs, the system is blocked. Suppose we modify the contract of the LCD to introduce this bug: on Figure 17, the transition from state l3 to l0 is now labeled by: $[\beta = ok]\{resp_L; \}op\{\}$. Suppose the simulation has reached the state $\{(c4,b0,m0,l3), Available = \{resp_L\}, \beta = ok\}$ (the processor is waiting for the interrupt, the memory is waiting for a READ/WRITE request, and the bus has just delivered the memory acknowledgment to the LCD). At this state, only the LCD may be activated, and the simulation moves to the state $\{(c4,b0,m0,l0), Available = \{\}\}$. At this state, all the components' transitions require inputs. But no inputs are available, which leads to a deadlock.

Other Bugs Other problems may be detected by the simulator. For instance, there are cases when a component is never activated. It's not necessarily a bug, but it deserves at least a warning. For example, when the LCD waits to be programmed, if the processor never does it, the LCD is never activated.

6.3   Simulation of the HW Platform Together with the Embedded Software

When the bugs that can be found with the execution of the hardware platform alone have been corrected, we start simulations together with the embedded software. As for the example in section 4.4, we need a set of wrapper functions (see Figure 15), and we may check the violation of the assertions.

One of the typical bugs mentioned previously is: the software omits to wait for the interrupt before reprogramming the LCD. So, suppose we omit the first occurrence of `wait_interrupt()` in the program of Figure 15. The simulation will report that the assertion associated with state c4 or c4' of the contract of the CPU is violated. This is a bug in the software, detected because it does not conform to its contract.

Despite the fact that the software respects its contract, there may be more bugs, related to the data. For instance, suppose the code of the lcd_print function is changed in the program of Figure 15: the condition of the loop is now y<HEIGHT+WIDTH, which means that the program writes 40 pixels instead of 400. This bug my be detected by observing the output on a simulated LCD, as shown on Figure 14-(d). The top of the LCD is colored whereas the bottom of it has the color corresponding to the initial memory value (white).

7   Related Work

We already gave some related work in the introduction, mainly on component models for embedded systems, and on the notion of contracts. A thorough comparison of all the component frameworks that could be applied for our purpose of building hardware abstract models is outside the scope of this paper.

The paper is focused on early execution of complex heterogeneous platforms. There is also related work in this direction.

The whole domain of transaction-level modeling for systems-on-a-chip is dedicated to this objective, but this is not yet possible to simulate the hardware with only the contract of the embedded software. A long cooperation with STMicroelectronics in Grenoble has led us to observe that, in some cases, people use TLM platforms to play with a very rough version of the embedded software, and the intention is clearly to use only the synchronization part of the software; but there are no tools to do that cleanly, the real embedded software cannot be compared to this rough version, etc.

There is also some academic work on early execution, especially for synchronous languages where the semantics is clear (see, for instance [19]).

Executable specifications have been advocated for a long time. In [7] they are illustrated with examples in the declarative language LSL (Larch Shared Language). The author claims that executing specifications allows early validation at an abstract level. This increases the correctness and the reliability of the software, and allows time and cost reduction. The same language is used as a target specification language for interpreting OCL (Object Constraint Language) constraints in UML [10].

The UML profile MARTE is defined for the analysis of real-time and embedded systems. [14] introduces a timing semantics expressed in CCSL (Clock Constraints Specification Language). CCSL constraints give a non-deterministic contract of a component, and the simulator produces execution scenarios of the system being modeled, non-deterministically. This is very similar to our approach, but more focused on time patterns (e.g., periodic inputs).

8   Conclusion

We have presented a notion of contract for a Ptolemy-like component model, usable for heterogeneous hardware/software concurrent systems. In this simple framework we suggest a solution to the following problem: how to design an abstract model of concurrent hardware platforms, to be exposed to software developers. This is inspired a lot by transaction-level modeling of systems-on-a-chip, but this is a first step towards *language-independent* TL models. This is useful because SystemC/TLM models, which have become a de facto standard, sometimes mix the semantics of the model with the peculiarities of the execution engine.

The 42 component framework is fully implemented. Basic components can be described in Java, the architecture of a composed component can be given in XML, and there is a small imperative language for describing the controllers, like the one in Figure 2. The framework has been used for other applications of 42, especially multi-MoCCs systems. For the application described in this paper, we added a way of describing contracts (also in XML) and the simulation controller which is reduced to a non-deterministic interpreter of the components' contracts. We also developed the mechanism of wrappers described in section 4.4. It is usable for the case when the implementation of a component is done in software. But it could be adapted to the case when the implementation is a piece of hardware. In this case, we would have to check the compatibility between the precise description of the hardware component (typically at the register-transfer level, given in VHDL or Verilog), and the contract. The principles of our wrappers could also be applied in this case; the essential point is that the wrapper has to produce the control outputs so that the assertions in the contracts can be checked.

Further work will be in three directions. First, We will investigate the languages used to describe contracts. Expressing a complex contract gives a big automaton. We can introduce finite-domain variables to keep small explicit automata; this would help in describing the general bus protocol of our example. But we also need products. The contract of the CPU we gave is in fact the synchronous product between a two-states automaton (the memory of the interrupt) and another automaton describing the cyclic behavior of the software. Note that these extensions do not increase the expressive power of the contracts. Second, we will concentrate on the expressivity of contracts, and precise comparisons with approaches like CCSL and the UML profile MARTE mentioned preciously. And, finally, further work on hardware models concentrates on the underlying modeling problem: *"what is the right granularity for models of hardware/software systems?"*. If it is too coarse, the model may hide bugs that will appear in the real system, because it does not show some important interleavings of the components' behaviors. If it is too fine grain, then it will expose a lot of behaviors and will be very slow, so it will be hard to exploit it for finding bugs. Finding the right compromise is quite hard, and there will be no theoretical answer (see [4] for a discussion). But we think that expressing the problem in a simple language-independent framework like 42 and its contracts, where the decision on atomicity is perfectly visible in the transitions of the contracts, is a good way to make progress.

References

1. Agha, G.: Actors: A Model of Concurrent Computation in Distributed Systems. Ph.D thesis. MIT, Cambridge (1985)
2. Alur, R., Henzinger, T.A.: Reactive modules. In: Proceedings, 11th Annual IEEE Symposium on Logic in Computer Science, New Brunswick, New Jersey, July 27–30, pp. 207–218. IEEE Computer Society Press, Los Alamitos (1996)
3. Buck, J., Ha, S., Lee, E.A., Messerschmitt, D.G.: Ptolemy: A framework for simulating and prototyping heterogenous systems. Int. Journal in Computer Simulation 4(2) (1994)
4. Cornet, J., Maraninchi, F., Maillet-Contoz, L.: A method for the efficient development of timed and untimed transaction-level models of systems-on-chip. In: Design Automation and Test in Europe (DATE), Munich, pp. 9–14 (March 2008)
5. Bartetzko, D., Fischer, C., Möller, M., Wehrheim, H.: Jass – Java with assertions. In: Havelund, K., Roşu, G. (eds.) Runtime Verification. Electronic Notes in Theoretical Computer Science, vol. 55. Elsevier, Amsterdam (2001)
6. de Alfaro, L., Henzinger, T.A.: Interface automata. In: Gruhn, V. (ed.) Proceedings of the Joint 8th ESEC/FSE and 9th ACM SIGSOFT, September 10–14, pp. 109–120. ACM Press, New York (2001)
7. Fuchs, N.E.: Fuchs. Specifications are (preferably) executable. Softw. Eng. J. 7(5), 323–334 (1992)
8. Ghenassia, F.: Transaction Level Modeling With SystemC: TLM Concepts And Applications for Embedded Systems. Springer, Heidelberg (2005)
9. Godefroid, P.: Model checking for programming languages using verisoft. In: POPL, pp. 174–186 (1997)
10. Hamie, A., Howse, J., Kent, S.: Interpreting the object constraint language. In: Software Engineering Conference, Proceedings. Asia Pacific, pp. 288–295 (December 1998)
11. Helmstetter, C., Maraninchi, F., Maillet-Contoz, L., Moy, M.: Automatic generation of schedulings for improving the test coverage of systems-on-a-chip. In: FMCAD, pp. 171–178. IEEE Computer Society, Los Alamitos (2006)
12. Leavens, G.T., Baker, A.L., Ruby, C.: JML: A notation for detailed design. In: Kilov, H., Rumpe, B., Simmonds, I. (eds.) Behavioral Specifications of Businesses and Systems, pp. 175–188. K.A Publishers, Boston (1999)
13. LeGuernic, P., Gautier, T., LeBorgne, M., LeMaire, C.: Programming real time applications with signal. Proceedings of the IEEE 79(9), 1321–1336 (1991)
14. Mallet, F.: Clock constraint specification language: specifying clock constraints with uml/marte. Innovations in SSE 4(3), 309–314 (2008)
15. Maraninchi, F., Bouhadiba, T.: 42: Programmable models of computation for a component-based approach to heterogeneous embedded systems. In: Sixth ACM International Conference on Generative Programming and Component Engineering (GPCE 2007), Salzburg, Austria (October 2007)
16. Maraninchi, F., Morel, L.: Logical-time contracts for the development of reactive embedded software. In: 30th Euromicro Conference, Component-Based Software Engineering Track (ECBSE), Rennes, France (September 2004)
17. Maraninchi, F., Bouhadiba, T.: 42: Programmable models of computation for the component-based virtual prototyping of heterogeneous embedded systems. Technical Report tr-2009-1, Verimag, Centre Équation, 38610 Gières (January 2009), http://www-verimag.imag.fr/index.php?page=techrep-list

18. McMillan, K.L.: Circular compositional reasoning about liveness. In: Pierre, L., Kropf, T. (eds.) CHARME 1999. LNCS, vol. 1703, pp. 342–345. Springer, Heidelberg (1999)
19. Morel, L., Mandel, L.: Executabe contracts for incremental prototypes of embedded systems. In: Workshop on Formal Foundations of Embedded Software and Component-Based Software Architectures (FESCA 2007), Braga (March 2007)
20. Plasil, S., Visnovsky, F.: Behavior protocols for software components. IEEE Transactions on Software Engineering 28, 1056–1076 (2002)
21. Devadas, S.: Optimizing interacting finite state machines using sequential don't cares. IEEE Transaction of Computer-Aided Design 10(12), 1473–1484 (1991)
22. van den Bos, J.: PROCOL: A protocol-constrained concurrent object-oriented language. Information Processing Letters 32(5), 221–227 (1989)

Coordination Model for Real-Time Collaborative Editors

Abdessamad Imine

INRIA Nancy-Grand Est & Nancy-Université, France
imine@loria.fr

Abstract. Real-time Collaborative Editors (RCE) are a class of distributed systems based on the interaction of several users trying to edit simultaneously shared documents, such as articles, wiki pages and programming source code. Operational Transformation (OT) is considered as the efficient and safe method for consistency maintenance in the literature of collaborative editors. Indeed, it is aimed at ensuring copies convergence even though the users's updates are executed in any order on different copies. Unfortunately, existing OT algorithms often fail to achieve this objective. Moreover, these algorithms have limited scalability with the number of users as they use vector timestamps to enforce causality dependency. In this paper, we present a novel coordination model for managing collaborative editing work in a scalable and decentralized fashion. It may be deployed easily on P2P networks as it supports dynamic groups where users can leave and join at any time.

Keywords: Collaborative editors, Optimistic replication, Consistency, Operational Transformation, Real-time collaboration.

1 Introduction

Motivations. Real-time Collaborative Editors (RCE) provide computer support for modifying simultaneously shared documents by dispersed users (*e.g.* Google Docs). To improve availability of data, each user has a local copy of the shared documents. In general, the collaboration is performed as follows: each user's updates are locally executed in nonblocking manner and then are propagated to other sites in order to be executed on other copies.

Although being distributed applications, RCE are specific in the sense that they must consider human factors. So, they are characterized by the following requirements: (i) *High local responsiveness*: the system has to be as responsive as its single-user editors [1, 17, 18]; (ii) *High concurrency*: the users must be able to concurrently and freely modify any part of the shared document at any time [1, 17]; (iii) *Consistency*: the users must eventually be able to see a converged view of all copies [1, 17]; (iv) *Decentralized coordination*: all concurrent updates must be synchronized in decentralized fashion in order to avoid a single point of failure; (v) *Scalability*: a group must be dynamic in the sense that users may join or leave the group at any time.

It is very difficult to meet these requirements when deploying RCE in networks with high communication latencies (*e.g.* Internet). Due to replication and arbitrary exchange of updates, consistency maintenance in a scalable and decentralized manner is a

J. Field and V.T. Vasconcelos (Eds.): COORDINATION 2009, LNCS 5521, pp. 225–246, 2009.
© Springer-Verlag Berlin Heidelberg 2009

challenging problem. Traditional concurrency control techniques, such as (pessimistic/optimistic) locking and serialization, turned out to be ineffective because they may ensure consistency at the expense of responsiveness and loss of updates [1, 7, 17].

To illustrate this problem, consider the scenario in Figure 1.(a) where two users work on a shared document represented by a sequence of characters. These characters are addressed from 1 to the end of the document. Initially, both copies hold the string "efecte". User 1 executes operation $o_1 = Ins(2, f)$ to insert the character 'f' at position 2. Concurrently, user 2 performs $o_2 = Del(6)$ to delete the character 'e' at position 6. When o_1 is received and executed on site 2, it produces the expected string "effect". But, at site 1, o_2 does not take into account that op_1 has been executed before it and it produces the string "effece". The result at site 1 is different from the result of site 2 and it apparently violates the intention of o_2 since the last character 'e', which was intended to be deleted, is still present in the final string. It should be pointed out that even if a serialization protocol [1] was used to require that all sites execute o_1 and o_2 in the same order (*i.e.* a global order on concurrent operations) to obtain an identical result *effece*, this identical result is still inconsistent with the original intention of o_2.

Operational Transformation (OT). To maintain consistency, an OT approach has been proposed in [1]. In general, it consists of application-dependent transformation algorithm, called IT, such that for every possible pair of concurrent updates, the application programmer has to specify how to integrate these updates regardless of reception order. In Figure 1.(b), we illustrate the effect of IT on the previous example. At site 1, o_2 needs to be transformed in order to include the effects of o_1: $o_2' = IT((Del(6), Ins(2, f)) = Del(7)$. The deletion position of o_2 is incremented because o_1 has inserted a character at position 1, which is before the character deleted by op_2.

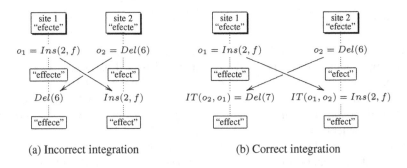

(a) Incorrect integration   (b) Correct integration

Fig. 1. Serialization of concurrent updates

Many collaborative applications are based on the OT approach such as Joint Emacs [13] (a groupware based on text editor Emacs), CoWord [18] (a collaborative Microsoft word processor) and CoPowerPoint [18] (a real-time collaborative multimedia slides creation and presentation system) and a file synchronizer [11] distributed with the industrial collaborative development environment LibreSource Community[1]. OT also has been proposed as a consistency model for replicated mobile computing [2].

---

[1] http://dev.libresource.org

OT aims at ensuring consistency in a decentralized way without need of any global order. It allows users to concurrently modify the shared document and exchange their updates in any order since the convergence of all copies must be ensured in all cases. Unfortunately, we have discovered that the most existing OT algorithms fail to guarantee consistency, because they contain bugs [5, 3]. Moreover, to our knowledge, the scalability requirement has never been dealt with in OT community research. All proposed OT frameworks rely on a fixed number of users during collaboration sessions. This is due in the fact that they use vector timestamps (to preserve causality relation) that do not scale well.

Contributions. In this paper, we propose a new framework for collaborative editing to address the weakness of previous OT works and to satisfy all requirements mentioned above. Our contributions are as follows:

1. Our framework supports an unconstrained collaborative editing work (without the necessity of central coordination). Using optimistic replication scheme, it provides simultaneous access to shared documents and an enhanced set of operations for editing these documents.
2. Instead of vector timestamps, we use a simple technique to preserve causality dependency. Our technique is minimal because only direct dependency information between updates is used. It is independent on the number of users and it provides high concurrency in comparison with vector timestamps.
3. Using OT approach, reconciliation of divergent copies is done automatically in decentralized fashion.
4. Our framework can scale naturally thanks to our minimal causality dependency relation. In other words, it may be deployed easily in Peer-to-Peer (P2P) networks.

Outline. This paper is organized as follows: In Section 2 we give an overview on the OT approach and we fix the main problems encountered in OT-based RCE. Section 3 presents the ingredients of our coordination model. Section 4 illustrates three kinds of OT algorithms that we use for transforming editing operations. Section 5 presents our concurrency control algorithm for managing collaborative editing sessions. Section 6 discusses related work and Section 7 summarizes contributions and future works.

2 Operational Transformation Approach and the Problems

2.1 Overview

OT is an optimistic replication technique which allows many users (or sites) to concurrently modify the shared data and next to synchronize their divergent replicas in order to obtain the same data. Every site stores all executed operations in a buffer also called a *log*. It is known that collaborative editors manipulate shared objects that own a linear data-structure [1, 16, 18] (*e.g.* a list). This list is a sequence of elements from some data type, such as a character, a paragraph, a page, an XML node, etc. In [18], it has been shown that this linear structure can be easily extended to a range of multimedia documents, such as MicroSoft Word and PowerPoint documents.

Two primitive operations are used to modify the shared document: (i) $Ins(p, e, s)$ to insert the element e at position p; (ii) $Del(p, s)$ to delete the element at position p. The parameter s is the identity of the site issuing the operation[2]. As a long established convention in collaborative editors [1, 16], the vector timestamps are used to determine the happened-before and concurrent relations between operations.

To deal with concurrent operations, OT uses an algorithm, called *inclusive transformation* [16] and denoted by function IT, to merge these operations regardless reception order. Let o_1 and o_2 be two concurrent operations. Intuitively, $IT(o_1, o_2)$ transforms o_1 against o_2 in order to *include the effect* of o_2 in o_1. The transformed form of o_1 is then executed after o_2. For instance, here are two transformation cases given in the IT algorithm proposed by Ressel et al. [13]:

$IT(Ins(p_1, e_1, s_1), Ins(p_2, e_2, s_2)) =$
if $(p_1 < p_2$ or $(p_1 = p_2$ and $s_1 < s_2))$ **then return** $Ins(p_1, e_1, s_1)$ **else return** $Ins(p_1 + 1, e_1, s_1)$

$IT(Ins(p_1, e_1, s_1), Del(p_2, s_2)) =$
if $(p_1 > p_2)$ **then return** $Ins(p_1 - 1, e_1, s_1)$ **else return** $Ins(p_1, e_1, s_1)$

The site identities are used to tie-break conflict situations (*e.g.* two concurrent operations inserting elements at the same position). Using an IT algorithm requires to satisfy two properties $TP1$ and $TP2$ in order to ensure convergence [13]. For all o, o_1 and o_2 pairwise concurrent operations with $o'_1 = IT(o_1, o_2)$ and $o'_2 = IT(o_2, o_1)$:

- **TP1**: $[o_1 ; o'_2] \equiv [o_2 ; o'_1]$, *i.e.* sequences $[o_1 ; o'_2]$ and $[o_2 ; o'_1]$ are equivalent.
- **TP2**: $IT(IT(o, o_1), o'_2) = IT(IT(o, o_2), o'_1)$.

Property $TP1$ defines a *state identity* and ensures that if o_1 and o_2 are concurrent, the effect of executing o_1 before o_2 is the same as executing o_2 before o_1. This property is necessary but not sufficient when the number of sites is greater than two. Property $TP2$ defines an *operation identity* and ensures that transforming o along equivalent and different operation sequences will give the same operation. Properties $TP1$ and $TP2$ are sufficient to ensure the convergence for *any number* of concurrent operations which can be executed in *arbitrary order* [13, 10]. Accordingly, by these properties, it is not necessary to enforce a global total order between concurrent operations because data divergence can always be repaired by operational transformation.

To better understand our work, all examples given in this paper use characters as elements to be inserted/deleted.

2.2 OT Problems

Here we summarize the main problems encountered in RCE based on OT approach:

Problem 1: Scalability issue. RCE must enable dynamic groups in the sense that users may enter and quit the groups at any time. Such editors rely on the vector timestamp technique to determine the happened-before and concurrent relations between

---

[2] Every site has a unique identity. The set of site identities is assumed totally ordered by relation $\leq$.

operations issued by users. Unfortunately, this technique does not scale well since each timestamp is a vector of integers with the number of entries equal to the number of sites.

Problem 2: TP2 Puzzle. Although in theory the OT approach is able to achieve convergence in the presence of arbitrary transformation orders, linear objects (such as text or ordered XML tree) still represent a serious challenge for the application of the OT approach. Indeed, all proposed IT algorithms [5, 3] for these datatypes fail to meet the property $TP2$, leading inevitably to data divergence situations. The "killer" scenario for these algorithms always consists of two insertion operations and a delete operation, like the one depicted in Figure 2). At site 2 (resp. site 3), o_1 is recursively transformed against the sequence $[o_2; o_3']$ (resp. $[o_3; o_2']$). As we can see $o_1' \neq o_1''$ and $TP2$ is violated. Therefore the data convergence is not achieved. This scenario is termed $TP2$ *puzzle* [16].

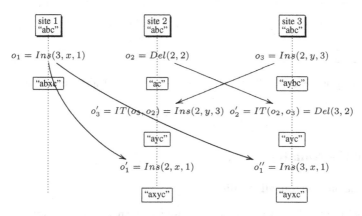

Fig. 2. Scenario of $TP2$ puzzle

Problem 3: Partial Concurrency. Two concurrent operations o_1 and o_2 are said to be *partially concurrent* iff o_1 and o_2 are generated from two different states [14]. In case of partial concurrency situation, naively applying the inclusive transformation IT may lead to data divergence.

Consider two users trying to correct the word "*fect*" as in Figure 3.(a). User 1 generates o_1 and o_2 (o_1 happens before o_2). User 2 concurrently generates o_3. It is clear that o_1 and o_3 are concurrent (as o_1 did not see the effect o_3 and vice-versa). However, o_2 and o_3 are partially concurrent as they are generated on different states: o_3 is generated on "*fect*" while o_2 is generated on "*afect*". Transforming directly o_2 against o_3 may lead to divergence situation (as illustrated in Figure 3.(a)). Indeed, $IT(o_2, o_3)$ requires that o_2 and o_3 be concurrent and defined on the same state.

To overcome this partial concurrency problem, the most existing OT frameworks, such that SOCT2 [14] and GOTO [16], impose to reorder local log into equivalent one before transforming o_2. Hence, the local log at site 2 must be reordered into a concatenation of two sequences L_h and L_c, where L_h contains all operations that happened before o_2 (*i.e.* o_1) and L_c includes operations that are concurrent with o_2 (*i.e.* $o_3' = IT(o_3, o_1)$). Next, o_2 is just inclusively transformed against L_c (see Figure 3.(b)).

In general, the above solution is very expensive because it may require several re-organizations inside local log in order to integrate each remote operation. As the log length can increase rapidly during collaboration sessions, these frequent reorganizations inevitably lead to performance degradation in RCE.

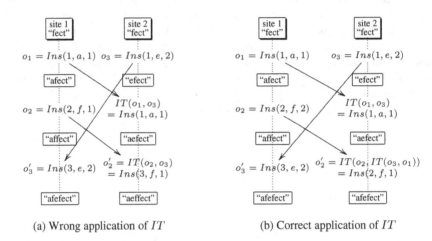

(a) Wrong application of IT (b) Correct application of IT

Fig. 3. Partial concurrency

3   Our Coordination Model

3.1   Model of Collaborative Editor

To deal with linear data-structure, we propose an enhanced set of operations to modify the shared state:(i) $Ins(p, e, \omega)$ where p is the insertion position, e the element to be added at position p and ω is the sequence of positions that contains all different positions occupied by e during the transformation process (see Section 4.1);(ii) $Del(p)$ which deletes the element at position p;(iii) $Up(p, e, e')$ which replaces the element e at position p by the new element e'. It is clear that combinations of these operations enable us to define complex operations, such as cut/copy and paste, intensively used in professional text editors.

We define a *request* q as a quadruple (c, r, a, o) where c is the identity of the collaborator site (or the user) issuing the request and $r \in \mathbb{N}$ is its serial number. Note that the concatenation of c and r is defined as the identity of q. The component a is the identity of the preceding request[3], and finally o is the operation to be executed on the shared state. If a is *null* then the request does not depend on any other request. The projections $q.c$, $q.r$, $q.a$, and $q.o$ will be used to denote the corresponding components of request q. We use q, q', q_1, q_2, ..., to denote all requests. We simply refer to *insert*, *delete* and *update* requests by respectively the letters i, d and u. Functions $old(u))$ and $new(u)$ return respectively the old element e and the new element e' for every update request with $u.o = Up(p, e, e')$. A *log* buffer is a request sequence which is maintained

---

[3] According to the dependency relation described in Definition 1.

on every site in order to keep all executed requests. Given a log L, $L[i]$ denotes the i-th request of L; $|L|$ is the length of L; $L[i,j]$ is the sub-log of L ranging from its i-th to j-th requests with $0 < i \leq j \leq n - 1$ such that $n = |L|$. Furthermore, we suppose that sites are interconnected by a reliable network. The propagation of requests is based on an epidemic style of communication.

3.2 Causal Dependency Relation

Given a log, a request may *depend on* previous requests according to the execution order. Tracking this dependency inside a log enables us to identify requests that must be executed on all sites according to the same order.

To address the *Scalability issue* (see **Problem 1** in Section 2.2), we propose a minimal dependency relation which is *independent* of the number of users, and accordingly, allows for dynamic groups. Studying the semantics of linear object (modified by insertion, deletion and update operations) allows us to provide the following dependency relation within a log:

Definition 1 *(Causal dependency relation). Let L be a log where $L[i] = q_i$ and $L[j] = q_j$ with $j = i + 1$. We define the transitive relation $\xrightarrow{s}$ on L as follows. We say that $q_i \xrightarrow{s} q_j$ iff one of the following conditions holds:*

1. $q_i.o = Ins(p, e, \omega)$, $q_j.o = Ins(p, e', \omega')$ and $q_i.c \leq q_j.c$; $\quad$ (df$_1$)
2. $q_i.o = Ins(p, e, \omega)$, $q_j.o = Ins(p + 1, e', \omega')$ and $q_j.c \leq q_i.c$; $\quad$ (df$_2$)
3. $q_i.o = Ins(p, e, \omega)$ and $q_j.o = Del(p)$; $\quad$ (df$_3$)
4. $q_i.o = Ins(p, e, \omega)$ and $q_j.o = Up(p, e, e')$; $\quad$ (df$_4$)
5. $q_i.o = Up(p, e, e')$, $q_j.o = Up(p, e', e'')$ and $q_j.c \leq q_i.c$; $\quad$ (df$_5$)

Otherwise, if $q_i \not\xrightarrow{s} q_j$ then q_i and q_j are independent *(or concurrent).*

When the added elements are adjacent (at positions p and/or $p + 1$), their respective insertion requests are considered as dependent provided that their site identities satisfy conditions imposed by **(df$_1$)** and **(df$_2$)**. Deleting an element depends on the request that has inserted this element. Thus, there is no dependency between delete requests and they can be executed among them in any order. Likewise, updating an element depends on the request inserting this element. At last, we consider two consecutive update requests as dependent if their update positions are equal and the condition on their site identities is satisfied.

Two adjacent requests within a log are independent means that they can commute backward in some sense (or they can be executed out-of-order). We only need to correctly compute this backward form. To do that we will use request transformations described in Section 4. Moreover, it is easy to show that our causal relation builds a *dependency tree* on the requests. In this case, each request has only to store the request identity whose it directly depends on. We will see in Section 4.2 how to detect this dependency between requests within a log.

3.3 Canonical Logs

To avoid the $TP2$ *puzzle* (see **Problem 2** in Section 2.2), we will define a class of logs which allows us to build transformation paths leading to data convergence.

Definition 2. *A log* L *is* canonical *iff* L *is the concatenation of two sub-logs* L_i *and* L_d *such that* L_i *does not contain deletion requests and* L_d *does not contain insertion requests.*

Of course, logs L_i and L_d can also contain update requests. In canonical logs, we impose an order on insertion and deletion requests: an insertion request should always be before deletion requests. Note that empty logs and logs containing only insert and/or update (resp. delete and/or update) requests are also canonical. For instance: $[u_1; i_1; u_2; d_1]$ and $[i_1; u_1; d_1; u_2]$ are canonical but $[u_1; d_1; u_2; i_1]$ is not. We will see in Section 4 how to build canonical logs.

3.4 Consistency Criteria

A stable state in a RCE is achieved when all generated requests have been performed at all sites. Our replication scheme must ensure the following criteria:

Definition 3. *(Consistency Model) A RCE is* consistent *iff it satisfies the following properties:*

1. Dependency preservation: *if* $q_1 \xrightarrow{s} q_2$ *then* q_1 *is executed before* q_2 *at all sites.*
2. Convergence: *when all sites have performed the same set of requests, the copies of the shared document are identical.*

To establish a causal dependency between requests, we use the relation given in Definition 1. This relation is minimal because every request has to know only the identity of the request it depends on directly. Nevertheless, an important issue remains and should be solved: how to serialize concurrent requests in order to achieve the convergence? The solution of this problem is given in the next section.

4   Building Canonical Logs

In our work, we use three kinds of transformation [14, 16]: Inclusive Transformation (IT), Exclusive Transformation (ET) and Permutation ($PERM$). In the following, we will present our IT and ET algorithms. For more details, see [3,6].

4.1   Inclusive Transformation

It should be noted that we have redefined the insertion operation by adding a new parameter (*i.e.* ω). This parameter is used as a *stack*: each time an insert request is transformed against a delete request we push the last position before transformation in the ω parameter. On the other hand, when an insert request is generated its ω is empty. For instance, consider requests i and d such that $i.o = Ins(3, x, \epsilon)$ and $d.o = Del(1)$ where ϵ denotes the empty stack: then $IT(i, d) = i'$ with $i'.o = Ins(2, x, [3])$.

Given requests i_j, u_j and d_j such that $i_j.o = Ins(p_j, e_j, \omega_j)$, $u_j.o = Up(p_j, e_j, e'_j)$ and $d_j.o = Del(p_j)$ for $j \in \{1, 2\}$. All cases for our IT are given in Algorithm 1. When two requests insert two elements at the same position (they are in conflict), a choice has to be done (lines 4-5): which element must be inserted before the other? In our IT function, when a conflict occurs, the element of an insertion request whose user identifier c is the highest is inserted before the other. On the other hand, when two requests delete at the same position, IT returns the idle request whose the operation parameter is $Nop()$[4] that has null effect on the shared state. The remaining cases of IT are quite simple.

Recall that IT algorithm is used to execute concurrent requests in any order. Using canonical logs we avoid the $TP2$ puzzle. Consequently, our IT algorithm is sufficient to achieve data convergence. For more details on our IT algorithm, see [6].

```
1:  IT(q₁, q₂) = q'₁
2:  q'₁ ← q₁
3:  Choice of q₁ and q₂
4:      Case: q₁ = i₁ and q₂ = i₂
5:          if (p₂ < p₁ or (p₂ = p₁ and q₂.c < q₁.c)) then q'₁.o ← Ins(p₁ + 1, e₁, ω₁)
6:      Case: q₁ = i₁ and q₂ = d₂
7:          if (p₂ < p₁) then q'₁.o ← Ins(p₁ − 1, e₁, p₁ω₁)
8:          else if (p₂ = p₁) then q'₁.o ← Ins(p₁, e₁, p₁ω₁)
9:      Case: q₁ = d₁ and q₂ = i₂
10:         if (p₂ ≤ p₁) then q'₁.o ← Del(p₁ + 1)
11:     Case: q₁ = d₁ and q₂ = d₂
12:         if (p₂ < p₁) then q'₁.o ← Del(p₁ − 1)
13:         else if (p₂ = p₁) then q'₁.o ← Nop()
14:     Case: q₁ = u₁ and q₂ = i₂
15:         if (p₂ ≤ p₁) then q'₁.o ← Up(p₁ + 1, old(u₁), new(u₁))
16:     Case: q₁ = u₁ and q₂ = u₂
17:         if (p₁ = p₂) and (q₂.c < q₁.c) then q'₁.o ← Up(p₁, new(u₂), new(u₁))
18:         else if (p₁ = p₂) and (q₂.c > q₁.c) then q'₁.o ← Nop()
19:     Case: q₁ = u₁ and q₂ = d₂
20:         if (p₂ < p₁) then q'₁.o ← Up(p₁ − 1, old(u₁), new(u₁))
21:         else if (p₂ = p₁) then q'₁.o ← Nop()
22: end choice
23: return q'₁
```

Algorithm 1. Inclusive transformation

4.2 Exclusive Transformation

Let $[q_1; q_2]$ be a request sequence so that q_2 is defined on the state produced by q_1. The *exclusive transformation* $ET(q_2, q_1)$ enables us to *exclude the effect* of q_1 from q_2 as if q_2 had not been executed after q_1. As a simple example, consider the scenario in Figure 4. Given q_1 defined in state "abc" and q_2 defined in state "ac" (produced by q_1): $ET(q_2, q_1) = q'_2$ with $q'_2.o = Ins(4, y, \epsilon)$ which is exactly the form of q_2 as defined relative to the state "abc".

Let i_j, u_j and d_j be three requests such that $i_j.o = Ins(p_j, e_j, \omega_j)$, $u_j.o = Up(p_j, e_j, e'_j)$ and $d_j.o = Del(p_j)$ with $j \in \{1, 2\}$. All different cases of our ET are given in Algorithm 2. For instance, when q_1 and q_2 have the same insertion positions, then the element added by q_1 must precede (or is before) the one added by q_2. If the relation between their positions or site identities reflects this precedence, $ET(q_1, q_2)$ returns q_1 as q_2 has no effect on the insertion position of q_1. On the other hand, when

---
[4] If $q.o = Nop()$ then $IT(q, q') = q$ and $IT(q', q) = q'$.

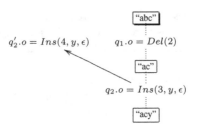

$$q_2'.o = Ins(4, y, \epsilon) \qquad q_1.o = Del(2)$$

$$q_2.o = Ins(3, y, \epsilon)$$

Fig. 4. Exclusive transformation

q_2 is before q_1 and their positions (or their site identities) give the same order, then we decrement the insertion position of q_1 for excluding the q_2's effect (lines 4-6).

Using ET algorithm enables us to detect causal dependency relation between requests (see Definition 1) inside a log. Indeed, when $ET(q_1, q_2)$ returns "Undefined" then $q_2 \xrightarrow{s} q_1$. Otherwise, ET algorithm allows requests to be executed out-of-order. In [3], we have shown that our algorithms IT and ET are reversible, in the sense that transforming in both directions preserves the data convergence.

```
1:  ET(q₁, q₂) = q₁'
2:  q₁' ← q₁
3:  Choice of q₁ and q₂
4:    Case: q₁ = i₁ and q₂ = i₂
5:      if (p₁ = p₂ and q₁.c ≥ q₂.c) or (p₁ = p₂ + 1 and q₁.c ≤ q₂.c)) then return "Undefined"
6:      else q₁'.o ← Ins(p₁ - 1, e₁, ω₁)

7:    Case: q₁ = i₁ and q₂ = d₂
8:      if (p₁ = p₂) then q₁'.o ← Ins(p₁, e₁, Tl(ω₁))  /* Function Tl returns the resulting stack without the top
        position */
9:      else if (p₁ > p₂) then q₁'.o ← Ins(p₁ + 1, e₁, Tl(ω₁))

10:   Case: q₁ = d₁ and q₂ = i₂
11:     if (p₁ ≥ p₂ + 1) then q₁'.o ← Del(p₁ - 1)
12:     else if (p₁ = p₂) then return "Undefined"

13:   Case : q₁ = d₁ and q₂ = d₂
14:     if (p₁ ≥ p₂) then q₁'.o ← Del(p₁ + 1)

15:   Case : q₁ = u₁ and q₂ = i₂
16:     if (p₁ > p₂) then q₁'.o ← Up(p₁ - 1, old(u₁), new(u₁))
17:     else if (p₁ = p₂) then return "Undefined"

18:   Case : q₁ = u₁ and q₂ = d₂
19:     if (p₁ > p₂) then q₁'.o ← Up(p₁ + 1, old(u₁), new(u₁))

20:   Case : q₁ = u₁ and q₂ = u₂
21:     if (p₁ = p₂ and q₁.c > q₂.c) then q₁'.o ← Up(p₁, old(u₂), new(u₁))
22:     else if (p₁ = p₂) return "Undefined"
23: end choice
24: return q₁'
```

Algorithm 2. Exclusive transformation

4.3   Reordering Logs

In this section we will give how to build canonical logs by combining ET and IT algorithms. Firstly, we refine Definition 1 on causal dependency relation between requests as follows.

Definition 4. *Let* $L = [q_1; q_2; \ldots; q_n]$ *be a log. We say that* $q_i \xrightarrow{s} q_j$, *where* $i, j \in \{1, \ldots, n\}$ *and* $i < j$, *iff there exists either (i)* $q' = ET^*(q_j, L[i + 1, j - 1])$ *such that* $q_i \xrightarrow{s} q'$; *or, (ii) a request* q_k *with* $i < k < j$ *and* $q_i \xrightarrow{s} q_k \xrightarrow{s} q_j$.

Function ET^* denotes the exclusive transformation of a request against a log. It is defined recursively as follows: (i) $ET^*(q, []) = q$ where $[]$ is the empty log; (ii) $ET^*(q, [q_1; \ldots; q_{n-1}; q_n]) = ET^*(ET(q, q_n), [q_1; \ldots; q_{n-1}])$. Definition 4 enables us to detect causal dependency between requests, that are not necessarily adjacent, by using recursively ET algorithm.

To build canonical logs, it is necessary to *reorder* (or *permute*) requests in a log without affecting the resulting state of this log [12, 14]. So we use function $PERM$ that enables a request to be moved back to the past in order to simulate it as being executed first.

Definition 5 *(Permuting requests).* *Let* $[q_1; q_2]$ *be a request sequence. We define function* $PERM$ *as follows: if* $q_1 \xnrightarrow{s} q_2$ *then* $PERM(q_2, q_1) = [q_2'; q_1']$ *such that (i)* $q_2' = ET(q_2, q_1)$; *and, (ii)* $q_1' = IT(q_1, q_2')$.

Note that the function $PERM$ is not defined when $q_1 \xrightarrow{s} q_2$. Given the reversibility of IT and ET, replacing $[q_1; q_2]$ by $PERM(q_2, q_1)$ means that we can get an equivalent sequence where another form of q_2 could be executed first. As a simple example, consider the scenario in Figure 5: $PERM(q_2', q_1) = [q_2; q_1']$ with $q_2 = ET(q_2', q_1)$ and $q_1' = IT(q_1, q_2)$ and so that $[q_2; q_1']$ and $[q_1; q_2']$ are equivalent. By using the ω parameter, we ensure that our ET algorithm "goes backward" in a deterministic way as ω contains the previous positions. We can build canonical logs by applying one or several request permutations.

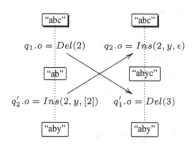

Fig. 5. Permutation of requests

4.4   How to Simplify Partial Concurrency

We present here how to alleviate the processing burden of *Partial Concurrency Situation* (see **Problem 3** in Section 2.2). Firstly, we give an interesting result when using our causal dependency relation.

Theorem 1. *For every request* q *concurrent with* q_1 *and* q_2:
if $q_1 \xrightarrow{s} q_2$ *then* $IT(q_1, q) \xrightarrow{s} IT(q_2, q')$ *where* $q' = IT(q, q_1)$.

Theorem 1 says that the causal dependency relation is still preserved when correctly applying the inclusive transformation for partial concurrent requests. Request q_1 is either an insertion request or an update (see Definition 1). Therefore, it is easy to generalize this result for canonical logs (*i.e.* q is replaced by a canonical log). The proof of Theorem 1 is given in Appendix A.

In our approach, we deal with the partial concurrency problem by avoiding the log reorganization. This is done, thanks to Theorem 1, by directly deducing the form to be executed of the remote request from its precedent request inside the local log. Consider the example of partial concurrency illustrated in Figure 3. We have $q_1 \xrightarrow{s} q_2$ at site 1 (*i.e.* df_2 form according to Definition 1). As this dependency is preserved by transformation at site 2, $q_1' \xrightarrow{s} q_2'$, we can deduce that $q_2'.o = q_2.o$.

5 Concurrency Control Algorithm

We have designed a new algorithm for managing all concurrent interactions occurring in RCE. This algorithm relies on (i) the replication of the shared documents in order to provide data access without constraints, and; (ii) the consistency model based on causal dependency. We will sketch the correctness of this algorithm in Appendix A.

5.1 Control Procedure

In our approach, a collaborative editor consists of a group of N sites (where N is variable in time) starting a collaboration session from the same initial state l_0. Each site stores all executed requests in canonical log L (*i.e.* insertions before deletions). Our control concurrency procedure is given in Algorithm 3.

Generation of Local Request. When an operation o is locally generated, it is immediately executed on its generation state (*i.e.* $Do(o, l)$ computes the resulting state when executing operation o on state l). Once the request $q = (c, r, null, o)$[5] is formed, function COMPUTEBF(q,L) is called (see Algorithm 4) in order to compute the minimal generation context of q. In other words, instead of considering q as being dependent of all L's requests, our procedure reduces this context by excluding as much as possible some requests of L by means of exclusive transformation ET. To well understand this step, consider the set $Dep(q) = \{q" \in L | q" \xrightarrow{s} q\}$ which is built according to Definition 4. If $Dep(q) = \emptyset$ then the new request q' is not dependent of L. Otherwise, $Dep(q) \neq \emptyset$, q' must be executed on all sites after the requests of $Dep(q)$. In this case, $q'.a$ contains only the identity of the direct preceding request plus the dependency form df_j (see Definition 1).

Integrating q after L may result in not canonical log. To transform $[L; q]$ in canonical form, we use function CANONIZE(q,L) that is given in Algorithm 5. It relies on function $PERM$ to applying successive permutations. Finally, the request q' (the result of COMPUTEBF) is propagated to all sites in order to be executed on other copies of the shared document.

---

[5] *null* means that q does not depend on any request.

```
1: COMPUTEBF(q,L) : q'
2: q' ← q
3: for (i = |L| − 1; i ≥ 0; i − −) do
4:     if q' is not dependent of L[i] then
5:         q' ← ET(q', L[i])
6:     else
7:         q'.a = (L[i].p, L[i].k, df_j)
           {df_j with j = 1, 2, 3, 4 or 5 according to the
           dependency form}
8:         return q'
9:     end if
10: end for
11: return q'
```

Algorithm 4. Detection of causal dependency

```
1: Main:
2: INITIALIZATION
3: while not aborted do
4:     if there is an input o then
5:         GENERATE_REQUEST(o)
6:     else
7:         RECEIVE_REQUEST
8:         INTEGRATE_REMOTE_REQUESTS
9:     end if
10: end while

11: INITIALIZATION:
12: Q ← []
13: L ← []
14: l ← l_0
15: r ← 1
16: c ← Identification of local user

17: GENERATE_REQUEST(o):
18: l ← Do(o, l)
19: q ← (c, r, null, o)
20: q' ← COMPUTEBF(q,L)
21: L ← CANONIZE(q,L)
22: broadcast q' to other users

23: RECEIVE_REQUEST:
24: if there is a request q from a network then
25:     Q ← Q + q
26: end if

27: INTEGRATE_REMOTE_REQUEST:
28: if there is q in Q that is causally-ready then
29:     Q ← Q − q
30:     q' ← COMPUTEFF(q,L)
31:     l ← Do(q'.o, l)
32:     L ← CANONIZE(q',L)
33: end if
```

Algorithm 3. Control Concurrency Algorithm

```
1: CANONIZE(q,L) : L'
2: L' ← [L; q]
3: i ← |L'| − 1
4: while L' is not canonical do
5:     < L'[i − 1], L'[i] >← PERM(L'[i], L'[i − 1])
6:     i ← i − 1
7: end while
8: return L'
```

Algorithm 5. Canonizing logs

```
1: COMPUTEFF(q,L) : q'
2: q' ← q
3: j ← −1
4: if q'.a ≠ null then
5:     Let L[j] be the request whose q' depends on
       (j ∈ {0, . . . , |L| − 1})
6:     Modify q'.o with respect to L[j].o and the
       dependency form
7: end if
8: for (i = j + 1; i ≤ |L| − 1; i + +) do
9:     q' ← IT(q', L[i])
10: end for
11: return q'
```

Algorithm 6. Transforming a request against a log

Integration of Remote Request. Each site has the use of queue Q to store the remote requests coming from other sites. Request q generated on site i is added to Q when it arrives at site j (with $i \neq j$). To preserve the causality dependency, q is extracted from the queue when it is *causally-ready*: if $q" \xrightarrow{s} q$ then $q"$ has been already integrated on site j. Next, function COMPUTEFF(q,L) (see Algorithm 6) is called in order to compute the transformed form q' to be executed on current state l. Let n be the length of L. Two cases are to be considered: (i) if $q.a = null$ then q is concurrent to all requests of L; (ii) if $q.a \neq null$ then there exists request $L[k]$ (with $k \in \{0, \ldots, n-1\}$) whose q depends on. In case (ii), unlike the others integration algorithms based on OT approach, our algorithm does not require to reorganize L in two sub-logs containing respectively precedent requests and concurrent requests with respect to q. Instead, only the parameter $q.o$ is updated with respect to $L[k]$ and the dependency form $\mathbf{df_j}$ contained in $q.a$ (see Definition 1). The obtained request is next inclusively transformed against $L[k+1, n-1]$. Finally, the transformed form of q, namely q', is executed on the current state and function CANONIZE is called in order to turn again $[L; q']$ in canonical form.

Asymptotic Time Complexities. We assume the time to execute IT, ET and $PERM$ transformations is constant. Let L be a canonical log. Let L_i be all insertion/update requests in L and L_d be all deletion/update requests in L. In the worst-case the complexity of COMPUTEBF(q,L) is $O(|L_i| + |L_d|)$. Indeed, if all requests concurrent with q are in L then q is exclusively transformed against all L's requests. When q is an insertion request and L_d is not empty, the function CANONIZE(q,L) takes time $O(|L_d|)$. If q is concurrent with all L's requests then the complexity of COMPUTEFF(q,L) is $O(|L_i| + |L_d|)$. Hence the generation of local request and the integration of remote request have the same complexity, $O(|L_i| + 2|L_d|)$, in the worst-case (*i.e.* q is an insertion request and L_d is not empty).

6   Related Work

The discovery of the $TP2$ puzzle [14, 16] gave birth to several works that have tried to address this problem. These works may be categorized in two approaches. The first one tries to avoid the $TP2$ puzzle scenario. This is done by constraining the communication among users in order to restrict the space of possible execution order. For instance, the SOCT4 algorithm [19] uses a sequencer, associated with a deferred broadcast and a sequential reception, to enforce a continuous global order on requests. This global order can also be obtained by using an undo/do/redo scheme like in GOT [17]. These ensure the data convergence but they cannot scale because they rely on client-server architecture in order to get a global and unique order of execution.

The second approach deals with resolution of $TP2$ puzzle. In this case, concurrent requests can be executed in any order, but the transformation algorithm requires to satisfy property $TP2$. This approach has been developed in adOPTed [13], SOCT2 [14], GOTO [16], and SDT [7]. Unfortunately, we have proved elsewhere [5,3] that all previously proposed transformation algorithms fail to satisfy $TP2$ when we deal with linear objects.

A first thought has been conducted in LBT environment [8] to build a total order on elements (*e.g.* characters) of the shared linear object. To establish such an order, each element must be uniquely identified. To achieve convergence, the integration of remote request consists in deducing the total order between elements. To do so, the following schemes are used: (i) a hash table containing all order relations between elements; (ii) vector timestamps for tracking causality dependency between requests; (iii) bidirectional (inclusive and exclusive) transformation algorithms; (iv) a particular class of transformation paths like the ones we have used in our integration algorithm, namely logs containing insertions before deletions. This approach is very complicated due to the number of schemes used to ensure convergence and it is also less practical even for small collaborative editors. In addition, LBT does not scale with the number of sites as the convergence is dependent on vector timestamps.

In ABT environment [9], the authors make up for the drawback of LBT. Indeed, ABT uses few schemes to ensure convergence. Besides using vector timestamps and canonical logs (insertions before deletions), ABT proceeds as follows: (i) only the effect of deletion requests are excluded from local request before to broadcast it; (ii) the integration of remote request requires the reorganization of local log to deal with the partial concurrency problem. Unlike ABT, our integration algorithm scales easily and it can provide a high degree of concurrency. Indeed, we propagate local request with minimal generation context. We also solve merely the problem of partial concurrency by integrating directly remote request without reorganizing the local log.

It should be noted that this work is an extension of our preliminary paper [4]. Indeed, in this work, we propose an enhanced set of operations and we present a new and optimized version of our concurrency control algorithm as well as its correctness.

7 Conclusion

In this paper, we have proposed a new framework for managing collaborative editing work in real-time context. It is based on optimistic replication. Using OT approach, it provides a simultaneous access to shared documents and an automatic reconciliation of divergent copies. A minimal causality between requests is given by means of a dependency relation based on semantics of the shared document. This causality relation is not tributary to the number of users and it allows to support dynamic groups. Thus, our framework may be deployed in P2P networks. Note that our work is the first that deals with the scalability and the consistency maintenance problems in OT research community. A prototype based on our OT framework has been implemented in Java. It supports the collaborative editing of wiki pages and it is deployed on P2P JXTA platform[6].

In future work, we intend to investigate the impact of our work when undoing requests [15]. As the length of local logs increases rapidly during collaboration sessions we plan to address the garbage collection problem.

References

1. Ellis, C.A., Gibbs, S.J.: Concurrency Control in Groupware Systems. In: SIGMOD Conference, vol. 18, pp. 399–407 (1989)
2. Guerraoui, R., Hari, C.: On the consistency problem in mobile distributed computing. In: Proceedings of the second ACM international workshop on Principles of mobile computing, pp. 51–57. ACM Press, New York (2002)
3. Imine, A.: Conception Formelle d'Algorithmes de Réplication Optimiste. Vers l'Edition Collaborative dans les Réseaux Pair-à-Pair. Ph.D thesis, University of Henri Poincaré, Nancy, France (December 2006)
4. Imine, A.: Flexible Concurrency Control for Real-time Collaborative Editors. In: 28th International Conference on Distributed Computing Systems Workshops, ICDCSW, Beijing, China, pp. 423–428. IEEE Computer Society, Los Alamitos (2008)

---

[6] http://www.sun.com/software/jxta/

5. Imine, A., Molli, P., Oster, G., Rusinowitch, M.: Proving Correctness of Transformation Functions in Real-Time Groupware. In: ECSCW 2003, Helsinki, Finland, September 14-18 (2003)
6. Imine, A., Rusinowitch, M.: Applying a Theorem Prover to the Verification of Optimistic Replication Algorithms. In: Comon-Lundh, H., Kirchner, C., Kirchner, H. (eds.) Jouannaud Festschrift. LNCS, vol. 4600, pp. 213–234. Springer, Heidelberg (2007)
7. Li, D., Li, R.: Ensuring Content Intention Consistency in Real-Time Group Editors. In: IEEE ICDCS 2004, Tokyo, Japan (March 2004)
8. Li, R., Li, D.: A landmark-based transformation approach to concurrency control in group editors. In: ACM GROUP 2005, New York, USA, pp. 284–293 (2005)
9. Li, R., Li, D.: A new operational transformation framework for real-time group editors. IEEE Trans. Parallel Distrib. Syst. 18(3), 307–319 (2007)
10. Lushman, B., Cormack, G.V.: Proof of correctness of ressel's adopted algorithm. Information Processing Letters 86(3), 303–310 (2003)
11. Molli, P., Oster, G., Skaf-Molli, H., Imine, A.: Using the transformational approach to build a safe and generic data synchronizer. In: Proceedings of the 2003 international ACM SIG-GROUP conference on Supporting group work, pp. 212–220. ACM Press, New York (2003)
12. Prakash, A., Knister, M.J.: A framework for undoing actions in collaborative systems. ACM Trans. Comput.-Hum. Interact. 1(4), 295–330 (1994)
13. Ressel, M., Nitsche-Ruhland, D., Gunzenhauser, R.: An Integrating, Transformation-Oriented Approach to Concurrency Control and Undo in Group Editors. In: ACM CSCW 1996, Boston, USA, November 1996, pp. 288–297 (1996)
14. Suleiman, M., Cart, M., Ferrié, J.: Concurrent operations in a distributed and mobile collaborative environment. In: IEEE ICDE 1998, pp. 36–45 (1998)
15. Sun, C.: Undo as concurrent inverse in group editors. ACM Trans. Comput.-Hum. Interact. 9(4), 309–361 (2002)
16. Sun, C., Ellis, C.: Operational transformation in real-time group editors: issues, algorithms, and achievements. In: ACM CSCW 1998, pp. 59–68 (1998)
17. Sun, C., Jia, X., Zhang, Y., Yang, Y., Chen, D.: Achieving Convergence, Causality-preservation and Intention-preservation in real-time Cooperative Editing Systems. ACM Trans. Comput.-Hum. Interact. 5(1), 63–108 (1998)
18. Sun, C., Xia, S., Sun, D., Chen, D., Shen, H., Cai, W.: Transparent adaptation of single-user applications for multi-user real-time collaboration. ACM Trans. Comput.-Hum. Interact. 13(4), 531–582 (2006)
19. Vidot, N., Cart, M., Ferrié, J., Suleiman, M.: Copies convergence in a distributed real-time collaborative environment. In: ACM CSCW 2000, Philadelphia, USA (December 2000)

A   Correctness

In this section we give the correctness of our concurrency control algorithm with respect to criteria consistency (see Definition 3). By lack of space, we only sketch some proofs.

A.1   Basic Definitions

The shared document can be modelled by the abstract data type *list*. A list is a sequence of elements from a data type $\mathcal{E}$. The element type is only a parameter and can be instantiated by each type needed. For instance, an element may be regarded as a character, a paragraph, a page, an XML node, etc. The set of operations modifying the list state is defined as follows:

$$\mathcal{O} = \{Ins(p, e, \omega) | e \in \mathcal{E}, p \in \mathbb{N} \text{ and } \omega \in \mathbb{N}^*\} \cup \{Del(p) | p \in \mathbb{N}\}$$
$$\cup \{Up(p, e, e') | p \in \mathbb{N}, e \in \mathcal{E} \text{ and } e' \in \mathcal{E}\} \cup \{Nop()\}$$

where $Nop()$ is the idle operation that has null effect on the list state. Each user's site has a local state l that is altered only by insertion, deletion and update operations. The initial state, denoted l_0, is the same for all sites. Let $\mathcal{L}$ be the set of list states. We use the function, $Do : \mathcal{O} \times \mathcal{L} \rightarrow \mathcal{L}$, for computing the resulting state l' when a user applies operation o to state l: $Do(o, l) = l'$. We extend this function to sequence of requests as follows: (i) $Do([], l) = l$ where $[]$ is the empty sequence and; (ii) $Do([q_1.o; q_2.o; \ldots; q_n.o], l) = Do(q_n.o, Do(\ldots, Do(q_2.o, Do(q_1.o, l))))$.

Every site stores all executed requests in a buffer also called a *log*.

Definition 6. *A log is a tuple $(L, \ll_L)$ where L is a finite set of requests together with a total order $\ll_L$ over L reflecting the execution order. For simplicity, we denote a log $(L, \ll_L)$ as the sequence $L = [q_1; q_2; \ldots; q_n]$ iff $L = \{q_1, q_2, \ldots, q_n\}$ and $(q_i, q_j) \in \ll_L$ whenever $i < j$.*

Every log can be divided into several sub-logs as follows.

Definition 7. *A log $(L', \ll_{L'})$ is a sub-log of $(L, \ll_L)$ iff $L' \subseteq L$ and for every requests $q, q' \in L'$ $(q, q') \in \ll_L$ iff $(q, q') \in \ll_{L'}$.*

The causal dependency relation given in Definition 1 allows us to define the following property on logs.

Definition 8. *A sub-log $(L', \ll_{L'})$ of log $(L, \ll_L)$ is closed iff for every requests $q \in L$ and $q' \in L'$ where $(q, q') \in \ll_L$ if $q \xrightarrow{s} q'$ then $q \in L'$.*

A closed sub-log contains for each request every preceding request it depends on. When exchanging requests between different sites, the closed-sublogs must be preserved. Permuting two successive requests in a log enables us to produce another log without altering the resulting state of the original log. So we can define an equivalence relation between logs:

Definition 9. *A log $(L, \ll_L)$ is equivalent by transformation to a log $(L', \ll_{L'})$, denoted $L \equiv_t L'$, iff the following conditions holds: (i) $Do(L, l_0) = Do(L', l_0)$ for every state l_0; (ii) $|L| = |L'|$; (iii) $(L', \ll_{L'})$ can be obtained from $(L, \ll_L)$ by applying a finite number of permutations.*

This equivalence by transformation is simply a bijective mapping $f : L \rightarrow L'$ that can be considered as a composition of a finite number of request permutations having the following form: $c_i : L \rightarrow L'$ (with $1 < i \leq |L|$) such that

$$\begin{cases} c_i(q_i) = q_i' & \text{where } q_i' = ET(q_i, q_{i-1}) \text{ and} \\ & (q_{i-1}, q_i) \in \ll_L \\ c_i(q_{i-1}) = q_{i-1}' & \text{where } q_{i-1}' = IT(q_{i-1}, q_i') \\ c_i(q) = q & \text{for all } q \neq q_i \text{ and } q \neq q_{i-1} \end{cases}$$

By abuse of notation we often write $f(L) = L'$.

Definition 10. *Two operations o_1, $o_2 \in \mathcal{O}$ are said* similar, *denoted by $o_1 \approx o_2$, iff one of the following conditions holds: (i) $o_1 = Ins(p, e, \omega_1)$ and $o_2 = Ins(p, e, \omega_2)$; (ii) $o_1 = Del(p)$ and $o_2 = Del(p)$; (iii) $o_1 = Up(p, e, e')$ and $o_2 = Ins(p, e, e')$; (iv) $o_1 = Nop()$ and $o_2 = Nop()$. We can extend this similarity relation to requests as follows: $q \approx q'$ iff $q.o \approx q'.o$, $q.c = q'.c$, $q.k = q'.k$ and $q.a = q'.a$.*

Two similar operations produce the same state when they are executed on the same initial state. For example, $o_1 = Ins(2, e, [3.4])$ and $o_2 = Ins(2, e, \epsilon)$ are similar.

A.2 Basic Properties

By abuse of notation, we also use IT (resp. ET) for transforming a request against a request sequence: (i) $IT(q, []) = q$ and $ET(q, []) = q$ where $[]$ is the empty log; (ii) $IT(q, [q_1; \ldots; q_{n-1}; q_n]) = IT(IT(q, q_1), [q_2; \ldots; q_n])$; (iii) $ET(q, [q_1; \ldots; q_{n-1}; q_n]) = ET(ET(q, q_n), [q_1; \ldots; q_{n-1}])$.

Property 1 expresses a relaxed form of $TP2$ property as it is based on canonical request sequences and the similarity relation. For example, consider two canonical sequences $[q_1; q_2']$ and $[q_2; q_1']$ where $q_1' = IT(q_1, q_2)$ and $q_2' = IT(q_2, q_1)$. Suppose that $q_1.o = Del(3)$ and $q_2.o = Del(2)$. By transformation, we have $q_1'.o = Del(2)$ and $q_2'.o = Del(2)$. Let q be an insertion request with $q.o = Ins(3, e, \epsilon)$. When transforming q against both sequences we obtain: $q' = IT(q, [q_1; q_2'])$ and $q'' = IT(q, [q_2; q_1'])$ with $q'.o = Ins(2, e, [3.3])$ and $q''.o = Ins(2, e, [2.3])$. It is clear that q' and q'' are not identical – unlike $TP2$ property – but they are similar.

Property 1. Let $[q_1; q_2']$ and $[q_2; q_1']$ be two canonical request sequences with $q_1' = IT(q_1, q_2)$ and $q_2' = IT(q_2, q_1)$. For every request q: if $q' = IT(q, [q_1; q_2'])$ and $q'' = IT(q, [q_2; q_1'])$ then $q \approx q'$.

Proof. Consider two cases:

(i) q_1 and q_2 are update requests: for every request q, the position parameter (*i.e.* insertion, deletion or update position) remains unchanged after transformation against both sequences.

(ii) q_1 and q_2 are pairwise deletion/insertion requests: if q is an update request, the position parameter evolves (*i.e.* it is increasing, decreasing, or unchanged) in the same way for both sequences.

The remaining cases where q, q_1 and q_2 are pairwise deletion/insertion requests have been proved in [3]. ∎

Property 2 stipulates that exclusively transforming a request against both canonical and equivalent sequences produces the same request.

Property 2. Let $[q_1; q_2']$ and $[q_2; q_1']$ be two canonical request sequences with $q_1' = IT(q_1, q_2)$ and $q_2' = IT(q_2, q_1)$. For every request q, if $q' = ET(q, [q_1; q_2'])$ then $q' = ET(q, [q_2; q_1'])$.

Proof. Consider two cases:

(i) q_1 and q_2 are update requests: if q is an insertion or deletion request, the position parameter (*i.e.* insertion or deletion position) remains unchanged after transformation.

(ii) q_1 and q_2 are pairwise deletion/insertion requests: if q is an update request, either its position parameter evolves (*i.e.* it is increasing, decreasing, or unchanged) in the same way or we get "undefined" value for both sequences.

The remaining cases where q, q_1 and q_2 are pairwise deletion/insertion requests have been proved in [3].   ■

A.3   Preservation of Causal Dependency Relation

Proof of Theorem 1.   Consider $q'_1 = IT(q_1, q)$ and $q'_2 = IT(q_2, q')$ with $q' = IT(q, q_1)$. We consider two dependency forms $\mathbf{df_4}$ and $\mathbf{df_5}$. The other forms have been proved in [3].

$\mathbf{df_4}$ **form:** We have $q_1.o = Ins(p, e, \omega)$ and $q_2.o = Up(p, e, e')$.

(i) $q.o = Ins(p_1, e_1, \omega_1)$ and $((p_1 = p$ and $q_1.c > q.c)$ or $(p_1 < p))$: $q'_1.o = Ins(p + 1, e, \omega)$ and $q'_2.o = Up(p + 1, e, e')$.

(ii) $q.o = Ins(p_1, e_1, \omega_1)$ and $((p_1 = p$ and $q_1.c < q.c)$ or $(p_1 > p))$: $q'_1 = q_1$ and $q'_2 = q_2$.

(iii) $q.o = Del(p_1)$ and $p_1 \geq p$: $q'_1 \approx q_1$ and $q'_2 = q_2$.

(iv) $q.o = Del(p_1)$ and $p_1 < p$: $q'_1.o = Ins(p - 1, e, p\omega)$ and $q'_2.o = Up(p - 1, e, e')$.

(v) $q.o = Up(p_1, e_1, e'_1)$: $q'_1 = q_1$ and $q'_2 = q_2$.

$\mathbf{df_5}$ **form:** We have $q_1.o = Up(p, e, e')$, $q_2.o = Up(p, e', e'')$ and $q_2.c \leq q_1.c$.

(i) $q.o = Ins(p_1, e_1, \omega_1)$ and $p_1 \leq p$: $q'_1.o = Up(p + 1, e, e')$ and $q'_2.o = Up(p + 1, e', e'')$.

(ii) $(q.o = Ins(p_1, e_1, \omega_1)$ or $q.o = Del(p_1))$ and $p_1 > p$: $q'_1 = q_1$ and $q'_2 = q_2$.

(iii) $q.o = Del(p_1)$ and $p_1 < p$: $q'_1.o = Up(p - 1, e, e')$ and $q'_2.o = Up(p - 1, e', e'')$.

(iv) $q.o = Del(p_1)$ and $p_1 > p$: $q'_1.o = Nop()$ and $q'_2.o = Nop()$.

(v) $q.o = Up(p, e, e'_1)$ and $q.c < q_1.c$: $q_1.o = Up(p, e'_1, e')$ and $q'_2 = q_2$.

(vi) $q.o = Up(p, e, e'_1)$ and $q.c > q_1.c$: $q_1.o = Nop()$ and $q'_2.o = Nop()$.   ■

In Lemma 1 we show how the causal dependency relation is preserved by permutation inside a log of three requests.

Lemma 1. *Let $L = [q_1; q_2; q_3]$ be a log formed by three requests. Then the following assertions hold:*

(i) *if $q_1 \xrightarrow{s} q_2$ and $q_2 \xrightarrow{s} q_3$ then $[q_1; q'_3; q'_2] \equiv_t L$ such that $PERM(q_2, q_3) = [q'_3; q'_2]$ and $q_1 \xrightarrow{s} q'_2$;*

(ii) *if $q_1 \xrightarrow{s} q_2$ and $q_2 \xrightarrow{s} q_3$ then $[q'_2; q'_1; q_3] \equiv_t L$ such that $PERM(q_1, q_2) = [q'_2; q'_1]$ and $q'_2 \xrightarrow{s} q_3$;*

(iii) if $q_1 \not\xrightarrow{s} q_2$ and $q_1 \xrightarrow{s} q_3$ then $[q'_2; q'_1; q_3] \equiv_t L$ such that $PERM(q_1, q_2) = [q'_2; q'_1]$ and $q'_1 \xrightarrow{s} q_3$;

(iv) (i) $\implies$ (iii);

(v) (ii) $\iff$ (iii).

Proof. We have to consider all different dependency forms according to Definition 1 (see [3]).   ∎

In Lemma 2 we show that the causal dependency between two requests inside canonical log is preserved in another equivalent log.

Lemma 2. *Let $L = [q_1; q_2; \ldots; q_n]$ be a canonical log. For every canonical log L' such that $L \equiv_t L'$, if $q_i \xrightarrow{s} q_j$ then $f(q_i) \xrightarrow{s} f(q_j)$ where $f(L) = L'$ and f is a bijective mapping.*

Proof. Suppose that f is the composition of p request permutations. Then we proceed by induction on p.

(i) *Induction base:* Let $p = 1$ and $L = [q_1; \ldots; q_i; \ldots; q_j; \ldots]$ such that $i < j$. Without a lost of generality we consider the case where $q_i \xrightarrow{s} q_j$ is a direct dependency, *i.e.* there is no q_k such that $i < k < j$ and $q_i \xrightarrow{s} q_k \xrightarrow{s} q_j$. Let $q'_j = ET(q_j, L[i+1, j-1])$ and $q''_j = ET(q_j, L[i+2, j-1])$. By definition, $q_i \xrightarrow{s} q_j$ implies $q_i \xrightarrow{s} q'_j$ and $q_i \xrightarrow{s} q''_j$. Let k be the position where the permutation is performed on L. We have the following cases:

   (a) $k < i$ or $k > j + 1$:
       $PERM(q_{k-1}, q_k)$ does not affect the requests between q_i and q_j;

   (b) $i + 1 < k < j$:
       As L' is canonical then q_{k-1} and q_k must be of the same type. From $L = [\ldots; q_i; \ldots; q_{k-1}; q_k; \ldots; q_j; \ldots]$ we get $L' = [\ldots; q_i; \ldots; q'_k; q'_{k-1}; \ldots; q_j; \ldots]$ such that $PERM(q_{k-1}, q_k) = [q'_k; q'_{k-1}]$. As $L[i+1, j-1] \equiv_t L'[i+1, j-1]$, then $q'_j = ET(q_j, L[i+1, j-1]) = ET(q_j, L'[i+1, j-1])$ using Property 2. Hence $q_i \xrightarrow{s} q_j$ is preserved.

   (c) $k = i$:
       From $L = [\ldots; q_{i-1}; q_i; \ldots; q_j; \ldots]$ we get $L' = [\ldots; q'_i; q'_{i-1}; \ldots; q_j; \ldots]$. As $q_{i-1} \not\xrightarrow{s} q_i$ and $q_i \xrightarrow{s} q'_j$ then $q'_i \xrightarrow{s} q_j$ using Lemma 1(ii).

   (d) $k = i + 1$:
       From $L = [\ldots; q_i; q_{i+1}; \ldots; q_j; \ldots]$ we get $L' = [\ldots; q'_{i+1}; q'_i; \ldots; q_j; \ldots]$. As $q_i \not\xrightarrow{s} q_{i+1}$ and $q_i \xrightarrow{s} q''_j$ then $q'_i \xrightarrow{s} q_j$ using Lemma 1(iii).

   (e) $k = j$:
       From $L = [\ldots; q_i; \ldots; q_{j-1}; q_j; \ldots]$ we get $L' = [\ldots; q_i; \ldots; q'_j; q'_{j-1}; \ldots]$. As $q_i \xrightarrow{s} q_j$ then $q_i \xrightarrow{s} ET(q_j, q_{j-1})$.

   (f) $k = j + 1$:
       If q_j and q_{j+1} are of the same type then from $L = [\ldots; q_i; \ldots; q_j; q_{j+1}; \ldots]$ we get $L' = [\ldots; q_i; \ldots; q'_{j+1}; q'_j; \ldots]$. As $q_i \xrightarrow{s} q_j$ and $q_j \not\xrightarrow{s} q_{j+1}$ then $q_i \xrightarrow{s} q'_j$ using Lemma 1(i).

(ii) *Induction hypothesis:* This lemma is true for $p \geq 1$.
(iii) *Induction step:* Let us show that this lemma holds for $p + 1$. Given L'' a canonical log built from L by applying p request permutations and L' a canonical log obtained by performed one request permutation to L''. Then this lemma holds for L' since it is true for L'' (by induction hypothesis) and it is true for one request permutation (by induction base). ∎

In Theorem 2 we show that all causal dependencies inside canonical logs are preserved by transformation.

Theorem 2. *Let L_1 and L_2 be two canonical logs such that $L_1 \equiv_t L_2$. If L_1' is a closed sub-log of L_1 then $f(L_1')$ is also a closed sub-log of L_2 such that $f(L_1) = L_2$ and f is a bijective mapping.*

Proof. Let $n = |L_1'|$. We proceed by induction on n.

(i) *Induction base:* for $n = 2$ we have $L_1' = [q_i; q_j]$ such that $q_i \xrightarrow{s} q_j$ with $i, j \in \{1, \ldots, |L_1|\}$ and $i < j$. Using Lemma 2, we can state that $f(L_1')$ is a closed sub-log of L_2.
(ii) *Induction hypothesis:* $f(L_1')$ is a closed sub-log of L_2 for $n \geq 2$.
(iii) *Induction step:* Let $L_1' = [q_{i_1}; \ldots; q_{i_n}]$ and $L_1'' = [L_1'; q]$ where q is a request and $q_{i_n} \xrightarrow{s} q$. As $f(q_{i_j}) \xrightarrow{s} f(q_{i_{j+1}})$ for $j \in \{1, \ldots, n\}$ (using the induction hypothesis) and $f(q_{i_n}) \xrightarrow{s} f(q)$ (using the induction base), then $f(L_1'')$ is a closed sub-log of L_2. ∎

As a consequence of Theorem 2, a closed sub-log containing only insertion (or update) requests can be reordered at the head of canonical log.

Corollary 1. *Let L_1' be a closed sub-log of a canonical log L_1 such that L_1' contains only insertion requests. There must exist a canonical log L_2 such that (i) $L_1 \equiv_t L_2$, and (ii) $L_2 = [L_2'; L_2'']$ where $L_2' = f(L_1')$ for every bijective mapping $f : L_1 \to L_2$.*

A.4 Data Convergence

By adding an insertion request to a canonical log it is still possible to build a new canonical log.

Lemma 3. *Suppose that L is a log which contains only deletion requests. Let i be an insertion request that is generated in state $s = Do(L, l_0)$. Then there exists a canonical log L' such that $L' \equiv_t [L; i]$.*

Proof. Let $|L| = n$. We proceed by induction on n.
Induction base: for $n = 1$ we have $L = [d]$ where d is a deletion request. By construction $[d; i] \equiv_t [i'; d']$ where $[i'; d'] = PERM(d, i)$. So $L' = [i'; d']$ is canonical.
Induction hypothesis: for $n > 1$ there exists a canonical log $L' \equiv_t [L; i]$.
Induction step: Let $L = [d_1; d_2; \ldots; d_n; d_{n+1}]$. Using induction hypothesis, we have: $L = [d_2; \ldots; d_n; d_{n+1}; i] \equiv_t [i'; d_2'; \ldots; d_n'; d_{n+1}']$ where i' is the result of permuting i

with requests $d_2, \ldots, d_{n+1}$. We have $[i''; d_1'] \equiv_t [d_1; i']$ as $PERM(d_1, i') = [i''; d_1']$. Consequently, $L' = [i''; d_1'; d_2'; \ldots; d_n'; d_{n+1}'; i] \equiv_t [L; i]$ and L' is canonical.   ∎

Theorem 3 concerns the generation step of our concurrency control algorithm.

Theorem 3. *Suppose that L is canonical log. Let q be a request generated in state $l = Do(L, l_0)$. There must exist a canonical log L' such that: $L' \equiv_t [L; q]$*

Proof. We consider two cases: either q is an insertion request or q is a deletion request.

1. q is a deletion or update request: We get L' by simply adding q to L, *i.e.* $L' = [L; q]$.
2. q is a insertion request: As L is canonical then $L = [L_i; L_d]$ where L_i contains insertions requests and L_d holds deletion requests. Using Lemma (3), we can permute q with every deletion requests in L_d and we get $[q'; L_d] \equiv_t [L_d; q]$. Hence, $L' = [L_i; q'; L_d'] \equiv_t [L; q]$ is canonical.   ∎

The following theorem concerns the integration of remote requests. It means that the integration of every remote request on every two equivalent logs produces also two equivalent logs.

Theorem 4. *At stable state any two sites have equivalent canonical logs.*

Proof. Let L_1 and L_2 be two canonical logs of peers P_1 and P_2, respectively, such that $L_1 \equiv_t L_2$. Let q be a remote request to be integrated in P_1 and P_2. Thus two cases are possible:

(i) *q is independent:* Let $q' = IT(q, L_1)$ and $q'' = IT(q, L_2)$. As $L_1 \equiv_t L_2$ then $q' \approx q''$ using Property 1 Thus, $Do([L_1; q'], l_0) = Do([L_2; q''], l_0)$.

(ii) *q is dependent:* Let $L_1' = [q_{i_1}; q_{i_2}; \ldots; q_{i_n}]$ be a closed log of L_1 such that $q_{i_n} \xrightarrow{s} q$. Note that L_1' contains only insertion deletions. In the following diagram we sketch the equivalent canonical logs we can build from L_1 and L_2 using bijective mappings f, f', g_1 and g_2:

$$
\begin{array}{ccc}
L_1 & \xrightarrow{\;f\;} & L_2 \\
\downarrow{\scriptstyle g_1} & & \downarrow{\scriptstyle g_2} \\
L_3 & \xrightarrow{\;f'\;} & L_4
\end{array}
$$

As $L_2' = f(L_1')$ is also a closed sub-log of L_2 then we deduce that $f(q_{i_n}) \xrightarrow{s} q$. By using Corollary 1, we have $L_3 = [L_3'; L_3'']$ such that $L_3' = g_1(L_1')$. In the same way, $L_4 = [L_4'; L_4'']$ such that $L_4' = g_1(L_2')$. It is easy to see that $f'(g_1(L_1')) = g_2(f(L_1'))$ and $L_3' = L_4'$ since they contains respectively the n first requests of L_3 and L_4 and they are closed sub-logs. In this case, the integration of q consists in transforming it along with L_3'' and L_4''. Let $q' = IT(q, L_3'')$ and $q'' = IT(q, L_4'')$. Since $L_3'' \equiv_t L_4''$ then $q' \approx q''$ according to Property 1. Thus, $Do([L_3; q'], l_0) = Do([L_4; q''], l_0)$.   ∎

A Uniform Framework for Modeling and Verifying Components and Connectors

Christel Baier, Tobias Blechmann, Joachim Klein, and Sascha Klüppelholz*

Faculty of Computer Science,
Technische Universität Dresden, Germany

Abstract. The purpose of this paper is to present a framework to model component interfaces and the component connectors that provide the glue code for the components. Our modeling approach is based on two input languages which rely on the same automata model. One of them is a scripting language which can serve to specify exogenous or endogenous coordination mechanisms. The other one is a guarded command language which has been designed to specify behavioral component interfaces, but can also be used to design component connectors. This hybrid approach allows nesting of the two specification languages, supports compositional design, modular verification and reusability of components or component connectors. It yields the input language of our verification toolset Vereofy which realizes several model checking algorithms for components, component connectors, and the composite system.

1 Introduction

The basic principle of component-based software engineering is to fragment a complex system into logical components with well-defined interfaces. In this context, a variety of coordination models and languages have been introduced that support the separation between computations inside the components and the interactions between the components. *Endogenous* coordination languages require to incorporate coordination primitives within the code that specifies the behavior of the components. A typical example is Linda [11] where components are described in a computational languages extended by operators to store or retrieve data objects from a global tuple space. A cleaner separation of computation and coordination is provided by *exogenous* coordination models where the components do not need to be aware of each other. Instead, they are controlled from "outside" via their interfaces. Several approaches for exogenous coordination have been suggested, e.g., an aspect-oriented approach [8], a variant of the π-calculus with anonymous peer-to-peer communication [13], and formalisms that rely on the construction of component connectors, such as interaction systems as in [12,17] or the declarative channel-based language Reo [2].

For providing tool support for the verification of systems specified in such coordination formalisms, one needs input languages which on the one hand cover the

---

* The authors are supported by the EU-project Credo and the DFG-project Syanco.

J. Field and V.T. Vasconcelos (Eds.): COORDINATION 2009, LNCS 5521, pp. 247–267, 2009.

major features of the coordination language and on the other hand have an operational semantics that can easily be implemented. For exogenous coordination languages, there is an additional aspect that should be taken into account. The objects specified in an exogenous coordination language typically just formalize the network that organizes the interactions of black-box components, but they do not make any restrictions on the behavior of the components. Such restrictions, however, might be essential to prove certain functional properties of the composite system consisting of several components and the network that serves as a component connector. Thus, what is needed for model checking tools are input languages that provide coordination primitives to specify the network and features to model the behavioral interfaces of the components. Beside constraints on the type of messages that can be send or received via the input and output ports, such behavioral interfaces can also specify local states of the components and impose (possibly data-dependent) conditions on the enabledness of sending and receiving messages via the I/O-ports. In the literature, there are several *automata-based models* that can be seen as "light-weight" formalisms for specifying the behavioral interfaces of components. Examples are I/O-automata that support compositional reasoning about asynchronous concurrent systems [16] or interface automata that have been introduced for reasoning about compatibility of components [10,9] or constraint automata which have been developed in the context of reasoning about exogenous coordination [5].

The goal of this paper is to present the uniform framework for specifying behavioral component interfaces and component connectors that we developed in the context of our toolkit Vereofy [7] (see Fig. 1). The verification constituents of Vereofy are symbolic BDD-based model checking tools for linear-, branching- and alternating-time temporal logics with special operators to reason about the data flow at I/O-ports of components or internal nodes of the network and a bisimulation checker. These logics LTL$_{IO}$, BTSL, ASL and verification algorithms for them and the bisimulation checking algorithm, together with some experimental results performed on the basis of a prototype implementation, have been presented elsewhere [6,15,4,14]. This work on model checking component-based systems uses *constraint automata* [5] as a uniform operational model for component connectors, behavioral component interfaces and the composite system. The focus of this paper is on the modeling approach of Vereofy which supports

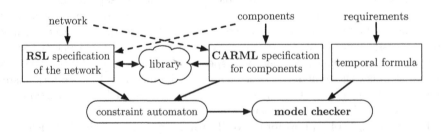

Fig. 1. Vereofy overview

exogenous and endogenous coordination. Vereofy deals with the combination of two languages, both equipped with a constraint automata semantics. One of them is a guarded command language, called CARML, that mainly serves to specify the I/O-ports of components and their stepwise "observable" behavior. The second input language of Vereofy, called RSL, is a *scripting language* which combines the major features of the exogenous coordination language Reo [2] with concepts to specify connectors with dynamically changing network topologies and some features of other languages (such as shared variables or data types). Reo's coordination primitives allow to reason about all kinds of coordination patterns with an arbitrary mixture of synchronous or asynchronous peer-to-peer communication. By combining Reo's coordination primitives with operators for the instantiation of component connectors or components which are specified in RSL or CARML, our approach offers an elegant way for the compositional, hierarchical construction of component connectors and components. While previous work on Reo and constraint automata relies on the assumption of a global data domain that serves as data type for all messages that can be send via the channels, our hybrid modeling approach with RSL and CARML supports the use of several data types. This allows using standard methods to ensure type consistency and to check compatibility via type checking.

Organization of the paper. Section 2 summarizes our notations concerning data types and constraint automata. The languages CARML and RSL are presented in Section 3 and 4, respectively. An example using our hybrid modeling approach is provided in Section 5 and experimental results with our toolkit Vereofy are presented in Section 6. The paper ends with some remarks on related work and a conclusion (Section 7).

2   Preliminaries

Data types with fixed semantics. Let DT denote a set of data types covering standard data types, such as Booleans or integers of fixed bit-size, or user-defined data types with a fixed semantics, such as arrays and unions over elements of a predefined data type or enumeration types. Let Op denote a set of operators on the data types in DT such as conjunction, disjunction, negation for Booleans and arithmetic operations like addition and multiplication for integers. Furthermore, Pred denotes a set of predicates, such as the standard binary comparison predicates $=$, $<$, $\leq$, and so on. Formally, the elements of DT are fixed finite nonempty sets and each operator $op \in Op$ is a function $op : T_1 \times \ldots \times T_k \rightarrow T$ where $(T_1, \ldots, T_k, T) \in DT^{k+1}$ and $k \in \mathbb{N}$. The tuple $(T_1, \ldots, T_k, T)$ is called the type of op, denoted $\mathfrak{type}(op)$. Each predicate $P \in Pred$ is a subset of $T_1 \times \ldots \times T_k$ where $k \geq 1$ and $T_1, \ldots, T_k \in DT$. We write $\mathfrak{type}(P)$ for the tuple $(T_1, \ldots, T_k)$.

Uninterpreted data types and signatures. Beside data types with fixed semantics, our languages also allow for uninterpreted symbols for data types, operators and predicates. These can be used as parameters for RSL and CARML specifications which then serve as templates for components or connectors.

A signature is a tuple $\mathfrak{Sig} = (\mathfrak{DT}, \mathfrak{Op}, \mathfrak{Pred}, \mathfrak{Var})$ where $\mathsf{DT} \subseteq \mathfrak{DT}$, $\mathsf{Op} \subseteq \mathfrak{Op}$ $\mathsf{Pred} \subseteq \mathfrak{Pred}$ and $\mathfrak{Var}$ is a set of typed variables, i.e., for each variable $V \in \mathfrak{Var}$ its type $\mathfrak{type}(V)$ is an element of $\mathfrak{DT}$. The uninterpreted symbols for data types, operators and predicates are then given by the elements of $\Theta = \mathfrak{DT} \setminus \mathsf{DT}$, $\Omega = \mathfrak{Op} \setminus \mathsf{Op}$ and $\Pi = \mathfrak{Pred} \setminus \mathsf{Pred}$, respectively. The data type symbols $T \in \Theta$ can be seen as placeholders for sets (data types). The operator symbols $op \in \Omega$ and predicate symbols $P \in \Pi$ are associated with a type. The type of an operator symbol $op \in \Omega$ is a tuple $\mathfrak{type}(op) = (T_1, \ldots, T_k, T) \in \mathfrak{DT}^{k+1}$ for some $k \in \mathbb{N}$. It declares that op takes as arguments k elements $v_1, \ldots, v_k$ where v_i is of type T_i and returns an element of type T. That is, op stands for a function $op : T_1 \times \ldots \times T_k \to T$. The number k is called the arity of op. Similarly, the type of a predicate symbol $P \in \Pi$ is a tuple $\mathfrak{type}(P) = (T_1, \ldots, T_k) \in \mathfrak{DT}^k$ for some $k \geq 1$, denoting that P has to be interpreted by a predicate consisting of tuples $(v_1, \ldots, v_k)$ where v_i is an element of data type T_i.

Terms and atomic propositions. Terms over $\mathfrak{Sig}$ are built by variables, constants, and the operator symbols in a type-consistent manner. Formally, terms over $\mathfrak{Sig}$ are defined recursively according to the following statements.

(1) Each variable $V \in \mathfrak{Var}$ is a term of type $\mathfrak{type}(V)$ and each constant $op \in \mathfrak{Op}$ (i.e., 0-ary operator in $\mathsf{Op} \cup \Omega$) is a term of type $\mathfrak{type}(op)$.
(2) If $t_1, \ldots, t_k$ are terms such that the type of t_i is T_i and $op \in \mathfrak{Op}$ with $\mathfrak{type}(op) = (T_1, \ldots, T_k, T)$ then $op(t_1, \ldots, t_k)$ is a term of type T.

Atomic propositions over $\mathfrak{Sig}$ are type-consistent expressions stating that a certain tuple of terms is an element of a predicate in $\mathfrak{Pred}$. Formally, if $P \in \mathfrak{Pred}$ with $\mathfrak{type}(P) = (T_1, \ldots, T_k)$ and $t_1, \ldots, t_k$ are terms over $\mathfrak{Sig}$ such that t_i is of type T_i then $P(t_1, \ldots, t_k)$ is called an atomic proposition over $\mathfrak{Sig}$.

Interpretations of signatures. For the semantics of terms and atomic propositions over a signature, we have to consider an interpretation $\mathcal{I}$ that provides type-consistent meanings for the uninterpreted data types, operator and predicate symbols and the variables. That is, $\mathcal{I}$ assigns a finite set $T^{\mathcal{I}} \neq \emptyset$ to each data type symbol T, an element of $V^{\mathcal{I}} \in T^{\mathcal{I}}$ to each variable of type T, a function $op^{\mathcal{I}} : T_1^{\mathcal{I}} \times \ldots T_k^{\mathcal{I}} \to T^{\mathcal{I}}$ to each operator symbol op of type $(T_1, \ldots, T_k, T)$ and a predicate $P^{\mathcal{I}} \subseteq T_1^{\mathcal{I}} \times \ldots T_k^{\mathcal{I}}$ to each predicate symbol P of type $(T_1, \ldots, T_k)$. (We treat $\mathcal{I}$ as an interpretation for all symbols of $\mathfrak{Sig}$ by putting $\mathsf{S}^{\mathcal{I}} = \mathsf{S}$ for all predefined symbols $\mathsf{S} \in \mathsf{DT} \cup \mathsf{Op} \cup \mathsf{Pred}$.) The semantics $t^{\mathcal{I}} \in T^{\mathcal{I}}$ of a term of type T and the truth value $P(t_1, \ldots, t_k)^{\mathcal{I}} \in \{\text{true}, \text{false}\}$ for an interpretation $\mathcal{I}$ and an atomic proposition $P(t_1, \ldots, t_k)$ are defined in the obvious way.

Locations and data-flow vocabulary. Locations are points in the network where data flow is observable, e.g., the I/O-ports of components or nodes of the network that serve as a router. In the sequel, $\mathcal{L}$ denotes a finite set of locations. The sets $\mathcal{L}^{src}$ and $\mathcal{L}^{snk}$ are disjoint subsets of $\mathcal{L}$ representing different kinds of locations. Intuitively, $\mathcal{L}^{src}$ stands for the set of input ports (sources), $\mathcal{L}^{snk}$ for the set of output ports (sinks). A data-flow vocabulary over a signature $\mathfrak{Sig}$ is a tuple $\mathfrak{Voc} = \langle \mathcal{L}, \mathcal{L}^{src}, \mathcal{L}^{snk}, \lambda \rangle$ where $\mathcal{L}$ is a set of locations and $\lambda : \mathcal{L} \to \mathfrak{DT}$ is a function that assigns to each location A its message-type $\lambda(A)$, i.e., the type of data items that can be passed via location A.

Concurrent I/O-operations (CIO) and Constraint automata (CA).
Constraint automata [5] serve as a compositional semantics for components and connectors specified in CARML or RSL. For the syntax of CA we slightly depart from [5] and use types for the messages that can be received or sent. The observable data flow is formalized in a CA by means of a concurrent I/O-operation. These can be understood as the potential actions of a component, a connector or as interactions between several components and the connector in the composite system. A concurrent I/O-operation specifies the locations where at some specific time instance data flow is observed simultaneously. In addition, it specifies the data items that are read or written at the I/O-ports of components or transmitted through locations of the connector. Formally, given an interpretation $\mathcal{I}$ for the signature $\mathfrak{Sig}$ then a concurrent I/O-operation over $\mathcal{I}$ is a function c that assigns to each location $A \in \mathcal{L}$ either a data item of type $\lambda(A)^{\mathcal{I}}$ or the special symbol $\bot$ indicating that there is no data flow at A. We write $Obs(c)$ for the set of locations $A \in \mathcal{L}$ such that $c(A) \neq \bot$. Let $CIO_{\mathcal{I}}$, or briefly CIO, denote the set of all concurrent I/O-operations over $\mathcal{I}$. A CA over an interpretation $\mathcal{I}$ for a signature $\mathfrak{Sig}$ is a tuple $\mathcal{A} = (Q, \mathfrak{Voc}, \to, Q_0)$, where Q is a finite set of states, $\mathfrak{Voc}$ a data-flow vocabulary over $\mathfrak{Sig}$, $\to \subseteq Q \times CIO_{\mathcal{I}} \times Q$ the transition relation, and $Q_0 \subseteq Q$ the set of initial states. Obviously, the interpretation $\mathcal{I}$ is irrelevant if all message-types have a fixed semantics, i.e, $\lambda(A) \in \mathsf{DT}$ for all $A \in \mathcal{L}$.

3   Constraint Automata Reactive Module Language

One of the input languages of Vereofy is a guarded command language, called CARML (constraint automata reactive module language), that describes the transitions of constraint automata in a symbolic way, i.e., by means of Boolean conditions on the states and the enabled concurrent I/O-operations. CARML provides a convenient way to specify the component interfaces and to provide a high-level description of the operational behavior of components. CARML supports channel-based message passing and communication over shared variables. The latter is irrelevant for exogenous coordination, but can be useful to incorporate the coordination primitives of an endogenous approach e.g. for existing systems where the coordination protocol is given in an imperative language. In this case, modeling the protocol by means of the coordination language can be much harder than providing a CARML specification. CARML is even expressive enough to specify complex component connectors. To ease the automatic translation of CARML specifications into a compact internal BDD-based representation, we adapted some concepts of reactive modules [1] for the syntax of CARML modules.

Standard data types such as Boolean, integers of fixed bit-size, arrays, unions and enumerations together with the usual operators and predicates on them can be used as data types for variables and message-types for I/O-ports. As in

Section 2, these sets of data types, operators and predicates with fixed semantics are denoted by DT, Op and Pred. CARML modules can also use uninterpreted symbols for data types, operators and predicates. That is, a CARML module $\mathcal{M}$ can be parameterized by a set Θ of data types, a set Ω of operator symbols, a set Π of predicate symbols, and a set Υ of variables with types in $\mathfrak{DT} = \mathsf{DT} \cup \Theta$.

MODULE $\mathcal{M}\langle$type $: \Theta,$ op $: \Omega,$ pred $: \Pi,$ var $: \Upsilon\rangle$ {

    // interface declaration: source ports
    in $: T_1^{\mathrm{in}} \ A_1;$
    $\vdots$ // A_i with message-types $T_i^{\mathrm{in}} \in \mathsf{DT} \cup \Theta$
    in $: T_k^{\mathrm{in}} \ A_r;$

    // interface declaration: sink ports
    out $: T_1^{\mathrm{out}} \ B_1;$
    $\vdots$ // B_i with message-types $T_i^{\mathrm{out}} \in \mathsf{DT} \cup \Theta$
    out $: T_\ell^{\mathrm{out}} \ B_s;$

    // definition of local variables X_i with data types $T_i^{\mathrm{var}} \in \mathsf{DT} \cup \Theta$
    // with initial value $init\_value_i \in T_i^{\mathrm{var}}$ (optional)
    var $: T_1^{\mathrm{var}} \ X_1$ init $:= init\_value_1;$
    $\vdots$
    var $: T_\ell^{\mathrm{var}} \ X_\ell$ init $:= init\_value_\ell;$

    // transition definitions
    $state\_guards_1 \ -\!\!\lfloor I/O\_guards_1 \rfloor\!\mapsto state\_assignments_1;$
    $\vdots$ $\vdots$ $\vdots$
    $state\_guards_n \ -\!\!\lfloor I/O\_guards_n \rfloor\!\mapsto state\_assignments_n;$ }

Fig. 2. Schema of a CARML module

The general schema of a CARML module is shown in Fig. 2. It consists of a (possibly empty) parameter list, the interface declaration where the source and sink ports of a component and its local variables are defined followed by the transition definitions specifying the behavioral interface. The shorthand notation "type $: \Theta,$ op $: \Omega,$ pred $: \Pi$" in Fig. 2 refers to a list where all uninterpreted symbols $S \in \Theta \cup \Omega \cup \Pi$ are encountered together with the corresponding keyword type, op or pred and their types in case of the operator and predicate symbols. Similarly, var $: \Upsilon$ stands short for an enumeration of all variables in Υ together with the keyword var and their types. All variables in Υ are passed according to the concept "call-by-value".

Let $\mathcal{M}$ be the name of the CARML module in Fig. 2. The data types with fixed semantics together with the parameters $\Theta, \Omega, \Pi, \Upsilon$ and the set $\mathfrak{Var}_{\mathcal{M}}$ of variables that can be used in $\mathcal{M}$ (see below) constitute the signature of $\mathcal{M}$ which is given by $\mathfrak{Sig}_{\mathcal{M}} = (\mathfrak{DT}, \mathfrak{Op}, \mathfrak{Pred}, \mathfrak{Var}_{\mathcal{M}})$ where $\mathfrak{DT} = \mathsf{DT} \cup \Theta$, $\mathfrak{Op} = \mathsf{Op} \cup \Omega$ and $\mathfrak{Pred} = \mathsf{Pred} \cup \Pi$. The variables that can be used in a CARML module $\mathcal{M}$ are *local variables* and the variables in Υ. The local variables together with their type have to be listed in the declaration part of $\mathcal{M}$. Thus, the CARML module in Fig. 2 has the local variables $X_1, \ldots, X_\ell$. The type of local variable X_i is $\mathfrak{type}(X_i) = T_i^{\text{var}}$ which has to be an element of $\mathfrak{DT}$. The specification of an initial value for the local variables is optional.

With our hybrid modeling approach where CARML specifications can be embedded in the scripting language RSL (see Section 4) a CARML module can also use *global variables* which have to be declared in the RSL (main) program. Let $\mathfrak{Var}_{\mathcal{M}}$ be the set of all local variables of $\mathcal{M}$, all variables in Υ and all global variables. We refer to the elements of $\mathfrak{Var}_{\mathcal{M}}$ as *accessible* variables of $\mathcal{M}$. The interface declaration in Fig. 2 induces the data-flow vocabulary $\mathfrak{Voc}_{\mathcal{M}} = \langle \mathcal{L}_{\mathcal{M}}, \mathcal{L}_{\mathcal{M}}^{src}, \mathcal{L}_{\mathcal{M}}^{snk}, \lambda_{\mathcal{M}} \rangle$ where $\mathcal{L}_{\mathcal{M}}^{src} = \{A_1, A_2, \ldots, A_r\}$, $\mathcal{L}_{\mathcal{M}}^{snk} = \{B_1, B_2, \ldots, B_s\}$, and $\mathcal{L}_{\mathcal{M}} = \mathcal{L}_{\mathcal{M}}^{src} \cup \mathcal{L}_{\mathcal{M}}^{snk}$. The type of source port A_i is $\lambda_{\mathcal{M}}(A_i) = T_i^{\text{in}}$, while sink port B_j is of type $\lambda_{\mathcal{M}}(B_j) = T_j^{\text{out}}$. Again, the types T_i^{in} and T_j^{out} are elements of $\mathfrak{DT}$. The sets $\mathcal{L}_{\mathcal{M}}^{snk}$ and $\mathcal{L}_{\mathcal{M}}^{src}$ are supposed to be disjoint.

Each *transition definition* consists of local conditions on the current state (a state guard), conditions on the concurrent I/O-operations to be fired (an I/O-guard) and the effect of firing such an I/O-operation on the states (formalized by the state assignments). A *state guard* is a (possibly empty) conjunction of atomic propositions $P(t_1, \ldots, t_k)$ over $\mathfrak{Sig}_{\mathcal{M}}$. An *I/O-guard* is a condition on the observable data flow, formalized by a Boolean combination of atomic propositions over an extended signature $\mathfrak{Sig}_{\mathcal{M}}^{\mathcal{L}}$ that allows to reason about the data items that are observable at the locations in $\mathcal{L}$. Formally, $\mathfrak{Sig}_{\mathcal{M}}^{\mathcal{L}}$ denotes the signature that results from $\mathfrak{Sig}_{\mathcal{M}}$ by adding

- a special type $T_{\text{I/O}}$ that serves for a characterization of the I/O-ports,
- a new monadic predicate symbol *active* with $\mathfrak{type}(active) = T_{\text{I/O}}$,
- constant symbols $data_A$ with $\mathfrak{type}(data_A) = \lambda_{\mathcal{M}}(A)$ for all $A \in \mathcal{L}_{\mathcal{M}}$.

The special type symbol $T_{\text{I/O}}$ is needed for technical reasons only. (Note that the location-symbol A is of type $T_{\text{I/O}}$, while its message-type is $\lambda_{\mathcal{M}}(A) = \mathfrak{type}(data_A)$.) For the interpretations $\mathcal{I}$ of $\mathfrak{Sig}_{\mathcal{M}}^{\mathcal{L}}$ we require that $T_{\text{I/O}}^{\mathcal{I}} = \mathcal{L}_{\mathcal{M}}$. The intuitive meaning of the atomic proposition $active(A)$ is a port activity flag which indicates that data flow at location A is observed. To avoid an overlap with state guards, we require that all atomic propositions $P(t_1, \ldots, t_k)$ in an I/O-guard contain at least one subterm $data_A$ for some $A \in \mathcal{L}_{\mathcal{M}}$.

A *state assignment* is a (possibly empty) sequence of assignments for accessible variables, i.e., state assignments have the form $V_1 := t_1 ; \ldots ; V_p := t_p$ where $V_1, \ldots, V_p$ are pairwise distinct variables in $\mathfrak{Var}_{\mathcal{M}}$ and t_j are terms over the extended signature $\mathfrak{Sig}_{\mathcal{M}}^{\mathcal{L}}$. Intuitively, when firing a transition via a concurrent I/O-operation c with a state assignment as above as then in the next state the value of the variables V_i agrees with the value of the term t_i under the interpretation given by the current state and the c. Variables $V \in \mathfrak{Var}_{\mathcal{M}} \setminus \{V_1, \ldots, V_p\}$ keep their value after the transition has been taken.

Example 1 (A railway track). The CARML module in Fig. 3 serves as a prototype definition for a railway track where trains may either pass or stop. It can be instantiated providing a data type for the trains and an element of that type indicating that there is no train in the track. The component has one source port A and one sink port B. Local variable "stat" keeps track of the status (free or occupied), while local variable "train" serves to remember which train actually stopped on the track when occupied by a train.   □

MODULE track⟨type : *Train Type*, var : *Train Type* no_train⟩{
   in : *Train Type* A;   // A is a source with $\mathfrak{type}(data_A) = $ *Train Type*
   out : *Train Type* B;   // B is a sink with $\mathfrak{type}(data_B) = $ *Train Type*
   var : enum{free, occupied} stat := free;
   var : *Train Type* train := no_train;
   stat = free−[active(A) ∧ active(B) ∧ $data_A = data_B$]↦;
   stat = free−[active(A) ∧ ¬active(B)]↦ stat := occupied ; train := $data_A$;
   stat = occupied−[active(B) ∧ ¬active(A) ∧ $data_B = $ train]↦
                                stat := free ; train := no_train;   }

Fig. 3. CARML module for a railway track

Semantics of a CARML module. The intuitive operational meaning of the transition definitions is as follows. Suppose that q is the current state, which means an evaluation of all accessible variables. Then, nondeterministically a concurrent I/O-operation c and one of the transition definition is chosen such that the state guard holds for q and the I/O-guard is fulfilled by c. The next state is then obtained by modifying q according to the state assignments of the chosen transition definition. This intuitive behavior can be formalized by means of constraint automata. As a CARML module $\mathcal{M}$ as in Fig. 2 serves as a template for components (or connectors), the constraint-automata semantics of $\mathcal{M}$ relies on an interpretation $\mathcal{J}$ for all parameters in $\Theta, \Omega, \Pi, \Upsilon$. For all predefined symbols $S \in DT \cup Op \cup Pred$ we write $S^{\mathcal{J}} = S$.

The constraint automaton $\mathcal{A}_{\mathcal{M},\mathcal{J}} = (Q, \mathfrak{Voc}_{\mathcal{M}}, \rightarrow, Q_0)$ over $\mathfrak{DT} = DT \cup \Theta$ is defined as follows. The data-flow vocabulary of $\mathcal{A}_{\mathcal{M},\mathcal{J}}$ is $\mathfrak{Voc}_{\mathcal{M}}$. The state space of $\mathcal{A}_{\mathcal{M},\mathcal{J}}$ is the set Q consisting of all evaluations of the variables that are accessible for $\mathcal{M}$, i.e., Q is the set of functions q that assign to each variable $V \in \mathfrak{Var}_{\mathcal{M}}$ a data item in $q(V)$ in $\mathfrak{type}(V)^{\mathcal{J}}$. The set Q_0 of initial states consists of all $q_0 \in Q$ such that $q_0(X_i) = init\_value_i$ for each local variable X_i where an initial value has been specified in the declaration part of $\mathcal{M}$. For all other variables V, $q_0(V)$ is an arbitrary element in $\mathfrak{type}(V)^{\mathcal{J}}$.

The transition relation $\rightarrow$ is defined as follows. Let $q, q' \in Q$ and $c \in CIO_{\mathcal{J}}$. Let $\mathcal{I} = (q, \mathcal{J})$ be the interpretation for $\mathfrak{Sig}_{\mathcal{M}}$ that agrees with q for all variables $V \in \mathfrak{Var}_{\mathcal{M}}$ and assigns to the symbols in the parameter list of $\mathcal{M}$ the same meaning as $\mathcal{J}$. The pair $(\mathcal{I}, c)$ denotes the interpretation for the extended signature $\mathfrak{Sig}_{\mathcal{M}}^{\mathcal{L}}$ that agrees with $\mathcal{I} = (q, \mathcal{J})$ on the symbols in $\mathfrak{Sig}_{\mathcal{M}}$, interprets the type symbol $T_{I/O}$ by $T_{I/O}^{\mathcal{I},c} = \mathcal{L}_{\mathcal{M}} = \{A_1, \ldots, A_r, B_1, \ldots, B_s\}$, and assigns $active^{\mathcal{I},c} = Obs(c) = \{D \in \mathcal{L}_{\mathcal{M}} : c(D) \neq \perp\}$ to the activity predicate.

For $D \in Obs(c)$ the interpretation of $data_D$ is the data element $data_D^{\mathcal{I},c} = c(D)$.
For $E \in \mathcal{L}_{\mathcal{M}}$ with $c(E) = \bot$, the interpretation $data_E^{\mathcal{I},c}$ is irrelevant.

Then, $q \xrightarrow{c} q'$ iff there is a transition definition $state\_guards_i \prec\! I/O\_guards_i \succ\!\!\mapsto state\_assignments_i$ in $\mathcal{M}$ such that the following conditions (1), (2) and (3) hold.

(1) state q fulfills the state guard, i.e., $state\_guards_i$ evaluates to true under $\mathcal{I}$
(2) the concurrent I/O-operation c satisfies the I/O-guard, i.e., I/O_guards_i evaluates to true when interpreted over $(\mathcal{I}, c)$
(3) the next state q' arises from q via executing the state assignments, i.e., if $state\_assignments_i$ has the form $V_1 := t_1 ; V_2 := t_2; \ldots V_p := t_p$ then $q'(V_j) = t_j^{\mathcal{I},c}$ for $1 \leq j \leq p$ and $q(V) = q'(V)$ for $V \in \mathfrak{Var}_{\mathcal{M}} \setminus \{V_1, \ldots, V_p\}$.

The picture on the right shows the reachable part of the CA for the railway track from Example 1 and interpretation $\mathcal{J}$ where $TrainType^{\mathcal{J}}$ is the set $\{train_1, train_2, no\_train\}$ and $no\_train^{\mathcal{J}} = no\_train$.

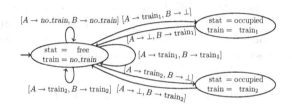

4   Reo Scripting Language

While the main purpose of CARML is to specify the behavioral interfaces of components, Reo scripting language (RSL) mainly serves to specify networks that provide the glue code for components. RSL is inspired by the exogenous coordination language Reo [2] which yields an elegant declarative framework for the compositional construction of connectors by creating channels and glueing their channels ends, the I/O-ports of components, or sub-connectors together. This is done via join-operations, resulting in a network called *Reo circuit*. The semantics of a Reo circuit is a CA which can be constructed in a compositional way by providing constraint automata models for each channel and component and mimicking Reo's operators by corresponding operators for CA [5].

The language RSL combines the Reo operators with operators for the instantiating of components, channels, and component connectors – that are either given by a parameterized CARML module or specified in RSL – and features to specify dynamic reconfigurations of the network topology. Indeed, RSL treats components, channels and component connectors in the same way. This means, that a channel is viewed as a primitive component connector and any component connector can use components or other connectors as "subroutines" via the instantiation mechanism. In what follows, the notion "module" will be used as an umbrella term for component, channel or component connector.

RSL programs. On the top-level, an RSL program consists of (1) a declaration part, (2) a list of include-instructions to access modules from a library, (3) a list of the CARML modules and RSL scripts that might be instantiated in the main system, and optionally (4) an instantiation of an RSL script that serves as the main system. When omitting (4), a non-parameterized module called "main" is required to be contained in (3). The declaration part of an RSL program contains the declarations of global variables and the definition of user-defined data types (like enumerations, arrays and unions over predefined or previously user-defined data types) as well as constants, operators of arity ≥ 1 and predicates. These together with the predefined data types and built-in operators and predicates constitute the sets DT, Op, Pred of data types, operators and predicates with fixed semantics and only these can be passed as meanings for the uninterpreted symbols (elements of $\Theta, \Omega, \Pi, \Upsilon$) in the parameter list of the instantiated module in (4). This ensures that the instantiation in (4) yields an interpretation for all free symbols in the RSL script for the main system. In (2) the library contains the CARML or RSL code for several predefined basic channel types, such as synchronous channels, FIFO channels, and so on, but also components connectors that serve as coordination units in many situations, like an exrouter or sequencer. It can be extended by user-defined modules.

CIRCUIT C $\langle$type : Θ, op : Ω, pred : Π, var : $\Upsilon\rangle$ {
    stmt;   // stepwise construction of a Reo circuit
    interface_decl   // declaration of the I/O-ports of the Reo circuit
}

Fig. 4. Schema of an RSL circuit

RSL scripts for networks with static topology. The schema for the RSL script of a Reo circuit without dynamic reconfiguration is shown in Fig. 4 where the parameterization by uninterpreted symbols for data types, operators, predicates and variables is as for CARML modules. The body of an RSL circuit consists of a *statement* that describes the stepwise construction of a Reo circuit and an *interface declaration* where the exported I/O-ports are specified.

Statements. The statement in the body of an RSL circuit is build by basic operations and control flow instructions (sequential composition, conditional branching and for-loops). The abstract syntax for statements is given by the grammar

$$stmt ::= instantiation \mid Reo\_operation \mid assignment \mid stmt; stmt \mid$$
$$\text{if } (bexpr) \; \{stmt\} \; \texttt{else} \; \{stmt\} \mid \texttt{for } (i = j, \ldots, k) \; \{stmt\}$$

Instantiation. The instantiation of a module (i.e., a component, a channel or a complex connector) specified in CARML or by a RSL circuit is performed via instructions of the form

$$\texttt{new module\_template}\langle\Theta', \Omega', \Pi', \Upsilon'\rangle(A_1, \ldots, A_r; B_1, \ldots, B_s)$$

where $\Theta', \Omega', \Pi', \Upsilon'$ are lists of data types, operators, predicates and variables or constants that provide meanings for the parameters in the CARML or RSL code for the module template. The elements of $\Theta', \Omega', \Pi', \Upsilon'$ have to be contained in the signature of $\mathcal{C}$ which is given by $\mathfrak{Sig}_{\mathcal{C}} = (\mathfrak{DT}, \mathfrak{Op}, \mathfrak{Pred}, \mathfrak{Var}_{\mathcal{C}})$ where $\mathfrak{DT} = \mathsf{DT} \cup \Theta$, $\mathfrak{Op} = \mathsf{Op} \cup \Omega$, $\mathfrak{Pred} = \mathsf{Pred} \cup \Pi$ and $\mathfrak{Var}_{\mathcal{C}} = \Upsilon$.[1] Optionally, the list of meanings for the uninterpreted symbols in the template for some module $\mathcal{M}$ is followed by a list $(A_1, \ldots, A_r; B_1, \ldots, B_s)$ of names for the source and sink ports of $\mathcal{M}$. Thus, A_i will serve as name for the i-th source port of the generated instance of $\mathcal{M}$, and B_j as name for the j-th sink port of that instance. The names A_i and B_j have to be pairwise distinct. They can be fresh names or can represent an existing location, in which case consistency of the message-types is required. If A_i is an already existing location then the message-types of A_i and the i-th source port of $\mathcal{M}$ must agree, and from now on location A_i is joined with the i-th source port of the created instance of $\mathcal{M}$. Analogous conditions are required for $B_1, \ldots, B_s$ and the sink ports of the created instance of $\mathcal{M}$.

The second type of instantiation is the creation of an entity that is called a *Reo node* [2] which plays a crucial role for the join-operation (explained below). A Reo node can combine zero or more channel ends or I/O-ports of components with the same message-type. Reo nodes can be understood as routers with a special routing strategy. The intuitive meaning is a merger semantics of all read operations performed at the sinks combined in a Reo node N and a replicator semantics of the write operations at the sources of N. That is, all pending read operations at the sinks of N are scheduled in an interleaved way and executed synchronously with writing the received value to all sources of N. The effect of an instantiation of a Reo node via the instruction $\mathtt{node}\langle\mathtt{type} : T\rangle$ is the creation of a fresh Reo node N without any channel end or I/O-port. The message-type of N is $T \in \mathfrak{DT}$ which indicates that only data items $v \in T$ can flow through N.

Reo operations. RSL supports Reo's main operations for the composition of complex circuits. The join operation $\mathtt{join}(N_1, \ldots, N_n)$ in RSL takes a list $N_1, \ldots, N_n$ of at least two I/O-ports or Reo nodes of the same message-type $T \in \mathfrak{DT}$ as arguments. It creates a new Reo node N of message-type T where all I/O-ports and channel ends of $N_1, \ldots, N_n$ are combined. If all N_i are sources then the resulting node N is called source (node). Similarly, N is called sink (node) if all N_i's are sinks. There are more operations offered by Reo, but any circuit which can be constructed by the complete list of Reo operations can also be obtained by a sequence of instantiations and join operations. Thus we omit explanations of additional Reo operations.

Script variables and assignments. I/O-ports, nodes created by a join-operation as well as the result of an instantiation (either a Reo node or module) can be stored into local script variables. Script variables can also be used to hold values of predefined data types (typically an integer value). The script variables are "dynamically typed" and do not have to be declared in advance. An assignment for a script variable sv has the syntax $sv := \mathcal{V}$ where

---

[1] There are the obvious side-constraints. If $\mathtt{type} : \Theta$ stands for $\mathtt{type} : T_1, \ldots, \mathtt{type} : T_n$ then Θ' must be a list $U_1, \ldots, U_n$ of elements in $\mathfrak{DT}$. If $\mathtt{op} : \Omega$ encounters m operator symbols then Ω' must be a list of m elements in $\mathfrak{Op}$, and if the i-th element in $\mathtt{op} : \Omega$ is $\mathtt{op} : (T_{i_1}, \ldots, T_{i_k}, T_j) f$ then the i-th element of Ω' has to be an element $f' \in \mathfrak{Op}$ of the type $(U_{i_1}, \ldots, U_{i_k}, U_j)$. Required conditions are required for Π' and Υ'.

$$\mathcal{V} ::= \textit{instantiation} \mid \texttt{join}(N_1, \ldots, N_n) \mid \textit{expression} \mid \textit{script\_variable}$$

and *expression* is a term over the signature induced by the predefined data types and the variables $V \in \Upsilon$ (typically arithmetic expressions). Script variables are dynamically sized arrays, with sv being shorthand for $sv[0]$. A script variable sv referring to an instantiated module $\mathcal{M}$ provides access to the interface I/O-ports via $sv.\texttt{source}[i]$ and $sv.\texttt{sink}[j]$. An RSL circuit can refer to its own source and sink ports via $\texttt{source}[i]$ and $\texttt{sink}[j]$ (see the explanations below).

Control flow instructions. The control flow features (sequential composition, conditional and repetitive commands) have the standard meaning. These and the script variables serve for the stepwise construction of a Reo circuit, and should not be confused with the operational behavior of the network given by the CA for the Reo circuit that results from executing the RSL script. The control flow statements make use of Boolean expressions (bexpr) that impose conditions on the values of script variables and variables in Υ. In the sloppy notation provided for the syntax of for-loops, we assume that i is an integer script variable and j and k are either integer script values or constants.

Interface declaration. In the schema sketched in Fig. 4, the body of an RSL circuit ends with a definition of the nodes that are exported to the higher level as source and sink ports. This can be done in an analogous way as in CARML via "in: A_1; ...; in: A_r; out: B_1; ...; out: B_s" to specify that the i-th source port is A_i and the j-th sink port is B_j. It is required that the A_i's are sources and the B_j's are sinks (I/O-ports or Reo nodes) that have been defined in *stmt* via an assignment or module instantiation. Furthermore, the A_i's and B_j's are required to be pairwise distinct. Alternatively, one may depart from the schema in Fig. 4 and define the interface ports in *stmt* via the references $\texttt{source}[i]$ and $\texttt{sink}[j]$, either by assignments ("$\texttt{source}[i] := \ldots$" and "$\texttt{sink}[j] := \ldots$") or instantiations ("$\texttt{new module}(\ldots, \texttt{source}[i], \ldots; \ldots, \texttt{sink}[j], \ldots)$"). The indices i and j for the exported source and sink ports have to be consecutive starting with 0. If there are two or more assignments for, e.g., $\texttt{source}[i]$ then the last one declares the i-th source port.

Semantics of an RSL circuit. Let $\mathcal{C}$ be an RSL circuit with the parameters Θ, Ω, Π and Υ as in Fig. 4. To provide an operational semantics for $\mathcal{C}$, we fix an interpretation $\mathcal{J}$ for the symbols in the parameter list of $\mathcal{C}$ (which yields an interpretation for the induced signature $\mathfrak{Sig}_\mathcal{C}$) and then construct a Reo circuit $\mathcal{R}_{\mathcal{C},\mathcal{J}}$ for $\mathcal{C}$ by means of the instructions given in *stmt*. Finally, we can apply the machinery presented in [5] to construct a constraint automaton $\mathcal{A}_{\mathcal{C},\mathcal{J}}$ from $\mathcal{R}_{\mathcal{C},\mathcal{J}}$. The data-flow vocabulary $\mathfrak{Voc}_\mathcal{C}$ of this constraint automaton $\mathcal{A}_{\mathcal{C},\mathcal{J}}$ is defined according to the interface declaration, i.e., $\mathfrak{Voc}_\mathcal{C} = (\mathcal{L}_\mathcal{C}, \mathcal{L}_\mathcal{C}^{src}, \mathcal{L}_\mathcal{C}^{snk}, \lambda_\mathcal{C})$ where $\mathcal{L}_\mathcal{C}^{src} = \{A_1, \ldots, A_r\}$ and $\mathcal{L}_\mathcal{C}^{snk} = \{B_1, \ldots, B_s\}$ if the interface declaration specifies $A_1, \ldots, A_s$ as source ports and $B_1, \ldots, B_s$ as sink ports. The function $\lambda_\mathcal{C}$ is the obvious one and assigns the message-type of A_i to the i-th source port ($\texttt{source}[i-1]$) and the message-type of B_j to the j-th sink port ($\texttt{sink}[j-1]$). The set of all observable locations of $\mathcal{C}$ is $\mathcal{L}_\mathcal{C} = \mathcal{L}_\mathcal{C}^{src} \cup \mathcal{L}_\mathcal{C}^{snk}$.

The Reo circuit $\mathcal{R}_{\mathcal{C},\mathcal{J}}$ is obtained by executing the RSL script given by the instructions in the body of $\mathcal{C}$. When instantiating a module the meanings of the uninterpreted data types, operator or predicate symbols are taken according to $\mathcal{J}$. The instantiation of a CARML module $\mathcal{M}(\Theta_0, \Omega_0, \Pi_0, \Upsilon_0)$ with n sources and m sinks via the instruction $comp := \text{new}\,\mathcal{M}(\Theta', \Omega', \Pi', \Upsilon')(D_1, \ldots, D_n, E_1,$ $\ldots, E_m)$ means binding an instance $comp$ of $\mathcal{M}$ where the i-th source of $comp$ is identified with the possibly already existing node D_i and the j-th sink of $comp$ with E_j. In the Reo circuit $\mathcal{R}_{\mathcal{C},\mathcal{J}}$, $comp$ is viewed as a black-box component. However, by applying the algorithm of [5] (extended to handle global variables) to construct a constraint automaton from $\mathcal{R}_{\mathcal{C},\mathcal{J}}$ we use a constraint automaton $\mathcal{A}_{comp,\mathcal{J}}$ as specification for the behavioral interface of that instance $comp$ of $\mathcal{M}$. Automaton $\mathcal{A}_{comp,\mathcal{J}}$ can be obtained as follows. Let $\mathcal{J}_0$ be the interpretation that arises from $\mathcal{J}$ by the substituting Θ_0 with Θ' (i.e., if the i-th data type symbol in Θ_0 is T and the i-th element of Θ' is U then $T^{\mathcal{J}_0} = U^{\mathcal{J}}$) and substituting Ω_0 with Ω', Π_0 with Π', and Υ_0 with Υ'. We now regard the constraint automaton $\mathcal{A}_{\mathcal{M},\mathcal{J}_0}$ and replace the i-th source port of $\mathcal{M}$ with D_i and the j-th sink port of $\mathcal{M}$ with E_j in the data-flow vocabulary of $\mathcal{A}_{\mathcal{M},\mathcal{J}_0}$ and the concurrent I/O-operations that appear as labels for the transitions of $\mathcal{A}_{\mathcal{M},\mathcal{J}_0}$. The resulting automaton is $\mathcal{A}_{comp,\mathcal{J}}$. The meaning of an instantiation of another RSL script $\mathcal{C}'$ via the instruction $comp := \text{new}\,\mathcal{C}'(\Theta', \Omega', \Pi', \Upsilon')(D_1, \ldots, D_n, E_1, \ldots, E_m)$ is analogous. It has the effect of including the Reo circuit associated with the generated instance of $\mathcal{C}'$.

```
CIRCUIT buffered_replicator ⟨type : T, var : integer k⟩ {
    // create channels
    F := new FIFO1⟨T⟩(A; R[0]);
    for (i = 1, ..., k){ new SYNC⟨T⟩(R[i]; B[i]); }
    // join channel-ends in a node N
    N := node⟨T⟩;
    for (i = 0, ..., k){ join(R[i], N); }
    // define the interface of the circuit
    source[0] := A;
    for (i = 0, ..., k−1){ sink[i] := B[i+1]; }
}
```

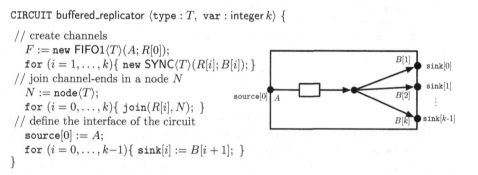

Fig. 5. RSL code for a Reo circuit for a buffered replicator of size k

Example 2. Fig. 5 shows the RSL code and its Reo circuit for a buffered replicator with k output ports where k is an integer variable passed in the parameter list. It uses modules FIFO1⟨type : T⟩ and SYNC⟨type : T⟩ from a built-in library that model a FIFO channel with one buffer cell and a synchronous channel, respectively, where both the input and output port of that channel have (uninterpreted) message-type T. For the instantiation of a buffered replicator circuit one has to provide an interpretation $T^{\mathcal{J}}$ for the data type symbol T to fix the type of data that may flow through the connector and an integer $k^{\mathcal{J}}$ for variable k which

Fig. 6. Three phases for creating a buffered-replicator of size 2. (a) create channels, (b) join channel ends, and (c) export the interface

determines the number of sink ports. (We assume here that $k^{\mathcal{J}} \geq 1$.) Fig. 6 illustrates the three phases in the construction of $\mathcal{R}_{repl,\mathcal{J}}$ (instantiation, composition via the join operations, and interface declaration) for $k^{\mathcal{J}} = 2$. In the first phase of the execution of the RSL script, a FIFO channel with one buffer cell and two synchronous channels are created. In a second phase the source ends of the synchronous channels are joined with the sink of the buffer in a new Reo node N. In the last phase the interface of the connector is defined by exporting the source end of the buffer and the sink ends of the synchronous channels.

// include predefined modules and prototype definition for a replicator and module $\mathcal{M}$:
#include "builtin", "buffered_replicator.rsl", "some_component.carml"
CIRCUIT main{
    $repl :=$ new buffered_replicator$\langle$Boolean$, 2\rangle(C; D1, D2)$;
    $S[0] :=$ new SYNC$\langle$Boolean$\rangle(B1; C)$;
    $S[1] :=$ new SYNC$\langle$Boolean$\rangle(D1; A1)$;
    $S[2] :=$ new SYNC$\langle$Boolean$\rangle(D2; E2)$;
    $comp :=$ new $\mathcal{M}\langle$Boolean$\rangle(A1, E1; B1)$;
    $in: E1;$ $out: E2;$ // equivalent to source$[0] := E1$; sink$[0] := E2$;
}

Fig. 7. RSL program for the circuit $\mathcal{R}_{\text{main}}$ depicted in Fig. 8

The replicator can be instantiated in another context like the RSL program in Fig. 7. The instantiation of the buffered replicator yields the interpretation $T^{\mathcal{J}} = $ Boolean and $k^{\mathcal{J}} = 2$. Thus, the first step in the construction of the Reo circuit $\mathcal{R}_{\text{main}}$ for the RSL program in Fig. 7 is running the script for the buffered replicator which yields the (sub)circuit $\mathcal{R}_{repl,\mathcal{J}}$. Then, the three synchronous channels $S[0], S[1]$, and $S[2]$ arise by the instantiation of the CARML module SYNC$\langle$type$:T\rangle$ taken from the built-in library. Finally, an instance $comp$ of a CARML module $\mathcal{M}$ (also taken from a library) is created. We assume here that $\mathcal{M}$'s parameter list consists of an uninterpreted data type symbol and that $\mathcal{M}$ has two input ports and one output port. The first input port of $comp$ is identified with node $A1$, the output port of $comp$ with $B1$, while the second input port $E1$ of $comp$ is a fresh node. Fig. 8 shows the resulting Reo circuit $\mathcal{R}_{\text{main}}$, where $comp$ is treated as a black-box component. The constraint automaton $\mathcal{A}_{comp}$ for the behavioral interface of $comp$ is obtained from the constraint automaton $\mathcal{A}_{\mathcal{M},\mathcal{J}_0}$ of its prototype module $\mathcal{M}$ and the interpretation $\mathcal{J}_0$ that assigns the type Boolean to the data type symbol T (i.e., $T^{\mathcal{J}_0} = $ Boolean) and replacing

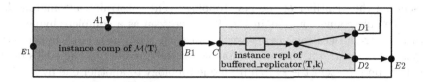

Fig. 8. Reo circuit $\mathcal{R}_{main}$ for the RSL program in Fig. 7

the names of the I/O-ports of $\mathcal{M}$ by the ones provided during the instantiation. The constraint automaton $\mathcal{A}_{main}$ for the RSL program in Fig. 7 is then obtained by using the algorithm of [5] to construct a constraint automaton $\mathcal{A}$ for the circuit $\mathcal{R}_{main}$ (where *comp* is treated as a black-box component), constructing the constraint automaton $\mathcal{A}_{comp} = \mathcal{A}_{\mathcal{M},\mathcal{J}_0}[^{\text{source}[0]}/_{A1}, {}^{\text{source}[1]}/_{E1}, {}^{\text{sink}[0]}/_{B1}]$, and finally building the product of $\mathcal{A}$ and $\mathcal{A}_{comp}$ as described in [5].   □

Dynamic reconfiguration. RSL provides support for specifying component connectors with multiple network topologies. The interface of a dynamic connector $\mathcal{C}$ contains a special input port $\mathcal{C}.\text{reconf}$, called *reconfiguration port*.

```
CIRCUIT C ⟨type : Θ, op : Ω, pred : Π, var : Υ⟩ {
    stmt;                       // construction of a common sub-circuit
    interface_decl     // declaration of the exported source/sink ports
    TOPO(id₁) = {stmt₁}        // additional sub-circuit for topology id₁
        ⋮
    TOPO(idₜ) = {stmtₜ}        // additional sub-circuit for topology idₜ
}
```

Fig. 9. Schema for RSL scripts with dynamic reconfiguration

The schema of RSL scripts with dynamic reconfigurations is shown in Fig. 9. The parameter list is the same as before. The body of a dynamic RSL circuit $\mathcal{C}$ consists of statement *stmt* that specifies a common (static) sub-circuit $\mathcal{C}_{stmt}$ of all network topologies, followed by the interface declaration and instructions of the form $\text{topo}(id_i)\{stmt_i\}$ for $i = 1, \ldots, t$. Here, id_i denotes an identifier for the i-th network topology and $stmt_i$ is a statement. The network topology with an identifier id_i is generated by the composite statement *stmt*; $stmt_i$, resulting in the (static) Reo circuit $\mathcal{C}'_i$. The interface declaration specifies the input and output ports of $\mathcal{C}$, except for the reconfiguration port $circ.\text{reconf}$ of the instances of the circuit $\mathcal{C}$ in Fig. 9. No special declaration is required for the reconfiguration port. The assignments in the interface declaration can only refer to the nodes and ports that appear in *stmt*, but not to entities created in $stmt_1, \ldots, stmt_t$. Any other RSL circuit $circ'$ creating an instance $circ$ of the circuit $\mathcal{C}$ in Fig. 9 can access the reconfiguration port $circ.\text{reconf}$ as any port in the interface of $circ$. Hence, any module that is connected in $circ'$ to the reconfiguration port $circ.\text{reconf}$ can serve as a driver and trigger switches in the topology of $circ$

by sending the identifier of the new topology. The constraint automaton $\mathcal{A}_{\mathcal{C},\mathcal{J}}$ for a dynamic connector $\mathcal{C}$ as in Fig. 9 can be seen as a complete hyper-graph with t hyper-vertices (one hyper-vertex for each topology). Each hyper-vertex stands for a constraint automaton for one of the circuits $\mathcal{C}'_i$. The edges of this hyper-graph represent the switch from one topology to another one by receiving a signal on the reconfiguration port. The formal definition of $\mathcal{A}_{\mathcal{C},\mathcal{J}}$ is as follows. The data-flow vocabulary $\mathfrak{Voc}_{\mathcal{C}}$ is defined according to the interface declaration completed with the reconfiguration port $\mathcal{C}.\mathtt{reconf}$ which is a source port of message-type $\{id_1, \ldots, id_t\}$. We use the aforementioned construction for each constraint automaton $\mathcal{A}'_i = \mathcal{A}_{stmt;stmt_i,\mathcal{J}} = (Q^{(i)}, \mathfrak{Voc}_{\mathcal{C}}, \rightarrow_i, Q_0^{(i)})$ for the circuit $\mathcal{C}'_i$ induced by the statement $stmt$; $stmt_i$. The states in $Q^{(i)}$ can be written in the form $\langle q, q^{(i)} \rangle$ where q stands for a state in the constraint automaton $\mathcal{A}_{stmt,\mathcal{J}}$ for the (static) common subcircuit $\mathcal{C}_{stmt}$ of all circuits $\mathcal{C}'_1, \ldots, \mathcal{C}'_t$ and $q^{(i)}$ a state of constraint automaton $\mathcal{A}_{stmt_i,\mathcal{J}}$ for the subcircuit induced by $stmt_i$. W.l.o.g. we can assume that $Q^{(i)} \cap Q^{(j)} = \emptyset$ for $1 \leq i < j \leq t$. The constraint automaton $\mathcal{A}_{\mathcal{C},\mathcal{J}} = (Q, \mathfrak{Voc}_{\mathcal{C}}, \rightarrow, Q_0)$ for the dynamic connector $\mathcal{C}$ is then obtained by combining $\mathcal{A}'_1, \ldots, \mathcal{A}'_t$ as follows. The state space Q of $\mathcal{A}_{\mathcal{C},\mathcal{J}}$ is the disjoint union of the state spaces of $\mathcal{A}'_1, \ldots, \mathcal{A}'_t$, that is, $Q = Q^{(1)} \cup \ldots \cup Q^{(t)}$. The set Q_0 of initial states in $\mathcal{A}_{\mathcal{C},\mathcal{J}}$ is the set of all states $\langle q, q^{(i)} \rangle$ where q is an initial state in the constraint automaton $\mathcal{A}_{stmt,\mathcal{J}}$ for $stmt$ and $q^{(i)}$ an initial state in the constraint automaton $\mathcal{A}_{stmt_i,\mathcal{J}}$ for $stmt_i$. The transitions $\rightarrow$ of $\mathcal{A}_{\mathcal{C},\mathcal{J}}$ are given by the following two rules, where the first stands for the receipt of the signal to switch to the j-th network topology and the second rule stands for the execution of a concurrent I/O-operation in the i-th topology:

$$\frac{q^{(j)} \text{ initial state of the CA } \mathcal{A}_{stmt_j,\mathcal{J}} \text{ for } stmt_j}{\langle q, q^{(i)} \rangle \xrightarrow{\mathcal{C}.\mathtt{reconf}?id_j} \langle q, q^{(j)} \rangle} \qquad \frac{\langle q, q^{(i)} \rangle \xrightarrow{c}_i \langle q, p^{(i)} \rangle}{\langle q, q^{(i)} \rangle \xrightarrow{c} \langle q, p^{(i)} \rangle}$$

where $\mathcal{C}.\mathtt{reconf}?id_j$ denotes the unique concurrent I/O-operation c with $\mathcal{L}(c) = \{\mathcal{C}.\mathtt{reconf}\}$ and $c(\mathcal{C}.\mathtt{reconf}) = id_j$.

5   Modeling a Railway Network

We demonstrate our hybrid approach with Vereofy's input languages CARML and RSL by means of a toy example modeling a simple railway network, composed out of basic building blocks (tracks, stations, switches). Trains are represented by unique identifiers and travel of a train is modeled by data flow of its identifier. We use the CARML module track (Fig. 3) as the basic (unidirectional) railway track, allowing a train to stop or to pass through instantaneously. A CARML module track_with_train is a variant of this basic track, initially occupied by a train. It has an additional parameter (var: $TrainType$ initial_train) used to specify the identifier of this train and can be derived from track by setting the initial values of variables "stat := occupied" and "train := initial_train". A CARML module for a train station (train_station) is obtained from track by removing the transition for an instantaneous pass-through.

Railway switches come in two variants, left-hand-side (lhs) with k entries and one exit and right-hand-side (rhs) with k exits and one entry. In Fig. 10, we show how to model two variants of right-hand-side switches with nondeterministic choice between the possible exits, one as a CARML module with two exits (simple_rhs_switch) and one as a RSL script with a parameterized number of k exits (rhs_switch), recursively built out of simpler switches. As an example for a left-hand-side switch, Fig. 10 also shows the RSL script for a switch with two entries, using dynamic reconfiguration (reconf_lhs_switch).

The CARML module for simple_rhs_switch ensures that a train leaves via exactly one exit and serves as the basic building block for the more general rhs_switch. Its RSL script has a parameter k specifying the number of exits (sink ports). The first two lines handle the base cases, by instantiating either a built-in synchronous channel or a simple_rhs_switch and exporting their ports. For $k > 2$, two instances of rhs_switch with half the number of exits are recursively instantiated (r_1, r_2) and a simple_rhs_switch (l) switches between r_1 and r_2. In the last three lines, the interface with one source port (that of l) and k sink ports (those of r_1 and r_2) is generated.

The RSL script for reconf_lhs_switch declares two sources and one sink as the common interface. In both topologies (having identifiers 0 and 1), one of the sources is connected via a synchronous channel to the sink, the other source is left unconnected (and thus blocks data flow). Upon receipt of topology identifier i at the reconfiguration port, the switch reconfigures to topology i, letting trains pass only from source i to the sink port.

The RSL program in Fig. 11 composes a simple railway network. A set of train identifiers is defined and the building blocks are included. In the RSL script main, instances of the building blocks are created and connected at the nodes L_i to yield the depicted network. To provide reconfiguration signals, an instance of the CARML module driver is connected to the reconfiguration port of sw_1, alternately sending the topology identifiers 0 and 1.

The given model of the railway example may now serve as input for our verification toolkit Vereofy. The tool allows to check safety or liveness conditions specified by temporal formula with classical modalities, but also to argue about the observable data flow at the locations of the network [4].

6 Implementation

Our toolkit Vereofy (see Fig. 1 and www.vereofy.de) supports modeling using RSL and CARML. Vereofy can be used as stand-alone tool or as an Eclipse plugin for the Eclipse Coordination Tools (ECT) [19] which allow to specify connectors in a graphical way. It currently supports all language features explained in Sections 3 and 4, except for the parameterization by uninterpreted symbols for data types, operators and predicates. Furthermore, global variables and locations of different message-types are not yet supported[2]. For model checking purposes,

---

[2] In Sections 3 and 4 we focused on a clear presentation of the core features of CARML and RSL and slightly departed from the syntax used in our implementation.

```
MODULE simple_rhs_switch⟨type : TrainType⟩ {
    in :   TrainType A;
    out : TrainType B;  out : TrainType C;
    ⊣[active(A) ∧  active(B) ∧ ¬active(C) ∧ dataₐ = data_B ]↦;
    ⊣[active(A) ∧ ¬active(B) ∧  active(C) ∧ dataₐ = data_C ]↦;
}  CIRCUIT rhs_switch⟨type : TrainType, var : integer k⟩ {
    if(k = 1){new SYNC⟨TrainType⟩(source[0]; sink[0]); }
    if(k = 2){new simple_rhs_switch⟨TrainType⟩(source[0]; sink[0], sink[1]); }
    if(k > 2){
        l := new simple_rhs_switch⟨TrainType⟩;
        r₁ := new rhs_switch⟨TrainType, ⌈k/2⌉⟩;
        r₂ := new rhs_switch⟨TrainType, k − ⌈k/2⌉⟩;
        join(l.sink[0], r₁.source[0]); join(l.sink[1], r₂.source[0]);
        source[0] := l.source[0]; out := 0;
        for(i = 1, . . . , ⌈k/2⌉) {sink[out] := r₁.sink[i − 1]; out := out + 1; }
        for(j = 1, . . . , k − ⌈k/2⌉) {sink[out] := r₂.sink[j − 1]; out := out + 1; }
    }
}  CIRCUIT reconf_lhs_switch⟨type : TrainType⟩ {
    source[0] := node⟨TrainType⟩; source[1] := node⟨TrainType⟩;
    sink[0] := node⟨TrainType⟩;
    TOPO(0) = {new SYNC⟨TrainType⟩(source[0]; sink[0]); }
    TOPO(1) = {new SYNC⟨TrainType⟩(source[1]; sink[0]); }
}
```

Fig. 10. Specifications for three variants of railway switches

```
TYPE Trains = enum{T₁, T₂, no_train};
#include "builtin", "railway_building_blocks"
MODULE driver {
    out :  int(0, 1) B;    var : int(0, 1) s := 0;
    ⊣[active(B) ∧ data_B = s]↦ s := (s + 1) mod 2;
}
CIRCUIT main {
    t₁ := new track_with_train⟨Trains, no_train, T₁⟩(L₆; L₁);
    t₂ := new track_with_train⟨Trains, no_train, T₂⟩(L₅; L₃);
    t₃ := new track⟨Trains, no_train⟩(L₂; L₄);
    st := new station⟨Trains, no_train⟩(L₄; L₇);
    sw₁ := new reconf_lhs_switch⟨Trains⟩;
    sw₂ := new rhs_switch⟨Trains, 2⟩;
    join(L₁, sw₁.source[0]); join(L₃, sw₁.source[1]);
    join(L₂, sw₁.sink[0]);
    join(L₅, sw₂.sink[0]); join(L₆, sw₂.sink[1]);
    join(L₇, sw₂.source[0]);
    d := new driver; L_r = join(d.sink[0], sw₁.reconf);

}
```

Fig. 11. Example RSL program for a railway network with two trains

RSL programs are translated into a symbolic BDD-based representation as presented in [6] of the corresponding constraint automaton. The translation is done by constructing the Reo circuit and applying the machinery presented in [5] and the enhancements for dynamic connectors explained in Section 4.

number of phils	reachable states	BDD nodes	building time (s)
100	$1,89 \cdot 10^{38}$	15618	7,29
200	$3,59 \cdot 10^{76}$	31418	31,15
400	$1,29 \cdot 10^{153}$	63018	148,87
600	$4,62 \cdot 10^{229}$	94618	364,35
800	$1,66 \cdot 10^{306}$	126218	706,12
1000	$> 10^{308}$	157818	1157,25

Fig. 12. Dining philosophers results

number of processes	reachable states	BDD nodes	building time (s)	reachable time (s)
(50, 29)	$2,54 \cdot 10^{21}$	2652	8,76	0,46
(50, 50)	$7,54 \cdot 10^{28}$	5298	10,13	0,95
(100, 61)	$1,22 \cdot 10^{45}$	8412	160,59	4,72
(100, 100)	$6,78 \cdot 10^{58}$	18123	192,61	13,25
(120, 79)	$5,00 \cdot 10^{56}$	12807	743,17	12,57
(120, 120)	$6,81 \cdot 10^{70}$	25353	785,89	164,97

Fig. 13. Mutual exclusion results

We illustrate the scalability of our approach by two examples. The first is a variant of a dining philosophers example [14]. The table in Fig. 12 shows the time in seconds needed to synthesize the scenario for a given number of philosophers, the number of reachable states as well as the number of BDD nodes necessary to store the composite system. Computing the reachable fragment of the state space finishes within one second for all depicted sizes. The second example is a mutual exclusion protocol using exogenous coordination, where n processes are present and k are allowed to enter their critical section at the same time. The table in Fig. 13 shows the time for the synthesis of the system and the time for computing the reachable fragment of the state space for different values of (n, k). The results for both examples have been achieved on a 2,2GHz CPU and 2GB memory.

7   Related Work and Conclusion

Related work. For the design of our languages RSL and CARML we borrowed ideas from many other modeling and coordination languages. We argue that there are rather natural transformations of many other languages into our hybrid modeling approach. Several formalisms have been embedded into Reo, such as Petri nets [20], the actor-based language Rebeca [21] or UML sequence diagrams [3], which can immediately encoded in RSL. The main features of process algebras can be mimicked by Reo operations and encoded in RSL. E.g., CCS-like parallel composition with synchronization over complementary actions can be modeled by synchronous channels and the join-operation. Nondeterministic choice operators can be modeled by a (RSL script for a) Reo circuit for an exrouter [2]. The concept of name-passing as in the π-calculus [18] is not yet supported by RSL, but intended for a future extension of RSL.

Interaction systems were introduced in [12] as a general model for component-based systems. In this approach, the behavioral interfaces of components are modeled by labeled transition systems and they offer ports to communicate with each other. Up to some syntactic adaptions for communication actions, they can easily be specified in CARML. Connectors of an interaction system are used to glue ports of different components together by enforcing some actions to be synchronized. They have a natural representation by an RSL script which instantiates several synchronous channels and performs several join operations on their channel ends.

Although the syntax of CARML is inspired by reactive modules [1] there are some crucial differences concerning the interactions of modules. Communication of reactive modules has to be realized via interface variables and the parallel composition of reactive modules is defined in terms of rounds. This round-based coordination principle of reactive modules can be modeled by a Reo circuit specified by an RSL script.

Conclusion. The presented approach is based on two modeling languages RSL and CARML which together permit formal reasoning about component-based systems relying on endogenous and exogenous coordination, possibly with dynamic reconfigurations of the network topology. It allows for compositional and hierarchical design and reusability of components and coordination units. In our opinion, our hybrid approach yields a good compromise between (1) the elegance and expressiveness of coordination languages and (2) meta-languages supporting an efficient generation of a compact system-representations that yield the basis for applying model checking routines.

To illustrate the main features of our hybrid approach, we presented a toy example and experimental results for the model generation with Vereofy for academic case studies. We are currently working on the modeling and verification of larger examples with our tool set, such as a peer-to-peer protocol with a dynamic network manager and a bio-medical sensor network. The embeddings of other languages as sketched in Section 7 together with the wide range of application areas of Reo (such as modeling of compliance-aware business processes, long-run business transactions, and orchestration of web services [19]) makes our modeling and verification approach with the tool set Vereofy applicable for many purposes.

References

1. Alur, R., Henzinger, T.: Reactive Modules. Formal Methods in System Design: An Intern. J. 15(1), 7–48 (1999)
2. Arbab, F.: Reo: A Channel-Based Coordination Model for Component Composition. MSCS 14(3), 329–366 (2004)
3. Arbab, F., Sun, M., Baier, C.: Synthesis of Reo circuits from scenario-based specifications. In: FOCLASA 2008. ENTCS (2008) (to appear)
4. Baier, C., Blechmann, T., Klein, J., Klüppelholz, S.: Formal verification for components and connectors (submitted for publication)
5. Baier, C., Sirjani, M., Arbab, F., Rutten, J.: Modeling Component Connectors in Reo by Constraint Automata. SCP 61, 75–113 (2006)
6. Blechmann, T., Baier, C.: Checking equivalence for reo networks. In: FACS 2007. ENTCS, vol. 215, pp. 209–226 (2008)

7. Blechmann, T., Klein, J., Klüppelholz, S.: Vereofy, http://www.vereofy.de/
8. Capizzi, S., Solmi, R., Zavattaro, G.: From endogenous to exogenous coordination using aspect-oriented programming. In: De Nicola, R., Ferrari, G.-L., Meredith, G. (eds.) COORDINATION 2004. LNCS, vol. 2949. Springer, Heidelberg (2004)
9. de Alfaro, L., Dias da Silva, L., Faella, M., Legay, A., Roy, P., Sorea, M.: Sociable interfaces. In: Gramlich, B. (ed.) FroCos 2005. LNCS, vol. 3717, pp. 81–105. Springer, Heidelberg (2005)
10. de Alfaro, L., Henzinger, T.: Interface Theories for Component-Based Design. In: Henzinger, T.A., Kirsch, C.M. (eds.) EMSOFT 2001. LNCS, vol. 2211, pp. 148–165. Springer, Heidelberg (2001)
11. Gelernter, D., Carriero, N., Chandran, S., Chang, S.: Parallel programming in linda. In: ICPP, pp. 255–263 (1985)
12. Gößler, G., Sifakis, J.: Component-based construction of deadlock-free systems: Extended abstract. In: Pandya, P.K., Radhakrishnan, J. (eds.) FSTTCS 2003. LNCS, vol. 2914, pp. 420–433. Springer, Heidelberg (2003)
13. Guillen-Scholten, J., Arbab, F., de Boer, F., Bonsangue, M.: MoCha-pi: an exogenous coordination calculus based on mobile channels. In: Proceedings of the 2005 ACM symposium on Applied computing (SAC), pp. 436–442. ACM, New York (2005)
14. Klüppelholz, S., Baier, C.: Symbolic Model Checking for Channel-based Component Connectors. In: Science of Computer Programming (2009)
15. Klüppelholz, S., Baier, C.: Alternating-time stream logic for multi-agent systems. In: Lea, D., Zavattaro, G. (eds.) COORDINATION 2008. LNCS, vol. 5052, pp. 184–198. Springer, Heidelberg (2008)
16. Lynch, N., Tuttle, M.: An Introduction to Input/Output Automata. CWI Quarterly 2(3), 219–246 (1989)
17. Majster-Cederbaum, M., Minnameier, C.: Everything is PSPACE-complete in interaction systems. In: Fitzgerald, J.S., Haxthausen, A.E., Yenigun, H. (eds.) ICTAC 2008. LNCS, vol. 5160, pp. 216–227. Springer, Heidelberg (2008)
18. Milner, R.: Communicating and Mobile Systems: The Pi-Calculus. Cambridge University Press, Cambridge (1999)
19. Reo website at CWI Amsterdam, http://reo.project.cwi.nl/
20. Scholten, J.-G., Arbab, F., de Boer, F., Bonsangue, M.: Modeling the exogenous coordination of mobile channel-based systems with Petri nets. In: FOCLASA 2005. ENTCS, vol. 154(1), pp. 83–99 (2006)
21. Sirjani, M., Jaghoori, M., Baier, C., Arbab, F.: Compositional semantics of an actor-based language using constraint automata. In: Ciancarini, P., Wiklicky, H. (eds.) COORDINATION 2006. LNCS, vol. 4038, pp. 281–297. Springer, Heidelberg (2006)

From Coordination to Stochastic Models of QoS

Farhad Arbab[1], Tom Chothia[2], Rob van der Mei[1,3], Sun Meng[1],
YoungJoo Moon[1], and Chrétien Verhoef[1]

[1] Centrum Wiskunde & Informatica (CWI), Amsterdam, The Netherlands
[2] School of Computer Science, Univ. of Birmingham, United Kingdom
[3] Vrije Universiteit Amsterdam, The Netherlands
{Farhad.Arbab,R.D.van.der.Mei,M.Sun,Y.J.Moon,C.G.Verhoef}@cwi.nl,
T.P.Chothia@cs.bham.ac.uk

Abstract. Reo is a channel-based coordination model whose operational semantics is given by Constraint Automata (CA). Quantitative
Constraint Automata extend CA (and hence, Reo) with quantitative
models to capture such non-functional aspects of a system's behaviour
as delays, costs, resource needs and consumption, that depend on the
internal details of the system. However, the performance of a system can
crucially depend not only on its internal details, but also on how it is
used in an environment, as determined for instance by the frequencies
and distributions of the arrivals of I/O requests. In this paper we propose Quantitative Intentional Automata (QIA), an extension of CA that
allow incorporating the influence of a system's environment on its performance. Moreover, we show the translation of QIA into Continuous-Time
Markov Chains (CTMCs), which allows us to apply existing CTMC tools
and techniques for performance analysis of QIA and Reo circuits.

Keywords: Performance evaluation, Coordination language, Reo,
Markov Chains.

1 Introduction

Service-oriented Computing (SOC) provides the means to design and deploy
distributed applications that span organization boundaries and computing platforms by exploiting and composing existing services available over a network.
Services are platform- and network-independent applications that support rapid,
low-cost, loosely-coupled composition. Services run on the hardware of their own
providers, in different containers, separated by fire-walls and other ownership and
trust barriers. Their composition requires additional mechanisms (e.g., process
work-flow engines, connectors, or glue code) to impose some form of coordination
(i.e., orchestration and/or choreography). Even if the quality of service (QoS)
properties of every individual service and connector are known, it is far from
trivial to build a model for and make statements about the end-to-end QoS of
a composed system. Yet, the end-to-end QoS of a composed service is often as
important as its functional properties in determining its viability in its market.

The coordination language Reo [3,6] provides a flexible, expressive model
for compositional construction of connectors that coordinate service behaviour.

J. Field and V.T. Vasconcelos (Eds.): COORDINATION 2009, LNCS 5521, pp. 268–287, 2009.
© Springer-Verlag Berlin Heidelberg 2009

CA [7] were introduced to express the operational semantics of Reo. Indeed, CA provide a unified model to capture the semantics of components and services, as well as Reo connectors and their composition. Quantitative Reo and Quantitative Constraint Automata (QCA) [4] extend Reo and CA with the means to describe and combine the QoS aspects of composed systems. The QCA model integrates the QoS aspects of components/services and connectors that comprise an application to yield the QoS properties of that application, ignoring the impact of the environment on its performance such as throughput and delays. While QCA provide a useful model for service selection and composition [20], the performance of a system can crucially depend not only on its internal details, but also on how it is used in an environment, as determined, for instance, by the frequencies and distributions of the arrivals of I/O requests which belong to stochastic aspects. However, such stochastic aspects are not investigated in [20]. Intentional Automata (IA) [15] take into account the influence of the environment as well as internal details of a system by describing the pending status of I/O operators interacting with the environment. A particular class of IA models, called the Reo Automata class, is defined in [15], which provides precise characterization of context-dependent connectors [7].

In this paper we propose QIA, an extension of IA that allows incorporating the influence of a system's environment on its performance. The QIA model extends the semantics of Reo by admitting annotations on its channel ends and the channels to represent the stochastic properties of request arrivals at those ends, data-flows, and data processing and transportation delays through those channels. The resulting *Stochastic Reo* model retains its compositional semantics through QIA: the QIA of a composed system is the product (composition) of the QIA of the individual channels and components/services used in its construction.

The QIA of a system typically has more states than its counterpart CA or QCA, reflecting the (epistemologically) intentional configurations of the system that CA and QCA abstract away. In addition to the synchronization and data constraints of the CA model, the transitions in QIA carry extra information in their labels to convey arrival and firing of data/requests, and their stochastic properties. This information is adequate to allow the analysis of the performance of a system in the context of the stochastic processes in its environment that determine the arrival of data/requests on its ports and their delays. In order to carry out such analysis, in this paper we show the translation of QIA into CTMCs [13], which allows us to apply existing CTMC tools and techniques for performance analysis of QIA and (Stochastic) Reo circuits.

The main contributions in this paper include:

- Stochastic Reo as a compositional model for specifying system behaviour that captures its non-functional (QoS) aspects and takes into account the influence of the environment on its performance,
- QIA as the operational semantics for Stochastic Reo which serves as an intermediate model for generating CTMCs, and
- translation from QIA specifications into CTMC models for performance evaluation.

The Reo and automata editors in the Eclipse Coordination Tools (ECT) [1] have been extended to support Stochastic Reo and QIA, and the automatic derivation of the QIA semantics of Reo circuits. We have implemented the translation of QIA to CTMCs described in this paper as a plug-in within this platform. We have also developed a bridge plug-in that generates the proper input for other stochastic analysis tools like PRISM [2,19] from our CTMC models to allow performance analysis of Stochastic Reo.

The remainder of this paper is organized as follows. In Section 2, we provide a short overview of Reo, CA, and their quantitative variants. In Section 3 we introduce Stochastic Reo. In Section 4 we define QIA and their composition through product and refinement. In Section 5, we show the translation from QIA into its corresponding CTMC. In Section 6, we show an example of how our CTMC model can be analyzed in PRISM. We review related work in Section 7. Conclusions and future work comprise Section 8. A crucial step in the translation of QIA into a CTMC, as described in Section 5, consists of the sequencing of the delays of synchronized actions that appear on the label of a single transition, and the algorithm of extracting the sequence is given in [5].

2 Preliminaries

2.1 Reo

Reo is a channel-based exogenous coordination model wherein complex coordinators, called connectors, are compositionally built out of simpler ones. We summarize only the main concepts of Reo and its CA semantics here. Further details about Reo and its semantics can be found in [3,7].

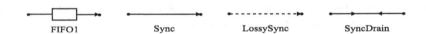

FIFO1   Sync   LossySync   SyncDrain

Fig. 1. Some basic Reo channels

Complex connectors in Reo are organised in a network of primitive connectors, called *channels*. Connectors serve to provide the protocol that controls and organises the communication, synchronization and cooperation among the components/services that they interconnect. Each channel has two *channel ends*, and there are two types of channel ends: *source* and *sink*. A source channel end accepts data into its channel, and a sink channel end dispenses data out of its channel. Reo places no restriction on the behaviour of a channel, so it is possible for the ends of a channel to be both sources or both sinks. Figure 1 shows the graphical representation of some simple channel types. A *FIFO1 channel* (FIFO1) represents an asynchronous channel with one buffer cell. A *synchronous channel* (Sync) has a source and a sink end and no buffer. It accepts a data item through its source end if it can simultaneously dispense it through its sink.

A *lossy synchronous channel* (LossySync) is similar to a synchronous channel except that it always accepts all data items through its source end. The data item is transferred if it is possible for the data item to be dispensed through the sink end, otherwise the data item is lost. A *synchronous drain* (SyncDrain) has two source ends and no sink end. It accepts a data item through one of its ends if and only if a data item is also available to be accepted simultaneously through the other end as well.

Connectors are constructed by composing simpler ones via the *join* operation. Channels are joined together in a node which consists of a set of channel ends. Nodes are categorised into source, sink and mixed nodes, depending on whether all channel ends that coincide on a node are source ends, sink ends or a combination of both. In remainder of this paper, we call source and sink nodes boundary nodes since they interact with the environment. Reo allows an open-ended set of user-defined channels with arbitrary behaviour, but it fixes the semantics of the nodes. A source node acts as a synchronous replicator. A sink node acts as a merger. A mixed node combines the behaviour of the the other two nodes and acts as a self-contained "pumping station" that atomically consumes an item out of one of its selected sink ends and replicates it to all of its source ends. Nodes have no memory or buffer and perform their actions atomically. This forces synchrony and exclusion constraints to propagate through the nodes, which causes the channels involved in each synchronous region of a circuit to synchronize their actions in atomic steps.

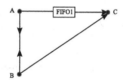

Fig. 2. Ordering circuit

For example, the connector shown in Figure 2 is an alternator that imposes an ordering on the flow of the data from its input nodes A and B to its output node C. The SyncDrain channel enforces that data flow through A and B only synchronously. The empty buffer together with the propagation of synchrony through the three nodes guarantee that the data item obtained from B is delivered to C while the data item obtained from A is stored in the FIFO1 buffer. After this, the buffer of the FIFO1 is full and propagation of exclusion from A through the SyncDrain channel to B guarantees that data cannot flow in through either A or B, but C can dispense the data stored in the FIFO1 buffer, which makes it empty again. Assume three independent processes (that follow no communication protocol and each of which knows nothing about the others) place I/O requests on nodes A, B, and C, each according to its own internal timing. By delaying the success of their requests, when necessary, this circuit guarantees that successive read operations at C obtain the values produced by the successive write operations at B and A alternately.

2.2   Constraint Automata

CA were introduced [7] as a formalism to capture the operational semantics of Reo, based on timed data streams, which also constitute the foundation of the coalgebraic semantics of Reo [6].

We assume a finite set $\mathcal{N}$ of nodes, and denote by *Data* a fixed, non-empty set of data that can be sent and received through these nodes via channels. CA use a symbolic representation of data assignments by data constraints, which are propositional formulas built from the atoms "$d_A \in P$", "$d_A = d_B$" and "$d_A = d$" using standard Boolean operators. Here, $A, B \in \mathcal{N}$, d_A is a symbol for the observed data item at node A and $d \in Data$. $DC(N)$ denotes the set of data constraints that at most refer to the observed data items d_A at node $A \in N$. Logical implication induces a partial order $\leq$ on DC: $g \leq g'$ iff $g \Rightarrow g'$.

A CA over the data domain *Data* is a tuple $\mathscr{A} = (S, S_0, \mathcal{N}, \rightarrow)$ where S is a set of states, also called configurations, $S_0 \subseteq S$ is the set of its initial states, $\mathcal{N}$ is a finite set of nodes, $\rightarrow$ is a finite subset of $S \times \{N\} \times DC(N) \times S$ with $N \in 2^{\mathcal{N}}$, called the transition relation. A transition fires if it observes data items in its respective ports/nodes of the component that satisfy the data constraint of the transition, and this firing may consequently change the state of the automaton.

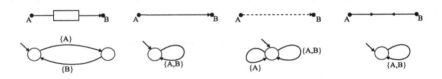

Fig. 3. Constraint Automata for basic Reo channels

Figure 3 shows the CA for the primitive Reo channels in Figure 1. In this figure and the remainder of this paper, for simplicity, we assume the data constraints of all transitions are **true** (which simply imposes no constraints on the contents of the data-flows) and omit them to avoid clutter. For proper full treatment of data constraints in CA, see [7].

As the counterpart for the join operation in Reo, the product of two CA $\mathscr{A}_1 = (S_1, S_{1,0}, \mathcal{N}_1, \rightarrow_1)$ and $\mathscr{A}_2 = (S_2, S_{2,0}, \mathcal{N}_2, \rightarrow_2)$ is defined as a constraint automaton $\mathscr{A}_1 \bowtie \mathscr{A}_2 \equiv (S_1 \times S_2, S_{1,0} \times S_{2,0}, \mathcal{N}_1 \cup \mathcal{N}_2, \rightarrow)$ where $\rightarrow$ is given by the following rules:

- If $s_1 \xrightarrow{\ N_1, g_1\ }_1 s_1'$, $s_2 \xrightarrow{\ N_2, g_2\ }_2 s_2'$, $N_1 \cap \mathcal{N}_2 = N_2 \cap \mathcal{N}_1$ and $g_1 \wedge g_2$ is satisfiable, then $\langle s_1, s_2 \rangle \xrightarrow{\ N_1 \cup N_2, g_1 \wedge g_2\ } \langle s_1', s_2' \rangle$.
- If $s_1 \xrightarrow{\ N_1, g_1\ }_1 s_1'$, where $N_1 \cap \mathcal{N}_2 = \emptyset$ then $\langle s_1, s_2 \rangle \xrightarrow{\ N_1, g_1\ } \langle s_1', s_2 \rangle$.
- If $s_2 \xrightarrow{\ N_2, g_2\ }_2 s_2'$, where $N_2 \cap \mathcal{N}_1 = \emptyset$ then $\langle s_1, s_2 \rangle \xrightarrow{\ N_2, g_2\ } \langle s_1, s_2' \rangle$.

2.3 Quantitative Constraint Automata and Quantitative Reo

Quantitative Reo and QCA are extensions of Reo and CA, respectively, with quantitative aspects by Q-algebra [14] and form the basis for compositional specification and reasoning on QoS issues for connectors. A Q-algebra is an algebraic structure $R = (C, \oplus, \otimes, \textcircled{D}, \mathbf{0}, \mathbf{1})$ such that $R_\otimes = (C, \oplus, \otimes, \mathbf{0}, \mathbf{1})$ and $R_\textcircled{D} = (C, \oplus, \textcircled{D}, \mathbf{0}, \mathbf{1})$ are both constraint semirings [10,21]. C is a set of QoS values and is called the *domain* of R. The operation $\oplus$ induces a partial order $\leq$ on C, which is defined by $c \leq c'$ iff $c \oplus c' = c'$. The other two operators $\otimes$ and $\textcircled{D}$ can combine QoS values when they occur, respectively, sequentially and concurrently. In these constraint semirings, $\mathbf{0}$ is the identity for $\oplus$, and $\mathbf{1}$ is the identity for $\otimes$ and $\textcircled{D}$.

A QCA is a tuple $\mathscr{A} = (S, S_0, \mathscr{N}, R, \longrightarrow)$ where S is a set of states, $S_0 \subseteq S$ is the set of its initial states, $\mathscr{N}$ is a finite set of nodes, $R = (C, \oplus, \otimes, \textcircled{D}, \mathbf{0}, \mathbf{1})$ is a Q-algebra with domain C of QoS values, $\longrightarrow$ is a finite subset of $S \times \{N\} \times DC(N) \times C \times S$ with $N \in 2^{\mathscr{N}}$.

The synchronous behaviour of each Quantitative Reo channel has a certain QoS value in its label, which is in the domain C of a Q-algebra. The following types of QoS for the basic channels in Reo are considered: t (execution time for data transmission), c (allocated memory cost for the message transmission) and p (reliability represented by the probability of successful transmission). The corresponding Q-algebras are given as:

- execution time: $(\mathbb{R}_+ \cup \{\infty\}, max, +, max, 0, 0)$
- memory cost: $(\mathbb{N}_+ \cup \{\infty\}, max, +, +, 0, 0)$
- reliability: $([0,1], min, \times, \times, 1, 1)$

Quantitative Reo keeps a compositional framework with the same *join* operation of Reo, and QCA, as operational semantics of Quantitative Reo, provide a corresponding composition method (product). Two QCA $\mathscr{A}$ and $\mathscr{B}$ with the same Q-algebra turn into a new QCA by the product operation. For $\mathscr{A} = (S_1, S_{0,1}, \mathscr{N}_1, R, \longrightarrow_1)$ and $\mathscr{B} = (S_2, S_{0,2}, \mathscr{N}_2, R, \longrightarrow_2)$, their product is defined as

$$\mathscr{A} \bowtie \mathscr{B} = (S_1 \times S_2, S_{0,1} \times S_{0,2}, \mathscr{N}_1 \times \mathscr{N}_2, R, \longrightarrow)$$

where $\longrightarrow$ is given by the following rules:

- If $s_1 \xrightarrow{N_1, g_1, c_1}_1 s_1'$, $s_2 \xrightarrow{N_2, g_2, c_2}_2 s_2'$, $N_1 \cap \mathscr{N}_2 = N_2 \cap \mathscr{N}_1 \neq \emptyset$ and $g_1 \wedge g_2$ is satisfiable, then $\langle s_1, s_2 \rangle \xrightarrow{N_1 \cup N_2, g_1 \wedge g_2, c_1 \textcircled{D} c_2} \langle s_1', s_2' \rangle$.
- If $s_1 \xrightarrow{N, g, c}_1 s_1'$, where $N \cap \mathscr{N}_2 = \emptyset$ then $\langle s_1, s_2 \rangle \xrightarrow{N, g, c} \langle s_1', s_2 \rangle$.
- If $s_2 \xrightarrow{N, g, c}_2 s_2'$, where $N \cap \mathscr{N}_1 = \emptyset$ then $\langle s_1, s_2 \rangle \xrightarrow{N, g, c} \langle s_1, s_2' \rangle$.

The quantitative version of the circuit in Figure 2 and its corresponding QCA are shown in Figure 5. The relevant QoS values are given by the tuple (t_i, c_i, p_i) that represents the QoS values for the basic channels, as specified in Figure 4.

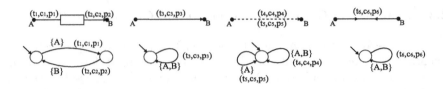

Fig. 4. Quantitative Constraint Automata for basic Quantitative Reo channels

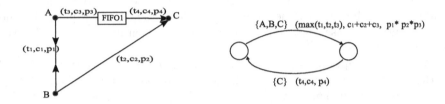

Fig. 5. Ordering circuit in Quantitative Reo and its QCA

3   Stochastic Reo

Stochastic Reo is an extension of Reo annotated with stochastic properties, such as processing delays on channels and arrival rates of data/requests at the channel ends, allowing general distributions. Figure 6 shows the primitive channels of Stochastic Reo that correspond to the primitives of Reo in Figure 1. In this figure and the remainder of this paper, for simplicity, we delete node names, but these names can be inferred from the names of their respective arrival processes: for instance, 'dA' means an arrival process at node 'A'. The labels annotating Stochastic Reo channels can be separated into the following two categories:

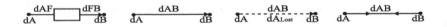

Fig. 6. Basic Stochastic Reo channels

- channel delays
  To model the stochastic behaviour of Reo channels, we assume every Reo channel has one or more associated delays represented by their corresponding random variables. Such a delay represents how long it takes for a channel to deliver or throw away its data. For instance, a LossySync has two associated variables 'dAB' and 'dA_{Lost}' for stochastic delays of, respectively, successful data-flow through the nodes 'A' and 'B' and losing data at node 'A' when a read request is absent at node 'B'. In a FIFO1 'dAF' means the delay

for data-flow from its source 'A' into the buffer, and 'dFB' for sending the data from the buffer to the sink 'B'. Similarly, the random variable of a Sync (and a SyncDrain) indicates the delay for data-flow from its source node 'A' to its sink node 'B' (and losing data at both ends, respectively).

− arrivals at nodes

I/O operations are performed on the source and sink nodes of a Reo circuit through which it interacts with its environment. We assume the time between consecutive arrivals of read and write requests at the sink and source nodes of Reo connectors depends on their associated stochastic processes. For instance, 'dA' and 'dB' in Figure 6 represent the associated arrival processes at nodes 'A' and 'B'. Furthermore, at most one request at each boundary node can wait for acceptance. If a boundary node is occupied by a pending request, then the node is blocked and consequently all further arrivals at that node are lost.

Stochastic Reo supports the same compositional framework of joining nodes as Reo. Most of the technical details of this *join* operation are identical to that of Reo. The nodes in Stochastic Reo have certain QoS information on them, hence joining nodes must accommodate their composition. Nodes are categorized into mixed, source, and sink nodes. Boundary nodes receive data/requests from the environment, after that mixed nodes are synchronized for data-flow and then merely pump data in the circuit, i.e., mixed nodes do not interact with the environment. This account shows the causality of the events happening in the circuit, such as arrivals of data/requests at its boundary nodes, synchronizing its mixed nodes, and occurrences of data-flow, sequentially. Besides, we assume that pumping data by mixed nodes is an immediate action and therefore mixed nodes have no associated stochastic variables[1]. Boundary nodes have their corresponding stochastic arrival processes, yet when they are combined into mixed nodes by a *join* operation, they lose their stochastic variables. As mentioned in Section 2, a source node and a sink node act as a replicator and a non-deterministic merger, respectively, and each activity, such as selecting a sink end or replicating data to its source ends, has its own stochastic property. In order to describe stochastic delays of a channel explicitly, we name the delay by the combination of a pair of (source, sink) nodes and the buffer of the channel. For example, the stochastic property 'dAF' of FIFO1 in Figure 6 stands for the data-flow from the source end 'A' into the buffer of the FIFO1. However, in cases where, for instance, a source node (as a replicator) A is connected to two different FIFO1s (buffers), then the corresponding stochastic processes have the same name, e.g., dAF. To avoid such an ambiguous situation, we rename the stochastic processes by adding a number after its node name like dA_1F and dA_2F when the node has more than one

---

[1] This assumption is not a real restriction. A mixed node with delay can be modelled by replacing this mixed node with a Sync channel with the delay. Moreover, according to the required level of specification detail, each input and output of the mixed node can be modelled by adding corresponding Sync channels with their stochastic values.

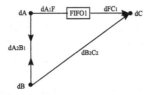

Fig. 7. Ordering circuit in Stochastic Reo

outgoing channel or one incoming channel. As an example of composed Stochastic Reo, Figure 7 shows the ordering circuit with the annotation of its stochastic variables.

4   Quantitative Intentional Automata

In this section we introduce the notion of QIA which is an extension of CA and provides operational semantics for Stochastic Reo. Whereas CA transitions describe system configuration changes, QIA transitions describe the changes of not only the system configuration but also the status of its pending I/O operations. In CA, configurations are shown as states, and processes causing state changes are shown in transition labels as a set of nodes where data are observed. Similarly, in QIA, system configurations and the status of pending I/O operations are shown as states. Data-flow or firing through nodes causes changes in the system configuration, and arrivals of data/requests at the nodes or synchronization of nodes changes the status of pending data/requests. These two different types of changes are shown in the transition labels by two different sets of nodes. Moreover, QIA transitions carry their relevant stochastic properties in their labels. We use such QIA as an intermediate model for translation Stochastic Reo into a homogeneous CTMC.

Definition 1. *QIA*
A Quantitative Intentional Automaton is a tuple $\mathscr{A} = (S, S_0, \mathscr{N}, \rightarrow)$ *where*

- $S \subseteq L \times 2^{\mathscr{N}}$ *is a finite set of states.*
  - *L is a set of system configurations.*
  - $R \in 2^{\mathscr{N}}$ *is a set of pending nodes, that describes the pending status in the current state.*
- $S_0 \subseteq S$ *is a set of initial states.*
- $\mathscr{N}$ *is a finite set of nodes.*
- $\rightarrow \subseteq \bigcup_{M,N \subseteq \mathscr{N}} S \times \{M\} \times \{N\} \times DC(N) \times 2^{DI} \times S$ *is the transition relation.*
  - $DI \subseteq 2^{\mathscr{N}} \times 2^{\mathscr{N}} \times \mathbb{R}^+$.

A transition in a QIA is represented as $\langle l, R \rangle \xrightarrow{M,N,g,D} \langle l', R' \rangle$ where M is the set of nodes that exchange data or synchronize for data-flow through the transition, N is the set of nodes to be released by the firing of the transition,

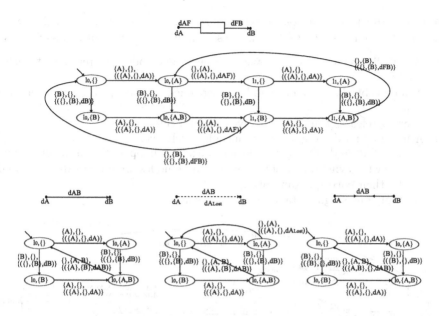

Fig. 8. QIA for each channel of Figure 6

and $D \subseteq DI$ is the set of delay information tuples (I, O, r) where I and O are sets of, respectively, source (input) and sink (output) nodes, and r indicates the stochastic delay rate for the data-flow from I to O or the arrival rate of data/request from the environment at nodes in $I \cup O$. Furthermore, let $D = \{(I_j, O_j, r_j)|1 \leq j \leq n\}$, then $\bigcup_{1 \leq j \leq n} (I_j \cup O_j) = N \cup M$.

Definition 1 is not enough to specify the system behaviour correctly. The causality of activities, such as arrivals of data/requests and firing, is not embraced in this definition. Moreover, in continuous time scale, all events occur one by one: only a single event, such as one request arrival or a single firing in a set of synchronized atomic firings, is taken into consideration at a time. Taking these features into account, we explore additional conditions that can be placed on QIA, and define the well-formedness condition of QIA. Hence, the QIA corresponding to the primitive Stochastic Reo channels are represented like Figure 8.

Definition 2. QIA Well-formedness

A QIA $\mathscr{A} = (S, S_0, \mathscr{N}, \rightarrow)$ is well-formed if $\forall \langle l, R \rangle \xrightarrow{M,N,g,D} \langle l', R' \rangle \in \rightarrow$ all following conditions are satisfied:

1. $N \subseteq R \cup M$
2. $M \cap R = \emptyset$
3. $(R \cup M) \setminus N = R'$
4. $((N \neq \emptyset \wedge M \subseteq N) \vee (N = \emptyset \wedge M \neq \emptyset \rightarrow |M| = 1))$

According to the assumption on synchronization and the causality of the activities in a Reo circuit, the well-formedness conditions are interpreted as follows:

1. A data-flow can occur only when all necessary nodes are ready to transfer the data.
2. A node is blocked when the node is suspended and occupied by another data item.
3. A firing releases the nodes involved in the firing.
4. A firing and a data arrival are mutually exclusive:
   - A firing and its relevant synchronization happen simultaneously, i.e., after the synchronization of nodes, those nodes are immediately released by their corresponding firing.
   - Only one single data/request arrives at a time.

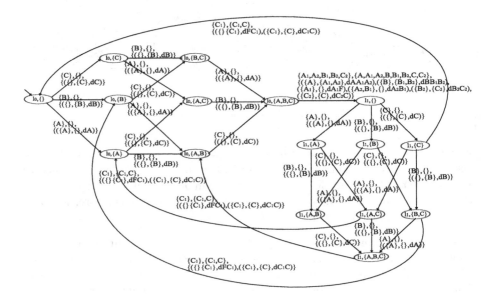

Fig. 9. Corresponding QIA to the ordering circuit in Figure 7

QIA provide a compositional framework for Stochastic Reo. Hence, the QIA corresponding to a circuit is obtained by the product of the QIA of all primitive channels that constitute the circuit, for example, the QIA model in Figure 9 corresponding to the ordering in Figure 7 is obtained by composing the QIA of its primitive channels. The mixed nodes from such a composition are obtained by a function $newMixed : \mathscr{A} \times \mathscr{A} \to 2^{\mathscr{N}}$. As mentioned above, the synchronization of its relevant mixed nodes has no associated stochastic property and occurs simultaneously with its corresponding firing. Hence, the mixed nodes involved in a certain firing must be considered as undergoing an atomic change through the firing, and the stochastic properties of the mixed nodes are deleted in the composed result. To represent such simultaneous occurrence, the relevant mixed nodes must be collected and shown in the label of their firing together.

Definition 3. *Synchronization of mixed nodes*
For two QIA $\mathscr{A} = (S_1, S_{0,1}, \mathscr{N}_1, \rightarrow_1)$, $\mathscr{B} = (S_2, S_{0,2}, \mathscr{N}_2, \rightarrow_2)$, the firing with synchronization of its mixed nodes is defined as $s \xrightarrow{\ C \cup M, N, g, D\ }{}^*_i s'$ for $C \subseteq newMixed(\mathscr{A}, \mathscr{B})$ such that there are consecutive transitions with the mixed nodes until its firing appears

$$s \xrightarrow{\ \{B_i\}, \emptyset, true, D_i\ }_i s_1 \xrightarrow{\ \{B_k\}, \emptyset, true, D_k\ }_i \cdots \xrightarrow{\ M, N, g, D\ }_i s'$$

where $B_i, B_k, \cdots \in C \wedge C \subseteq N$ for $i = 1, 2$.

Definition 4. *QIA Product*
Given two QIA $\mathscr{A} = (S_1, S_{1,0}, \mathscr{N}_1, \longrightarrow_1)$ and $\mathscr{B} = (S_2, S_{2,0}, \mathscr{N}_2, \longrightarrow_2)$, their product is defined as $\mathscr{A} \bowtie \mathscr{B} = (S_1 \times S_2, S_{1,0} \times S_{2,0}, \mathscr{N}_1 \cup \mathscr{N}_2, \longrightarrow)$ where $\longrightarrow$ is given by the following set of rules:

1. for every $\langle l_1, R_1 \rangle \xrightarrow{\ M_1, N_1, g_1, D_1\ }_1 \langle l_1', R_1' \rangle$ and $\langle l_2, R_2 \rangle \xrightarrow{\ M_2, N_2, g_2, D_2\ }_2 \langle l_2', R_2' \rangle$
   - if $M_1 \cap \mathscr{N}_2 = \emptyset \wedge N_1 \cap \mathscr{N}_2 = \emptyset$, then
   $$\langle (l_1, l_2), R_1 \cup R_2 \rangle \xrightarrow{\ M_1, N_1, g_1, D_1\ } \langle (l_1', l_2), R_1' \cup R_2 \rangle.$$
   - if $M_2 \cap \mathscr{N}_1 = \emptyset \wedge N_2 \cap \mathscr{N}_1 = \emptyset$, then
   $$\langle (l_1, l_2), R_1 \cup R_2 \rangle \xrightarrow{\ M_2, N_2, g_2, D_2\ } \langle (l_1, l_2'), R_1 \cup R_2' \rangle.$$
2. for every $\langle l_1, R_1 \rangle \xrightarrow{\ C_1 \cup M_1, N_1, g_1, D_1\ }{}^*_1 \langle l_1', R_1' \rangle$ and $\langle l_2, R_2 \rangle \xrightarrow{\ C_2 \cup M_2, N_2, g_2, D_2\ }{}^*_2 \langle l_2', R_2' \rangle$
   with $\forall C_1, C_2 \subseteq newMixed(\mathscr{A}, \mathscr{B})$
   - if $N_1 \neq \emptyset \neq N_2 \wedge N_1 \cap \mathscr{N}_2 = N_2 \cap \mathscr{N}_1$, then
   $$\langle (l_1, l_2), R_1 \cup R_2 \rangle \xrightarrow{\ C_1 \cup C_2 \cup M_1 \cup M_2, N_1 \cup N_2, g_1 \wedge g_2, D_1 \cup D_2\ } \langle (l_1', l_2'), R_1' \cup R_2' \rangle$$

The product of two QIA generates all possible compositions of transitions, though some of the generated transitions are irrelevant. For instance, in the product of the automata LossySync AB and Sync BC (cf. the first automaton in Figure 10), the state $\langle l_0, \{A, C\} \rangle$ has two possible firing transitions: one for losing the data at A and the other for the data-flow from A to C via the mixed node B. However, this state says that some requests are pending on nodes A and C, therefore, only data-flow between A and C can occur in the next step. We define a notion of refinement in the following that can be used to delete such unnecessary transitions from a product.

Definition 5. *QIA Refinement*
For a QIA $\mathscr{A} = (S, S_0, \mathscr{N}, \rightarrow)$, the refinement of $\mathscr{A}$, $Ref(\mathscr{A})$, is defined as $(S, S_0, \mathscr{N}, \rightarrow')$ with $\rightarrow' = \rightarrow \setminus T$, where T is defined as

$$T = \{s \xrightarrow{\ M, N, g, D\ } s' \mid \exists s \xrightarrow{\ M_1, N_1, g_1, D_1\ } s_1 \in \rightarrow \ s.t. \ P\}$$

, P is the conjunction of the following conditions:

1. $g \wedge g_1$ is satisfiable.
2. $M \subseteq M_1 \wedge \emptyset \neq N \subseteq N_1$

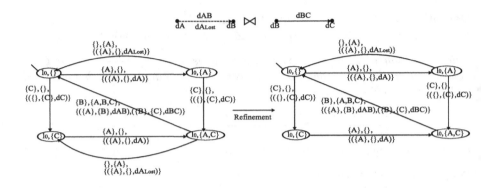

Fig. 10. QIA product of LossySync AB and Sync BC

3. $N \setminus M \subseteq N_1 \setminus M_1$

4. $\nexists s \xrightarrow{M_2, N_2, g_2, D_2} s_2$ s.t. $(N_1 \setminus M_1) \setminus (N \setminus M) \subseteq (N_2 \setminus M_2) \neq \emptyset$
   $\wedge (N \setminus M) \cap (N_2 \setminus M_2) = \emptyset$

Intuitively, conditions 1, 2, and 3 in Definition 5 guarantee that a transition with less pending and firing nodes than another transition from the same source state will be removed, and condition 4 ensures that transitions with independent firings of pending nodes are kept. Now we apply such refinement to the product of LossySync AB and Sync BC in Figure 10. The transition from $\langle l_0, \{A, C\} \rangle$ with losing data at node A has less pending and firing nodes than the other transition from the same source state with a data-flow from A to C via the mixed node B, and also there is no independent firing through the node C ($\in \{A, C\} \setminus \{A\}$), which means the firing of pending requests at nodes A and C are dependent. Hence the transition of losing data at node A with pending data at nodes A and C will be removed from the product result. A QIA model specifies the system behaviour with considering the influence of the environment, and provides a compositional framework, i.e., the QIA version of a complex connector is obtained by applying the product to primitive channels which comprise the connector. However, the context-dependency [7] of the connector is ignored in the product, hence we apply the refinement to the product result to retain the dependency.

5   From QIA to CTMC

A CTMC is a stochastic discrete-state process, often used to model and analyse system performance. A CTMC process is defined as $\{X(t)|t \geq 0\}$. $X(t) \in S$ denotes the state in state space S at time t. Let $\mathbf{P}\{X(t) = i\}$ be the probability that the process is in state i at time t. The stochastic process $X(t)$ is a homogeneous CTMC if, for ordered times $t_0 < \cdots < t_n < t_n + \Delta t$, the conditional probability of staying in any state j satisfies:

$$\mathbf{P}\{X(t_n + \Delta t) = j | X(t_n) = i_n, X(t_{n-1}) = i_{n-1}, \cdots, X(t_0) = i_0\} = $$
$$\mathbf{P}\{X(t_n + \Delta t) = j | X(t_n) = i_n\}$$

In this section we propose an approach for translating QIA into CTMC to carry out performance evaluation. Through this translation, we can specify a system in Stochastic Reo, provide its operational semantics with QIA, and then evaluate its performance via the CTMC derived from its QIA. A Markov Chain (MC) is not compositional and it is difficult to obtain a MC model for a complex system. In our approach, QIA provide a compositional framework for the specification, and the corresponding CTMC model even for a complex system can be subsequently derived from the composed QIA by translation.

In a CTMC, all the stochastic variables on each of its transitions must be exponentially distributed. Hence every stochastic event occurs one by one. In QIA, each transition corresponds to an atomic behaviour, i.e., an arrival of a single data item or synchronized multiple events (especially firings). Such synchronized multiple events happen together, and this is where QIA and CTMC differ. Therefore, for our translation, we need to spread and divide such synchronized multi-event firings into micro-step single-event transitions.

Principle 1. *A data-flow in a channel takes place from its input node to its output node.*

Principle 2. *Mixed nodes send and receive data instantaneously.*

Recall that a D in a QIA transition label is a set of delay information tuples (I, O, r) in $2^{\mathcal{N}} \times 2^{\mathcal{N}} \times \mathbb{R}^+$. Each such tuple describes a data-flow from its input nodes in I to its output nodes in O with the stochastic delay r. The above principles impose a causality-based sequence on the events in D. For example, in $D = \{(\{A\}, \{B\}, dAB), (\{B\}, \{C\}, dBC)\}$, the two tuples directly indicate that data-flow occurs from A to B, with delay dAB, and from B to C, with delay dBC. Moreover, since B appears in the output set of one tuple and the input set of the other, B must be a mixed node, which implies that the data-flow between A and B occurs before data-flow between B and C. From such causality-based sequences we derive a delay-sequence d for each firing, capturing the sequential or parallel properties of each element in its D. The concrete algorithm of extracting such a delay-sequence from D is given in [5]. Syntactically, a delay sequence is:

$$d ::= \epsilon \mid delay \mid d; d \mid d|d \qquad (1)$$

where ϵ is the empty sequence, $delay \in D$, '$d; d$' is the sequential composition of delays, and '$d|d$' is the parallel composition of delays. We also use parentheses '(' and ')' to indicate the highest priority for grouping, where more deeply nested groups have higher precedence. The empty sequence ϵ is an identity element for the ';' and '|' operations, i.e., $\epsilon|d = d = d|\epsilon$, $\epsilon; d = d = d; \epsilon$, and '|' is commutative, associative, and idempotent, i.e., $A|B = B|A$, $(A|B)|C = A|(B|C)$, $A|A = A$.

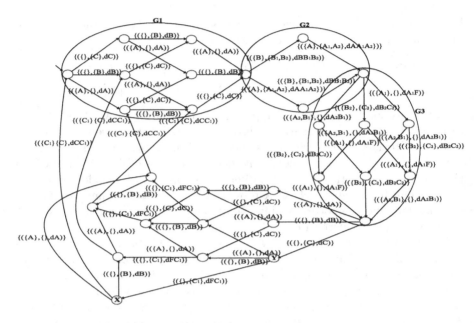

Fig. 11. Derived MC from ordering circuit

In the translation from QIA to CTMC, a single *delay* causes no change to a transition. A synchronized multi-event firing in the '$d; d$' or '$d|d$' form is divided into micro-step single-event transitions by, respectively, enumerating each *delay* element in a sequential delay-sequence and considering the interleaving of all single delays in a parallel delay-sequence. For example, in Figure 11, the consecutive transitions from state Y to the initial state via state X correspond to the result of splitting the synchronized multi-event firing from state $\langle l_1, \{C\}\rangle$ to state $\langle l_0, \{\}\rangle$ in Figure 9, into micro-step single-event transitions. Similarly, the second and third diamond-shaped clusters of transitions (G_2 and G_3 in Figure 11, respectively) represent the result of splitting the synchronized multi-event firing from state $\langle l_0, \{A, B, C\}\rangle$ to state $\langle l_1, \{\}\rangle$ in Figure 9. This splitting is applied until no multi-event firing remains. Consequently, every transition in the result corresponds to a single event with its stochastic property.

In QIA, a synchronized multi-event firing is considered atomic, hence other events cannot interfere with it. However, as we split multiple synchronized events, we cannot guarantee their atomicity any more. A transition having the same source state as another transition that involves a synchronized multi-event firing represents an event that can preempt the sequence of transitions that result from splitting the multi-event firing. For example, state $\langle l_1, \{C\}\rangle$ of the QIA in Figure 9 is connected to the initial state by the transition labeled with the synchronized multi-event firing $\{(\{\}, \{C_1\}, dFC_1), (\{C_1\}, \{C\}, dC_1C)\}$, and there are two other transitions of data arrivals at nodes A and B out of $\langle l_1, \{C\}\rangle$. These arrivals are preemptible events for the sequence of micro-step transitions that result from the splitting of this synchronized multi-event firing. State $\langle l_1, \{C\}\rangle$

in Figure 9 corresponds to state Y in Figure 11, and hence its preemptible events are added as extra transitions tracing the split single-event transitions, like the transitions from state X labeled with data arrivals at nodes A and B.

6   Stochastic Analysis

Our QIA to CTMC translation tool has been incorporated as a plug-in in our ECT environment and can generate input files for analysis in other existing tools like PRISM. For instance, PRISM can be used on a CTMC for the analysis of its steady-state distributions to gain insight not only into the essential states of a system but also about principal performance measures such as delays, through-put, bottlenecks, and blocking probabilities. Moreover, by adjusting values of some stochastic variables, we can perform sensitivity analysis on the system. To illustrate the relevance of our method and the usefulness of our tool, we briefly consider an example, and show the results of a simple analysis of our generated model.

Consider the ordering circuit in Figure 7. As mentioned in Section 3, a bound-ary node or a buffer in a connector is blocked when it is occupied by another pending request. Figure 12 shows the blocking probabilities of nodes A, B, and C and the buffer of the FIFO1 channel when the arrival rate dA at node A increases (i.e., the arrival frequency of requests at node A is increasing) while the arrival rates of requests at nodes B and C, and all processing delays are fixed to 1. A blocking probability is calculated by accumulating steady-state probabilities of its corresponding states, i.e., the blocking probability of node A is obtained as the summation of the steady-state probabilities of all the states whose configurations show that node A is blocked. The arrival rate λ is distributed exponentially and its mean is $1/\lambda$ time units. Hence, as dA increases, the blocking probability of node A also increases, which increases the probability that the FIFO1 is full since

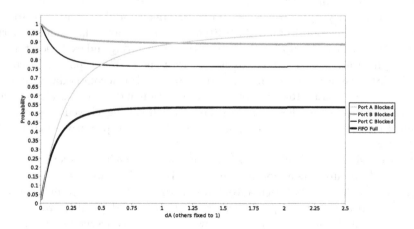

Fig. 12. Blocking probabilities of ordering circuit in Figure 7

the request at node A is delivered to its buffer. A request at node B is consumed together with a request at node A, and a request at node C is consumed together with another at node B or the FIFO1 buffer, alternately. Hence as requests arrive at node A more frequently, the probabilities that nodes B and C are released increase (i.e., their blocking probabilities decrease). Because node C is released by both node B and the buffer, its blocking probability decreases more quickly than that of node B. However all probabilities reach a certain threshold after a while, because of the fixed stochastic values.

7   Related Work

The research in formal specification of a system with quantitative aspects encompasses many developments such as Stochastic Process Algebras (SPAs) [12], Stochastic Automata Networks (SANs) [16,23,25], Stochastic Petri nets (SPNs) [17,24]. SPA is a model for both qualitative and quantitative specification and analysis with a compositional and hierarchical framework, and has algebraic laws (or so called static laws) and expansion laws which express a parallel composition in terms of its operators. In SPA the interpretation of the parallel composition is a vexed one, which allows various interpretations such as Performance Evaluation Process Algebra (PEPA) [18], Extended Markovian Process Algebra (EMPA) [8,9]. SPA describes 'how' each process behaves, but (Stochastic) Reo directly describes 'what' communication protocols connect and coordinate the processes in a system, in terms of primitive channels and their composition. Therefore, QIA and (Stochastic) Reo explicitly model the pure coordination and communication protocols including the impact of real communication networks on software systems and their interactions. Compared to SPA, our approach more naturally leads to a formulation using queueing models like SPNs.

SPN is a directed, weighted, and bipartite graph with an associate exponentially distributed firing delay on each transition. SPN is widely used for modelling concurrency, synchronization, and precedence, and is conducive to both top-down and bottom-up modelling. Stochastic Reo shares the same properties with SPN and natively supports composition of synchrony and exclusion together with asynchrony, which is not possible in Petri nets. The topology of connectors in (Stochastic) Reo is inherently dynamic, and it accommodates mobility. Moreover, (Stochastic) Reo supports a liberal notion of channels and is more general than data-flow models and Petri nets, which can be viewed as specialized channel-based models that incorporate certain specific primitive coordination constructs.

SAN consists of a couple of stochastic automata which act independently. In other words, it supports a modular approach. Hence the state of SAN at time t is expressed by the states of each automaton at time t. The concept of a collection of individual automata helps modelling distributed and parallel systems more easily. SAN might be viewed as SPA. However, SPA is concerned with structural properties such as compositionality and equivalence, and mapping of the specification onto Markov Chains for the computation of performance measures. On the other hand, the original purpose of SAN is to provide an efficient and convenient methodology for computing performance measures rather than a means of deriving algebraic properties of complex systems. The interactions in SAN are rather limited to patterns like synchronizing events or operating at different rates. Compared with the SAN approach, the expressiveness of (Stochastic) Reo makes it possible to model different interaction patterns involving both asynchronous and synchronous communications.

In general, the reachability graphs or MCs derived from the above formalisms have a large state space that prohibits the computation of a solution. In case of SAN the state space explosion problem is relieved by a modular approach to modelling and efficient numerical treatment of the generator matrix [23]. Ameliorating the state explosion problem in other models is still ongoing research, and we are also concerned with the efficient solution technique for the MC derived from Stochastic Reo. The compositional nature of Reo encourages a modular design approach that can, as in the case of SAN, help the state explosion problem. Moreover, the Markov Chains generated by our translation method from Stochastic Reo and QIA consistently show certain interesting structural properties that can be exploited for modular solution and composition through re-scaling. We are currently investigating these alternative solution techniques.

QCA and Quantitative Reo deal with various kinds of non-functional aspects of the system's behaviour and provide a computational and reasoning model with Q-algebra, as used for selection and composition of services/components [20]. The QoS aspects concerned in QCA, such as delays, costs, and resource, depend on the internal details of the system, and accordingly ignore the influence of the environment. However, the performance of a system depends not only on its internal details but also on how it is used in its environment like the the frequency and distribution of request arrivals, and QCA do not concern these stochastic aspects. QIA and Stochastic Reo cover both the internal details of a system as well as the influence of the environment, and hence support a comprehensive approach for specification and performance analysis of a system.

8 Conclusion and Future Work

In this paper, we propose Stochastic Reo and QIA by adding quantitative support in our coordination model and its operational semantics to account for the influence of the environment on the performance of a coordination protocol (i.e., connector). We provide an approach to translate QIA into CTMC for performance analysis when the performance properties are distributed exponentially in QIA. The Reo and automata editors in the Eclipse Coordination Tools [1] have been extended to support Stochastic Reo and QIA, and the automatic derivation of the QIA semantics of Stochastic Reo circuits. We have implemented the translation from QIA to CTMC, and also the generation of the input files for PRISM, and have incorporated them within this platform.

As future work, we want to consider non-exponential distributions, for example, by considering phase-type distributions [22] as an approximation of non-exponential distributions or using (generalized) semi-Markov processes [26] as a target model of the translation. We have found that the CTMCs that are derived from Reo circuits frequently contain a pattern of essentially feed-forward clusters of states. We are investigating methods to exploit these patterns for more efficient compositional solution techniques. A recent semantic model for Reo captures the context-dependent behaviour of Reo connectors in a very small automata model [11]. We expect that using these automata as a basis can provide a more abstract model with significantly smaller numbers of states and transitions compared to the QIA. This can make translating a Reo connector to a MC considerably more efficient.

Acknowledgment

The work reported in this paper is supported by a grant from the GLANCE funding program of NWO, through project CooPer (600.643.000.05N12); project SYANCO (DN 62-613) funded by the DFG-NWO bilateral program; and by the European IST-33826 STREP project CREDO. The authors are indebted to the members of SEN3 for helpful discussions on various aspects of this work. Specifically, the authors are thankful for the assistance of Christian Koehler and Ziyan Maraikar for their cooperation in the implementation of the QIA tools.

References

1. Eclipse Coordination Tools, http://reo.project.cwi.nl/
2. Probabilistic model checker, http://www.prismmodelchecker.org/
3. Arbab, F.: Reo: a channel-based coordination model for component composition. MSCS 14(3), 329–366 (2004)
4. Arbab, F., Chothia, T., Meng, S., Moon, Y.-J.: Component Connectors with QoS Guarantees. In: Murphy, A.L., Vitek, J. (eds.) COORDINATION 2007. LNCS, vol. 4467, pp. 286–304. Springer, Heidelberg (2007)
5. Arbab, F., Chothia, T., van der Mei, R., Meng, S., Moon, Y.-J., Verhoef, C.: From Coordination to Stochastic Models of QoS. Technical report, CWI
6. Arbab, F., Rutten, J.J.M.M.: A Coinductive Calculus of Component Connectors. In: Wirsing, M., Pattinson, D., Hennicker, R. (eds.) WADT 2002. LNCS, vol. 2755, pp. 34–55. Springer, Heidelberg (2003)
7. Baier, C., Sirjani, M., Arbab, F., Rutten, J.J.M.M.: Modeling component connectors in Reo by constraint automata. Sci. Comput. Program. 61(2), 75–113 (2006)
8. Bernardo, M., Gorrieri, R.: Extended Markovian Process Algebra. In: Sassone, V., Montanari, U. (eds.) CONCUR 1996. LNCS, vol. 1119, pp. 315–330. Springer, Heidelberg (1996)
9. Bernardo, M., Gorrieri, R.: A Tutorial on EMPA: A Theory of Concurrent Processes with Nondeterminism, Priorities, Probabilities and Time. Theor. Comput. Sci. 202(1-2), 1–54 (1998)
10. Bistarelli, S., Montanari, U., Rossi, F.: Semiring-based constraint satisfaction and optimization. J. ACM 44(2), 201–236 (1997)
11. Bonsangue, M., Clarke, D., Silva, A.: Automata for context-dependent connectors. In: COORDINATION 2009. LNCS, vol. 5521, pp. 183–202. Springer, Heidelberg (2009)

12. Calzarossa, M.C., Tucci, S. (eds.): Performance 2002. LNCS, vol. 2459. Springer, Heidelberg (2002)
13. Ching, W.-K., Ng, M.K.: Markov Chains: Models, Algorithms and Applications. Springer, Heidelberg (2005)
14. Chothia, T., Kleijn, J.: Q-Automata: Modelling the Resource Usage of Concurrent Components. Electr. Notes Theor. Comput. Sci. 175(2), 153–167 (2007)
15. Costa, D.: Formal Models for Context Dependent Connectors for Distributed Software Components and Services. Ph.D thesis, Vrije Universiteit Amsterdam (2009)
16. Fernandes, P., Plateau, B., Stewart, W.J.: Efficient Descriptor-Vector Multiplications in Stochastic Automata Networks. J. ACM 45(3), 381–414 (1998)
17. Haverkort, B.R., Marie, R., Rubino, G., Trivedi, K.S. (eds.): Performability Modelling: Techniques and Tools. Wiley, Chichester (2001)
18. Hillston, J.: A Compositional Approach to Performance Modelling. Cambridge University Press, Cambridge (1996)
19. Kwiatkowska, M.Z., Norman, G., Parker, D.: PRISM: Probabilistic Symbolic Model Checker. In: Field, T., Harrison, P.G., Bradley, J., Harder, U. (eds.) TOOLS 2002. LNCS, vol. 2324, pp. 200–204. Springer, Heidelberg (2002)
20. Meng, S., Arbab, F.: QoS-Driven Service Selection and Composition. In: ACSD, pp. 160–169. IEEE Computer Society, Los Alamitos (2008)
21. Nicola, R.D., Ferrari, G.L., Montanari, U., Pugliese, R., Tuosto, E.: A Process Calculus for QoS-Aware Applications. In: Jacquet, J.-M., Picco, G.P. (eds.) COORDINATION 2005. LNCS, vol. 3454, pp. 33–48. Springer, Heidelberg (2005)
22. O'Cinneide, C.: Characterization of phase-type distributions. Stochastic Models 6(1), 1–57 (1990)
23. Plateau, B., Stewart, W.J.: Stochastic automata networks: product forms and iterative solutions. Technical Report RR-2939, INRIA
24. Sahner, R.A., Trivedi, K.S., Puliafito, A.: Performance and reliability analysis of computer systems: an example-based approach using the SHARPE software package. Kluwer Academic Publishers, Norwell (1996)
25. Stewart, W.J., Atif, K., Plateau, B.: The numerical solution of stochastic automata networks. EOR 86(3), 503–525 (1995)
26. Younes, H., Simmons, R.: Solving Generalized Semi-Markov Decision Processes using Continuous Phase-Type Distributions. In: Proceedings of the 19th National Conference on Artificial Intelligence, California, pp. 742–747. AAAI Press, Menlo Park (2004)

Assume-Guarantee Verification of Concurrent Systems

Liliana D'Errico and Michele Loreti

Dipartimento di Sistemi e Informatica
Università di Firenze

Abstract. Process algebras are a set of mathematically rigourous languages with well defined semantics that permit modelling behaviour of concurrent and communicating systems. Verification of concurrent systems within the process algebraic approach can be performed by checking that processes enjoy properties described by some temporal logic's formulae. In this paper we present a formal framework that permits verifying properties of concurrent and communicating systems by using an assumption-guarantee approach. Each system component is not considered in isolation, but in conjunction with assumptions about the context of the component. In the paper we introduce a sound and complete proof system that permits verifying whether a process, when it is executed in an environment for which we provide some assumptions, satisfies a given formula. It is also ensured that property satisfaction is preserved whenever the context is partially instantiated (implemented) as a concrete process that verifies the assumptions we have for the environment.

1 Introduction

Process algebras [4,5,19,20] are a set of mathematically rigourous languages with well defined semantics that permit describing and verifying properties of concurrent communicating systems. They can be seen as mathematical models of processes, regarded as agents that act and interact continuously with other similar agents and with their common environment. The agents may be real-world objects (even people), or they may be artefacts, embodied perhaps in computer hardware or software systems.

Process algebras provide a number of constructors for system descriptions and are equipped with an operational semantics that describes systems evolution. Moreover, they often come equipped with observational mechanisms that permit identifying (through behavioural equivalencies) those systems that cannot be taken apart by external observations. In some cases, process algebras have also complete axiomatisations, that capture the relevant identifications.

Verification of concurrent systems within the process algebraic approach is performed either by resorting to behavioural equivalencies for proving conformance of processes to specifications that are expressed within the notation of the same algebra or by checking that processes enjoy properties described by some temporal logic's formulae [10,17].

In the former case two descriptions of a given system, one very detailed and close to the actual concurrent implementation, the other more abstract describing the abstract tree of relevant actions the system has to perform, are provided and tested for equivalence.

J. Field and V.T. Vasconcelos (Eds.): COORDINATION 2009, LNCS 5521, pp. 288–305, 2009.

In the latter case, concurrent systems are specified as terms of a process description language while properties are specified as temporal logic formulae. Labelled Transition Systems are associated with terms via a set of structural operational semantics rules and model checking is used to determine whether the transition systems associated with those terms enjoy the property specified by the given formulae.

Process algebras and modal logics have been largely used as tools for specifying and verifying properties of concurrent systems. This also thanks to model checking algorithms that permit verifying whether a given specification satisfies the expected properties.

However, it is not always possible to specify (or know) all the details of a system. Typical examples are network and distributed systems. These are composed of heterogeneous computational units that interact with each other following a predefined protocol. Even if the protocol governing the interactions among the system components is completely specified, the precise implementation of each component is not known.

In this paper we will consider *mixed specifications* of the form $\Gamma \rhd P$, where Γ is a set of formulae describing the properties we assume satisfied by the environment where the process is executed, while P is a process that describes the behaviour of a part of the system we completely know. Our aim is to introduce a proof system that permits verifying whether a given process P satisfies φ whenever it is executed in an environment satisfying assumptions Γ. In the case, we will guarantee that for each Q satisfying Γ, $P|Q$ will satisfy φ.

The idea is to verify the behaviour of a subset of the system components (P). These components are not considered in isolation, but in conjunction with assumptions (Γ) on the behaviour of the context where the components will be executed.

The proposed framework naturally induces a notion of *refinement*. Indeed, $\Gamma_2 \rhd Q$ refines assumption Γ_1 if and only if $\Gamma_2 \rhd Q$ satisfies Γ_1. At the same time, if $\Gamma_1 \rhd P$ satisfies φ the same is for $\Gamma_2 \rhd Q|P$. By iterating the proposed approach we obtain a methodology that permits obtaining a complete description of a system starting from an high level logical based specification. In each step of the refinement procedure, the satisfaction of the expected properties is preserved.

The rest of the paper is organised as follows. In Section 2 we recall basic the *Calculus of Communication Systems* and the *Hennessy-Milner logic*. In Section 3 we present the dialect of HML that we use for specifying the properties we assume satisfied by the environment. Section 4 presents the proposed proof system. Section 5 concludes the paper with a few final considerations. In the present paper all the proof are only sketched, detailed proofs can be found in [13].

2   Calculus of Communicating Systems

The *Calculus of Communicating Systems* (CCS) [19,20], one of the most popular process calculi, provides a set of operators that permit describing the behaviour of a system starting from the specification of its subcomponents. Components interact with each other by means of *actions*, atomic and not interruptible steps, which represent input/output operations on communication ports or internal computations of the system.

Let Λ be an infinite numerable set of channels or ports, a CCS action α can be: an input over $a \in \Lambda$, denoted by a; an output on $a \in \Lambda$, denoted by $\bar{a}$; an internal computational step, denoted by τ. We assume $\bar{\bar{\alpha}} \triangleq \alpha$, where $\alpha \in \Lambda \cup \{\bar{a} \mid a \in \Lambda\} \cup \{\tau\}$. Actions $\bar{\alpha}$ and α are said complementary, they represent input and output actions on the same channel.

The syntax of CCS processes is defined by means of the following grammar:

$$P, Q ::= nil \mid X \mid \alpha.P \mid P + Q \mid Q \mid P \mid P \mid P \backslash A \mid P[f]$$
$$\alpha ::= \bar{a} \mid a \mid \tau$$

CCS operators have the following meaning:

- nil is the *inactive* process.
- X is a *constant* which is assumed defined by an appropriate equation $X \triangleq P$ for some process term P, where *constants* occur only guarded in P, i.e. under the scope of an action prefix.
- $\alpha.Q$ is the *action prefixing* and describes a process that after the execution of action α behaves like P
- $P + Q$ is the *choice or sum* operator and identifies a process that can behaves either like P or like Q.
- $P \mid Q$ is the *parallel composition* operator and represents the concurrent execution of processes P and Q. A synchronisation, generating a τ action, can occur when P and Q execute complementary actions.
- $P \backslash A$ is the *restriction* operator and models a process that behaves like P, but for the impossibility of interacting using actions in $A \subseteq \Lambda$.
- $P[f]$ is the *relabelling* operator where $f : \Lambda \to \Lambda$ is a function that "renames" actions performed by P (we let $\hat{f}$ be such that $\hat{f}(\tau) = \tau$ while $\hat{f}(\bar{a}) = \overline{f(a)}$).

Table 1. CCS Operational Semantics

$$\frac{}{\alpha.P \xrightarrow{\alpha} P} \qquad \frac{P \xrightarrow{\alpha} P'}{P + Q \xrightarrow{\alpha} P'} \qquad \frac{Q \xrightarrow{\alpha} Q'}{P + Q \xrightarrow{\alpha} Q'}$$

$$\frac{P \xrightarrow{\alpha} P'}{P|Q \xrightarrow{\alpha} P'|Q} \qquad \frac{Q \xrightarrow{\alpha} Q'}{P|Q \xrightarrow{\alpha} P|Q'} \qquad \frac{P \xrightarrow{\alpha} P' \quad Q \xrightarrow{\bar{\alpha}} Q'}{P|Q \xrightarrow{\tau} P'|Q'}$$

$$\frac{P \xrightarrow{\alpha} P'}{P \backslash A \xrightarrow{\alpha} P' \backslash A}(\alpha, \bar{\alpha} \notin A) \qquad \frac{P \xrightarrow{\alpha} P'}{P[f] \xrightarrow{\hat{f}(\alpha)} P'[f]} \qquad \frac{P \xrightarrow{\alpha} P'}{X \xrightarrow{\alpha} P'}(X \triangleq P)$$

The operational semantics of CCS is formally defined in Table 1. In the rest of the paper we will use $P \xrightarrow{\alpha}$ to denote that exists P' such that $P \xrightarrow{\alpha} P'$. Similarly, $P \not\xrightarrow{\alpha}$ if $\neg(P \xrightarrow{\alpha})$. We will also write $P \to P'$ if exists α such that $P \xrightarrow{\alpha} P'$ while $\to^*$ is the transitive and reflexive closure of $\to$. Finally, we adopt the following notation:

- $\text{Ch}(P)$ denotes the set of channels occurring in P;
- $\text{Act}(P)$ denotes the set of actions P can perform during a computation;
- $\text{Init}(P)$ denotes the set of actions P can immediately perform;
- $\text{Der}(P) = \{Q | P \to^* Q\}$.

Example 1 (Dining Philosophers). The dining philosophers problem is a classical example proposed by Edsger Dijkstra to illustrate resource sharing, fairness and synchronisation in concurrent systems. There are n philosophers sitting at a circular table. Each philosopher can do one of two activities: eating or thinking. A fork is placed in between each philosopher. A philosopher must obtain the use of his left and right forks concurrently to be able to eat, which means two neighbouring philosophers can not eat simultaneously since they share the resource, the fork. After a philosopher finishes eating, he puts down the forks and starts to think.

The i-th philosopher can be modelled in CCS as follows:

$$Ph_i = pick_i.pick_{i+1\bmod n}.\overline{eat_i}.\overline{rel_i}.\overline{rel}_{i+1\bmod n}.Ph_i$$

while the i-th fork is rendered as:

$$F_i = \overline{pick_i}.rel_i.F_i$$

2.1 Hennessy-Milner Logic

Hennessy-Milner Logic (HML) is a modal logic introduced by Hennessy and Milner to provide a logical characterisation of bisimulation [14]. The syntax of HML formulae is the following:

$$\varphi ::= tt \mid ff \mid \langle \alpha \rangle \varphi \mid \neg \varphi \mid \varphi_1 \vee \varphi_2 \mid X \mid \nu X.\varphi$$

A process satisfies $\langle \alpha \rangle \varphi$ if and only if action α can be executed leading to process satisfying φ. Greatest fix-point ($\nu X.\varphi$) can be used for specifying recursive properties. Greatest fix-point operator $\nu X.\varphi$ acts as a binder for the recursive variable occurring in φ. We said that X occurs *free* in φ if it does not occur under the scope of $\nu X.$. A formula φ is *closed* if no free variable occurs in φ; φ is *well-formed* if it is closed and in each sub-formula of the form $\nu X.\varphi$, X is *positive*, i.e. X appears under an even number of symbols of negation. From now on we will consider only well-formed formulae.

Other operators can be defined as macro in the HML. In the sequel, we let $\varphi_1 \wedge \varphi_2$ be $\neg(\neg \varphi_1 \vee \neg \varphi_2)$ and $[\alpha]\varphi$ be $\neg \langle \alpha \rangle \neg \varphi$. The former is the logical conjunction operator while the latter is a modal operator satisfied by all the process that, after α, satisfy φ.

Semantics of HML formulae is formally defined by means of an interpretation function $[\![\cdot]\!]$ that takes a formula φ and a *recursion environment* δ, i.e. a function mapping recursion variable to set of processes, and yields the set of processes satisfying φ. Function $[\![\cdot]\!]$ is formally defined as follows:

- $[\![tt]\!]\delta = Proc$
- $[\![ff]\!]\delta = \emptyset$
- $[\![\neg \varphi]\!]\delta = Proc - [\![\varphi]\!]\delta$
- $[\![\varphi_1 \vee \varphi_2]\!]\delta = [\![\varphi_1]\!]\delta \cup [\![\varphi_2]\!]\delta$

Table 2. Formulae proof system

$$\frac{P \vdash \varphi}{P \vdash \neg\neg\varphi} \qquad \frac{P \vdash \neg\varphi_1 \quad P \vdash \neg\varphi_2}{P \vdash \neg(\varphi_1 \vee \varphi_2)} \qquad \frac{P \vdash \varphi_i}{P \vdash \varphi_1 \vee \varphi_2}(i = 1, 2)$$

$$\frac{Q \vdash \varphi}{P \vdash \langle\alpha\rangle\,\varphi}(\exists Q : P \xrightarrow{\alpha} Q) \qquad\qquad \frac{\{Q \vdash \neg\varphi \mid P \xrightarrow{\alpha} Q\}}{P \vdash \neg\langle\alpha\rangle\,\varphi}$$

$$\frac{P \vdash \varphi[vX\{P,\vec{r}\}\varphi/X]}{P \vdash vX\{\vec{r}\}\varphi}(P \notin \{\vec{r}\}) \qquad \frac{P \vdash \varphi[\mu X\{P,\vec{r}\}\varphi/X]}{P \vdash \mu X\{\vec{r}\}\varphi}(P \notin \{\vec{r}\})$$

- $\llbracket\,\langle\alpha\rangle\,\varphi\,\rrbracket\delta = \left\{P\,\middle|\,\exists P' : P \xrightarrow{\alpha} P' \ \& \ P' \in \llbracket\,\varphi\,\rrbracket\delta\right\}$
- $\llbracket\,X\,\rrbracket\delta = \delta(X)$
- $\llbracket\,vX.\varphi\,\rrbracket\delta = \bigcup\left\{S\,\middle|\,S \subseteq \llbracket\,\varphi\,\rrbracket\delta\left[^S/_X\right]\right\}$

where if δ is a recursion environment, $\delta[S/X]$ denotes the function associating S to X and $\delta(Y)$ to each variable $Y \neq X$ while [] denotes the function associating $\emptyset$ to each variable. A process P satisfies a formula φ ($P \models \varphi$) if and only if $P \in \llbracket\,\varphi\,\rrbracket[]$.

Example 2. For the *dining philosophers*, two properties are classically considered: absence of deadlock and absence of starvation. The former requires that the system never reaches a configuration where no action can be performed while the latter asks that each philosopher can eventually eat. In HML these properties can be rendered as follows:

Absence of deadlock:

$$vX. \langle\mathcal{A}\rangle\,tt \wedge [\mathcal{A}]\,X$$

Absence of starvation (for i-th philosopher):

$$\neg vX. \left[\overline{eat_i}\right] ff \wedge \langle\mathcal{A}\rangle\,X$$

where $\mathcal{A} = \{\tau\} \cup \{\overline{eat_i} | 0 \leq i < n\}$ and $\langle\mathcal{A}\rangle\,\varphi$ (resp. $[\mathcal{A}]\,\varphi$) stands for $\bigvee_{\alpha\in\mathcal{A}} \langle\alpha\rangle\,\varphi$ (resp. $\bigwedge_{\alpha\in\mathcal{A}} [\alpha]\,\varphi$).

2.2 A Proof System

Satisfaction of HML formulae can be verified by using a *local model-checking* technique [24,23,11] that is based on *tableau*. Tableau systems are finite families of deduction rules which sanction reduction of goals to subgoals. They are similar in style to structured operational semantics.

To verify whether a process satisfies a formula, we consider the proof system of Table 2 already presented in [24]. The proof system operates on *sequents* (denoted by $\pi_1, \pi_2, \ldots$) of the form $P \vdash \psi$ where ψ is a logic formula and P is a process. Derivation rules have the following form:

$$\frac{\{\pi_1, \ldots, \pi_n\}}{\pi} cond$$

where $\{\pi_1, \ldots, \pi_n\}$ is the (finite) set of sequents to prove in order to assess *validity* of π and *cond* is a side condition. A rule like the above can be applied only when the side condition is satisfied.

We say that Π is a *derivation from* π if and only if it has π as root and it is maximal, in the sense that no rule can be applied from *leaves*.

Definition 1. *A sequent* $\pi = P \vdash \psi$ *is* successful *when one of the following conditions holds:*

1. $\psi \equiv tt$;
2. $\psi \equiv \nu X\{\vec{r}\}\varphi$ *and* $P \in \{\vec{r}\}$;
3. π *is derivable from* $\{\}$.

A derivation Π is successful if all its leaves are successful. A sequent π is provable if there exists a successful derivation Π from it. In the case we said that Π is a *proof* for π.

Notice that, to properly handle recursive properties, the syntax of HML has been enriched in order to annotate recursive variables with set of processes:

$$\nu X\{P_1, \ldots, P_n\}.\varphi$$

where $\nu X.\varphi$ can be viewed as a shorthand for $\nu X\{\ \}.\varphi$. Interpretation function is then modified as follows:

$$[\![\, \nu X\{\mathcal{P}\}.\varphi \,]\!]\delta = \mathcal{P} \cup \bigcup \left\{ S \;\middle|\; S \subseteq [\![\, \varphi \,]\!]\delta\left[{}^S/_X\right] \right\}$$

Termination of proofs is ensured by the fact that assertions are strictly smaller after reductions and for recursive assertions an assumption on finite-state processes is done. The Lemma below is the key result on which is based the proof of soundness and completeness of the proof system.

Lemma 1 (Reduction lemma [24]). *For each set of processes* $\mathcal{P}$,

$$P \models \nu X.\varphi \Leftrightarrow P \models \varphi[\nu X\{\mathcal{P}\}.\varphi/X]$$

Theorem 1 (Soundness and Completeness [24]). *Let* P *be a process such that* $\mathsf{Der}(P)$ *is finite, and* φ *is a closed formula,* $P \vdash \varphi$ *is provable if and only if* $P \models \varphi$.

Example 3. The proof system of Table 2 can be used for proving that the following system Sys composed of 2 philosophers and 2 forks:

$$Sys \triangleq Ph_0|F_0|Ph_1|F_1$$

does not satisfy neither *absence of deadlock* nor *absence of starvation*.

Deadlock can be avoided when we let one of the two philosophers taking forks in a reverse order. If we let:

$$Ph_1^* = pick_0.pick_1.\overline{eat}_1.\overline{rel}_0.\overline{rel}_1.Ph_i$$

and

$$Sys^* \triangleq Ph_0|F_0|Ph_1^*|F_1$$

we have that Sys^* satisfies *absence of deadlock* while *absence of starvation* is still unsatisfied. Indeed, there exists an infinite computation in which Ph_0 (resp. Ph_1) never eats.

3   Formalising Assumptions for Process Environments

In the previous section we have presented a proof system that permits verifying whether a process P satisfies or not a given property φ. However, when distributed or network systems are taken into account, all the details of a system are typically not known. Indeed, these systems are composed of heterogeneous computational units that interact with each other following a predefined protocol. Even if the protocol governing the interactions among the system components is completely specified, the precise implementation of each component is not known.

In this section we present a dialect of HML thought for specifying the set of properties we assume satisfied by the environment where a process is executed. Indeed, we will consider system specifications composed of two parts: a CCS process P that specifies the behaviour of a known component, and a set of formulae Γ that identifies the set of properties we assume satisfied by the environment where P is executed.

In the example of *Dining Philosophers* introduced in previous sections, desired properties can be verified only on a specific instance of the problem. On the contrary, by relying on the framework introduced in this section, behaviour of a philosopher, namely Ph_i, will be analysed by considering a given set of assumptions we let satisfied by the context where Ph_i operates. Satisfaction of verified properties will be preserved each time Ph_i will be immersed in an environment satisfying the considered assumptions. This, for instance, independently from the number of philosophers considered in the particular instance of the system.

Assumptions on the environment will be formalised by means of a dialect of HML for which we will be able to define a precise operational semantics, i.e. a relation of the form $\Gamma \xrightarrow{\alpha} \Gamma'$. The proposed semantics will guarantee that a Γ exhibits a given behaviour if and only if it is shared among all the processes satisfying Γ

We let $\mathcal{L}_\chi$ be the set of formulae Φ, Ψ, ... defined by the following syntax:

$$\Phi, \Psi ::= tt \mid ff \mid \prec \alpha \succ \Phi \mid \dagger(\alpha) \mid (\!| \alpha |\!) \Phi \mid \neg\Phi \mid \Phi \vee \Psi \mid X \mid \nu X.\Phi$$

where for each $\nu X.\Phi$ we assume each free occurrence of X in Φ always occurring under the scope of a modal operator, even and never under the scope of a $\prec \cdot \succ$.

In $\mathcal{L}_\chi$, modal operators of HML are replaced by $\dagger(\cdot)$, $(\!| \cdot |\!)$, $\prec \cdot \succ$ that have the following meaning: $\dagger(\alpha)$ states that action α cannot be performed, while both $(\!| \alpha |\!)\Phi$

and $\ll \alpha \gg \Phi$ guarantees the execution of action α. However, while the former ensures that after α, Φ is always satisfied, the latter is satisfied by those processes that can evolve with α both to states satisfying Φ and to states satisfying $\neg\Phi$. For instance, $(\!|\,\alpha\,|\!)\dagger(\beta)$ is satisfied by $\alpha.nil$ and it is not satisfied by $\alpha.\beta.nil|\alpha.nil$. Conversely, $\ll \alpha \gg \dagger(\beta)$ is is satisfied by $\alpha.\beta.nil|\alpha.nil$ and it is not satisfied by $\alpha.nil$.

Interpretation function of *HML* is then extended in order to consider new modal operators:

$$- [\![\ll \alpha \gg \Phi]\!]\delta = \left\{ P \,\middle|\, \exists P_1, P_2 : P \xrightarrow{\alpha} P_1, P_1 \in [\![\Phi]\!]\delta \,\&\, P \xrightarrow{\alpha} P_2, P_2 \in [\![\neg\Phi]\!]\delta \right\}$$

$$- [\![\dagger(\alpha)]\!]\delta = \left\{ P \,\middle|\, P \overset{\alpha}{\nrightarrow} \right\}$$

$$- [\![(\!|\,\alpha\,|\!)\Phi]\!]\delta = \left\{ P \,\middle|\, P \xrightarrow{\alpha} \,\&\, \forall P' : P \xrightarrow{\alpha} P', P' \in [\![\Phi]\!]\delta \right\}$$

Notice that the proposed logic is a dialect of HML in the sense that it can be completely specified by using HML formulae. Indeed, it is easy to prove that modal operators $\langle\cdot\rangle$ and $[\cdot]$ can be easily expressed, and then considered as macros, by using the ones in $\mathcal{L}_\chi$:

$$\langle\alpha\rangle\,\varphi \equiv \neg((\!|\,\alpha\,|\!)\neg\varphi \vee \dagger(\alpha)) \qquad [\alpha]\,\varphi \equiv (\!|\,\alpha\,|\!)\varphi \vee \dagger(\alpha)$$

at the same time, it is easy to prove that modal operators in $\mathcal{L}_\chi$ can be expressed by using HML operators:

$$(\!|\,\alpha\,|\!)\Phi \equiv [\alpha]\,\Phi \wedge \langle\alpha\rangle\,tt \qquad \ll \alpha \gg \Phi \equiv \langle\alpha\rangle\,\Phi \wedge \langle\alpha\rangle\,\neg\Phi \qquad \dagger(\alpha) \equiv [\alpha]\,ff$$

Assumptions on environments are then specified by means of a set Γ of sets of formulae in $\mathcal{L}_\chi$. A process P satisfies an assumption Γ if and only if for each $\Phi \in \Gamma$, $P \models \Phi$. Formally:

$$[\![\Gamma]\!]\delta = \bigcap_{\Phi \in \Gamma} [\![\Phi]\!]\delta$$

Even if HML could be used for specifying the properties we assume for an environment, this approach is not suitable for deriving the possible behaviours of the specified environment. On the contrary, the proposed dialect permits directly characterising the behaviour that is shared among all the processes satisfying given assumptions Γ.

We let $\rightarrow\, \subseteq \mathcal{L}_\chi \times \mathsf{Act} \times \mathcal{L}_\chi$ be the transition relation defined in Table 3. Notice that, a transition can be derived for a Γ only when each $\Phi \in \Gamma$ has only modal operators at top level. We will refer to this kind of assumptions as *determined*.

Definition 2. *An environment Γ is determined if and only if $\Gamma \neq \emptyset$ and for each $\Phi \in \Gamma$, $\Phi = \ll \alpha \gg \Psi, (\!|\,\alpha\,|\!)\Psi, \dagger(\alpha)$.*

Indeed, we cannot directly derive a transition for every Γ. For instance, let Γ be:

$$((\!|\,\alpha\,|\!)\Phi_1 \wedge \dagger(\beta)) \vee ((\!|\,\beta\,|\!)\Phi_1 \wedge \dagger(\alpha))$$

This identifies all the environments where either α or β can be executed. In both the cases, after α (or β), satisfaction of Φ_1 is guaranteed. The point is that $\vee$ can

Table 3. Formulae operational semantics

$$\{\lessdot \alpha \gtrdot \Phi\} \overset{\alpha}{\to} \{\Phi\} \qquad\qquad \{\lessdot \alpha \gtrdot \Phi\} \overset{\alpha}{\to} \{\neg\Phi\} \qquad\qquad \{(\!|\,\alpha\,|\!)\Phi\} \overset{\alpha}{\to} \{\Phi\}$$

$$\frac{\Gamma \overset{\beta}{\to} \Gamma'}{\Gamma \cup \{\lessdot \alpha \gtrdot \Phi\} \overset{\beta}{\to} \Gamma'}(\alpha \neq \beta) \quad \frac{\Gamma \overset{\alpha}{\to} \Gamma'}{\Gamma \cup \{\lessdot \alpha \gtrdot \Phi\} \overset{\alpha}{\to} \Gamma' \cup \{\Phi\}} \quad \frac{\Gamma \overset{\alpha}{\to} \Gamma'}{\Gamma \cup \{\lessdot \alpha \gtrdot \Phi\} \overset{\alpha}{\to} \Gamma' \cup \{\neg\Phi\}}$$

$$\frac{\Gamma \overset{\beta}{\to} \Gamma'}{\Gamma \cup \{\dagger(\alpha)\} \overset{\beta}{\to} \Gamma'}(\alpha \neq \beta) \quad \frac{\Gamma \overset{\alpha}{\to} \Gamma'}{\Gamma \cup \{(\!|\,\alpha\,|\!)\Phi\} \overset{\alpha}{\to} \Gamma' \cup \{\Phi\}} \quad \frac{\Gamma \overset{\beta}{\to} \Gamma'}{\Gamma \cup \{(\!|\,\alpha\,|\!)\Phi\} \overset{\beta}{\to} \Gamma'}(\alpha \neq \beta)$$

---

combine "behaviours" that do not provide a "coherent" specification. In the example above, $(\!|\,\alpha\,|\!)\Phi_1 \wedge \dagger(\beta)$ states that α can be executed and β can not, while $(\!|\,\beta\,|\!)\Phi_1 \wedge \dagger(\alpha)$ does the contrary.

In the rest of the paper $\Gamma \to \Gamma'$ indicates that exists α such that $\Gamma \overset{\alpha}{\to} \Gamma'$ and $\Gamma \to^* \Gamma'$ is the transitive and reflexive closure of $\to$.

The following lemma permits guarantee that if $\Gamma \overset{\alpha}{\to} \Gamma'$ then each process satisfying Γ can perform the same action leading to a state satisfying Γ'.

Lemma 2. *For each* $\Gamma \subseteq \mathcal{L}_\chi$, $|\Gamma| > 0$, *and for each process P such that $P \models \Gamma$:*

$$\exists \Gamma', \alpha : \Gamma \overset{\alpha}{\to} \Gamma' \implies \exists P' : P \overset{\alpha}{\to} P' \wedge P' \models \Gamma'$$

Proof. The proof easily proceeds by induction on the size of Γ.   □

The reverse implication does not hold in the general case. For instance, let $\Gamma = \{\dagger(\alpha)\}$ and $P = \beta.nil$ $(\alpha \neq \beta)$: $P \models \Gamma$ and $P \overset{\beta}{\to} P'$ while $\Gamma \overset{\beta}{\nrightarrow}$. However, if one considers an action α that is *initial* in Γ, it holds that if $P \models \Gamma$ (Γ determined) and $P \overset{\alpha}{\to} P'$ then $\Gamma \overset{\alpha}{\to} \Gamma'$ and $P' \models \Gamma'$.

Definition 3.

– *For each $\Phi \in \mathcal{L}_\chi$,* $\mathsf{Init}(\Phi)$ *is inductively defined as follows:*

$$\mathsf{Init}(tt) = \mathsf{Init}(ff) = \mathsf{Init}(X) = \emptyset$$
$$\mathsf{Init}(\neg\Phi) = \mathsf{Init}(\Phi)$$
$$\mathsf{Init}(\Phi_1 \vee \Phi_2) = \mathsf{Init}(\Phi_1) \cup \mathsf{Init}(\Phi_2)$$
$$\mathsf{Init}(\lessdot \alpha \gtrdot \Phi) = \mathsf{Init}((\!|\,\alpha\,|\!)\Phi) = \mathsf{Init}(\dagger(\alpha)) = \{\alpha\}$$
$$\mathsf{Init}(\nu X.\Phi) = \mathsf{Init}(\Phi)$$

– *For each $\Gamma \subseteq \mathcal{L}_\chi$:*

$$\mathsf{Init}(\Gamma) = \bigcup_{\Phi \in \Gamma} \mathsf{Init}(\Phi)$$

Lemma 3. *For each $\Gamma \subseteq \mathcal{L}_\chi$ determined and for each process P such that $P \models \Gamma$ and for each $\alpha \in \text{Init}(\Gamma)$:*

$$\exists P' : P \xrightarrow{\alpha} P' \implies \exists \Gamma' : \Gamma \xrightarrow{\alpha} \Gamma' \wedge P' \models \Gamma'$$

Proof. The proof easily proceeds by induction on the size of Γ.   □

Another important point is that an assumption Γ can be inconsistent, i.e. either $ff \in \Gamma$ or both $\dagger(\alpha)$ and $(\!(\alpha)\!)\Phi$ (or $\triangleleft \alpha \triangleright \Phi$) belong to Γ, for some α and Φ. This can be either a consequence of a bad specification or due to the fact that some combinations of assumptions in Γ can never be satisfied. For instance, let Γ be $\{(\!(\alpha)\!)\Phi_1 \vee \dagger(\beta), (\!(\beta)\!)\Phi_2\}$. A process satisfies Γ if and only if it satisfies either $\{(\!(\alpha)\!)\Phi_1, (\!(\beta)\!)\Phi_2\}$ or $\{\dagger(\beta), (\!(\beta)\!)\Phi_2\}$. However, the latter is inconsistent and is never satisfied.

The following lemma guarantees that, if a Γ can reach an inconsistent Γ', then no process satisfies Γ.

Lemma 4. *For each $\Gamma \subseteq \mathcal{L}_\chi$, if $\Gamma \to^* \Gamma' \subseteq \mathcal{L}_\chi$ and Γ' is inconsistent, then $[\![\Gamma]\!] = \emptyset$.*

Proof. By induction on the length of the derivation $\to^*$.   □

We now introduce some macros that simplify the specification of environment assumptions:

$$\text{Always}(\mathcal{A}, \Phi) = \nu X.\Phi \wedge \bigwedge_{\alpha \in \mathcal{A}} [\alpha] X \quad \text{Eventually}(\mathcal{A}, \Phi) = \neg\text{Always}(\mathcal{A}, \neg\Phi)$$

Let $\mathcal{A} \subseteq \text{Act}$ be a finite set of actions, $\text{Always}(\mathcal{A}, \Phi)$ is satisfied by those processes that *always* satisfy Φ in each state reachable with actions in $\mathcal{A}$. A process satisfies $\text{Eventually}(\mathcal{A}, \Phi)$ if a state satisfying Φ is reachable by executing a finite sequence of actions in $\mathcal{A}$.

Interpretation function of Section 2.1 can be extended in order to consider the assumptions where a process is executed. The set of processes satisfying φ under the assumptions Γ ($[\![\varphi]\!]_\Gamma$) can be defined as:

$$[\![\varphi]\!]_\Gamma =_{def} \left\{ P \,\middle|\, \forall Q.\ Q \models \Gamma,\ P|Q \in [\![\varphi]\!] \right\} \tag{1}$$

Let $\mathcal{A} \subset \text{Act}$, we can limit our attention to only those processes that can perform only action in $\mathcal{A}$:

$$[\![\varphi]\!]_\Gamma^{\mathcal{A}} =_{def} \left\{ P \,\middle|\, \forall Q.\ \text{Act}(Q) \subseteq \mathcal{A} \wedge Q \models \Gamma,\ P|Q \in [\![\varphi]\!] \right\}$$

Notice that, if Γ is inconsistent, $[\![\Gamma]\!] = \emptyset$ and, for each P and φ, $P \in [\![\varphi]\!]_\Gamma$.

Example 4. Logic $\mathcal{L}_\chi$ can be used for formalising the properties we assume satisfied by each environment where philosopher Ph_0 could be executed. First of all we assume that these environments can only interact with Ph_0 by performing a finite set of actions in $\mathcal{A}$ containing $\{\tau, \overline{pick_0}, \overline{pick_1}, rel_0, rel_1\}$. Properties we assume for the environment of Ph_0 are:

– Two forks, F_0 and F_1, are available in the environment. Then $\overline{pick}_0$ (resp. $\overline{pick}_1$) can be performed leading to a state where action rel_0 (resp. rel_1) is always available until fork F_0 (resp. F_1) is released. We let Φ_F^i ($i = 0, 1$) be:

$$\Phi_F^i = \nu X.\mathsf{Always}(\mathcal{A} - \overline{pick}_i, (\!|\, \overline{pick}_i \,|\!)\mathsf{Always}(\mathcal{A} - rel_i, (\!|\, rel_i \,|\!)X))$$

– A fork can be used by another philosopher. In that case, it will return eventually available:

$$\Phi_B^i = \nu X.((\!|\, \tau \,|\!)\mathsf{Eventually}(\mathcal{A} - \{\overline{pick}_i, rel_i\}, (\!|\, \tau \,|\!)(\Phi_F^i \wedge X))$$
$$\wedge$$
$$(\!|\, \overline{pick}_i \,|\!)\mathsf{Always}(\mathcal{A} - \{rel_i\}, (\!|\, rel_i \,|\!)X)$$
$$)\vee ($$
$$\bigwedge\nolimits_{\alpha \in \mathcal{A} - \{\overline{pick}_i\}} [\alpha]\,X$$
$$)$$

– Never both $\overline{pick}_i$ and rel_i are enabled at the same time in the environment:

$$\Phi_C^i = \neg\mathsf{Always}(\mathcal{A}, (\!|\, \overline{pick}_i \,|\!)tt \wedge (\!|\, rel_i \,|\!)tt)$$

The overall assumptions are:

$$\Gamma_{DF} = \{\Phi_F^0, \Phi_F^1, \Phi_B^0, \Phi_B^1, \Phi_C^0, \Phi_C^1\}$$

4   An Assume-Guarantee Based Proof System

In this section we present a proof system that permits verifying whether a process P satisfies a formula φ under the assumption that the environment where P is executed satisfies a given set of formulae $\Gamma \subseteq \mathcal{L}_\chi$.

The proposed proof system, formally defined in Table 4, operates on sequents of the form $S \vdash \varphi$ where S is a *specification* of the form $\Gamma \triangleright P$ and φ a formula of HML. Operational semantics of Table 1 is extended in order to consider specifications S with the following rule:

$$\frac{P \xrightarrow{\alpha} P'}{\Gamma \triangleright P \xrightarrow{\alpha} \Gamma \triangleright P'} \qquad \frac{\Gamma \xrightarrow{\alpha} \Gamma'}{\Gamma \triangleright P \xrightarrow{\alpha} \Gamma' \triangleright P} \qquad \frac{\Gamma \xrightarrow{\alpha} \Gamma' \quad P \xrightarrow{\bar{\alpha}} P'}{\Gamma \triangleright P \xrightarrow{\tau} \Gamma' \triangleright P'} \qquad (2)$$

Proof system of Table 2 is extended with the rules for handling logical connectives on the assumptions. Rule E-Not states that if $\Gamma \cup \{\neg\neg\Phi\}$ is assumed, then the proof proceeds with assumption $\Gamma \cup \{\Phi\}$. Rule E-And and E-Or are used for handling conjunctions and disjunctions in the assumptions. The former states that assuming $\neg(\Phi_1 \vee \Phi_2)$ is the same to assume both $\neg\Phi_1$ and $\neg\Phi_2$. The latter states that to prove $\Gamma \cup \{\Phi_1 \vee \Phi_2\} \triangleright P \vdash \varphi$ we have to prove both $\Gamma \cup \{\Phi_1\} \triangleright P \vdash \varphi$ and $\Gamma \cup \{\Phi_2\} \triangleright P \vdash \varphi$ separately.

Rules E-Fix and E-NotFix are used when a fixed point ($\nu X.\Phi$), or its negation ($\neg\nu X.\Phi$), is in the assumptions. In both the cases we proceed in a proof by replacing each occurrence of X in Φ (resp. $\neg\Phi$) with $\nu X.\Phi$.

Table 4. Tableau based Proof System

$$\frac{S \vdash \psi}{S \vdash \neg\neg\psi} \text{ (Not)} \qquad \frac{\Gamma \cup \{\Phi\} \triangleright P \vdash \psi}{\Gamma \cup \{\neg\neg\Phi\} \triangleright P \vdash \psi} \text{ (E-Not)}$$

$$\frac{\Gamma \triangleright P \xrightarrow{\alpha} S \quad S \vdash \psi}{\Gamma \triangleright P \vdash \langle \alpha \rangle \psi} \text{ (Dia)}^* \qquad \frac{\left\{ S \vdash \neg\psi \mid \Gamma \triangleright P \xrightarrow{\alpha} S \right\}}{\Gamma \triangleright P \vdash \neg \langle \alpha \rangle \psi} \text{ (Box)}^*$$

$$\frac{S \vdash \neg\psi_1 \quad S \vdash \neg\psi_2}{S \vdash \neg(\psi_1 \vee \psi_2)} \text{ (And)} \qquad \frac{S \vdash \psi_i \quad i \in \{1,2\}}{S \vdash \psi_1 \vee \psi_2} \text{ (Or)}$$

$$\frac{\Gamma \cup \{\neg\Phi_1, \neg\Phi_2\} \triangleright P \vdash \psi}{\Gamma \cup \{\neg(\Phi_1 \vee \Phi_2)\} \triangleright P \vdash \psi} \text{ (E-And)} \qquad \frac{\Gamma \cup \{\Phi_1\} \triangleright P \vdash \psi \quad \Gamma \cup \{\Phi_2\} \triangleright P \vdash \psi}{\Gamma \cup \{\Phi_1 \vee \Phi_2\} \triangleright P \vdash \psi} \text{ (E-Or)}$$

$$\frac{S \vdash \psi[\nu X\{\mathcal{H}, S\}.\psi/X]}{S \vdash \nu X\{\mathcal{H}\}.\psi} (S \notin \mathcal{H})(\text{Fix}) \qquad \frac{S \vdash \neg\psi[\neg\nu X\{\mathcal{H}, S\}.\psi/X]}{S \vdash \neg\nu X.\psi} (S \notin \mathcal{H})(\text{NotFix})$$

$$\frac{\Gamma \cup \{\Phi[\nu X.\Phi/X]\} \triangleright P \vdash \psi}{\Gamma \cup \{\nu X.\Phi\} \triangleright P \vdash \psi} \text{ (E-Fix)} \qquad \frac{\Gamma \cup \{\neg\Phi[\neg\nu X.\Phi/X]\} \triangleright P \vdash \psi}{\Gamma \cup \{\neg\nu X.\Phi\} \triangleright P \vdash \psi} \text{ (E-NotFix)}$$

$$\frac{\Gamma \triangleright P \vdash \psi}{\Gamma \cup \{tt\} \triangleright P \vdash \psi} \text{ (E-True)} \qquad \frac{\Gamma \cup \{(\!|\,\alpha\,|\!) tt\} \triangleright P \vdash \psi}{\Gamma \cup \{\neg\dagger(\alpha)\} \triangleright P \vdash \psi} \text{ (E-NotNeg)}$$

$$\frac{\Gamma \cup \{\dagger(\alpha)\} \triangleright P \vdash \psi \quad \Gamma \cup \{(\!|\,\alpha\,|\!)\Phi\} \triangleright P \vdash \psi \quad \Gamma \cup \{(\!|\,\alpha\,|\!)\neg\Phi\} \triangleright P \vdash \psi}{\Gamma \cup \{\neg < \alpha > \Phi\} \triangleright P \vdash \psi} \text{ (E-NotPos)}$$

$$\frac{\Gamma \cup \{\dagger(\alpha)\} \triangleright P \vdash \psi \quad \Gamma \cup \{< \alpha > \Phi\} \triangleright P \vdash \psi \quad \Gamma \cup \{(\!|\,\alpha\,|\!)\neg\Phi\} \triangleright P \vdash \psi}{\Gamma \cup \{\neg(\!|\,\alpha\,|\!)\Phi\} \triangleright P \vdash \psi} \text{ (E-NotNec)}$$

(*) Γ is *determined*.

Finally, rules E-NotDis, E-NotPos and E-NotNec handle assumptions where a negation of a modal formula is assumed. In all these rules the proof proceeds with the corresponding positive assumptions on the considered environment. For instance, if $\neg(\!|\,\alpha\,|\!)\Phi$ is assumed, then we have that either α can not be executed ($\dagger(\alpha)$ is assumed), after α both states satisfying Φ and states satisfying $\neg\Phi$ can be reachable ($< \alpha > \Phi$ is assumed), or each state after α satisfies $\neg\Phi$ ($(\!|\,\alpha\,|\!)\neg\Phi$ is assumed).

Like for the proof system of Section 2.2, we say that Π is a *derivation from* $\pi = S \vdash \varphi$ if and only if has π as root and it is maximal, in the sense that nothing can be derived from its *leaves*. Sequent successfulness is also extended in order to consider *inconsistent* assumptions:

Definition 4. *A sequent* $\Gamma \triangleright P \vdash \varphi$ *is successful if and only if either one of the conditions of Definition 1 holds or* Γ *is inconsistent.*

A derivation Π is successful if all its leaves are successful. If Π is a successful derivation from π, then Π is a *proof* for π.

Table 5. Relation ≻

$$\Gamma \cup \{\Phi_1 \vee \Phi_2\} \succ \Gamma \cup \{\Phi_i\} \qquad \Gamma \cup \{\neg(\Phi_1 \vee \Phi_2)\} \succ \Gamma \cup \{\neg\Phi_1, \neg\Phi_2\}$$

$$\Gamma \cup \{\neg\neg\Phi\} \succ \Gamma \cup \{\Phi\} \qquad \Gamma \cup \{vX.\Phi\} \succ \Gamma \cup \{\Phi[vX.\Phi/X]\}$$

$$\frac{\Gamma_1 \succ \Gamma_2}{\Gamma_1 \overset{\alpha}{\to} \Gamma_2}$$

$$\Gamma \cup \{\neg vX.\Phi\} \succ \Gamma \cup \{\neg\Phi[vX.\Phi/X]\}$$

$$\Gamma \cup \{\neg\dagger(\alpha)\} \succ \Gamma \cup \{(\!|\,\alpha\,|\!)tt\} \qquad \Gamma \cup \{\neg \prec \alpha \succ \Phi\} \succ \Gamma \cup \{\dagger(\alpha)\}$$

$$\Gamma \cup \{\neg \prec \alpha \succ \Phi\} \succ \Gamma \cup \{(\!|\,\alpha\,|\!)\Phi\} \qquad \Gamma \cup \{\neg \prec \alpha \succ \Phi\} \succ \Gamma \cup \{(\!|\,\alpha\,|\!)\neg\Phi\}$$

$$\Gamma \cup \{\neg(\!|\,\alpha\,|\!)\Phi\} \succ \Gamma \cup \{\dagger(\alpha)\} \qquad \Gamma \cup \{\neg(\!|\,\alpha\,|\!)\Phi\} \succ \Gamma \cup \{\prec \alpha \succ \Phi\}$$

$$\Gamma \cup \{\neg(\!|\,\alpha\,|\!)\Phi\} \succ \Gamma \cup \{(\!|\,\alpha\,|\!)\neg\Phi\}$$

In the rest of this section we show how soundness and completeness can be proved for our system. We will show that, $\Gamma \triangleright P \vdash \varphi$ is provable if and only if $P \in [\![\, \varphi \,]\!]_\Gamma^{\mathcal{A}}$ where $\mathcal{A}$ is the set of actions we assume performed by the environment. However, to obtain this result we have to guarantee that all the actions the environment can perform are properly considered in the assumptions Γ. We let $\mathsf{Der}(\Gamma)$ denoting the set of assumptions we have to consider in a proof involving assumptions Γ:

Definition 5. *We let:*

- $\succ$ *be the smallest relation satisfying the rule of Table 5;*
- $\geq$ *be the transitive and reflexive closure of* $\succ$;
- $\mathsf{Der}(\Gamma) = \{\Gamma' | \Gamma \geq \Gamma'\}$.

It is important to notice that, for each Γ, $\mathsf{Der}(\Gamma)$ is finite.

Lemma 5. *For each* Γ, $\mathsf{Der}(\Gamma)$ *is finite.*

Proof. The proof proceeds by induction on the cardinality of Γ and by showing that for each $\Gamma_1 \neq \emptyset$ and $\Gamma_2 \neq \emptyset$, $\mathsf{Der}(\Gamma_1 \cup \Gamma_2) \subseteq \{\Gamma'_1 \cup \Gamma'_2 | \Gamma'_1 \in \mathsf{Der}(\Gamma_1) \wedge \Gamma'_2 \in \mathsf{Der}(\Gamma_2)\}$. □

Definition 6. Γ *is* complete *for* $\mathcal{A} \subseteq \mathsf{Act}$ *if and only if for each* $\Gamma' \in \mathsf{Der}(\Gamma)$, $\mathsf{Init}(\Gamma') = \mathcal{A}$.

Notice that, if Γ is complete for $\mathcal{A} \subseteq \mathsf{Act}$ then the assumptions of Lemma 3 are always verified in each proof involving Γ.

Theorem 2 (Soundness). *For each* Γ *complete for* $\mathcal{A} \subseteq \mathsf{Act}$, *if* $\Gamma \triangleright P \vdash \varphi$ *is provable then* $P \in [\![\, \varphi \,]\!]_\Gamma^{\mathcal{A}}$.

Proof. The proof proceeds by induction on the length of a proof Π for $\Gamma \triangleright P \vdash \varphi$ and by showing that, for each P, Γ and φ the following hold:

a. $P \in [\![\, \varphi \,]\!]_{\Gamma \cup \{tt\}} \Leftrightarrow P \in [\![\, \varphi \,]\!]_\Gamma$
b. $P \in [\![\, \varphi \,]\!]_{\Gamma \cup \{\Phi_1 \vee \Phi_2\}} \Leftrightarrow P \in \left([\![\, \varphi \,]\!]_{\Gamma \cup \{\Phi_1\}} \cap [\![\, \varphi \,]\!]_{\Gamma \cup \{\Phi_2\}}\right)$
c. $P \in [\![\, \varphi \,]\!]_{\Gamma \cup \{\Phi_1 \wedge \Phi_2\}} \Leftrightarrow P \in [\![\, \varphi \,]\!]_{\Gamma \cup \{\Phi_1\} \cup \{\Phi_2\}}$

d. $P \in [\![\varphi]\!]_{\Gamma \cup \{\neg\neg\Phi\}} \Leftrightarrow P \in [\![\varphi]\!]_{\Gamma \cup \{\Phi\}}$

e. $P \in [\![\varphi]\!]_{\Gamma \cup \{vX.\Phi\}} \Leftrightarrow P \in [\![\varphi]\!]_{\Gamma \cup \{\Phi[vX.\Phi/X]\}}$

f. $P \in [\![\varphi]\!]_{\Gamma \cup \{\neg vX.\Phi\}} \Leftrightarrow P \in [\![\varphi]\!]_{\Gamma \cup \{\neg\Phi[\neg vX.\Phi/X]\}}$

g. $P \in [\![\varphi]\!]_{\Gamma \cup \{\neg\dagger(\alpha)\}} \Leftrightarrow P \in [\![\varphi]\!]_{\Gamma \cup \{(\!|\alpha|\!)tt\}}$

h. $P \in [\![\varphi]\!]_{\Gamma \cup \{\neg < \alpha > \Phi\}} \Leftrightarrow P \in \left([\![\varphi]\!]_{\Gamma \cup \{\dagger(\alpha)\}} \cap [\![\varphi]\!]_{\Gamma \cup \{(\!|\alpha|\!)\Phi\}} \cap [\![\varphi]\!]_{\Gamma \cup \{(\!|\alpha|\!)\neg\Phi\}}\right)$

i. $P \in [\![\varphi]\!]_{\Gamma \cup \{\neg(\!|\alpha|\!)\Phi\}} \Leftrightarrow P \in \left([\![\varphi]\!]_{\Gamma \cup \{\dagger(\alpha)\}} \cap [\![\varphi]\!]_{\Gamma \cup \{(\!|\alpha|\!)\neg\Phi\}} \cap [\![\varphi]\!]_{\Gamma \cup \{< \alpha > \Phi\}}\right)$

$\square$

To prove completeness we use the following schema. First we prove that for each P, Γ and φ, if $\mathsf{Der}(P)$ is finite then we can have only finite maximal derivations for $\Gamma \rhd P \vdash \varphi$. From that we can derive that only one between $\Gamma \rhd P \vdash \varphi$ and $\Gamma \rhd P \vdash \neg\varphi$ is provable. This, with the soundness result, guarantees the completeness (and the decidability) of the proposed proof system.

Definition 7. *We let* $\mathsf{Der}(\Gamma \rhd P) = \{\Gamma' \rhd Q | \Gamma' \in \mathsf{Der}(\Gamma) \wedge Q \in \mathsf{Der}(P)\}$

Definition 8. *Let* $S = \Gamma \rhd P$, *for each* φ *and* ψ *we will write* $\varphi <_S \psi$ *if and only if:*

- *either* ψ *is a proper subformula of* φ;
- *or* $\psi = \neg\psi'$, $\varphi = \neg\varphi'$ *and* $\psi' <_S \varphi'$;
- *or* $\varphi = vX\{\vec{S}\}.\varphi'$ *and* $\psi = \varphi'[vX\{\vec{S}, S'\}.\varphi'/X]$ *where* $S' \in \mathsf{Der}(S) - \{\vec{S}\}$.

It is clear that, if $\mathsf{Der}(P)$ is finite then, for each Γ $\mathsf{Der}(\Gamma \rhd P)$ is finite too. The following lemma guarantees that if $\mathsf{Der}(\Gamma \rhd P)$ is finite than we cannot find an infinite ascending chain of formulae for a derivation involving $\Gamma \rhd P$.

Lemma 6. *For each* S *such that* $\mathsf{Der}(S)$ *is finite does not exist an infinite sequence of formulae* φ_i $(i \in \mathbb{N})$ *such that, for each* i, $\varphi_i <_S \varphi_{i+1}$.

Proof. Directly from the fact that $vX\{\mathsf{Der}(S)\}.\psi$ is a maximum. $\square$

Since $\varphi_1 <_{\Gamma \rhd P} \varphi_2$ means that φ_2 is a formula that can occur in a proof for φ_1, we can conclude that only a finite number of formulae can occur in a derivation.

Definition 9. *For each formula* Φ *we let weight(Φ) as follows:*

- *weight(tt) = weight(ff) = weight$(\dagger(\alpha))$ = weight$(< \alpha > \Phi)$ = weight$((\!|\alpha|\!)\Phi)$ = 0;*
- *weight$(\Phi_1 \vee \Phi_2)$ = 2 + weight(Φ_1) + weight(Φ_2)*
- *weight$(vX.\Phi)$ = 1 + weight(Φ)*
- *weight$(\neg\Phi)$ = 1 + weight(Φ)*

Definition 10. *Let* π_1 *and* π_2 *be two sequents, we will write* $\pi_1 \sqsubset \pi_2$ *if and only if* π_1 *immediately precedes* π_2 *in a proof.*

The following lemma shows that, if sequent π_1 can be proved through sequent π_2 then either the weight of assumptions, i.e. the number of logical connectives in front of modal operators, or the formula subject of the derivation decrease in π_2. These means that, if we find an infinite derivation from π then we have also an infinite chain of formulae.

Lemma 7. *If $\Gamma_1 \triangleright P_1 \vdash \varphi_1 \sqsubseteq \Gamma_2 \triangleright P_2 \vdash \varphi_2$ then either $weight(\Gamma_1) < weight(\Gamma_2)$ or $\varphi_1 \prec_{\Gamma_1 \triangleright P_1} \varphi_2$.*

Proof. Directly from rules of Table 4. □

Lemma 8. *For each P such that $\mathsf{Der}(P)$ is finite and for each Γ and φ, does not exist infinite derivation starting from $\Gamma \triangleright P \vdash \varphi$.*

Proof. Suppose that there exists an infinite derivation for $\Gamma \triangleright P \vdash \varphi$.

$\Longrightarrow$ $\{Def.\pi_1 \sqsubseteq \pi_2\}$

   $\exists$ infinite chain of sequents $\pi_i : \forall k, \pi_k \sqsubseteq \pi_{k+1} \quad (i \in \mathbb{N})$

$\Longrightarrow$ $\{Lemma\ 7\}$

   $\exists$ infinite sequence of formulae $\varphi_j : \forall k, \varphi_k \prec_{\Gamma \triangleright P} \varphi_{k+1} \quad (j \in \mathbb{N})$

$\Longrightarrow$ $\{Lemma\ 6, \mathsf{Der}(\Gamma \triangleright P)$ is finite$\}$

   $\nexists$ infinite sequence of formulae $\varphi_j : \forall k, \varphi_k \prec_{\Gamma \triangleright P} \varphi_{k+1} \quad (j \in \mathbb{N})$

$\Longrightarrow$ $\{$Reductio ad absurdum$\}$

   $\nexists$ infinite derivation from $\Gamma \triangleright P \vdash \varphi$ □

We can now introduce our final result:

Theorem 3. *For each process P, Γ, φ and $\mathcal{A}$, where $\mathsf{Der}(P)$ is finite and Γ is complete for $\mathcal{A}$, if $P \in [\![\varphi]\!]^{\mathcal{A}}_\Gamma$ then $\Gamma \triangleright P \vdash \varphi$ is provable.*

Proof. $\mathsf{Der}(P)$ is finite

$\Longrightarrow$ $\{Lemma\ 8\}$

   $\nexists$ infinite derivation from $\Gamma \triangleright P \vdash \varphi$

$\Longrightarrow$ $\{$Each maximal derivation is finite$\}$

   one between $\Gamma \triangleright P \vdash \varphi$ and $\Gamma \triangleright P \vdash \neg\varphi$ is provable

$\Longrightarrow$ $\{$Theorem 2$\}$

   $\Gamma \triangleright P \vdash \varphi$ is provable   □

Example 5. The proposed proof system can be used for verifying that, when we consider the assumptions Γ_{DF} of Example 4, process Ph_0 guarantees absence of deadlock. However, absence of starvation is not guaranteed. Indeed, $\Phi^0_F | Ph_1 | \Phi^1_F$ does not satisfy Γ_{DF} that, on the contrary, is satisfied by Ph^*_1 (see Example 3). Moreover, in the former specification it is not guaranteed that fork F_1 will be released after that it is acquired by the environment.

   The proposed assumptions can be *refined* by considering a concrete specification for forks F_0 and F_1. In this case we have:

$$\Gamma^2_{DF} = \{\Phi_0, \Phi_1, \Phi_C\}$$

Where each Φ_i identifies the protocol used by the environment for interacting with fork F_i, while Φ_C states that $pick_i$ and $\overline{rel}_i$ ($i = 1, 0$) can not be enabled at the same time. If $\mathcal{A}$ is the (finite) set of actions that can be performed by the environment, where $\{\tau, pick_0, pick_1, \overline{rel}_0, \overline{rel}_1\} \subseteq \mathcal{A}$, Φ_i and Φ_C are defined as follows:

$$\Phi_i = \nu X.(\!|\; pick_i \;|\!)\mathsf{Eventually}(\mathcal{A} - \{pick_i, \overline{rel}_i\}, (\!|\; \overline{rel}_i \;|\!)X)$$

$$\Phi_C = \neg\mathsf{Always}(\mathcal{A}, ((\!|\; pick_0 \;|\!)tt \wedge (\!|\; \overline{rel}_0 \;|\!)tt) \vee ((\!|\; pick_1 \;|\!)tt \wedge (\!|\; \overline{rel}_1 \;|\!)tt))$$

The proposed proof system can be used for verifying that $\Gamma_{DF}^2 \triangleright F_0|F_1$ satisfies Γ_{DF}. Therefore, $\Gamma_{DF}^2 \triangleright Ph_0|F_0|F_1$ guarantees that deadlock is never reached. However, both Ph_1 and Ph_1^* do not satisfies Γ_{DF}^2. Indeed, these processes assume a prefixed order in which forks are retrieved, while in the assumed behaviour, forks can be retrieved by the environment in any order. A correct implementation of Γ_{DF}^2 is a process that, non deterministically, can select the first picked fork and, at the same time, can always decide to release the first without taking the second.

5   Conclusions, Related Works and Future Works

In this paper we have presented a formal framework that permits verifying properties of concurrent and communicating systems by using an assumption-guarantee approach [16]. Each system component under the analysis is not considered in isolation, but in conjunction with assumptions about the context of the component. In the paper we have also introduced a sound and complete proof system that permits verifying whether a process, when it is executed in an environment for which we provide some assumptions, satisfies a given formula. It is also ensured that property satisfaction is preserved whenever the context is partially instantiated (implemented) as a concrete process that verifies the assumptions we have for the environment. Even if the proposed approach can be used for modular/compositional verification, it is important to remark that this is only a consequence of our approach and it is not the main objective. Indeed, differently from existing compositional proof systems [2,12,18], process specification and the investigated property are not (automatically) *decomposed* in components and sub-formulae that are verified separately.

The proposed framework is somehow reminiscent of the one proposed in [21] where the logical implication $(-\!\ast)$ on monoids $\mathcal{M} = (M, \cdot, e, \sqsubseteq)$ has been introduced. This implication is defined as $m \models \varphi -\!\ast\psi \Leftrightarrow \forall n \in M(n \models \varphi \Rightarrow n \cdot m \models \psi)$. However, elements in M are not processes but memory locations. Moreover, $\cdot$ is not a parallel composition but a Cartesian product.

In the same line of [21] we recall the *Separation Logic* presented in [22]. In this work each process has a storage space. Processes are composed by using the separating conjunction $P \ast Q$ asserting that P and Q use disjoint portions of the addressable storage. The same approach has been used in [6,15] to concurrent processes sharing access to mutable data.

However, while in [21,22] concurrent programs mainly interact by means of shared memory, in our work, on the contrary, we consider processes that interact by using channels. Moreover, we also consider an explicit interaction between the environment and the considered process.

In [8,9] a *spatial implication* (▷) is used for relating the satisfaction of a formula to the properties satisfied by the context. Indeed, P satisfies $\mathcal{A} \triangleright \mathcal{B}$ if and only if for each Q satisfying $\mathcal{A}$, $P|Q$ satisfies $\mathcal{B}$. However, this very interesting and powerful logical framework makes the operator undecidable [7]. In our approach, we do not perform any *separation* of components running in parallel.

Other existing solutions for partical/compositional specification rely on mixed specifications or on the use of intuitionistic/linear logics. *Mixed specifications* [3] have been also introduced to describe a system where transitions *must* or *may* happen. The context is then specified by means of Modal Transition Systems that, combined with a process specification, are used by model checking algorithms to verify the satisfiability of temporal logics. In [1], two logics, one intuitionistic and the other linear, have been introduced for specifying reactive systems and for studying compositional rules. In this approach, process semantics is defined in term of a logical framework where process composition is derived in term of tensor product and linear implications. Even if these works and the present paper share the same aim, the final results are quite different. Indeed, in the case of Modal Transition Systems, different tools have to be used for verifying the compliance between the abstract specification with the refined implementation. On the contrary, in the case of [1] the actual implementation of the system (i.e. the process describing the behaviour of the considered system) is hidden inside the logical specification. Moreover, property verification, as well as system refinement, is performed in term of propositional reasoning. Our approach, by relying on Hennessy-Milner Logic/mu Calculus, permits exploiting standard and well studied model checking algorithms.

In the future, we aim at defining a methodology that, starting from a process P and a formula φ, aims at deriving the most general assumptions we have to impose to the environment to see φ be satisfied by P.

References

1. Abadi, M., Plotkin, G.D.: A logical view of composition. Theoretical Computer Science 114(1), 3–30 (1993)
2. Andersen, H.R., Stirling, C., Winskel, G.: A compositional proof system for the modal mu-calculus. In: Proceedings, Ninth Annual IEEE Symposium on Logic in Computer Science, Paris, France, July 4-7, pp. 144–153. IEEE Computer Society, Los Alamitos (1994)
3. Antonik, A., Huth, M., Larsen, K.G., Nyman, U., Wasowski, A.: 20 years of modal and mixed specifications. Bulletin of the EATCS 95, 94–129 (2008)
4. Bergstra, J.A., Klop, J.W.: Process algebra for synchronous communication. Information and Control 60(1-3), 109–137 (1984)
5. Brookes, S.D., Hoare, C.A.R., Roscoe, A.W.: A theory of communicating sequential processes. J. ACM 31(3), 560–599 (1984)
6. Brookes, S.: A semantics for concurrent separation logic. Theoretical Computer Science 375(1-3), 227–270 (2007); Festschrift for John C. Reynolds's 70th birthday
7. Caires, L., Lozes, É.: Elimination of quantifiers and undecidability in spatial logics for concurrency. Theor. Comput. Sci. 358(2-3), 293–314 (2006)
8. Caires, L., Cardelli, L.: A spatial logic for concurrency (part I). In: Information and Computation, pp. 1–37. Springer, Heidelberg (2001)

9. Caires, L., Cardelli, L.: A spatial logic for concurrency (part II). In: Brim, L., Jančar, P., Křetínský, M., Kucera, A. (eds.) CONCUR 2002. LNCS, vol. 2421, pp. 209–225. Springer, Heidelberg (2002)
10. Clarke, E.M., Emerson, E.A.: Design and synthesis of synchronization skeletons using branching-time temporal logic. In: Kozen, D. (ed.) Logic of Programs 1981. LNCS, vol. 131, pp. 52–71. Springer, Heidelberg (1982)
11. Cleaveland, R.: Tableau-based model checking in the propositional mu-calculus. Acta Inf. 27(8), 725–747 (1989)
12. Dam, M., Gurov, D.: Compositional verification of CCS processes. In: Bjorner, D., Broy, M., Zamulin, A.V. (eds.) PSI 1999. LNCS, vol. 1755, pp. 247–256. Springer, Heidelberg (2000)
13. D'Errico, L., Loreti, M.: Assume-guarantee verification of concurrent systems. Technical report, Università di Firenze (2009), http://www.dsi.unifi.it/~loreti/
14. Hennessy, M., Milner, R.: Algebraic laws for nondeterminism and concurrency. J. ACM 32(1), 137–161 (1985)
15. Hoare, T., O'Hearn, P.: Separation logic semantics for communicating processes. Electronic Notes in Theoretical Computer Science 212, 3–25 (2008); Proceedings of the First International Conference on Foundations of Informatics, Computing and Software (FICS 2008)
16. Jones, C.B.: Tentative steps toward a development method for interfering programs. ACM Transactions on Programming Languages and Systems 5(4), 596–619 (1983)
17. Kozen, D.: Results on the propositional μ-calculus. Theor. Comput. Sci. 27, 333–354 (1983)
18. Larsen, K.G., Xinxin, L.: Compositionality through an operational semantics of contexts. J. Log. Comput. 1(6), 761–795 (1991)
19. Milner, R.: A Calculus of Communication Systems. LNCS, vol. 92. Springer, Heidelberg (1980)
20. Milner, R.: Communication and concurrency. Prentice-Hall, Inc., Upper Saddle River (1989)
21. O'hearn, P.W., Pym, D.J.: The logic of bunched implications. Bulletin of Symbolic Logic 5, 215–244 (1999)
22. Reynolds, J.C.: Separation logic: A logic for shared mutable data structures. In: Symposium on Logic in Computer Science, p. 55 (2002)
23. Stirling, C., Walker, D.: Local model checking in the modal mu-calculus. In: Díaz, J., Orejas, F. (eds.) CAAP 1989 and TAPSOFT 1989. LNCS, vol. 351, pp. 369–383. Springer, Heidelberg (1989)
24. Winskel, G.: The formal semantics of programming languages: an introduction. MIT Press, Cambridge (1993)

Author Index